I0016852

The Quantum of

C

Programming Language:

From Syntax to Systematic Solutions

By

Mike Zephalon

Copyright © 2025 by Mike Zephalon

Book Title: The Quantum of C Language: From Syntax to Systematic Solutions

All rights reserved. No part of this book may be reproduced, distributed, or transmitted in any form or by any means, including photocopying, recording, or other electronic or mechanical methods, without the prior written permission of the publisher, except in the case of brief quotations embodied in critical reviews and certain other non-commercial uses permitted by copyright law. For permission requests, write to the publisher at the address below:

For permissions or inquiries, please contact: **mikezephalon@gmail.com.**
Published by **Mike Zephalon**

Legal Notice:

This book is intended for informational purposes only. The author and publisher have made every effort to ensure the accuracy of the information contained in this book. However, they make no representations or warranties regarding the completeness, accuracy, or suitability of this information for any purpose. Neither the author nor the publisher shall be held liable for any damages arising from the use of this book.

About Author

Mike Zephalon was born in Toronto, Canada, and developed a passion for technology and programming at an early age. His journey into the world of coding began when he was just a teenager, experimenting with simple scripts and exploring the vast possibilities of web development. Mike pursued his studies at the University of Toronto, where he majored in Computer Science. During his time at university, he became deeply interested in JavaScript, captivated by its versatility and power in building dynamic, interactive web applications.

Over the years, Mike has worked with several tech startups and companies, where he honed his skills as a front-end developer. His dedication to mastering JavaScript and its frameworks has made him a respected voice in the developer community. Through his books and tutorials, Mike aims to empower new and experienced developers alike, helping them unlock the full potential of JavaScript in their projects.

Table of Contents

1. Introduction to C Programming

The Importance of C Programming Language

Begin by introducing the C programming language, explaining its influence on modern programming, and why it remains widely used despite the emergence of newer languages. Discuss how C's performance efficiency, portability, and foundational principles have made it a cornerstone in systems programming and embedded systems. Explain how learning C can provide a strong foundation for understanding low-level operations, memory management, and developing an appreciation for programming fundamentals.

Role of C in Technology and Applications

Provide examples of how C is used in operating systems (like Unix and Linux), embedded systems, software development, and even gaming. This can help the reader connect with the practical applications of C, adding context to why they are studying the language.

2. History and Origin of C

Origins of C and Its Development

Trace the origins of C back to the early 1970s. Explain how it was developed by Dennis Ritchie at Bell Labs for Unix operating system development, which required a more efficient programming language. Discuss its predecessors (like BCPL and B), highlighting what motivated the transition to C.

Evolution of C and Standardization

Describe the evolution of C, focusing on key milestones:

- **K&R C**: Named after Brian Kernighan and Dennis Ritchie, this version set the initial standards.
- **ANSI C**: Standardized in 1989 (known as C89 or ANSI C) by the American National Standards Institute to bring uniformity.
- **ISO C**: In 1990, the International Organization for Standardization adopted ANSI C, further refining it.
- **Modern C Versions**: Mention updates in C99, C11, and C18, explaining how newer standards have introduced features like inline functions, variable-length arrays, and improved compatibility and safety.

Impact of C on Other Programming Languages

Highlight how C influenced languages like C++, Java, C#, and JavaScript, especially in syntax, structure, and foundational principles.

3. Overview of C Language Features

Low-Level Access

Explain how C allows direct manipulation of hardware through pointers and memory allocation, making it ideal for system programming.

Portability

Discuss C's portability across different platforms and operating systems, one of its most defining characteristics. Explain how its simplicity allows C programs to be compiled on various architectures with minimal modification.

Efficiency and Performance

Emphasize C's efficiency in terms of speed and performance, as its operations closely mirror the capabilities of the underlying hardware. Describe how this feature has made C a top choice for applications where speed is crucial.

Modularity with Functions

Explain the concept of modularity in C, where complex programs can be broken down into functions, making code more manageable and reusable.

Rich Library Support

Mention the availability of standard libraries in C, which offer a range of functionalities, from I/O operations to string handling and mathematical functions.

Syntax and Structure

Briefly introduce the syntax and structure of C programs, noting how its simple, straightforward syntax has influenced many other languages. Introduce the concept of control statements, loops, functions, and data types.

4. Setting Up the Environment and Tools

Choosing a Compiler

Explain the role of a compiler in translating C code into executable machine code. Recommend popular C compilers like GCC (GNU Compiler Collection), Clang, and MSVC (Microsoft Visual C++), highlighting key features of each and providing guidance on choosing one based on the reader's operating system.

Setting up on Different Operating Systems

Provide a step-by-step guide on installing a C compiler on:

- **Windows**: Walk through installing GCC using MinGW or an IDE like Code::Blocks.
- **MacOS**: Introduce Xcode's command-line tools and installation of GCC or Clang.

- **Linux**: Explain how GCC can be installed on Linux distributions using package managers like apt for Ubuntu or yum for Fedora.

Introduction to IDEs and Text Editors

Introduce Integrated Development Environments (IDEs) like Code::Blocks, Visual Studio, and Eclipse, along with text editors like VS Code and Sublime Text. Explain the advantages of each, helping beginners decide on an environment.

Using the Command Line for Compilation

Walk readers through compiling a C program using the command line to familiarize them with this approach. Show commands like gcc program.co program and how to run the compiled executable.

5. Writing and Running the First C Program

Understanding the "Hello, World!" Program

Begin with a simple "Hello, World!" example to introduce readers to the syntax and structure of a C program. Explain each line of code in detail, including the purpose of #include <stdio.h> for input/output functionality, the main function as the entry point, and printf for displaying output.

Steps for Writing, Compiling, and Running the Program

Guide readers through writing the code in an editor, saving it with a .c extension, and compiling and running the program. Include detailed steps for using a compiler (e.g., GCC) and executing the program on the command line or in an IDE.

Troubleshooting Common Errors

Cover typical errors beginners may encounter, such as missing semicolons, unrecognized symbols, and syntax issues. Provide simple troubleshooting tips and encourage good practices, like saving code frequently and reviewing error messages carefully.

6. Basic Structure of a C Program

Breaking Down the C Program Structure

Explain the typical structure of a C program, including:

- **Preprocessor Directives**: Describe directives like #include for library imports and #define for defining constants.

- **Main Function**: Detail the importance of the main function, its purpose as the program's starting point, and return types like int with return 0; to indicate successful execution.

- **Variable Declarations**: Show how variables are declared at the beginning of functions, covering basic types like int, float, char, and double.

- **Statements and Expressions**: Explain how statements (e.g., arithmetic operations, assignments) and expressions function in C.

Comments in C

Explain the use of comments (// for single-line and /* */ for multi-line) to document code, making it easier to understand and maintain.

Control Flow Statements

Briefly introduce control structures like conditionals (if, else) and loops (for, while), providing examples of each to illustrate how they work in a basic program.

Let's Start

Computer is an electronic device which works on the instructions provided by the user. As the computer does not understand natural language, it is required to provide the instructions in some computer understandable language. Such a computer understandable language is known as Programming language.

A computer programming language consists of a set of symbols and characters, words, and grammar rules that permit people to construct instructions in the format that can be interpreted by the computer system Computer Programming is the art of making a computer do what you want it to do. Computer programming is a field that has to do with the analytical creation of source code that can be used to configure computer systems. Computer programmers may choose to function in a broad range of programming functions, or specialize in some aspect of development, support, or maintenance of computers for the home or workplace. Programmers provide the basis for the creation and ongoing function of the systems that many people rely upon for all sorts of information exchange, both businesses related and for entertainment purposes.

Programming Language

Different programming languages support different styles of programming. The choice of language used is subject to many considerations, such as company policy, suitability to task, availability of third-party packages, or individual preference. Ideally, the programming language best suited for the task at hand will be selected. Trade-offs from this ideal involve finding enough programmers who know the language to build a team, the availability of compilers for that language, and the efficiency with which programs written in a given language execute.

The basic instructions of programming language are:

Input: Get data from the keyboard, a file, or some other device.

Output: Display data on the screen or send data to a file or other device.

Math: Perform basic mathematical operations like addition and multiplication.

Conditional execution: Check for certain conditions and execute the appropriate sequence of statements.

Repetition: Perform some action repeatedly, usually with some variation.

Machine Level Language

Computer language, also known as machine code, is a low-level programming language made up of binary digits (ones and zeros). Before a computer can run code written in high-level languages like Swift and C++, the code must be converted into machine language.

Since computers are digital devices, they only recognize binary data. Every program, video, image, and character of text is represented in binary. This binary data, or machine code, is processed as input by the CPU. The resulting output is sent to the operating system or an application, which displays the data visually. For example, the ASCII value for the letter "A" is 01000001 in machine code, but this data is displayed as "A" on the screen. An image may have thousands or even millions of binary values that determine the color of each pixel.

While computers can be programmed to understand a variety of computer languages, there is only one language that the computer understands without the use of a translation program; this language is known as the computer's machine language or machine code. Machine code is the fundamental language of a computer and is normally written as strings of binary 1s and 0s. The circuitry of a computer is wired in such a way that it immediately recognizes the machine language and converts it into the electrical signals needed to run the computer.

An instruction prepared in any language has two parts. The first part is command or operation, and it tells the computer what function to perform. Every computer has an operation code or op-code for each of its functions. The second part of the instruction is the operand, and it tells the computer where to find or store the data or other instructions that are to be maintained. Thus, each instruction tells the control unit of the CPU what to do and the length and location of the data field are involved in the operation. Typical operations involve reading, adding, subtracting, writing and so on.

Discuss Example of Machine Level Language

Instruction Format

We already know that all commuters use binary digits (0s and 1s) for performing operations. Hence, most computers machine language consists of strings of binary numbers and is the only one the CPU directly understands. When stored inside the computer, the symbols which make up the machine language program are made up of 1s and 0s.

A typical program instruction to print out a number on the printer might be.
10110011111101001101100110000111001

The program to add two numbers in memory and print the result look something like the Following:

00100000000001100111001

00111000000111111000111

10011110001110110011010110101

10110001010101010111 0000

00000000000000000000000000

This is obviously not a very easy language to learn, partly because it is difficult to read and understand and partly because it is written in a number system with which we are not familiar. But it will be surprising to note that some of the first programmers, who worked with the first few computers, actually wrote their programs in binary form as above. Since human programmers are more familiar with the decimal number system, most of them preferred to write the computer instructions in decimal, and leave the input device to convert these to binary. In fact, without too much effort, a computer can be wired so that instead of using long numbers.

With this change, the preceding program appears as follows:

10001471

14002041

30003456

50773456

00000000

The set of instruction codes, whether in binary or decimal, which can be directly understood by the CPU of a computer without the help of a translating program, is called a machine code or machine language. Thus, a machine language program need not necessarily be coded as strings of binary digits (1s and 0s). It can also be written using decimal digits if the circuitry of the computer being used permits this.

Advantages and Limitations of Machine Language

Programs written in machine language can be executed very fast by the computer. This is mainly because machine instructions are directly understood by the CPU writing a program in machine language has several disadvantages which are discussed below.

Machine dependent

Because the internal design of every type of commuter is different from every other type of computer and needs different electrical signals to operate, the machine language also is different from computer to computer. It is determined by the actual design or construction of the LU, the control unit, and the size as well as the word length of the memory unit. Hence, suppose after becoming proficient in the machine code of a particular computer, a company decides to change to another computer, the programmer may be required to learn a new machine language and would have to rewrite all the existing programs.

Difficult to program

Although easily used by the computer, machine language is difficult to program, it is necessary for the programmer either to memorize the dozens of code numbers for the commands in the machine's instruction set or to constantly refer to keep track of the storage location of data and instructions. Moreover, a machine language programmer must be an expert who knows about the hardware structure of the computer.

Error code

For writing programs in machine language, since a programmer has to remember the opcodes and he must also keep track of the storage location of data and instructions, it becomes very difficult for him to concentrate fully on the logic of the problem. This frequently results in program errors. Hence, it is easy to make errors while using machine code.

Difficult to modify

It is difficult to correct or modify machine language programs. Checking machine instructions to locate errors is about as tedious as writing them initially. Similarly, modifying a machine language program at a later date is so difficult that many programmers would prefer to code the new logic afresh instead of incorporating the necessary modifications in the old program.

Assembly Language

Assembly languages are also known as second generation languages. These languages substitute alphabetic symbols for the binary codes of machine language. In assembly language, symbols are used in place of absolute addresses to represent memory locations. Mnemonics are used for operation code, i.e., single letters or short abbreviations that help the programmers to understand what the code represents.

MOV AX, DX.

Here mnemonic MOV represents 'transfer' operation and AX, DX are used to represent the registers. One of the first steps in improving the program preparation process was to substitute letter symbols mnemonics for the numeric operation codes of machine language. A mnemonic is any kind of mental trick we use to help us remember. Mnemonics come in various shapes and sizes, all of them useful in their own way.

All computers have the power of handling letters as well as numbers. Hence, a computer can be taught to recognize certain combination of letter or numbers. It can be taught to substitute the number 14 every time it sees the symbol ADD, substitute the number 15 every time it sees the symbol SUB, and so forth. In this way, the computer can be trained to translate a program written with symbols instead of numbers into the computer's own machine language. Then we can write program for the computer using symbols instead of numbers, and have the computer do its own translating. This makes it easier for the programmer, because he can use letters, symbols, and mnemonics instead of numbers for writing his programs.

The preceding program that was written in machine language for adding two numbers and printing out the result could be written in the following way:

```
CLA   A
ADD   B
```

```
STA    C
TYP    C
```

Which would mean "take A, add B, store the result in C, type C, and halt." The computer by means of a translating program, would translate each line of this program into the corresponding machine language program.

Advantages of Assembly Language

Assembly language is easier to use than machine language.

An assembler is useful for detecting programming errors.

Programmers do not have to know the absolute addresses of data items.

Assembly languages encourage modular programming.

Disadvantages of Assembly Language

Assembly language programs are not directly executable.

Assembly languages are machine dependent and, therefore, not portable from one machine to another.

Programming in assembly language requires a higher level of programming skill.

Assembly Program Execution

An assembly program is written according to a strict set of rules. An editor or word processor is used for keying an assembly program into the computer as a file, and then the assembler is used to translate the program into machine code.

There are two ways of converting an assembly language program into machine language:

Manual assembly

By using an assembler.

Manual Assembly

It was an old method that required the programmer to translate each opcode into its numerical machine language representation by looking up a table of the microprocessor instructions set, which contains both assembly and machine language instructions. Manual assembly is acceptable for short programs but becomes very inconvenient for large programs. The Intel SDK-85 and most of the earlier university kits were programmed using manual assembly.

Using an Assembler

The symbolic instructions that you code in assembly language is known as - Source program.

An assembler program translates the source program into machine code, which is known as object program.

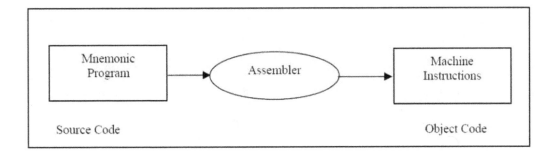

The steps required to assemble, link and execute a program are:

The assembly step involves translating the source code into object code and generating an intermediate .OBJ (object file) or module. The assembler also creates a header immediately in front of the generated .OBJ module; part of the header contains information about incomplete addresses. The .OBJ module is not quite in executable form.

The link step involves converting the .OBJ module to an .EXE machine code module. The linker's tasks include completing any address left open by the assembler and combining separately assembled programs into one executable module.

The linker

Combines assembled module into one executable program

Generates an .EXE module and initializes with special instructions to facilitate its

Subsequent loading for execution

The last step is to load the program for execution. Because the loader knows where the program is going to load in memory, it is now able to resolve any remaining address still left incomplete in the header. The loader drops the header and creates a program segment prefix (PSP) immediately before the program is loaded in memory.

Tools Required for Assembly Language Programming

The tools of the assembly process described may vary in details.

The editor is a program that allows the user to enter, modify, and store a group of instructions or text under a file name. The editor programs can be classified in two groups.

- Line editors

- Full screen editors

Line editors, such as EDIT in MS DOS, work with the manage one line at a time. Full screen editors, such as Notepad, WordPad etc. manage the full screen or a paragraph at a time. To write text, the user must call the editor under the control of the operating system. As soon as the editor program is transferred from the disk to the system memory, the program control is transferred from the operating system to the editor program. The editor has its own command and the user can enter and modify text by using those commands. Some editor programs such as WordPerfect are very easy to use.

At the completion of writing a program, the exit command of the editor program will save the program on the disk under the file name and will transfer the control to the operating system. If the source file is intended to be a program in the 8086-assembly language the user should follow the syntax of the assembly language and the rules of the assembler.

Linker

For modularity of your programs, it is better to break your program into several sub routines. It is even better to put the common routine, like reading a hexadecimal number, writing hexadecimal number, etc., which could be used by a lot of your other programs into a separate file. These files are assembled separately. After each file has been successfully assembled, they can be linked together to form a large file, which constitutes your complete program. The file containing the common routines can be linked to your other program also. The program that links your program is called the linker.

Loader

Loader is a program which assigns absolute addresses to the program. These addresses are generated by adding the address from where the program is loaded into the memory to all the offsets. Loader comes into action when you want to execute your program. This program is brought from the secondary memory like disk. The file name extension for loading is .exe or .com, which after loading can be executed by the CPU.

Differences between Machine-Level language and Assembly language

Machine-level language	Assembly language
The machine-level language comes at the lowest level in the hierarchy, so it has zero abstraction level from the hardware.	The assembly language comes above the machine language means that it has less abstraction level from the hardware.
It cannot be easily understood by humans.	It is easy to read, write, and maintain.
The machine-level language is written in binary digits, i.e., 0 and 1.	The assembly language is written in simple English language, so it is easily understandable by the users.
It does not require any translator as the machine code is directly executed by the computer.	In assembly language, the assembler is used to convert the assembly code into machine code.

It is a first-generation programming language.	It is a second-generation programming language.

High Level Languages

We have talked about programming languages as COBOL, FORTRAN and BASIC. They are called high level programming languages. The program shown below is written in BASIC to obtain the sum of two numbers.

```
LET    X      =      7
LET    Y      =      10
LET    sum    =      X+Y
PRINT SUM
END
```

The time and cost of creating machine and assembly languages was quite high. And this was the prime motivation for the development of high level languages. Because of the difficulty of working with low-level languages, high-level languages were developed to make it easier to write computer programs. High level programming languages create computer programs using instructions that are much easier to understand than machine or assembly language code because you can use words that more clearly describe the task being performed.

When writing a program in a high-level language, then the whole attention needs to be paid to the logic of the problem. A compiler is required to translate a high-level language into a low-level language.

High-level languages include FORTRAN, COBOL, BASIC, PASCAL, C, C++ and JAVA.

Advantages of a high-level language

Readability: Programs written in these languages are more readable than assembly and machine language.

Portability: Programs could be run on different machines with little or no change. We can, therefore, exchange software leading to creation of program libraries.

Easy debugging: Errors could easily be removed (debugged).

Easy Software development: Software could easily be developed. Commands of programming language are similar to natural languages (ENGLISH).

Differences between Low-Level language and High-Level language

Low-level language	High-level language

It is a machine-friendly language, i.e., the computer understands the machine language, which is represented in 0 or 1.	It is a user-friendly language as this language is written in simple English words, which can be easily understood by humans.
The low-level language takes more time to execute.	It executes at a faster pace.
It requires the assembler to convert the assembly code into machine code.	It requires the compiler to convert the highlevel language instructions into machine code.
The machine code cannot run on all machines, so it is not a portable language.	The high-level code can run all the platforms, so it is a portable language.
It is memory efficient.	It is less memory efficient.
Debugging and maintenance are not easier in a low-level language.	Debugging and maintenance are easier in a high-level language.

Introduction to C Programming

The programming language C was originally developed by Dennis Ritchie of Bell Laboratories and was designed to run on a PDP-11 with a UNIX operating system. Although it was originally intended to run under UNIX, there has been a great interest in running it under the MS-DOS operating system on the IBM PC and compatibles. It is an excellent language for this environment because of the simplicity of expression, the compactness of the code, and the wide range of applicability.

Also, due to the simplicity and ease of writing a C compiler, it is usually the first high level language available on any new computer, including microcomputers, minicomputers, and mainframes. It allows the programmer a wide range of operations from high level down to a very low level, approaching the level of assembly language. There seems to be no limit to the flexibility available.

Origin and Development of C Language

C is a general-purpose, structured programming language. Structured Languages have a characteristic program structure and associated set of static scope rules. C was originated in Bell Telephone Laboratories presently known as AT & T Bell Laboratories by Dennis Ritchie in 1970. The Kernighan and Ritchie description is commonly referred to as "K&R C". Following the publication of the K & R description, computer professionals, impressed with C's many desirable features, began to promote the use of the language. Since 1980's, the popularity of C has become widespread. The American National Standards Institute (ANSI) proposed a standardized definition of the C language (ANSI committee X3J11). Most commercial C compilers and interpreters are expected to adopt the ANSI standard.

C has the feature of high-level programming language as well as the low-level programming. It works as a bridging gap between machine language and the more conventional high-level languages. This feature of C Language made it most popular for system programming as well as application programming.

Applications of C Language

Mainly C Language is used for Develop Desktop application and system software. Some application of C language is given below.

C programming language can be used to design the system software like operating system and Compiler.

To develop application software like database and spread sheets.

For Develop Graphical related application like computer and mobile games.

To evaluate any kind of mathematical equation, use c language.

C programming language can be used to design the compilers.

UNIX Kernel is completely developed in C Language.

For Creating Compilers of different Languages which can take input from other language and convert it into lower-level machine dependent language.

C programming language can be used to design Operating System.

C programming language can be used to design Network Devices.

To design GUI Applications. Adobe Photoshop, one of the most popularly used photo editors since olden times, was created with the help of C.

Evolution of C

By the late fifties, there were many computer languages into existence. However, none of them were general purpose. They served better in a particular type of programming application more than others. Thus, while FORTRAN was more suited for engineering programming, COBOL was better for business programming. At this stage people started thinking that instead of learning so many languages for different programming purposes, why not have a single computer language that can be used for programming any type of application.

In 1960, to this end, an international committee was constituted which came out with a language named ALGOL-60. This language could not become popular because it was too general and highly abstract.

In 1963, a modified ALGOL-60 by reducing its generality and abstractness, a new language, CPL (Combined Programming Language) was developed at Cambridge University. CPL, too turned out to be very big and difficult to learn.

In 1967, Martin Richards, at Cambridge University, stripped down some of the complexities from CPL retaining useful features and created BCPL (Basic CPL). Very soon it was realized that BCPL was too specific and much too less powerful.

In 1970, Ken Thompson, at AT&T labs. Developed a language known by the name B as another simplification to CPL. B, too, like its predecessors, turned out to be very specific and limited in application.

In 1972, Ritchie, at AT&T, took the best of the two BCPL and B, and developed the language C. C was truly a general-purpose language, easy to learn and very powerful.

In 1972, Ritchie, at AT&T, took the best of the two BCPL and B, and developed the language C. C was truly a general-purpose language, easy to learn and very powerful.

Give two examples of high-level languages.

Compiler and Interpreter

Note that the only language a digital computer understands is binary coded instructions. Even the above implementation will not execute on a computer without further translation into binary (machine) code. This translation is not done manually, however. There are programs available to do this job. These translation programs are called compilers and interpreters.

Compilers and interpreters are programs that take a program written in a language as input and translate it into machine language. Thus, a program that translates a C program into machine code is called C compiler; BASIC program into machine code is called a BASIC compiler and so on.

Compilers and interpreters are programs that take a program written in a language as input and translate it into machine language. Thus, a program that translates a C program into machine code is called C compiler; BASIC program into machine code is called a BASIC compiler and so on.

A number of different compilers are available these days for C language. GCC, ANSI, Borland C, Turbo C, etc. are only few of the popular C compilers. As a matter of fact, these software tools are little more than just compiler. They provide a complete environment for C program development. They include, among others, an editor to allow Program writing, a Compiler for compilation of the same, a debugger for debugging/testing the program, and so forth. Such tools are referred to as IDE (Integrated Development Environment) or SDK (Software Development Kit).

Code blocks is an IDE for running C and C++ programs on different operating systems like Windows, Linux and Mac OS.

Program Development in C

The development of a "C" program involves the use of the following programs in the order of their usage.

Editor

This program is used for writing the Source Code, the first thing that any programmer writing a program in any language would be doing.

Debugger

This program helps us identify syntax errors in the source code.

Pre-Processor

There are certain special instructions within the source code identified by the # symbol that are carried on by a special program called a preprocessor. Compiler

The process of converting the C source code to machine code and is done by a program called Compiler.

Linker

The machine code relating to the source code you have written is combined with some other machine code to derive the complete program in an executable file. This is done by a program called the linker.

Writing a C Program

The following rules are applicable to all C-statements:

Blank spaces may be inserted between two words to improve the readability of the statement. However, no blank space is allowed within a word.

Most of the C-compilers are case-sensitive, and hence statements are entered in small case letters.

C has no specific rules about the position at which different parts of a statements be written. Not only can a C statement be written anywhere in a line, it can also be split over multiple lines. That is why it is called free-format language.

A C-statement ends with a semi-colon (;)

Every C program contains one main() function.

```
#include<stdio.h> main(){
printf("Hello World");
}
```

Creating and Compiling a C Program

Creating a compiling a C program on operating system use compiler and an integrated development environment. Code blocks is used for create and execute program of C language. File name is hello.c and save in windows operating system using code blocks IDE.

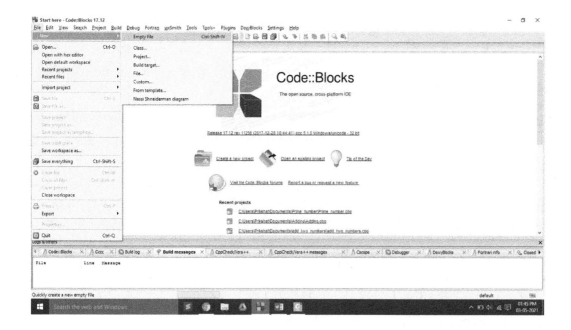

Click on empty file link and save that file with name hello.c and write code.

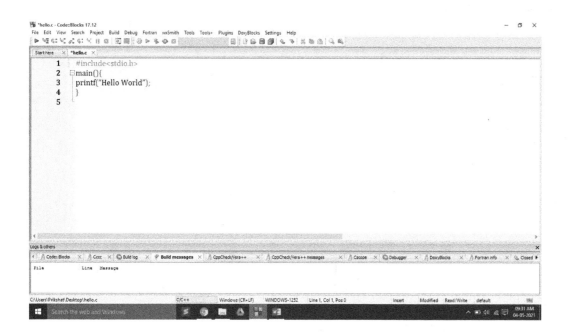

After write code in code blocks,

Gcc compiler is used for compiling code using code blocks

For compile press CTRL+F9 or click on build option and click on build

To run C program in code blocks after write code press first compile program than run (CTRL+F10).

Output will be

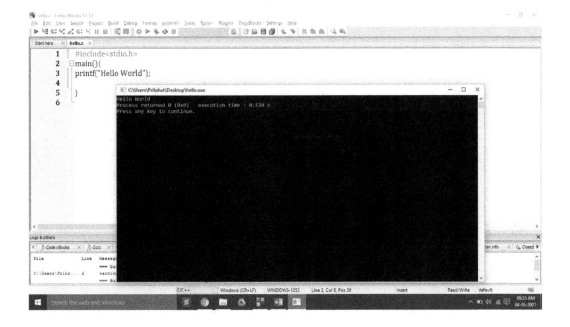

C Character set

Like each other language, 'C' additionally has its own character set. A program is a bunch of directions that, when executed, produce a yield. The information that is prepared by a program comprises of different characters and images. The yield produced is additionally a mix of characters and images.

A character set in 'C' is divided into

Letters

Numbers

Special characters

White spaces (blank spaces)

Letters

Uppercase characters (A-Z)

Lowercase characters (a-z)

Numbers

All the digits from 0 to 9

White spaces

Blank space

New line

Carriage return

Horizontal tab

Special characters

Special characters in 'C' are shown in the given table,

, (comma)	{ (opening curly bracket)
. (period)	} (closing curly bracket)
; (semi-colon)	[(left bracket)
: (colon)	] (right bracket)
? (question mark)	((opening left parenthesis)
' (apostrophe)	) (closing right parenthesis)
" (double quotation mark)	& (ampersand)
! (exclamation mark)	^ (caret)
|(vertical bar)	+ (addition)
/ (forward slash)	- (subtraction)
\ (backward slash)	* (multiplication)
~ (tilde)	/ (division)
_ (underscore)	> (greater than or closing angle bracket)
$ (dollar sign)	< (less than or opening angle bracket)
% (percentage sign)	# (hash sign)
, (comma)	{ (opening curly bracket)

Identifiers and keywords

Keywords have fixed meanings, and the meaning cannot be changed. They act as a building block of a 'C' program. There are a total of 32 keywords in 'C'. Keywords are written in lowercase letters.

auto	double	int	struct
break	else	long	switch
case	enum	register	typedef
char	extern	return	union
const	short	float	unsigned
continue	for	signed	void

An identifier is nothing but a name assigned to an element in a program. Example, name of a variable, function, etc.

Conclusion to "Introduction to C Programming"

1. Summarizing the Journey Through C Programming Fundamentals

Reflect on the major elements covered, underscoring the importance of each:

- **History and Evolution of C**: Summarize how C, created in the early 1970s by Dennis Ritchie at Bell Labs, quickly gained traction as the preferred language for system programming and later for other domains like embedded systems and applications due to its efficiency, portability, and ease of use. Acknowledge how understanding the history provides context and appreciation for the language's longevity and relevance.

- **C Language Features**: Highlight key features like portability, efficiency, modularity, and low-level access, explaining how these traits make C ideal for programming across a broad range of applications. Reinforce the importance of modular programming and how breaking code into manageable functions makes both development and debugging easier.

- **Setting up the Environment and Tools**: Acknowledge that setting up the environment and choosing the right tools is an essential step in learning any programming language. Reiterate how working with compilers, IDEs, and text editors enables efficient coding and builds confidence. Mention how practicing with the command line strengthens understanding of the compilation process and error troubleshooting.

- **Writing the First C Program**: Describe how writing the "Hello, World!" program is a universal rite of passage for programmers. Emphasize the value of understanding each line in this simple program, as it forms a foundation for writing more complex code. Highlight the importance of compiling, running, and troubleshooting errors as part of the learning process.

- **Basic Structure of a C Program**: Reinforce the foundational structure of C, including preprocessor directives, the main function, variable declarations, and basic statements. Explain that having a good grasp of this structure sets the stage for deeper dives into more advanced topics in programming.

2. Reflecting on the Benefits of Learning C

C is not just a language but a gateway to understanding the architecture of programming itself. Point out how learning C provides a strong foundation for learning other languages, particularly those heavily influenced by C, like C++, Java, and even newer languages like Rust. Here's how learning C helps in various aspects:

- **Efficiency and Problem Solving**: Explain that C is well-regarded for its ability to perform tasks efficiently. Mastering C forces programmers to think about memory management, pointers, and data types in ways that are often abstracted away in higher-level languages. This focus on problem-solving at the memory and hardware level makes for sharper programming skills overall.

- **Direct Hardware Interaction and System-Level Programming**: Describe how working with C brings a deeper understanding of the inner workings of computers. C is particularly valuable for those interested in system-level programming, as it allows for direct memory access and control over system resources. Explain that this experience is critical for fields like operating systems, embedded systems, and real-time applications were understanding how the hardware works is crucial.

- **Portability and Cross-Platform Development**: Emphasize the portability of C, which allows programs written in C to be compiled and run across multiple platforms with minimal changes. This portability provides programmers with a strong skill in adapting code across different operating systems, which can be highly beneficial in software development and deployment.

3. Addressing Common Challenges and Overcoming Them

Learning C is not without its challenges. Discuss some common challenges beginners face and how to address them:

- **Syntax and Semantics**: C's syntax is relatively strict and can lead to errors like missing semicolons, mismatched braces, or incorrect variable declarations. Encourage readers to pay close attention to detail and to learn from these mistakes as they arise.

- **Memory Management**: One of the more challenging aspects of C is managing memory, particularly with pointers and dynamic allocation. Explain that while these topics may seem complex, they are fundamental to understanding efficient coding practices, and mastery over them offers powerful control in programming.

- **Troubleshooting and Debugging**: Error messages in C may initially seem cryptic, and understanding them takes practice. Encourage readers to embrace debugging as a part of the learning journey, recommending strategies like breaking down code, using comments for clarity, and consulting documentation to identify and resolve errors effectively.

4. Building a Strong Foundation for Advanced Topics

The fundamentals covered so far lay the groundwork for diving into advanced topics. Describe how each area of learning in C programming leads naturally to the next level:

- **Control Structures and Logic**: Understanding the basics of control structures—such as if-statements, loops, and switch statements—sets the stage for more complex logic in programming, which is crucial for algorithms and problem-solving.

- **Data Structures**: Knowing C's data types and control flow forms a basis for understanding and implementing data structures like arrays, linked lists, stacks, and queues. Emphasize that these structures are fundamental in efficient data handling and manipulation.

- **Memory and Pointers**: Introduce pointers as a concept that will recur throughout advanced C programming. Explain how pointers, dynamic memory allocation, and memory management allow for efficient data handling and open doors to complex topics like linked data structures and memory-efficient programming.

- **Modularity and Code Organization**: The concept of breaking down tasks into functions prepares the reader to explore modular programming, code reuse, and even the basics of multi-file programs and libraries.

5. Encouraging a Growth Mindset in C Programming

Programming, especially in C, is a skill that improves with persistence and continuous practice. Encourage readers to approach programming with patience, noting that proficiency comes through consistent application and curiosity. Outline ways to practice effectively:

- **Start with Simple Projects**: Suggest that readers reinforce their skills by working on small projects, like calculators, simple games, or file-handling programs. Building something tangible can boost confidence and provide a sense of accomplishment.

- **Solve Problems**: Recommend engaging in coding challenges or problem-solving exercises on platforms like HackerRank, LeetCode, or CodeSignal, as these can improve logical thinking and understanding of algorithms.

- **Read and Analyze Code**: Encourage readers to explore open-source C projects or example programs to see how other programmers structure and solve problems. Analyzing real-world code can provide insights into best practices and techniques.

6. Charting the Path Forward: Next Steps in C Programming

After mastering the basics, outline some logical next steps to build upon their foundational knowledge:

- **Exploring C Libraries**: Suggest that readers explore standard libraries in C, such as stdlib.h, string.h, math.h, and others, to expand their toolbox and capabilities within the language.

- **Data Structures and Algorithms**: Emphasize the importance of learning data structures and algorithms, as they are crucial for efficient problem-solving and are highly applicable in software development.

- **File I/O and File Management**: Introduce file handling as the next step for working with real-world data. Explain how handling files in C enables readers to build applications that store data persistently.

- **Networking and Concurrent Programming**: Mention advanced topics like networking (using sockets) and concurrency (using threads). These are essential in fields like systems programming and can open doors to more specialized applications.

- **Contributing to Open Source**: Recommend exploring open-source projects written in C, as contributing to or learning from real-world projects can deepen understanding and provide hands-on experience.

7. Final Words of Encouragement

Conclude with encouragement to stay motivated and enjoy the process. Programming in C, while challenging, offers a rewarding journey through problem-solving and logical thinking. Remind readers that every step they take in C builds a skill set that is foundational to many other programming languages and technologies.

Emphasize that the road to mastery in C is long, but every challenge overcome, and every project completed will bring them closer to becoming proficient and confident in programming. This language not only builds technical skills but also cultivates a disciplined approach to problem-solving, an invaluable skill in any field of software development.

2. Basic Concepts Of C

Structure of a C Program

A C program's structure consists of specific components that work together to form a complete executable program. Let's break down the structure:

Header Files and Libraries

Every C program begins with preprocessor directives, typically the inclusion of header files such as <stdio.h>, <stdlib.h>, and <math.h>. These files contain declarations for standard functions and macros used throughout the program.

For example:

#include <stdio.h>

Preprocessor Directives

Preprocessor directives, marked by #, instruct the compiler to process commands before actual compilation. The #include directive tells the compiler to include specific libraries, while #define allows the creation of constants:

#define PI 3.14159

Main Function

The main() function is the entry point for any C program. It's where program execution begins. A basic main() function looks like this:

```
int main() {
    // Code statements
    return 0;
}
```

Returning 0 signals that the program has executed successfully. Code within main() and other functions is enclosed in braces {} to define the scope.

Code Blocks and Statements

Code blocks in C are defined by curly braces {}. Each statement in C ends with a semicolon; and blocks are often nested within each other, particularly in control structures or functions. For example:

```
if (condition) {
```

```
    // code block
}
```

Function Definitions

Functions are reusable blocks of code defined outside main(). Each function has a return type, a name, parameters (if any), and a code block. Example:

```
int add(int a, int b) {
    return a + b;
}
```

Functions allow for modular, readable, and reusable code.

3. Syntax and Coding Conventions

C syntax has specific rules that define how code is written and interpreted.

Syntax Basics

- **Case Sensitivity:** C is case-sensitive, meaning Var and var are different identifiers.
- **Statement Endings:** Each statement ends with a semicolon;
- **Comments:** Use // for single-line comments and /* ... */ for multi-line comments.

Naming Conventions

In C, identifiers (names of variables, functions, etc.) should be meaningful and follow consistent naming conventions.

Common styles include:

- **Camel Case:** camelCaseExample
- **Snake Case:** snake_case_example

Code Indentation and Style

For readability, C code follows indentation and bracket alignment conventions. Tools like clang-format can automatically format code.

Example style:

```
int main() {
    int number = 5;
```

```
    if (number > 0) {
        printf("Positive\n");
    }
}
```

This clarity becomes especially important in large, multi-developer projects.

4. Data Types, Variables, and Constants

Data types, variables, and constants are fundamental in defining the kind of data your program will handle and store.

Built-in Data Types

C provides several built-in data types to accommodate different kinds of data:

- **int:** Stores integers (whole numbers), typically 4 bytes.
- **float:** Stores floating-point numbers (decimals) with single precision.
- **double:** Stores floating-point numbers with double precision.
- **char:** Stores single characters, usually 1 byte, with ASCII representation.

Variable Declaration and Initialization

Variables in C must be declared before use, specifying the data type. Variables can be declared and initialized in a single line:

```
int age = 25;
float temperature = 98.6;
```

Variables can also be declared without immediate initialization, though they will contain garbage values until assigned.

Constants and Literals

Constants are fixed values that do not change during program execution. Use the const keyword to declare constants, ensuring they remain unaltered:

```
const int MAX_SCORE = 100;
```

Literals like 5, 3.14, and 'A' directly represent values of specific data types.

5. Input and Output Functions (printf and scanf)

The C Standard Library provides printf and scanf functions for handling input and output.

Overview of Standard I/O

Standard I/O functions like printf and scanf are part of the <stdio.h> library. They enable interaction with the user through text-based input and output.

Using printf for Formatted Output

printf is used to print text and variable values to the console. It supports various formatting options:

```
printf("Hello, World!\n");
int age = 25;
printf("I am %d years old.\n", age);
```

- %d for integers
- %f for floats
- %c for characters
- %s for strings

You can control the precision and width of displayed values, especially useful for floating-point numbers:

```
float price = 10.5;
printf("The price is $%.2f\n", price); // Output: 10.50
```

Using scanf for Input

scanf reads user input from the console, storing it in variables. Each format specifier in scanf corresponds to the expected input type:

```
int age;
scanf("%d", &age); // Note the use of `&` to pass the variable's address
```

Common format specifiers include:

- %d for integers
- %f for floats
- %c for characters
- %s for strings

Using & in scanf is crucial because scanf needs the variable's memory address to store the input. However, & is not used with strings, as they are inherently pointers.

Formatting Specifiers and Error Handling

Formatting specifiers in printf and scanf ensure the correct data types are used. Here's a list of commonly used specifiers:

- **%d**: Integers
- **%f**: Floating-point numbers
- **%lf**: Double-precision floats
- **%c**: Characters
- **%s**: Strings

Example Program: Combining Input and Output

Here's a sample program using both printf and scanf to take user input and display output:

```
#include <stdio.h>

int main() {
    int age;
    float height;

    // Prompt the user for input
    printf("Enter your age: ");
    scanf("%d", &age);

    printf("Enter your height in meters: ");
    scanf("%f", &height);

    // Display the input
    printf("You are %d years old and %.2f meters tall.\n", age, height);

    return 0;
}
```

This program introduces basic interactions with the user, leveraging input/output functions effectively.

Now that you have a solid understanding of the history and structure of C programming, it's time to roll up your sleeves and dive into the practical aspects of the language. In this chapter, we will guide you through the fundamental concepts and techniques that form the backbone of C programming.

We will begin by introducing you to the basic syntax of C. This includes the structure of a C program, how to declare variables, and how to write comments. Understanding the syntax is crucial as it forms the rules of the language, much like grammar in spoken languages.

Next, we will explore data types and variables. In C, every variable has a type, which determines the size and layout of the variable's memory, the range of values that it can hold, and the set of operations that can be applied to it. We will discuss the basic data types provided by C, such as integers, floating-point numbers, and characters, and show you how to declare and use variables of these types.

Following that, we will delve into operators and expressions. Operators are symbols that tell the compiler to perform specific mathematical or logical manipulations. C has a wide range of operators, including arithmetic operators, relational operators, and logical operators. We will discuss how to use these operators to form expressions, which are the building blocks of C programs.

Finally, we will discuss control structures, which allow you to control the flow of your program. This includes conditional statements such as if and switch, and loops such as for and while. Understanding control structures is key to writing programs that can make decisions and perform repetitive tasks.

By the end of this chapter, you will have the knowledge and skills to write simple C programs. You will understand the basic syntax of C, know how to use various data types and operators, and be able to control the flow of your program using control structures. So, let's get started with C!

Basic Syntax

The syntax of a programming language is the set of rules that define the combinations of symbols that are considered to be correctly structured programs in that language. In this section, we will cover the basic syntax of C programming.

Structure of a C Program

A typical C program consists of one or more functions, one of which must be named `main`. The `main` function serves as the starting point of the program.

Here's the simplest possible C program:

```
int main() {    return 0;
}
```

This program does nothing but return an exit status of 0, which generally indicates that the program has run successfully.

Comments

Comments are used to explain the code and improve its readability. They are ignored by the compiler. In C, there are two types of comments: - Single-line comments, which start with `//`. Everything from the `//` to the end of the line is a comment.

Multi-line comments, which start with `/*` and end with `*/`. Everything in between is a comment.

Here's an example:

```
// This is a single-line comment
/* This is a
   multi-line comment */
```

Variables and Data Types

In C, every variable has a type, which determines the size and layout of the variable's memory, the range of values that it can hold, and the set of operations that can be applied to it.

Here's an example of declaring an integer variable:

```
int myVariable;
```

Statements and Blocks

A statement is a simple or compound instruction that can include expressions and declarations. Each statement must end with a semicolon (`;`).

Here's an example of a statement:

```
int myVariable = 5;
```

A block is a group of statements enclosed in curly braces (`{}`), and can be used wherever a single statement is allowed.

Here's an example of a block:

```
{
int myVariable = 5;
```

```
myVariable = myVariable + 1;
}
```

Control Structures

Control structures determine the flow of a program. They include conditionals like `if` and `switch`, and loops like `for` and `while`.

Here's an example of an `if` statement:

```
if (myVariable > 5) {
// This block is executed if myVariable is greater than 5
}
```

This is just a brief overview of the basic syntax of C. As you continue to learn C, you will encounter more complex syntax and more powerful features.

Data Types and Variables

In C programming, every variable has a type, which determines the size and layout of the variable's memory, the range of values that it can hold, and the set of operations that can be applied to it. Understanding data types and how to use them is fundamental to programming in C.

Basic Data Types

In C programming, data types are declarations for variables. This determines the type and size of data associated with variables.

The C language provides several basic data types, including:

1. **Integers**: In the C language, one of the fundamental types used to represent numerical data is the integer data type. Integer types are integral data types that can hold whole numbers, both positive and negative, excluding decimal or fractional parts. This chapter delves into the understanding of integer data types in C and outlines their different variations, including signed char, short, int, long, long long, unsigned char, unsigned short, unsigned int, unsigned long, unsigned long long, and fixed width integer types like int8_t, int16_t, int32_t, uint8_t, uint16_t, and uint32_t.

Signed Integer Types

Signed Char

The 'signed char' data type in C is used to store signed character or small integers. It has a size of 1 byte, which translates to 8 bits. This means it can hold values from -128 to 127.

Short

The 'short' data type, or more formally 'short int', is used to store signed integers. The size of the 'short' data type is 2 bytes, which allows it to store values from -32,768 to 32,767.

Int

The 'int' data type is the most commonly used data type for storing signed integers. The size of 'int' usually is 4 bytes, which allows it to store values from -2,147,483,648 to 2,147,483,647.

Long

The 'long' or 'long int' data type is used for larger integers. The size of a 'long' is typically 4 bytes, allowing it to store values from -2,147,483,648 to 2,147,483,647. Note that on some platforms and compilers, 'long' may have a size of 8 bytes.

Long Long

The 'long long' or 'long long int' data type is used for storing very large integers. The size of 'long long' is 8 bytes, allowing it to store values from -9,223,372,036,854,775,808 to 9,223,372,036,854,775,807.

Unsigned Integer Types

The unsigned integer types only represent non-negative numbers (zero and positive integers).

Unsigned Char

The 'unsigned char' type is used to store unsigned small integers or characters. It has a size of 1 byte and can hold values from 0 to 255.

Unsigned Short

The 'unsigned short' or 'unsigned short int' type is used for storing unsigned small integers. It has a size of 2 bytes, allowing it to store values from 0 to 65,535.

Unsigned Int

The 'unsigned int' type is used for storing unsigned integers. Typically, the size of 'unsigned int' is 4 bytes, allowing it to store values from 0 to 4,294,967,295.

Unsigned Long

The 'unsigned long' or 'unsigned long int' type is used for larger unsigned integers. The size of 'unsigned long' is usually 4 bytes, but it can be 8 bytes on some platforms and compilers. For a size of 4 bytes, it can store values from 0 to 4,294,967,295.

Unsigned Long Long

The 'unsigned long long' or 'unsigned long long int' type is used for very large unsigned integers. It has a size of 8 bytes, allowing it to store values from 0 to 18,446,744,073,709,551,615.

Fixed Width Integer Types

C99 introduced fixed-width integer types. These types have specified widths, making them platform-independent. They are defined in the `<stdint.h>` library.

int8_t, int16_t, int32_t

These are signed integer types with widths of 8, 16, and 32 bits respectively. For example, 'int8_t' can hold values from -128 to 127, while 'int32_t' can store values from -2,147,483,648 to 2,147,483,647.

uint8_t, uint16_t, uint32_t

These are unsigned integer types with widths of 8, 16, and 32 bits respectively. For example, 'uint8_t' can hold values from 0 to 255, while 'uint32_t' can store values from 0 to 4,294,967,295.

In conclusion, when programming in C, it is essential to understand the ranges and limitations of each integer type. Using the appropriate integer type based on your needs can lead to more efficient memory usage and prevent unexpected behaviors due to integer overflow or underflow.

2. **float, double** and **long double**: The C language provides three distinct data types for representing real numbers (numbers that can have a decimal fraction), i.e., floating-point numbers. These types are `float`, `double`, and `long double`.

Float

A `float` type in C is used to represent real numbers, providing significant digits of about six decimal places. The range of values can be approximately from 1.2E-38 to 3.4E+38. The exact limits depend on the implementation, but you can retrieve them in your program using the `FLT_MIN` and `FLT_MAX` constants from the `<float.h>` library. The `float` type is a good choice when your program requires fractional precision, but not extreme accuracy. For example, it is often used in graphics libraries because the precision provided is sufficient for screen resolutions and the memory savings are beneficial.

Double

A `double` type in C is a double-precision floating-point type. It provides roughly double the precision of a `float`, about 15 decimal places. The range of values can be approximately from 2.3E-308 to 1.7E+308. You can retrieve the exact limits in your program using the `DBL_MIN` and `DBL_MAX` constants from the `<float.h>` library.

The `double` type is often the default choice for calculations involving real numbers as it provides a good balance between precision and performance. It is used in scientific calculations that require high precision and can tolerate larger memory usage.

Long Double

A `long double` type in C provides even more precision than a `double`. The actual size and range of a `long double` can vary between platforms and compilers, but it is at least as large as `double`. This type is usually used when extremely high precision is required.

The precision and range of `long double` can also be accessed using the `LDBL_MIN` and `LDBL_MAX` constants from the `<float.h>` library.

It's important to note that while `long double` offers more precision, it does come with a cost. The memory requirement is higher and arithmetic operations can be slower. Therefore, it's typically used in scientific and mathematical applications where the extra precision is critical.

In conclusion, the choice between `float`, `double`, and `long double` should be dictated by the specific needs of your program. While a `float` might be more efficient in terms of memory usage, `double` and `long double` provide higher precision, which might be necessary for certain calculations. Understanding the trade-offs between these types is key to writing efficient and accurate C programs.

char: This is a character type, used to represent individual characters. `char` variables are typically 1 byte in size, and can represent a character using ASCII encoding. For example, the character 'A' is represented by the number 65. `char` can be signed or unsigned, affecting its range. An unsigned `char` type can represent values from 0 to 255, while a signed `char` can represent values from -128 to 127.

void: This is a special type that represents the absence of a type. It is typically used to indicate that a function does not return a value or does not take any parameters. For example, a function with a `void` return type does not return a value.

bool: This is a boolean type, used to represent true or false values. In C, `bool` is not a built-in data type. Instead, it is defined in the `stdbool.h` header file. A `bool` variable can store either `true` (which is equivalent to integer 1) or `false` (which is equivalent to integer 0).

These basic data types form the foundation of data storage in C. Understanding these types and how they work is crucial to writing effective C code.

Variables

In C programming, a variable is a named location in memory where a value can be stored for use by a program. Variables are the basic units of storage in a program. The value stored in a variable can be changed during program execution. A variable is only readable and writable piece of memory.

Variables in C must be declared before they can be used. This is done using a declaration statement, which specifies the type of the variable and its name.

The general syntax for declaring a variable is:

type variable_name;

Here, `type` is one of C's data types, and `variable_name` is any valid identifier. For example, to declare an integer variable named `myVariable`, you would write:

int myVariable;

In this case, `int` is the data type (representing an integer), and `myVariable` is the name of the variable.

You can also initialize a variable at the time of declaration. Initialization means assigning a value to the variable when you declare it.

The syntax for this is:

type variable_name = value;

For example, to declare an integer variable named `myVariable` and initialize it with the value 10, you would write:

int myVariable = 10;

In this case, `myVariable` is being initialized with the value `10`. This means that the memory location named `myVariable` now contains the integer value `10`.

It's important to note that each variable in C has a specific type, which determines the size and layout of the variable's memory, the range of values that can be stored within that memory, and the set of operations that can be applied to the variable.

Constants

In C programming, constants refer to fixed values that do not change during the execution of a program. Constants can be of any basic data type like `int`, `char`, `double`, etc., and can be divided into Integer Numerals, Floating-Point Numerals, Characters, Strings, and Defined Constants.

Defined constants are created using the `#define` preprocessor directive. This directive tells the C preprocessor to replace instances of the defined constants with the specified value before the actual compilation process begins.

The syntax for defining a constant using `#define` is:

#define constant_name value

Here, `constant_name` is the name of the constant you want to define, and `value` is the value of the constant.

For example, to define a constant that represents the mathematical constant pi, you could write:

#define PI 3.14159

In this example, `PI` is a constant that represents the value of pi. Anywhere the preprocessor sees `PI` in the code, it will replace it with `3.14159`. This means you can use `PI` in your program as if it were a variable that holds the value `3.14159`, but unlike a variable, you cannot change the value of `PI`.

Another way to define constants in C is using the `const` keyword. The `const` keyword allows you to specify that a variable's value is constant and tells the compiler to prevent the programmer from modifying it.

const double pi = 3.14159;

In this case, `pi` is a constant with the value `3.14159`. Any attempt to change the value of `pi` later in the program will result in a compile error.

Understanding data types and variables is crucial to writing effective C code. As you continue to learn C, you will encounter more complex data types, such as arrays, pointers, and structures.

The `const` keyword can also be used with pointers to create "constant pointers" and "pointers to constants".

Constant Pointers

A constant pointer is a pointer that cannot change the address it is pointing to. Here's how you can declare a constant pointer:

int x = 10; int * const p = &x;

In this example, `p` is a constant pointer to an integer. You can change the value of `x` through `p`, but you cannot change `p` to point to a different integer.

Pointers to Constants

A pointer to a constant is a pointer that cannot change the value it is pointing to. Here's how you can declare a pointer to a constant:

const int x = 10;

const int *p = &x;

In this example, `p` is a pointer to a constant integer. You can change `p` to point to a different integer, but you cannot change the value of `x` through `p`.

Conclusion

In this introduction to C programming, we've journeyed through the foundational components that define the language. By understanding C's **basic concepts, program structure, syntax and coding conventions, data types, variables, and constants**, and **input/output functions**, you've built a toolkit that's essential for moving forward with more advanced topics in C and programming in general.

Each of these concepts plays a critical role in writing efficient, functional C programs. C's syntax may seem straightforward, but the language demands clarity, structure, and discipline, as it offers very little in the way of built-in safeguards compared to newer languages. This discipline in coding becomes a valuable skill that translates well into other languages and contexts. Let's dive deeper into each area, reinforcing their significance in programming with C and beyond.

1. The Power of C's Basic Concepts

The **basic concepts of C** revolve around understanding the language's purpose and its low-level capabilities, which make it unique. C is celebrated for its efficiency and control over memory and system resources. It's often referred to as a "portable assembly language," meaning it bridges the gap between machine code and higher-level abstractions. Learning C introduces fundamental computer science concepts like pointers, memory management, and low-level I/O handling, which are often abstracted away in other languages.

One of the reasons C has remained relevant over decades is its portability.

Programs written in C can run on various hardware architectures with minimal modification, making it a preferred language in systems programming. This legacy of portability, combined with the fact that C underpins many modern languages (like C++, Java, Python), makes learning C an investment in long-term programming skills.

In summary: Understanding C's foundational purpose and structure grants you a unique ability to appreciate how computer systems work at a granular level and fosters skills in writing high-performance code.

2. Structure of a C Program: The Blueprint of Execution

A well-structured C program follows a specific layout that ensures readability, maintainability, and efficiency. Every program begins with **header files** and **preprocessor directives** that set up the necessary environment for compiling. By incorporating standard libraries (e.g., <stdio.h> for input/output), C programs can leverage pre-defined functions and constants, reducing redundant code and focusing efforts on program-specific functionality.

The **main() function** acts as the entry point for execution. This structure not only aids in understanding the flow of a program but also allows for modularity by separating different functionalities into different functions. This functional organization is foundational not only to C but to programming in general. In large-scale programs, this modular approach aids in debugging, testing, and enhancing individual program segments without impacting the rest of the codebase.

In summary: Learning to structure a C program is akin to learning the basics of architecture in building design—it provides the scaffolding for creating more complex systems while ensuring efficiency and clarity in smaller programs.

3. Syntax and Coding Conventions: Crafting Readable, Consistent Code

Syntax and coding conventions are critical in C programming due to its explicit and strict nature. Unlike more recent languages, C does not provide extensive error-checking or syntactic sugar, which means programmers must adhere strictly to syntax rules. The language is case-sensitive, requires precise punctuation, and demands clear separation of statements, variables, and data types.

Coding conventions in C, such as using meaningful variable names, indentation, and consistent styling, make code more readable and maintainable. Well-written C code is easier to debug and enhances collaboration, as other programmers can quickly understand the logic and structure. Furthermore, adhering to conventions early on helps build habits that will be beneficial in any programming environment.

In summary: The importance of syntax and conventions in C teaches precision, discipline, and clarity—qualities that transcend C programming and are valuable in any coding or problem-solving context.

4. Data Types, Variables, and Constants: Building Blocks of C

Data types, variables, and constants form the foundation for data storage and manipulation in C. C offers several **primitive data types** such as int, float, double, and char, each serving a specific role in storing and representing data efficiently. Understanding the different data types, as well as the storage they require and the limits they impose, helps programmers make efficient choices, particularly in memory-constrained environments.

Variables are the names associated with storage locations that hold data values, and their correct declaration and initialization are essential to prevent bugs or undefined behavior. **Constants** provide a way to define fixed values that remain unchanged throughout a program's execution, helping avoid magic numbers in code, making programs more readable, and preventing accidental modification.

In C, where direct memory access through pointers is possible, it is essential to have a strong understanding of data types to prevent undefined behavior, memory leaks, or crashes. The language's design enforces a rigorous approach to data handling, preparing you to tackle more complex topics like pointers, arrays, and memory allocation.

In summary: Mastering data types, variables, and constants in C is essential not only for managing data efficiently but also for laying the groundwork for more advanced memory handling techniques.

5. Input and Output Functions (printf and scanf): Interacting with the User

The **input/output (I/O) functions** printf and scanf provide a direct way to interact with the user. C, as a low-level language, lacks the advanced I/O handling seen in some higher-level languages, but printf and scanf cover the basics needed for formatted output and user input. Understanding how to use these functions, especially in conjunction with format specifiers, is critical for working with different data types and ensuring accurate, formatted data processing.

Learning to use printf for formatted output is beneficial, as it introduces basic data formatting concepts that apply to various programming environments and languages. scanf, although powerful, requires careful handling due to its lack of built-in error handling and potential pitfalls when reading different types of input. Developing an understanding of these functions—and the importance of managing input/output carefully—builds skills in basic data handling, formatted output, and user interaction.

In summary: Proficiency in printf and scanf equips you with essential tools for handling user interaction, preparing you to manage more complex I/O operations in C or other languages.

The Broader Impact of Learning C Programming

Learning C goes beyond understanding syntax and structure; it introduces critical thinking in terms of **efficiency, problem-solving, and debugging**. C doesn't offer as many safeguards as modern programming languages, which makes it essential for programmers to write code that's safe, optimized, and understandable. Each concept we covered has contributed to building these qualities in your approach to programming.

For example:

- Understanding **data types and memory allocation** helps avoid memory leaks.
- Mastering the **structure of a C program** enables you to build well-organized, modular programs.
- Following **coding conventions** ensures readability and maintainability, which are crucial in collaborative environments.

By building a foundation in C, you've also gained insight into the underlying principles that shape computer science and systems programming. As you continue learning, you'll find that many of these skills and practices apply to languages like C++, Python, and Java, albeit with more abstraction. This versatility and foundational knowledge allow C programmers to adapt to various environments and challenges.

What's Next?

After understanding these fundamentals, the next logical step is to explore more advanced topics:

1. **Control Structures** (if-else, loops, switch statements) for decision-making and repetition.
2. **Functions and Scope** to deepen understanding of modular programming.
3. **Pointers and Dynamic Memory Allocation** to manage memory directly.
4. **Data Structures** such as arrays, linked lists, and structs for managing collections of data.
5. **File Handling** for more complex input/output operations.

Advanced topics like **pointers**, **dynamic memory management**, and **file handling** will require a solid understanding of what we've covered, as they build on these foundational principles. For example, pointers rely on a deep understanding of data types and variables, and dynamic memory allocation necessitates precise control over variable scope and lifecycle.

3. Control Structures in C

Introduction to Control Structures

Control structures in C determine the flow of program execution based on conditions or repetition. These structures enhance program flexibility, allowing for decision-making and looping processes. This section provides a foundation for writing efficient, readable, and maintainable C code.

1. Conditional Statements

Conditional statements control the flow based on specific conditions. They are essential for decision-making, where actions are performed if certain criteria are met.

1.1 if Statement

- Syntax and usage.

- Examples:

  - Checking if a number is positive.
  - Using an if statement within functions.

- Common mistakes (e.g., missing braces in single-line if statements).

1.2 if-else Statement

- When and how to use the else branch.

- Examples:

  - Classifying a score as pass/fail.
  - Using if-else for error handling.

- Tips for readability in nested if-else structures.

1.3 else if Ladder

- Explanation of multiple condition handling.

- Examples:

- o   Grade classification (A, B, C, etc.).
- o   Handling multiple scenarios in input validation.

- Potential pitfalls in deeply nested if-else if ladders.

1.4 switch Statement

- Syntax and purpose.

- Examples:

  - o   Menu selection in programs.
  - o   Handling input commands.

- Best practices:

  - o   Using break statements to prevent fall-through.
  - o   The role of the default case.

2. Looping Structures

Loops allow repetition, reducing code duplication and enabling complex iterative processes.

2.1 for Loop

- Syntax and structure.

- Examples:

  - o   Summing numbers.
  - o   Iterating through arrays.

- Use cases and when to prefer for loops.

2.2 while Loop

- Syntax and purpose.

- Examples:
  - o   Calculating factorials.

- o Waiting for a specific condition.

- Differences from for loops and ideal use cases.

2.3 do-while Loop

- Syntax and examples.

- Example scenarios:

  - o Menu-driven programs requiring user input.

- When to use do-while over while.

2.4 Nesting Loops

- Explanation with syntax.

- Examples:

  - o Multiplication tables.
  - o Working with multi-dimensional arrays.

- Performance considerations.

What is a statement?

A statement is an expression ending with a semicolon symbol (;).
For example, x + y is an expression, but x + y; is a statement. Let us list a few simple statements we have used so far:

int x; – a statement containing a declaration int x = 123; – a statement containing an initialization x = 123; – a simple assignment statement z = x + y; – a statement with multiple expressions x++; – a statement having a postfix increment expression printf("Hello World!"); – a function call statement.

Every statement except the last one is called an expression statement because they consist solely of expressions. The last statement is a function call statement. We often say that statements are executed and expressions are evaluated.

Let us write a simple source code example to explain the terminology:

```
#include <stdio.h>
int main(void)
```

```
{
    int x = 123; int y = 456;     int z = x + y;
    printf("The result is: %d\n", z);
}
```

Output:

The result is: 579

In this example, statements inside the function main() are executed in a sequence, one after the other. Statements inside the function body marked with {} are also called compound statements. The entire block is often referred to as a block of statements or code block.

Now, with the terminology out of the way, let us learn about the built-in statements. These statements are part of the C programming language itself. They have reserved names and special syntax and can be divided into several categories:

Selection statements (conditional statements):

if statement
if-else statement
switch statement

Iteration statements or loops:

for statement

while statement

do-while statement

Selection Statements

Selection statements execute other statements based on some expression (condition). If that expression evaluates to anything other than 0, they proceed to execute other statements. Here we will explain the following selection statements:

if statement
if-else statement
switch statement

if statement

The if statement is of the following syntax:

```
if (some_condition) some_statement;
```

The if statement checks an expression (a condition) first. The condition is surrounded by parentheses (). If that condition (expression) evaluates to true (anything other than 0), the specified statement is executed. If the condition is false (the condition evaluates to 0), the statement will not be executed.

The following example uses an if statement to execute a single printf statement:

```
#include <stdio.h>
int main(void)
{
    int x = 123;     if (x < 150)
        printf("The x is less than 150.\n");
}
```

The if statement checks the condition first. In our case, it checks if x is less than some arbitrary number 150. If so, the condition is true, and the printf statement is executed. If the condition is false, the printf call will not be executed.

The if statement can also execute a block of statements/multiple statements marked with braces {}.

The syntax is:

```
if (some_condition)
{
    some_statement_1;     some_statement_2;     some_statement_3;
    // ...
}
```

An example that uses the if statement to execute a block of statements:

```
#include <stdio.h>
int main(void)
{
    int x = 123; if (x < 150)
    {
        printf("The x is less than 150.\n"); printf("This is a second statement.\n");
    }
}
```

Output:

The x is less than 150.

This is a second statement.

The if statement is a perfect use case for logical operators && and || where these operators can appear as part of the condition expression.

An example that uses the logical AND operator &&:

```
#include <stdio.h>
int main(void)
{
    int x = 123; int y = 456;
    if (x < 150 && y > 150)
    {
        printf("The condition is true.\n");
    }
}
```

Output:

The condition is true.

The condition in this if statement says: If both x is less than 150 and y is greater than 150, the entire condition is true, and the printf statement gets executed.

Let us now write a similar example that uses a logical OR operator || instead:

```
#include <stdio.h>
int main(void)
{
    int x = 123;     int y = 456;
    if (x < 150 || y > 150)
    {
        printf("The condition is true.\n");
    }
}
```

Output:

The condition is true.

This condition checks if either x is less than 150 or y is greater than 150. If either of these is true, the entire expression is true, and the printf function gets called/executed inside the code block.

To use a negation operator! inside the if statement condition, we write:

```
#include <stdio.h>
int main(void)
{
    int x = 0; if (!x)
    {
        printf("The condition is true.\n");
    }
}
```

Output:

The condition is true.

In this example, the negation operator! negates the value of x. Since x was 0, the negation operator turns it into 1, which stands for true, rendering the entire! x expression true. Since now the condition is true, the if statement executes the code block with our printf function in it.

Note   It is a good practice always to use the code block marked with {} inside the if and other conditional statements, even when the code block contains only one statement. This is for readability reasons.

if-else statement

In addition to an if statement, there is also an if-else variation.

The if-else statement is of the following syntax:

if (some_condition) some_statement_1; else   some_statement_2;

The if-else statement checks the condition value, and if the condition is true, it executes some_statement1. If the condition is false, it executes some_statement_2 coming after the else keyword.

Example:

```
#include <stdio.h>
int main(void)
{
    int x = 123;     if (x < 150)
```

```c
        printf("The condition is true. X is less than 150.\n");      else
        printf("The condition is false. X is not less than 150.\n");
}
```

Output:

The condition is true. X is less than 150.

This example uses a simple condition to check if x is less than some arbitrary number 150. If the condition is true, the first printf function executes. Otherwise, when x is not less than 150, (when the condition is false), the second printf statement executes.

To execute more than one statement in either if or else sections, we surround the statements with code blocks {}:

```c
#include <stdio.h>
int main(void)
{
    int x = 123;      if (x < 150)
    {
        printf("The condition is true. X is less than 150.\n");
printf("This is the second statement in the if-block\n");
    }    else
    {
        printf("The condition is false. X is not less than 150.\n");
printf("This is the second statement in the else-block\n");
    }
}
```

Output:

The condition is true. X is less than 150.

This is the second statement in the if-block

As before, when executing statement(s) from conditional statements, it is a good practice to use the code blocks {}, even if there is only one statement to be executed:

```c
#include <stdio.h>
int main(void)
{
    int x = 123;      if (x < 150)
    {
```

```
        printf("The condition is true. X is less than 150.\n");
    }      else
    {
        printf("The condition is false. X is not less than 150.\n");
    }
}
```

Output:

The condition is true. X is less than 150.

Switch statement

The switch statement executes a code based on integral expression value.

It is of the following syntax:

```
switch (expression)
{ case value_1: statements;
break;
case value_2: statements;

break;

case value_3: statements;
break;
    default:
        statement;
    break;
}
```

The code above is a switch statement blueprint. Let us break the above wordy syntax into pseudo-code segments and analyze the switch statement structure, one segment at a time.

The switch statement evaluates the value of an expression inside parentheses followed by a switch statement body marked with {}. The expression inside parentheses must be of type char, int, signed, unsigned, or enum (we cover enums later in the book).

So far, it looks like the following:

```
switch (expression) {

}
```

The switch statement body can have one or more case: labels. Each case label has a constant expression that is of char, int, signed, unsigned, or enum type followed by a colon sign (:).

Now the switch statement looks like this:

```
switch (expression)
{
case value_1:
case value_2:
case value_3:
}
```

If the constant-expression value inside the case: label matches the value of the expression, the statement inside that case label is executed. The statement needs to be followed by a break; statement. A break or return statement exits the switch statement. If we leave out the break; statement, the code would fall through, meaning the code in the next case label would also execute.

Now, our switch statement looks like:

```
switch (expression)
{
case value_1: some_statement;
break;
case value_2: some_statement;
break;
case value_3: some_statement;
break;
}
```

And finally, there is a default: label. If none of the case label values match the expression value, the statement inside the default: label gets executed. It is good practice to put a break statement inside the default label as well.

Our full pseudo-code switch statement now looks like:

```
switch (expression)
{
case value_1: statements;
break;
case value_2: statements;
break;
    default:
        statement;
break;
}
```

Now we are ready to write a complete source code example that uses the switch statement:

```
#include <stdio.h>
```

```c
int main(void)
{
    int x = 123;
switch (x)
{
case 100:
printf("The value of x is 100.\n");
break;
case 123:
printf("The value of x is 123.\n");
break;
case 456:
printf("The value of x is 456.\n");
break;
    default:
        printf("None of the above values matches the value of x.\n");
break;
    }
}
```

Output:

The value of x is 123.

This example initializes an integer variable x to the value of 123. Then, it uses the switch statement to check if the value of x is equal to either 100, 123, or 456. Since the second case label indeed checks for the value of 123, the printf statement in that label is executed.

Let us now write an example that uses type char:

```c
#include <stdio.h>
int main(void)
{
    char c = 'a';
switch (c)
{
case 'a':
printf("The value of c is 'a'.\n");
break;
case 'b':

printf("The value of c is 'b'.\n");

break;
case 'c':
printf("The value of x is 'c'.\n");
break;
```

```
        default:
            printf("None of the above values matches the value of c.\n");
break;
        }
}
```

Output:

The value of c is 'a'.

We initialize a char variable to the value of 'a'. The switch statement checks for matching value and executes the code in the appropriate case label. We are now using the type char. This means the constant expressions inside the case labels can now use character   constants marked with single quotes ''. Here, the value inside the first case label matches the value of the variable c, and the statement inside this label is executed.

We use the switch statement when we want to check for multiple values and then act accordingly. The switch statement is equivalent to having multiple if branches.

Iteration Statements

Iteration statements allow us to execute other statements multiple times/repeatedly. These statements are also called loops.

There are three different loops in C:

while loop
do-while loop
for loop

While statement

The while statement is of the following syntax:

```
while(some_expression)

{

    some_statements;
}
```

The while statement executes one or more statements while the expression inside the parentheses is true/not equal to 0.

A simple example that prints out a message 5 times:

#include <stdio.h>

```
int main(void)
{
    int mycounter = 0; while (mycounter < 5)
    {
        printf("Hello World from a while loop.\n");
mycounter++;
    }
}
```

Explanation: we initialize a variable that represents a counter to a value of 0. The while statement evaluates the expression mycounter < 5 inside the parentheses. If the expression is true/other than 0, the while loop executes the code inside the while loop body. This process repeats until the mycounter < 5 becomes false/0.

In this example, there are two statements inside the while loop body. The first statement prints out a simple message, and the second statement mycounter++; increases the counter by one. At some point, the mycounter will get the value of 5, causing the condition mycounter < 5 to become 0 and the while statement to end. In general, the while loop may execute 0 or more times as its condition is at the beginning.

do-while statement

The do-while statement is of the following syntax:

do { some_statements; } while (some_expression);

The do-while loop continues to execute statements until the condition/expression while the condition is true/ other than 0. In different words, it repeatedly executes a code block until the condition becomes equal to 0/false. The do-while statement is guaranteed to execute the statements inside its body at least once. This is because the condition is placed at the end, after the do-while code block.

Let us write an example that uses a do-while loop to display a message 5 times:

```
#include <stdio.h>
int main(void)
{
    int mycounter = 0;
do {
        printf("Hello World from a do-while loop.\n");
mycounter++;
    } while (mycounter < 5);
}
```

Explanation: the example initializes the integer variable to 0. Then the do-while code block executes the printf and the mycounter++ statements. Then it checks the condition mycounter < 5. If the condition evaluates to anything other than 0, the code inside the code block is executed again. Once the mycounter reaches the value of 5, the condition mycounter < 5 evaluates to 0 and the do-while loop exits.

for statement

The for loop has the following blueprint:

```
for (initialization; condition; iteration;)
{
    // loop body
}
```

The for loop repeatedly executes the statements in its loop body as long as the condition is true. In addition to a condition, the for loop also has its initialization and iteration parts.

The for loop initializes a counter variable in the initialization part, checks the condition, executes the loop body, and then increments or decrements the counter in the iteration part. The loop continues to execute the statements in the loop body as long as the condition is true.

In plain words, the for loop is like a while loop, but with its own counter, a condition, and an iteration part.

Let us write an example that prints out a message 5 times:

```
#include <stdio.h>
int main(void)
{
    for (int i = 0; i < 5; i++)
    {
        printf("Hello World from a for loop.\n");
    }
}
```

Explanation: in the for-loop section, we declare an integer variable called I and initialize it to 0. This variable will serve as our counter, and this expression is evaluated only once. Next, the condition i < 5 is evaluated. If it evaluates to true/other than 0, the statement in the for-loop body is executed. Then the i variable is incremented by one in the i++; part. Now the entire process (except the initialization part) repeats itself. When i reaches 5, the condition i < 5 evaluates to 0 and the for loop exits.

To execute a loop body 10 times, we would rewrite the condition to i < 10 and so on.

The counter can also use the prefix variation in the iteration segment:

```
#include <stdio.h>
int main(void)
{
    for (int i = 0; i < 5; ++i)
    {
        printf("Hello World from a for loop.\n");
    }
}
```

To print out the value of a counter, we write:

```
#include <stdio.h>
int main(void)
{
    for (int i = 0; i < 5; i++)
    {
        printf("Counter value: %d\n", i);
    }
}
```

The type of the counter variable i can also be size_t (which stands for unsigned integer type), unsigned.

The counter itself does not have to start from 0, it can start from any number. It is zero by convention. for loops are often used to print out array elements which themselves are indexed from 0. We will cover this in more detail when we learn about arrays and array indexes.

In a nutshell, the for loop is a convenient way to repeatedly execute statements a given (fixed) number of times while having access to an index/counter. One example is iterating over array elements.

Conclusion: Mastering Control Structures in C

Control structures form the fundamental core of programming in C, enabling programmers to write logical, organized, and efficient code that responds to a variety of conditions and repetitive tasks. Without control structures, a program would execute linearly from start to finish without variation, severely limiting its usefulness and adaptability. By incorporating conditional statements and looping mechanisms, control structures allow C programs to make decisions and repeat processes, opening the door to building complex applications and solving sophisticated problems.

In this discussion, we examined the key components of control structures in C, exploring **conditional statements** (if, else if, else, and switch) and **looping structures** (for, while, and do-while). Understanding and utilizing these constructs effectively is essential for any C programmer, as they are applicable in nearly every C application—from simple scripts to complex, data-driven software.

The Role of Conditional Statements in Decision-Making

Conditional statements are a pillar of programming logic, as they enable programs to evaluate conditions and determine an appropriate course of action based on those conditions.

Here's how each type of conditional statement contributes to a program's flexibility:

1. **if Statements**: The if statement is one of the simplest yet most essential tools in C programming. It allows for a single condition to be evaluated, executing code only when the condition is true. This basic construct enables programmers to create decision points in their code, adding responsiveness to user inputs, data states, or real-time events. The if statement also provides a foundation for more complex structures, like if-else and else if ladders.

2. **if-else Statements**: When a program requires alternative actions for different outcomes, the if-else statement is ideal. By providing a secondary path of execution if the initial condition is false, it ensures that a program can handle multiple scenarios. This structure is particularly useful for error handling, status checking, and scenarios where only one of two possible paths should be executed.

3. **else if Ladder**: For decision-making with multiple conditions, the else if ladder extends the if-else construct, allowing several conditions to be checked in sequence. Each else if condition provides an additional layer of complexity, enabling programs to evaluate a series of scenarios and take the appropriate action. This is particularly beneficial when working with categorized data, grading systems, or dynamic user inputs. However, it is essential to manage else if ladders carefully, as deeply nested structures can reduce readability and increase the chance of logic errors.

4. **switch Statements**: The switch statement offers an efficient alternative to multiple if-else statements, especially when dealing with discrete, constant values. By comparing a single expression against various cases, switch statements streamline the code and improve readability, especially for menu-driven programs, input handling, and control-flow decisions based on discrete states. One of the best practices in using switch statements is to include a default case, which acts as a catch-all for unmatched conditions. This practice is critical for robust error handling, ensuring that all possible values are accounted for in the program.

Together, these conditional statements allow developers to create C programs that respond dynamically to different conditions, adapting based on user input, data values, or environmental variables. By mastering these structures, a programmer can create flexible code that is both reactive and intuitive.

The Power of Loops in Repetitive Tasks

Loops are the driving force behind repetitive tasks in C, allowing programs to execute the same block of code multiple times without redundancy. This capability is particularly useful in scenarios where operations need to be repeated based on the size of data, the number of user inputs, or until a certain condition is met.

1. **for Loop**: The for loop is highly structured and ideal for scenarios where the number of iterations is known in advance. This makes it a go-to tool for traversing arrays, iterating through data collections, and performing operations a specific number of times. With its defined initialization, condition, and update sections, the for loop provides concise, readable code. One best practice is to ensure that the termination condition is clear and achievable, as an incorrectly defined condition can lead to infinite loops or premature termination.

2. **while Loop**: The while loop checks a condition before each iteration, making it suitable for situations where the loop should continue until a specific condition changes. This flexibility is advantageous for tasks where the number of repetitions is not known beforehand, such as reading user input until a certain value is provided, processing data until an error flag is set, or waiting for an external event. Given its conditional structure, it is critical to ensure that the condition will eventually become false; otherwise, the program will enter an infinite loop, consuming system resources unnecessarily.

3. **do-while Loop**: Unique in that it evaluates the condition after executing the loop body, the do-while loop ensures that the code inside the loop runs at least once. This is useful in user-interactive programs where an initial action should occur regardless of the condition, such as prompting a user for input until valid data is entered. However, developers should use do-while loops judiciously, as their structure can sometimes make logic difficult to follow, especially for more complex conditions.

4. **Nested Loops**: Nested loops, where one loop resides inside another, allow for multi-dimensional iteration, such as processing elements in a matrix or handling a list of lists. While nested loops can be powerful, they are also computationally expensive, particularly for large data sets, as they exponentially increase the number of iterations. To maintain efficiency, programmers should consider alternatives like breaking down nested operations or using more advanced data structures if appropriate.

Best Practices for Using Control Structures in C

As a programmer's toolkit expands, so does the importance of writing clean, efficient code. The effective use of control structures is central to achieving this goal:

1. **Code Readability**: Structure code with indentation, comments, and clear variable names to enhance readability. This practice is especially valuable in conditional and nested statements, where logical flow can quickly become confusing.

2. **Avoid Deep Nesting**: Overly nested loops and conditions reduce readability and maintainability. For complex structures, consider breaking code into functions, using switch statements, or applying other design patterns that simplify logic flow.

3. **Optimize Condition Evaluation**: Arrange conditions logically, placing the most likely conditions or simplest checks first to reduce unnecessary evaluations.

4. **Mind Performance**: For large-scale applications, loops and conditional checks can impact performance. Using break statements in loops, minimizing loop operations, and limiting function

calls within conditions are techniques that help maintain efficiency.

5. **Error Handling with Defaults**: Incorporating a default case in switch statements or a final else in conditional ladders enhances error-handling robustness. This practice prevents the program from encountering unexpected inputs or states without an appropriate response.

6. **Test for Infinite Loops**: While loops must be carefully controlled to avoid infinite execution, which can lead to crashes. Ensure that loop conditions will eventually be false and that exit strategies are built in.

Conclusion: The Strategic Application of Control Structures

By understanding and strategically applying control structures, programmers unlock a wide range of possibilities in C. These constructs enable not only the execution of logical conditions and repetitive actions but also the implementation of sophisticated algorithms, dynamic applications, and adaptable systems. The power of control structures in C lies in their flexibility, efficiency, and clarity, as they shape how the code interacts with data, handles conditions, and manages tasks. Through consistent practice and adherence to best practices, developers can use control structures to create high-quality, maintainable, and scalable C applications.

Control structures bridge the gap between static code and dynamic functionality, making them an indispensable aspect of programming in C. For aspiring developers and experienced programmers alike, mastering these tools is essential for building efficient, responsive applications that meet user needs and adapt to changing requirements.

4. Operators and Expressions in C

Introduction

In C programming, operators and expressions are fundamental tools that allow developers to manipulate data and control program flow effectively. Operators are symbols that instruct the compiler to perform specific operations on one or more operands. An operand is a value or variable on which the operation is performed. This introduction covers various types of operators in C, including arithmetic, relational, logical, bitwise, assignment, compound assignment, and ternary operators, as well as the size of operator. It also delves into the concepts of operator precedence and associativity to help you structure complex expressions in C.

1. Arithmetic Operators

Arithmetic operators are used to perform mathematical operations like addition, subtraction, multiplication, division, and modulus. These operators work on both integer and floating-point values, allowing a wide range of arithmetic computations.

Operator	Symbol	Description
Addition	+	Adds two operands
Subtraction	-	Subtracts second operand from the first
Multiplication	*	Multiplies two operands
Division	/	Divides first operand by second
Modulus	%	Returns the remainder of division

Example:

```
int a = 10, b = 3;
int sum = a + b;        // sum = 13
int difference = a - b; // difference = 7
int product = a * b;    // product = 30
int quotient = a / b;   // quotient = 3
int remainder = a % b;  // remainder = 1
```

2. Relational and Logical Operators

Relational and logical operators allow you to compare values and make decisions based on those comparisons, returning either true (1) or false (0).

Relational Operators

Operator	Symbol	Description
Equal to	==	Checks if two values are equal
Not equal to	!=	Checks if two values are not equal
Greater than	>	Checks if the left operand is greater than the right
Less than	<	Checks if the left operand is less than the right
Greater than or equal to	>=	Checks if left operand is greater than or equal to the right
Less than or equal to	<=	Checks if left operand is less than or equal to the right

Logical Operators

Logical operators are used in expressions involving multiple conditions. They allow combining two or more relational expressions and return true if certain conditions are met.

Operator	Symbol	Description
Logical AND	&&	Returns true if both operands are true
Logical OR	`	
Logical NOT	!	Reverses the truth value of the operand

Example:

```
int x = 5, y = 10;
if (x < y && y > 0) {
    printf("Both conditions are true.\n");
}
if (x != y || y == 10) {
    printf("At least one condition is true.\n");
}
if (!(x == y)) {
    printf("x is not equal to y.\n");
}
```

3. Bitwise Operators

Bitwise operators perform operations on individual bits of integer values. They are particularly useful in low-level programming, such as hardware manipulation, cryptography, and data compression.

Operator	Symbol	Description
Bitwise AND	&	Sets each bit to 1 if both bits are 1
Bitwise OR	`	`
Bitwise XOR	^	Sets each bit to 1 if only one of the bits is 1
Bitwise NOT	~	Inverts all the bits
Left Shift	<<	Shifts bits to the left, filling with zeros
Right Shift	>>	Shifts bits to the right, filling with the leftmost bit's original value (sign bit for signed integers)

Example:

```
int a = 5;  // Binary: 0101
int b = 3;  // Binary: 0011
int result = a & b;  // Bitwise AND result: 0001 (1 in decimal)
result = a | b;      // Bitwise OR result: 0111 (7 in decimal)
result = a ^ b;      // Bitwise XOR result: 0110 (6 in decimal)
result = ~a;         // Bitwise NOT result: 1010 (in two's complement)
result = a << 1;     // Left shift result: 1010 (10 in decimal)
result = a >> 1;     // Right shift result: 0010 (2 in decimal)
```

4. Assignment and Compound Assignment Operators

Assignment operators are used to assign values to variables. The simple assignment operator is =, but C also provides compound assignment operators that combine arithmetic operations with assignment.

Operator	Symbol	Description
Simple Assignment	=	Assigns the right-hand operand to the left-hand variable
Add and Assign	+=	Adds right-hand operand to the left-hand variable and assigns the result

Operator	Symbol	Description
Subtract and Assign	-=	Subtracts right-hand operand from left-hand variable and assigns the result
Multiply and Assign	*=	Multiplies left-hand variable by the right-hand operand and assigns the result
Divide and Assign	/=	Divides left-hand variable by the right-hand operand and assigns the result
Modulus and Assign	%=	Takes modulus of left-hand variable by the right-hand operand and assigns the result

Example:

int a = 10;

a += 5; // a = a + 5 -> a = 15

a -= 3; // a = a - 3 -> a = 12

a *= 2; // a = a * 2 -> a = 24

a /= 4; // a = a / 4 -> a = 6

a %= 3; // a = a % 3 -> a = 0

5. Ternary Operator

The ternary operator is a shorthand for an if-else statement, and it's often used for simple conditional assignments.

The syntax is:

condition? expression_if_true : expression_if_false;

Example:

int x = 5, y = 10;

int max = (x > y) ? x : y; // max will be assigned the value of y (10)

6. sizeof Operator

The sizeof operator returns the size, in bytes, of a data type or variable. This is useful for memory allocation and understanding how much space a variable occupies.

Example:

int a;

```c
printf("Size of int: %zu bytes\n", sizeof(int));
printf("Size of variable a: %zu bytes\n", sizeof(a));
```

7. Operator Precedence and Associativity

Operator precedence determines the order in which operators are evaluated in an expression, while associativity determines the direction in which operators of the same precedence are processed. Understanding these concepts is crucial to correctly interpreting complex expressions.

Example of Operator Precedence

In an expression 3 + 5 * 2, multiplication (*) has a higher precedence than addition (+), so the result is 3 + (5 * 2) = 13.

Associativity Rules

Operators have either left-to-right or right-to-left associativity. For example, in an expression like a - b + c, both - and + operators have left-to-right associativity, so it is evaluated as (a - b) + c.

Operator Type	Operators	Associativity
Unary	+ - ! ~ ++ -- sizeof	Right-to-left
Multiplicative	* / %	Left-to-right
Additive	+ -	Left-to-right
Relational	< <= > >=	Left-to-right
Equality	== !=	Left-to-right
Logical AND	&&	Left-to-right
Logical OR	`	
Conditional	?:	Right-to-left
Assignment	`= += -= *= /= %= &= ^=	= <<= >>=`

So far, we have seen how values are stored to and from variables. Simply storing and retrieving values to and from variables, while important, is only a small part of handling values. What is far more important is the ability to manipulate values in useful ways, which corresponds to the ways we manipulate real-world values, such as adding up our restaurant bill or calculating how much further we have to go to get to grandma's house and how much longer that might take.

The kinds of manipulations that are reasonable to perform on one or more values depend entirely on what kinds of values they are, that is, their data types. What makes sense for one data type may not make sense for another. In this chapter, we will explore the myriad ways that values can be manipulated.

Understanding expressions and operations

What are expressions? Well, in simple terms, an expression is a way of computing a value. We've seen how to do this with functions and return values. We will now turn to C's basic set of arithmetic operators for addition, subtraction, multiplication, and division, which are common in most programming languages. C adds to this a large number of operations that includes incrementation/decrementation, relational operators, logical operators, and bitwise manipulation. C further extends assignment operations in useful ways. Finally, C includes some unusual operators that are not commonly found in other languages, such as conditional and sequence operators.

The expressions we will explore in this chapter consist of one or more values as variables or constants combined with the help of operators. Expressions can be complete statements; however, just as often, expressions are components of complex statements. Operators work on one or more expressions, where an expression can be simple or complex, as shown in the following examples:

5 is a literal expression that evaluates to the value of **5**.

5 + 8 is an arithmetic expression of two simple expressions (literal constants), which, with the addition operator, evaluates to **13**.

A more complex expression, **5 + 8 - 10**, is really two binary arithmetical operations where **5** and **8** are first evaluated to produce an intermediate result, and then **10** is subtracted from it.

5; is an expression statement that evaluates to 5 and then moves on to the next statement. A more useful version of this would be **aValue = 5;** which is really two expressions – the evaluation of **5** and then the assignment of that value to the **aValue** variable.

Each value of an expression can be one of the following:

A literal constant

A variable or constant variable

The returned value from a function call

An example expression using all of these would be as follows:

5 + aValue + feetToInches (3.5) Consider the following statement: aLength = 5 + aValue + feetToInches (3.5);

The preceding statement is, in reality, five distinct operations in one statement:

The retrieval of the value from the **aValue** variable

The function call to **feetToInches()**

The addition of the literal **5** value, with the value of **aValue** giving an intermediate result

The addition of the function call result to the intermediate result

The assignment of the intermediate result to the **aLength** variable

An alternative way in which to calculate the same result can involve three simple statements instead of one complex statement, as follows:

aLength = 5;

aLength = aLength + aValue; aLength = aLength + feetToInches (3.5);

In this way, the different values are evaluated and added to the **aLength** variable. Instead of one assignment, there are three. Instead of a temporary intermediate result, the results of the additions are accumulated explicitly in the **aLength** variable as a result of each statement.

A simple program, **calcLength.c**, that applies each method of using simple and complex expressions is as follows:

```
#include <stdio.h>
int feetToInches( double feet ) {   int inches = feet * 12;   return inches; }
int main( void ) {   int aValue  = 8;   int aLength  = 0;
  aLength = 5 + aValue + feetToInches( 3.5 );   printf( "Calculated length = %d\n" , aLength );   aLength = 5;
  aLength = aLength + aValue;   aLength = aLength + feetToInches( 3.5 );   printf( "Calculated length = %d\n" , aLength );   return 0; }
```

This program calculates **aLength** from the sum of a literal value, which, in this case, is **5**, an **aValue** variable, and the result of the **feetToInches()** function. It then prints out the result to the terminal. The program itself is not very useful – we have no idea what we are calculating, nor do we know why the values that were chosen are significant. For now, however, let's just focus on the expression of **aLength**. This is a value calculated by adding three other values together in one complex statement and again with three simple statements.

Now, create the **calcLength.c** file, type in the program, and then save the file. Compile the program and run it.

You should see the following output:

```
> cc calcLength.c -o calcLength
> ./calcLength
Calculated length = 55
Calculated length = 55
>
```

Figure – Screenshot of calcLength.c output

As you can see, the single statement for calculating **aLength** is far less verbose than using the three statements to do so. However, neither approach is incorrect, nor is one method always preferred over the other. When calculations are relatively simple, the first method might be clearer and more appropriate. On the other hand, when calculations become much more complex, the second method might make each step of the computation clearer and more appropriate. Choosing which method to employ can be a challenge, as you are trying to find a balance between brevity and clarity. Whenever you have to choose one over the other, always choose clarity.

Introducing operations on numbers

The basic arithmetic operators on numbers are addition (+), subtraction (-), multiplication (*), and division (/). They are binary operations, as they work on one pair of expressions at a time. They work largely as you would expect them to for both integers (whole numbers) and real numbers (numbers with fractions). Division of two real numbers results in a real number. Division of two whole numbers results in a whole number; any possible fraction part is discarded from the result. There is also the modulo operator (%) that will provide the integer remainder of the division of two integers.

For example, 12.0 / 5.0 (two real numbers) evaluates to 2.5, whereas 12 / 5 (two integers) evaluates to 2. If we were working only with integers and we needed the remainder of 12 / 5, we would use the remainder operator, %. Thus, 12 % 5 evaluates to another integer, 2.

Many languages have an exponent operator. C does not. To raise an expression to a power, standard C provides the **pow(x , y)** library function. The prototype for this function is **double pow(double x , double y);**, which raises the value of **x** to the power of value **y** and yields **double** as its result. To use this function in your program, include the **<math.h>** header file wherever the prototype is declared.

Let's create a new file, **convertTemperature.c**, where we will create two useful functions, **celsiusToFahrenheit()** and **fahrenheitToCelsius()**, as follows:

```
// Given a Celsius temperature, convert it to Fahrenheit.
```

```
double celsiusToFahrenheit( double degreesC )  {   double degreesF = (degreesC * 9.0 / 5.0 ) + 32;
return degreesF; }   // Given a Fahrenheit temperature, convert it to Celsius.
double fahrenheitToCelsius( double degreesF )  {   double degreesC = (degreesF - 32 ) * 5.0 / 9.0 ;
return degreesC;
}
```

Each function takes a **double** value type as an input parameter and returns the converted value as **double**.

There are a couple of things to take note of regarding these functions.

First, we could have made them single-line functions by combining the two statements in each function body into one, as follows:

```
return (degreesC * 9.0 / 5.0) + 32;
```

Here is another example:
```
return (degreesF - 32) * 5.0 / 9.0;
```

Many programmers would do this. However, as your programming skills advance, this actually becomes a needless practice – it doesn't really save much of anything, and it makes debugging with a debugger (an advanced topic) far more difficult and time-consuming.

Many programmers are further tempted to turn these functions into **#define** macro symbols (another advanced topic), as follows:

```
#define celsiusToFahrenheit( x )  (((x) * 9.0  / 5.0 ) + 32)
#define fahrenheitToCelsius( x )  (((x) - 32 ) * 5.0 / 9.0)
```

Using macros can be dangerous because we could lose type information or the operations in such a macro might not be appropriate for the type of value given. Furthermore, we would have to be extremely careful about how we craft such preprocessor symbols to avoid unexpected results. Note that in this example, there is an extra set of $()$ around each **x**; this is to avoid misinterpretation of any value of **x**, for instance, **x** being given as **aValue + 5**. For the few characters of typing saved, neither the single-line complex return statement nor the macro definitions are worth the potential hassle.

Second, we use the grouping operator, $()$, to ensure our calculations are performed in the correct order. For now, just know that anything inside $()$ is evaluated first. We will discuss this in more detail later on in this chapter.

A Note About the Use of The Preprocessor

There are many temptations to use the preprocessor as much as possible – that is, to overuse the preprocessor. There lies the road to perdition! Instead, if you find yourself being pulled by such temptations for whatever reason, Working with Multi-File Programs. Understanding Scope. We can now finish the program that uses the two functions we created.

Add the following to **convertTemperature.c** before the two function definitions:

```
#include <stdio.h>
double celsiusToFahrenheit(double degreesC );
double fahrenheitToCelsius (double degreesF );
int main( void )
{
int c = 0;   int f = 32;
printf( "%4d Celsius  is %4d Fahrenheit\n" , c , (int)celsiusToFahrenheit( c ) );
printf( "%4d Fahrenheit is %4d Celsius\n\n" , f , (int)fahrenheitToCelsius( f ) );
c = 100;   f = 212;
printf( "%4d Celsius   is %4d Fahrenheit\n" , c , (int)celsiusToFahrenheit( c ) );
printf( "%4d Fahrenheit is %4d Celsius\n\n" , f , (int)fahrenheitToCelsius( f ) );
c = f = 50;
printf( "%4d Celsius   is %4d Fahrenheit\n" , c , (int)celsiusToFahrenheit( c ) );
printf( "%4d Fahrenheit is %4d Celsius\n\n" , f , (int)fahrenheitToCelsius( f ) );
return 0;
} // function definitions here...
```

With all of the parts in place, save the file, compile it, and then run it. You should see the following output:

```
> cc convertTemperature.c -o convertTemperature
> ./convertTemperature
   0 Celsius    is   32 Fahrenheit
  32 Fahrenheit is    0 Celsius

 100 Celsius    is  212 Fahrenheit
 212 Fahrenheit is  100 Celsius

  50 Celsius    is  122 Fahrenheit
  50 Fahrenheit is   10 Celsius

>
```

Figure – Screenshot of convertTemperature.c output

Note how we exercised our functions with known values to verify that they are correct. First, freezing values for each scale were converted to the other scale. Then, boiling values for each scale were converted to the other scale.

We then tried a simple middle value to see the results.

You may be wondering how to perform the conversions if we pass values other than doubles into the function. You might even be inclined to create several functions whose only difference is the type of variables. Take a look at the **convertTemperature_NoNo.c** program. Try to compile it for yourself and see what kind of errors you get. You will find that, in C, we cannot overload function names, that is, use the same function name but with different parameter and return types. This is possible with other languages but not with C.

In C, each function is simply called by its name; nothing else is used to differentiate one function call from another. A function having one name with a given type and two parameters cannot be distinguished from another function of the same name with a different type and no parameter.

We could try to embed the type names into the function names, such as **fahrenheithDblToCelsiusInt()** and **celsiusIntToCelsiusDbl()**, but this would be extremely tedious to declare and define for all data types.

Additionally, it would be extremely difficult to use in our programs. Compiler errors, due to mistyping the function names and even mistyping the calling parameters, would be highly likely and time-consuming to work through in a large or complicated program.

So, how does C deal with this?

Don't fret! We will consider this very topic in the next section, along with a complete program showing how to use these functions.

Considering the special issues resulting from operations on numbers

When performing calculations with any numbers, the possible ranges of both the inputs and outputs must be considered. For each type of number, there is a limit to both its maximum values and minimum values. These are defined on each system in the C standard library for that system in the header file, **limits.h**.

As the programmer, you must ensure that the results of any arithmetic operation are within the limits of the range for the data type specified or your program must check for valid inputs, thereby preventing invalid outputs. There are four types of invalid outputs – **Not a Number (NaN)**, **Infinity (Inf)**, **underflow**, and **overflow**.

Understanding NaN and Inf

NaN and **Inf** outputs can occur as a result of expressions upon floating-point numbers. There are two **NaN** types, one that is quiet and allows computations to continue, and one that signals an exception. What happens when such an exception occurs depends upon the C implementation; it may continue, halt the program, or perform some other behavior.

A **NaN** result occurs when the result of an operation is an undefined or unrepresentable number.

An **Inf** result occurs when the result of an operation is an inexpressibly large number or infinity.

Consider this equation – y = 1 / x. What is the value of y as x approaches zero from the positive side? It will become an infinitely large positive value. This results in a positive Inf result. What then is the value of y as x approaches zero from the negative side? It will become an infinitely large negative value and result in a negative Inf output.

A **NaN** result also occurs when the data types are real but the result of the computation is a complex number, for example, the square root of a negative number or the logarithm of a negative number. A **NaN** result can also occur where discontinuities appear in inverse trigonometric functions.

Consider the following program, **Inf_Nan.c**:

```
#include <stdio.h> #include <math.h> int main( void ) {   double y = 1 / 0.0;   printf( " 1 / 0.0 = %f\n" ,
y );    y = -1/0.0;

  printf( "-1 / 0.0 = %f\n" , y );    y = log( 0 );

  printf( "log( 0 ) = %f\n" , y );

  y = sqrt( -1 );

  printf( "Square root of -1 = %f\n" , y );   return 0;
}
```

This program will generate a positive **Inf** output and two negative **Inf** outputs, as well as a **NaN**. We need to include **<math.h>**, a standard library file that will enable us to call the **log()** and **sqrt()** functions.

When you enter, save, compile, and run this program, you will see the following output:

```
> cc Inf_Nan.c -o Inf_Nan
> ./Inf_Nan
 1 / 0.0 = inf
-1 / 0.0 = -inf
log( 0 ) = -inf
Square root of -1 = nan
>
```

Figure – Screenshot of Inf_Nan.c output

Understanding underflow

Underflow occurs when the result of an arithmetic operation is smaller than the smallest value that can be represented by the type specified.

For integers, this would mean either a number less than **0** if the integer is **unsigned** or a very large negative number if the integer is **signed** (for instance, **-2** is smaller than **-1**).

For real numbers, this would be a number very, very close to zero (that is, an extremely small fractional part), resulting from the division of an extremely small number by a very large number, or the multiplication of two extremely small numbers.

Understanding overflow

Overflow occurs when the result of an arithmetic operation is greater than the greatest value that can be represented for the type specified.

This would occur with both the addition and multiplication of two extremely large numbers or the division of a very large number by an extremely small number.

In the following program, **Overflow_Underflow.c**, we can see how overflow and underflow can occur:

```
#include <stdio.h>
#include <inttypes.h>
#include <float.h>
int main (void)
{
 uint16_t biggest = UINT16_MAX;
uint16_t overflow = biggest + 1;
printf( "Biggest=%d and overflow=%d\n" , biggest , overflow );
int16_t smallest = INT16_MIN;
int16_t underflow = smallest - 1;
printf("Biggest=%d and underflow=%d\n" , smallest , underflow );
float   fBiggest  = FLT_MAX;   float    fOverflow = fBiggest * 2;
printf( "FloatBiggest = %g FloatOverflow (FloatBiggest * 2) = %g\n" , fBiggest , fOverflow );
float   fSmallest  = FLT_MIN;
float   fUnderflow = fBiggest / fSmallest;
printf( "FloatSmallest = %g FloatUnderflow (FloatBiggest/FloatSmallest) = %g\n", fSmallest ,
fUnderflo   return 0;
}
```

We need to include **inttypes.h** and **float.h**, both C standard library headers, to declare variables of known size regardless of your system or C implementation. **uint16_t** is an unsigned 16-bit integer and **int16_t** is a signed 16-bit integer. Overflow occurs when we add 1 to the largest possible 16-bit unsigned integer.

Underflow occurs when we subtract 1 from the smallest 16-bit signed integer; note how the value became positive. We then demonstrate overflow and underflow with floats (floats and doubles already have an implementation-independent size).

Note that these are not the only expressions that may cause overflow and underflow.

If you create, save, compile, and run **Overflow_Underflow.c**, you will see the following output:

```
> cc OverFlow_Underflow.c -o OverFlow_Underflow
> ./OverFlow_Underflow
Biggest=65535 and overflow=0
Biggest=-32768 and underflow=32767
FloatBiggest  = 3.40282e+38 FloatOverflow (FloatBiggest * 2) = inf
FloatSmallest = 1.17549e-38 FloatUnderflow (FloatBiggest/FloatSmallest) = inf
>
```

Figure – Screenshot of Overflow_Underflow.c output

For integers, we can see that when we add **1** to the largest 16-bit unsigned integer, we don't get **65536**, but instead get **0** because **65537** cannot be represented in 16 bits. Likewise, when we subtract **1** from the smallest 16-bit signed integer, we don't get **–32769** but instead get **32767** (the sign bit becomes **0** instead of **1** and we get a very large number as a result).

Likewise, for floating-point numbers, when we multiply the largest **float** by **2**, we get an overflow value that becomes **inf**. When we divide the largest **float** by the smallest **float**, we should get a very large number. But it cannot be represented in a **float**, so we get an **inf** result.

When we reach these overflow/underflow conditions, unpredictable results can happen. One way to mitigate this problem is to assign the results of one size computation (two 16-bit ints or two floats) to a larger data type (32-bit **int** or **double**, respectively).

Considering precision

When performing calculations with real numbers, we need to be concerned with the exponential difference between the two of them. When one exponent is very large (positive) and the other very small (negative), we will likely produce either insignificant results or a **NaN** output. This happens when the calculated result will either represent an insignificant change to the largest exponent value via addition and subtraction therefore, precision will be lost – or be outside the possible range of values via multiplication and division therefore, a **NaN** or **Inf** output will result. Adding a very, very small value to a very, very large value may not give any significant change in the resulting value – again, precision in the result will be lost.

It is only when the exponents are relatively close, and the calculated result is within a reasonable range, that we can be sure of the accuracy of our result.

With 64-bit integer values and up to 128-bit real values, the ranges of values are vast, even beyond ordinary human conception. More often, however, our programs will use data types that do not provide the extreme limits of possible values. In those cases, the results of operations should always be given some consideration.

Exploring type conversion

C provides mechanisms that allow you to convert one type of value into another type of the same value. When there is no loss of precision – in other words, when the conversion of values results in the same value C operates without complaining. However, when there is a possible loss of precision, or if the resulting value is not identical to the original value, then the C compiler does not provide any such warning.

Understanding implicit type conversion and values

So, what happens when expressions are performed with operands of different types, for example, the multiplication of an **int** with a **float**, or the subtraction of a **double** from a **short**?

There, we saw how different data types took different numbers of bytes; some are 1 byte, some are 2 bytes, some are 4 bytes, and most values are 8 bytes.

When C encounters an expression of mixed types, it first performs an implicit conversion of the smallest data type (in bytes) to match the number of bytes in the largest data type size (in bytes). The conversion occurs in such a way that the value with the narrow range would be converted into the other with a wider range of values.

Consider the following calculation:

int   feet = 11; double yards = 0.0; yards = feet / 3;

In this calculation, both the **feet** variables and **3** are integer values. The resulting value of the expression is an integer. However, the integer result is implicitly converted into a double upon assignment. The **feet** integer divided by the **3** integer is not **3.2** but **3** because an integer cannot have a fractional part. The value of **yards** is then **3.0** (3 converted to a double is **3.0**), which is clearly incorrect.

This error can be corrected by either **type casting feet** or by using a decimal literal, as follows:

yards = (double)feet / 3; // type casting
yards = feet / 3.0;   // forcing proper type with a   // float literal

The first statement casts **feet** to **double** and then performs the division; the result is **double**. The second statement specifies a decimal literal, which is interpreted as **double** and performs the division; the result is double. In both statements, because the result is **double**, there is no conversion needed upon assignment to **yards**; that now has the correct value of **3.66667**.

Implicit conversion also occurs when the type of the actual parameter value is different from the defined parameter type.

A simple conversion is when a smaller type is converted into a larger type. This would include short integers being converted into long integers or **float** being converted into **double**.

Consider the following function declaration and the statement that calls it:

```
long int add (long int i1, long int i2)
{
return i1 + i2;
}
int main (void)
{
unsigned char b1 = 254;
unsigned char b2 = 253;
long int r1;
r1 = add (b1, b2);
printf ("%d + %d = %ld\n", b1, b2, r1);
return 0;
}
```

The **add()** function has two parameters, which are both long integers of 8 bytes each. Later, **add()** is called with two variables that are 1 byte each. The single-byte values of **254** and **253** are implicitly converted into the wider **long int** when they are copied into the function parameters. The result of the addition is **507**, which is correct.

The output of this program, **bytelong.c**, is as follows:

```
> cc bytelong.c -o bytelong
> ./bytelong
254 + 253 = 507
>
```

Figure – Screenshot of bytelong.c output

Most integers can easily be converted into a **float** or **double**. In the multiplication of an **int** (4 bytes) with a **float** (4 bytes), an implicit conversion will happen – **int** will be converted into a **float**. The implicit result of the expression would be a **float**.

In the subtraction of a **double** (8 bytes) from a **short** (2 bytes), one conversion happens on the **short** – it is converted into a **double** (8 bytes). The implicit result of the expression would be a **double**. Depending on what happens next in the compound expression, the implicit result may be further converted. If the next operation involves an explicit type, then the implicit result will be converted into that type, if necessary.

Otherwise, it may again be converted into the widest possible implicit type for the next operation.

However, when we assign an implicit or explicit result type to a narrower type in the assignment, a loss of precision is likely. For integers, loss involves the high-order bits (or the bits with the largest binary values).

A value of **32,000,000** assigned to a **char** (**signed** or **unsigned**) will always be **0**. For real numbers, truncation and rounding occur. Conversion from a **double** to a **float** will cause rounding or truncation, depending upon the compiler implementation. Conversion from a **float** to an **int** will cause the fractional part of the value to be lost.

Consider the following statements:

```
long int add( long int i1 , long int i2 )
{
return i1 + i2;
}
int main (void)
{
unsigned char b1 = 254;
```

```
unsigned char b2 = 253;

unsigned char r1;

r1 = add (b1, b2);

printf("%d + %d = %d\n" , b1 , b2 , r1 );

return 0;
}
```

The only change in these statements is the type of the **r1** variable; it is now a single byte. So, while **b1** and **b2** are widened to **long int**, **add()** returns a **long int**, but this 8-byte return value must be truncated into a single byte. The value assigned to **r1** is incorrect; it becomes **251**. Note that we also changed the format specifier from **%ld** to just **%d**.

When we create, edit, save, compile, and run this program, **longbyte.c**, we will see the following output:

```
> cc longbyte.c -o longbyte
> ./longbyte
254 + 253 = 251
>
```

Figure – Screenshot of longbyte.c output

As you can see, **254 + 253** is clearly not **251**. This shows the result of incorrect results from having to narrow a value from a **long int** to a single byte (**unsigned char**).

When performing complicated expressions that require a high degree of precision in the result, it is always best to perform the calculations in the widest possible data type and only at the very end convert the result into a narrower data type.

Let's test this with a simple program. In **truncRounding.c**, we have two functions – one that takes a **double** as a parameter and prints it, and one that takes a **long int** as a parameter and prints it. The following program illustrates implicit type conversion, in which the parameter values are assigned to actual values:

```
#include <stdio.h>

void doubleFunc (double   dbl );

void longintFunc (long int li);
```

```c
int main (void)
{
float floatValue   = 58.73;
short int intValue = 13;
longintFunc( intValue );
longintFunc( floatValue ); // possible truncation
doubleFunc( floatValue );
doubleFunc( intValue );
return 0;
}
void doublFunc (double dbl )
{
printf("doubleFunc %.2f\n" , dbl );
}
void longintFunc (long int li)
{
printf("longintFunc %ld\n" , li );
}
```

We have not yet explored the ways in which **printf()** can format values. For now, simply take for granted that **%.2f** will print a **double** value with two decimal places, and that **%ld** will print out a **long int**. Exploring Formatted Output.

Enter, compile, and run **truncRounding.c**. You should see the following output:

```
> cc truncRounding.c -o truncRounding
> ./truncRounding
longIntFunc      13
longIntFunc      58
doubleFunc  58.73
doubleFunc  13.00
>
```

Figure – Screenshot of truncRounding.c output

Note that no rounding occurs when **58.73** is converted into a **long int**. However, we do lose the fractional part; this is called **truncation**, where the fractional part of the value is cut off. A **short int** is properly converted into a **double** just as a **float** is properly converted into a **double**.

Also, note that when you compiled and ran **truncRounding.c**, no compiler error nor runtime warning was given when the **float** was converted into a **long int**, resulting in the loss of precision.

Using explicit type conversion – casting

If we rely on implicit casting, our results may go awry or we may get unexpected results. To avoid this, we can cause an explicit, yet temporary, type change. We do this by **casting**. When we explicitly cast a variable to another type, its value is temporarily converted into the desired type and then used. The type of the variable and its value does not change.

Any expression can be prefixed by **(type)** to change its explicit type to the indicated type for the lifetime of the expression. This lifetime is only a single statement. The explicit type is never changed, nor is the value stored in that explicitly typed variable.

An example of this is given in the following program, **casting.c**:

```
#include <stdio.h>
int main (void)

{
int numerator = 33;

int denominator = 5;

double result   = 0.0;

result = numerator / denominator;

printf ("Truncation: %d / %d = %.2g\n" , numerator , denominator , result );

result = (double) numerator / denominator;

printf( "No truncation: %.2f / %d = %.2f\n" , (double)numerator , denominator , result );

result = numerator / (double)denominator;

printf( " %d / %.2f = %.2f\n" , numerator , (double)denominator , result );

return 0;
}
```

Enter, compile, and run **casting .c**. You should see the following output:

```
> cc casting.c -o casting
> ./casting
Truncation:          (int) 33   /    (int) 5    = 6

No truncation: (double) 33.0 /     (int) 5    = 6.6
                    (int) 33   / (double) 5.0  = 6.6
>
```

Figure – Screenshot of casting.c output

In **casting.c**, we can see, in the first division expression, that there is no casting and no implicit conversion. Therefore, the result is an **int** output and the fractional part is truncated. When the **int** result is assigned to a **double**, the fractional part has already been lost. In the second and third division statements, we guarantee that the operation is done on **double** values by casting either one of them to **double**. The other value is then implicitly converted to **double**. The result is a **double**, so when it is assigned to a **double**, there is no truncation.

The types of numerators and denominators are not changed permanently but only within the context of the expression where casting occurs.

Introducing operations on characters

The integer value of the letter **'a'** is **97**. When we treat that value as a char, the **97** value becomes **'a'**. Since characters are internally represented as integers, any of the integer operations can be applied to them too. However, only a couple of operations make sense to apply to characters – the additive operators (that is, addition and subtraction). While multiplying and dividing characters are legal, those operations never produce any practical or useful results:

char - char yields **int**. The result represents the distance between characters. **char + int** yields **char**. This yields the character that is the specified distance from the original character. **char - int** yields **char**. This also yields the character that is the specified distance from the original character.

So, **'a'** + **5** is **'f'**; that is, **97** + **5** is **102**, which as a character is **'f'**. **'M'** - **10** is **'C'**; that is, **77 – 10** is **67**, which as a character is **'C'**. And finally, **'a'** - **'A'** is **32**; that is, **97 – 65** is **32**, the distance between **a** and **A**.

Remember that a **char** is only one unsigned byte, so any addition or subtraction outside of the range of **0.255** will yield unexpected results due to the truncation of high-order bits.

A common use of the addition and subtraction of characters is the conversion of a given ASCII character to uppercase or lowercase. If the character is uppercase, then simply adding 32 to it will give you its lowercase version. If the character is lowercase, then simply subtracting 32 from it will give you its uppercase version.

An example of this is given in the following program, **convertUpperLower.c**:

```
#include <stdio.h>
int main (void)
{
char lowerChar = 'b';
char upperChar = 'M';
char anUpper = lowerChar - 32;
char aLower = upperChar + 32;
printf ("Lower case '%c' can be changed to upper case '%c'\n", lowerChar, anUpper);
printf ("Upper case '%c' can be changed to lower case '%c'\n", upperChar, aLower);
return 0;
}
```

Given a lowercase **'e'**, we convert it into uppercase by subtracting **32** from it. Given an uppercase **'S'**, we convert it into lowercase by adding **32** to it. Working with Strings.

In your editor, create a new file and enter the **convertUpperLower.c** program. Compile and run it in a terminal window.

You should see the following output:

```
> cc convertUpperLower.c -o convertUpperLower
> ./convertUpperLower
Lower case 'e' can be changed to upper case 'E'
Upper case 'S' can be changed to lower case 's'
>
```

Figure – Screenshot of convertUpperLower.c output

Another common use of operations on characters is to convert the character of a digit (**'0'** to **'9'**) into its actual numerical value. The value of **'0'** is not **0** but some other value that represents that character. To convert a character digit into its numerical value, we simply subtract the **'0'** character from it.

An example of this is given in the following program, **convertDigitToInt.c**:

```
int main(void )
{
```

```c
char digit5 = '5';
char digit8 = '8';
int sumDigits = digit5 + digit8;
printf ("digit5 + digit8 = '5' + '8' = %d (oh, dear!)\n", sumDigits );
char value5 = digit5 - '0';  // get the numerical value  // of '5'
char value8 = digit8 - '0';   // get the numerical value // of '8'
sumDigits = value5 + value8;
printf ("value5 + value8 = 5 + 8 = %d\n", sumDigits );
return 0;
}
```

When we simply add characters together, unexpected results are likely to occur. What we really need to do is to convert each digit character into its corresponding numerical value and then add those values. The results of that addition are what we want.

In your editor, create a new file and enter the **convertDigitToInt.c** program. Compile and run it in a terminal window.

You should see the following output:

```
> cc convertDigitToInt.c -o convertDigitToInt
> ./convertDigitToInt
digit5 + digit8 = '5' + '8' = 109 (oh, dear!)
value5 + value8 = 5 + 8 = 13
>
```

Figure – Screenshot of convertDigitToInt.c output

In order to understand the difference between a character and its value, Working with Strings.

Logical operators

A Boolean value is one that has either the value of **true** or **false** and no other value. Early versions of C did not have explicit Boolean (**true** and **false**) data types. To handle boolean values, C implicitly converts any zero value into the Boolean **false** value and implicitly converts any non-zero value into the Boolean **true** value. This implicit conversion comes in handy very often but must be used with care.

However, when we use **#include <stdbool.h>**, the official **bool** types and **true** and **false** values are available to us.

We will explore later how we might choose to define our own Boolean values with enumerations or with custom types.

There are three Boolean operators:

||: The binary logical **OR** operator

&&: The binary logical **AND** operator

^: The binary logical **XOR** operator

!: The unary logical **NOT** operator

These are logical operators whose results are always Boolean **true** (non-zero) or **false** (exactly zero). They are so named in order to differentiate them from bitwise operators whose results involve a different bit pattern, which we shall learn about shortly.

The first two logical operators evaluate the results of two expressions:

expressionA

expressionB

The result of logical **AND** is **TRUE** only if both **expressionA** and **expressionB** are **TRUE**; it is **FALSE** if either or both are **FALSE**.

The result of logical **OR** is **FALSE** only if both **expressionA** and **expressionB** are **FALSE**; it is **TRUE** if either or both are **TRUE**.

In this Boolean expression, it would seem that both **expressionA** and **expressionB** are both always evaluated. This is not the case; we must consider what is known as **short-circuit evaluation** or **minimal evaluation** of Boolean expressions. When there are two or more Boolean expressions, only those expressions are evaluated with results that satisfy the Boolean comparison. Once satisfied, the rest of the expression is ignored.

When the operator is logical **AND** (**&&**), and if **expressionA** evaluates to **false**, then **expressionB** is not evaluated. It does not need to be since regardless of what the second result is, the **AND** condition will still be **false**. However, when **expressionA** is true, **expressionB** must then be evaluated.

When the operator is logical **OR** (||), if **expressionA** evaluates to **true**, then **expressionB** is not evaluated. It does not need to be since regardless of what the second result is, the **OR** condition will still be **true**.

However, when **expressionA** is false, **expressionB** must then be evaluated.

The unary logical **NOT** (!) operator is employed, therefore, as! expressionC.

It takes the result of **expressionC**, implicitly converting it into a Boolean result and evaluating it with its opposite Boolean result. Therefore, true becomes **false**, and **!false** becomes **true**.

In the **logical.c** program, three tables are printed to show how the logical operators work. They are known as **truth tables**. The values are printed as either 1 or 0 decimals, but they are really Boolean values.

The first truth table is produced with the **printLogicalAND()** function, as follows:

```c
void printLogicalAND( bool z, bool o )
{
bool zero_zero = z && z ;
bool zero_one  = z && o ;
bool one_zero  = o && z ;
bool one_one   = o && o ;
printf( "AND | %1d | %1d\n"    , z , o );
printf( " %1d | %1d | %1d \n"  , z , zero_zero , zero_one );
printf( " %1d | %1d | %1d \n\n", o , zero_one  , one_one );
}
```

The next truth table is produced with the **printLogicalOR()** function, as follows:

```c
void printLogicalOR( bool z, bool o )
{
bool zero_zero = z || z ;
bool zero_one  = z || o ;
bool one_zero  = o || z ;
bool one_one   = o || o ;
printf( "OR | %1d | %1d\n", z , o );
printf( " %1d | %1d | %1d \n", z , zero_zero , zero_one );
printf( " %1d | %1d | %1d \n\n" , o , zero_one , one_one );
}
```

The next truth table is produced with the **printLogicalXOR()** function, as follows:

```c
void printLogicalXOR( bool z, bool o )
{
bool zero_zero = z ^ z ;
```

```c
bool zero_one  = z ^ o ;
bool one_zero  = o ^ z ;
bool one_one   = o ^ o ;
printf( "XOR | %1d | %1d\n", z , o );
printf( " %1d | %1d | %1d\n", z, zero_zero, zero_one );

printf( " %1d | %1d | %1d\n\n" , o , one_zero, one_one  );

printf( "\n" );

}
```

Finally, the **printLogicalNOT()** function prints the **NOT** truth table, as follows:

```c
void printLogicalNOT (bool z, bool o)

{

bool not_zero = !z ;

bool not_one = !o ;

printf( "NOT \n" );

printf( " %1d | %1d \n", z , not_zero );

printf( " %1d | %1d \n\n" , o , not_one );
}
```

Create the **logicals.c** file and enter the three truth table functions. Then, add the following program code to complete **logicals.c**:

```c
#include <stdio.h>

#include <stdbool.h>

void printLogicalAND (bool z, bool o);

void printLogicalOR (bool z, bool o);

void printLogicalXOR (bool z, bool o);

void printLogicalNOT (bool z, bool o);

int main (void)

{

 bool one = 1;

bool zero = 0;

printLogicalAND( zero , one );

printLogicalOR( zero , one );

PrintLogicalXOR( zero , one );

printLogicalNOT( zero , one );
```

```
return 0;
}
```

Save, compile, and run **logicals.c**. You should see the following output:

```
> cc logicals.c -o logicals
> ./logicals
AND | 0 | 1
  0 | 0 | 0
  1 | 0 | 1


 OR | 0 | 1
  0 | 0 | 1
  1 | 1 | 1

XOR | 0 | 1
  0 | 0 | 1
  1 | 1 | 0


NOT 0 | 1
    1 | 0

> █
```

Figure – Screenshot of logicals.c output

These are known as truth tables. When you perform the **AND, OR, XOR,** or **NOT** operations on a value in the top row and a value in the left column, the intersecting cell is the result. So, **1 AND 1** yields **1**, **1 OR 0** yields **1**, and **NOT 0** yields **1**.

Not all operations can be simply expressed as strictly Boolean values. In these cases, there are the relational operators that produce results that are convenient to regard as **true** and **false**. Statements such as **if** and **while**, as we shall learn, test those results.

Relational operators

Relational operators involve the comparison of the result of one expression with the result of a second expression.

They have the same form as the binary logical operators shown previously. Each of them gives a Boolean result.

They are as follows:

> (greater than operator): **true** if **expressionA** is greater than **expressionB**

>= (greater than or equal operator): **true** if **expressionA** is greater than or equal to **expressionB**

< (less than operator): **true** if **expressionA** is less than **expressionB**

<= (less than or equal operator): **true** if **expressionA** is less than or equal to **expressionB**

== (equal operator (note that this is different from the = assignment operator)): **true** if **expressionA** is equal to **expressionB**

• **!= (not equal operator)**: **true** if **expressionA** is not equal to **expressionB**

Bitwise operators

Bitwise operators manipulate bit patterns in useful ways. The bitwise **AND (&)**, **OR** (|), and **XOR** (^) operators compare the two operands bit by bit. The bitwise shifting operators shift all of the bits of the first operand left or right. The bitwise complement changes each bit in a bit pattern to its opposite bit value.

Each bit in a bit field (8, 16, or 32 bits) could be used as if it was a switch, or flag, determining whether some feature or characteristic of the program was off (0) or on (1). The main drawback of using bit fields in this manner is that the meaning of the bit positions can only be known by reading the source code, assuming that the proper source code is both available and well commented!

Bitwise operations are less valuable today, not only because memory and CPU registers are cheap and plentiful but because they are now expensive operations computationally. They do, occasionally, find a useful place in some programs but not often.

The bitwise operators are as follows:

&: Bitwise **AND** – for example, 1 if both bits are 1.

|: Bitwise **OR** – for example, 1 if either bit is 1.

^: Bitwise **XOR** – for example, 1 if either but not both are 1.

<<: Bitwise shift left. Each bit is moved over to the left (the larger bit position). It is equivalent to **value * 2** – for example, **0010** becomes **0100**.

>>: Bitwise shift right. Each bit is moved over to the right (the smaller bit position). It is equivalent to **value / 2** – for example, **0010** becomes **0001**.

~: Bitwise complement. Change each bit to its other – for example, **1** to **0**, and **0** to **1**.

The following is an example of bitwise operators and flags:

```
/* flag name */  /* bit pattern */ const unsigned char lowercase 1;
/* 0000 0001 */ const unsigned char bold 2;
/* 0000 0010 */ const unsigned char italic 4;
```

```
/* 0000 0100 */ const unsigned char underline 8;
/* 0000 1000 */ unsigned char flags = 0;
```

flags = flags | bold; /* switch on bold */ flags = flags & ~italic; /* switch off italic; */

if((flags & underline) == underline) ... /* test for underline bit 1/on? */ if(flags & underline) ... /* test for underline */

Instead of using bitwise fields, custom data types called **enumerations** and more explicit data structures, such as hash tables, are often preferred.

The conditional operator

This is also known as the ternary operator. This operator has three expressions – **testExpression**, **ifTrueExpression**, and **ifFalseExpression**.

It looks like this: testExpression ? ifTrueExpression : ifFalseExpression

In this expression, **testExpression** is evaluated. If the **testExpression** result is **true**, or non-zero, then **ifTrueExpression** is evaluated and its result becomes the expression result. If the **testExpression** result is **false**, or exactly zero, then **ifFalseExpression** is evaluated and its result becomes the expression result. Either **ifTrueExpression** or **ifFalseExpression** is evaluated – never both.

This operator is useful in odd places, such as setting switches, building string values, and printing out various messages. In the following example, we'll use it to add pluralization to a word if it makes sense in the text string:

```
printf( "Length = %d meter%c\n" , len, len == 1 ? '' : 's' );
```

Or, we can use it to print out whole words:

```
printf( "Length = %d %s\n" , len, len == 1 ? "foot" : "feet" );
```

The following program uses these statements:

```
#include <stdio.h>
const double inchesPerFoot = 12.0;
const double inchesPerMeter = 39.67;
void printLength (double meters);
int main( void )
{
printLength( 0.0 );
printLength( 1.0 );
printLength( inchesPerFoot / inchesPerMeter );
printLength( 2.5 );
```

```
    return 0;

}

void printLength (double meters)
{

double feet = meters * inchesPerMeter / inchesPerFoot;
printf( "Length = %f meter%c\n", meters, meters == 1.0 ? ' ' : 's' );

printf( "Length = %f %s\n\n", feet, 0.99995 < feet && feet < 1.00005 ? "foot" : "feet" );

}
```

In the preceding program, you might be wondering why the statement for determining **"foot"** or **"feet"** has become so much more complex. The reason is that the **feet** variable is a computed value. Furthermore, because of the precision of the **double** data type, it is extremely unlikely that any computation will be exactly **1.0000...**, especially when division is involved. Therefore, we need to consider values of **feet** that are reasonably close to zero but might never be exactly zero. For our simple example, four significant digits will suffice.

When you type in the **printLength.c** program, save it, compile it, and run it, you should see the following output:

```
> cc printLength.c -o printLength
> ./printLength
Length = 0.000000 meters
Length = 0.000000 feet

Length = 1.000000 meter
Length = 3.305833 feet

Length = 0.302496 meters
Length = 1.000000 foot

Length = 2.500000 meters
Length = 8.264583 feet

>
```

Figure – Screenshot of printLength.c output

Be careful, however, not to overuse the ternary operator for anything other than simple value replacements. In the next chapter, we'll explore how more explicit solutions are commonly used for general conditional executions.

The sequence operator

Sometimes, it makes sense to perform a sequence of expressions as though they were a single statement. This would rarely be used or make sense in a normal statement.

We can string multiple expressions together in sequence using the, operator. Each expression is evaluated from left to right in the order they appear. The value of the entire expression is the resultant value of the rightmost expression.

For instance, consider the following:

```
int x = 0, y = 0, z = 0;  // declare and initialize. ... ...
x = 3 , y = 4 , z = 5; ... ...
x = 4; y = 3; z = 5; ... ... x = 5; y = 12; z = 13;
```

The single line assigning all three variables is perfectly valid. However, in this case, there is little value in doing it.

The three variables are either loosely related or not related at all from what we can tell in this snippet. Note that this use of the comma is not a sequence operator but is used to declare a list of variables. Furthermore, commas in function parameter lists are also not sequence operators.

The next line shows the comma as a sequence operator. It makes each assignment its own expression and condenses the code from three lines to one. While it is also valid, there is seldom a need for this.

The sequence operator, however, does make sense in the context of iterative statements, such as **while()** **…, for() …**, and **do … while()**.

Compound assignment operators

As we have already seen, expressions can be combined in many ways to form compound expressions. There are some compound expressions that recur so often that C has a set of operators that make them shorter. In each case, the result is formed by taking the variable on the left of the operator, performing the operation on it with the value of the expression on the right, and assigning it back to the variable on the left.

Compound operations are of the **variable operator= expression** form.

The most common of these is incrementation with an assignment: counter = counter + 1;

With the += compound operator, this just becomes the following: counter += 1;

The full set of compound operators is as follows:

+=: assignment with addition to a variable

-=: assignment with subtraction to a variable

*=: assignment with multiplication to a variable

/=: assignment with division (integer or real) to a variable

%=: assignment with an integer remaindering to a variable

<<=: assignment with bitwise shift left

>>=: assignment with bitwise shift right

&=: assignment with bitwise **AND**

^=: assignment with bitwise **XOR** (exclusive **OR**)

|=: assignment with bitwise **OR**

These operators help to make your computations a bit more condensed and somewhat clearer.

Multiple assignments in a single expression

We have learned how to combine expressions to make compound expressions. We can also do this with assignments. For example, we could initialize variables, as follows:

int height, width, length; height = width = length = 0;

The expressions are evaluated from right to left, and the final result of the expression is the value of the last assignment. Each variable is assigned a value of **0**.

Another way to put multiple assignments in a single statement is to use the, sequence operator. We could write a simple swap statement in one line with three variables, as follows:

int first, second, temp; // Swap first & second variables. temp = first, first = second, second = temp;

The sequence of three assignments is performed from left to right. This would be equivalent to the following three statements:

temp = first; first = second; second = temp;

Either way is correct. Some might argue that the three assignments are logically associated because of their commonality to being swapped, so the first way is preferred. Ultimately, which method you choose is a matter of taste and appropriateness in the given context. Always choose clarity over obfuscation.

Incremental operators

C provides even shorter shorthand (shortest shorthand?) operators that make the code even smaller and clearer.

These are the autoincrement and autodecrement operators.

Writing the **counter = counter + 1;** statement is equivalent to a shorter version, **counter += 1;** as we have already learned. However, this simple expression happens so often, especially when incrementing or decrementing a counter or index, that there is an even shorter shorthand way to do it. For this, there is the unary increment operator of **counter++;** or **++counter;**

In each case, the result of the statement is that the value of the counter has been incremented by one.

Here are the unary operators:

- ++: autoincrement by 1, prefix or postfix
- --: autodecrement by 1, prefix or postfix

Postfix versus prefix incrementation

There are subtle differences between how that value of the counter is incremented when it is prefixed (++ comes before the expression is evaluated) or postfixed (++ comes after the expression).

In prefix notation, ++ is applied to the result of the expression before its value is considered. In postfix notations, the result of the expression is applied to any other evaluation and then the ++ operation is performed.

Here, an example will be useful.

In this example, we set a value and then print that value using both the prefix and postfix notations. Finally, the program shows a more predictable method, that is, perform either method of incrementation as a single statement.

The result will always be what we expect:

```
int main( void )
{
int aValue = 5;    // Demonstrate prefix incrementation.
printf( "Initial: %d\n" , aValue );
printf( " Prefix: %d\n" , ++aValue );  // Prefix incrementation.
printf( " Final: %\n"  , aValue );
aValue = 5;  // Reset aValue.    // Demonstrate postfix incrementation.
printf( "Initial: %d\n" , aValue );
printf( " Prefix: %d\n" , aValue++ );  // Postfix incrementation.
printf( " Final: %\n"  , aValue );    // A more predictable result: increment in isolation.
aValue = 5;  ++aValue;
printf( "++aValue (alone) == %d\n" , aValue );
aValue = 5;  aValue++;
printf( "aValue++ (alone) == %d\n" , aValue );
return 0;
}
```

Enter, compile, and run **prefixpostfix.c**.

You should see the following output:

```
> cc prefixPostfix.c -o prefixPostfix
> ./prefixPostfix
Initial: 5
 Prefix: 6
  Final: 6

Initial: 5
Postfix: 5
  Final: 6

++aValue (alone) == 6
aValue++ (alone) == 6
>
```

Figure – Screenshot of prefixPostfix.c output

In the output, you can see how the prefix and postfix notations affect (or not) the value passed to **printf()**. In prefix autoincrement, the value is first incremented and then passed to **printf()**. In postfix autoincrement, the value is passed to **printf()** as is, and after **printf()** is evaluated, the value is then incremented. Additionally, note that when these are single, simple statements, both results are identical.

Some C programmers relish jamming together as many expressions and operators as possible. There is really no good reason to do this. I often go cross-eyed when looking at such code. In fact, because of the subtle differences in compilers and the possible confusion if and when such expressions need to be modified, this practice is discouraged. Therefore, to avoid the possible side effects of the prefix or postfix incrementations, a better practice is to put the incrementation on a line by itself, when possible, and use grouping (we will discuss this in the next section).

Order of operations and grouping

When an expression contains two or more operators, it is essential to know which operation will be performed first, next, and so on. This is known as the **order of evaluation**. Not all operations are evaluated from left to right.

Consider 3 + 4 * 5. Does this evaluate to 35 – 3 + 4 = 7 * 5 = 35? Or does this evaluate to 23 – 4 * 5 = 20 + 3 = 23?

If, on the other hand, we explicitly group these operations in the manner desired, we remove all doubt. Either 3 + (4 * 5) or (3 + 4) * 5 is what we actually intend.

C has built-in precedence and associativity of operations that determine how and in what order operations are performed. Precedence determines which operations have a higher priority and are, therefore, performed before those with a lower priority. Associativity refers to how operators of the same precedence are evaluated – from left to right or from right to left.

The following table shows all the operators we have already encountered along with some that we will encounter in later chapters (such as postfix **[]** **.** **->** and unary * **&**). The highest precedence is the postfix group at the top and the lowest precedence is the sequence operator at the bottom:

Linux/Unix	Download URL
Text editors (pick one)	
Nano	`https://www.nano-editor.org/download.php`
Vim or vi	Built-in
gedit	`https://wiki.gnome.org/Apps/Gedit`
Emacs	`https://www.gnu.org/software/emacs/download.html`
Compiler	
GCC	`https://gcc.gnu.org/install/` (see the notes following this table for certain Linux versions)
Terminal	
Terminal	Built-in

Table – Operator precedence table

What is most interesting here is that (1) grouping happens first, and (2) assignment typically happens last in a statement. Well, this is not quite true. Sequencing happens after everything else. Typically, though, sequencing is not often used in a single statement. It can, however, be quite useful as a part of the **for** complex statement.

While it is important to know precedence and associativity, I would encourage you to be very explicit in your expressions and use grouping to make your intentions clear and unambiguous. As we encounter additional operators in subsequent chapters, we will revisit this operator precedence table.
Conclusion

In the context of C programming, operators and expressions form the backbone of computational logic, allowing developers to write concise, effective, and powerful code. Mastering how to use different types of operators—such as arithmetic, relational, logical, bitwise, assignment, compound assignment, ternary, and sizeof—is essential for any C programmer. Additionally, understanding operator precedence and associativity is crucial for structuring expressions correctly, ensuring they are interpreted in the desired manner, and avoiding logical errors.

Recap of Key Operator Types

1. **Arithmetic Operators**

   Arithmetic operators provide the core functions of mathematical calculations. By understanding how to use addition, subtraction, multiplication, division, and modulus operators, developers can manipulate numerical data with ease, whether for simple calculations or for handling complex algorithms.

2. **Relational and Logical Operators**

   These operators are fundamental for decision-making in programs, enabling comparison between values and checking conditions. Relational operators allow comparisons (e.g., equal to, greater than, less than), while logical operators let developers combine multiple conditions efficiently. Together, they help control the flow of a program by forming the basis of if statements, loops, and other control structures.

3. **Bitwise Operators**

   Bitwise operators perform operations on individual bits, which can be particularly beneficial in fields like embedded systems, cryptography, and network programming. Understanding bitwise AND, OR, XOR, NOT, and shift operations helps developers manipulate binary data and optimize memory usage. Although bitwise operations are not as commonly used in high-level programming, they are indispensable in low-level programming for efficient data processing.

4. **Assignment and Compound Assignment Operators**

   Assignment operators, including compound assignment operators, streamline code by combining arithmetic operations with assignment. Instead of writing repetitive expressions, developers can use compound assignments to achieve concise, readable, and maintainable code. This aspect of operator usage can simplify variable manipulation significantly, making code more expressive.

5. **Ternary Operator**

   The ternary operator (?:) offers a compact syntax for simple conditional evaluations, acting as a shorthand for basic if-else statements. Though it may seem minor, the ternary operator is often preferred for short, straightforward assignments based on conditions. However, it should be used judiciously to maintain readability, as complex ternary expressions can become difficult to understand.

6. **sizeof Operator**

   The sizeof operator helps determine memory allocation by returning the size in bytes of data types or variables. It's a valuable tool for memory management and structuring data, especially in cases where memory optimization is critical. With sizeof, developers can calculate the storage requirements of data structures, a key aspect when working with arrays, pointers, and dynamic memory allocation.

Importance of Precedence and Associativity

Operator precedence and associativity are essential for interpreting expressions accurately. Precedence determines the order in which operators are evaluated, while associativity dictates the direction of evaluation when operators have the same precedence level. Misinterpreting precedence or associativity can lead to incorrect results and subtle bugs, so understanding these rules is critical, especially in complex expressions.

Consider the expression a + b * c. If precedence were not clear, we might misinterpret it as (a + b) * c, resulting in an unintended calculation. In C, multiplication has higher precedence than addition, so the expression is evaluated as a + (b * c). Associativity complements precedence by specifying the evaluation order for operators of the same precedence, like addition and subtraction. For instance, a - b + c is evaluated from left to right as (a - b) + c, respecting the left-to-right associativity of addition and subtraction.

Practical Applications of Operators

Operators have applications in nearly every aspect of programming, from simple calculations to complex algorithms:

- **Arithmetic and Assignment in Calculations**

  Arithmetic operators are essential for all types of calculations, whether in game development, statistical analysis, financial software, or data science. Compound assignments streamline repetitive operations, making code both shorter and easier to follow.

- **Relational and Logical Operators in Control Structures**

  Relational and logical operators are indispensable for conditional statements and loops. In any application requiring decision-making—such as user authentication, menu navigation, or data validation—these operators provide the foundation for comparing values and conditions. Complex conditionals can be simplified with logical operators, allowing multiple conditions to be evaluated in a single statement.

- **Bitwise Operators in System Programming and Data Encoding**

  Bitwise operations are frequently used in low-level programming, including systems programming, where direct memory manipulation is required. For example, developers might use bitwise shifts to encode data compactly, perform cryptographic functions, or communicate with hardware at the binary level. By manipulating individual bits, programs can operate faster and reduce memory usage, optimizing both performance and resource allocation.

- **Memory Management with sizeof**

  Knowing the size of variables and data structures is crucial in memory management, particularly when working with dynamic memory. The sizeof operator helps allocate appropriate memory amounts, especially for structures, unions, and arrays. For instance, when using malloc for dynamic allocation, sizeof ensures that the exact memory needed is reserved, preventing under- or overallocation.

- **Compact Conditional Checks with the Ternary Operator**

  The ternary operator provides a quick way to assign values based on simple conditions, making code cleaner and more efficient. For instance, instead of using an if-else block, the ternary operator can assign values directly within an expression, as seen in GUI programming where color or text changes depend on a user's input or system state.

Advantages of a Deep Understanding of Operators

Mastering operators in C provides a programmer with numerous benefits, including:

1. **Optimized Code**: Efficient use of operators leads to optimized code that performs well and runs faster. For example, replacing multiplication and division with bitwise shifts (where appropriate) can result in significant performance gains in computationally intensive applications.

2. **Improved Readability and Maintainability**: Concise expressions improve readability, especially in codebases shared among multiple developers. Compound assignment operators, the ternary operator, and clear understanding of operator precedence help make the code more readable, easier to maintain, and less error-prone.

3. **Memory and Resource Efficiency**: Using operators like sizeof and bitwise operators can help manage memory effectively, which is especially important in resource-constrained environments like embedded systems. Knowing how to manipulate memory efficiently allows developers to optimize applications for devices with limited resources.

4. **Enhanced Debugging Skills**: Understanding operators, precedence, and associativity can greatly aid in debugging complex expressions, as it's easier to identify errors related to improper evaluation order or incorrect use of operators. This skill is invaluable when optimizing or troubleshooting code.

Common Pitfalls and Best Practices

While operators are powerful, certain pitfalls can arise if not used carefully:

- **Misunderstanding Precedence and Associativity**: Misinterpreting operator precedence can lead to logic errors. To avoid ambiguity, use parentheses to clarify the intended order of operations, particularly in complex expressions.

- **Overusing the Ternary Operator**: Although the ternary operator is useful for simple conditional assignments, overusing it in complex conditions can make code harder to read. It's best used sparingly and avoided for nested conditions.

- **Avoiding Excessive Bitwise Operations**: While bitwise operators are powerful, excessive use can make code difficult to understand, especially for developers unfamiliar with binary arithmetic. Use bitwise operations when necessary, and consider adding comments for clarity.

- **Ensuring Proper Use of sizeof**: When working with pointers and dynamic memory, using sizeof correctly is vital. Always apply sizeof to the data type rather than hardcoding values, as this ensures portability and maintains accuracy across different platforms.

Conclusion

In summary, operators in C are indispensable for performing calculations, comparing data, managing memory, and controlling program flow. They range from the basic arithmetic operators to the more complex bitwise and ternary operators, each offering unique functionality that allows C programs to be efficient and powerful. Understanding operator precedence and associativity helps avoid logic errors, and using operators thoughtfully can lead to code that is not only functional but also optimized, readable, and maintainable.

A solid grasp of these operators will empower you to write more expressive, efficient, and optimized C code, whether working on small scripts or large applications. Whether you're crafting simple arithmetic expressions or manipulating bits for hardware-level programming, the skilful use of operators transforms the way you approach problem-solving in C, opening up opportunities to write high-performance and memory-efficient applications. By embracing best practices, avoiding common pitfalls, and applying a structured approach, you can maximize the potential of C's operators and expressions in any programming endeavour.

5. Functions in C

Introduction

In C programming, functions are essential for creating modular and reusable code. They allow programmers to break down complex tasks into manageable subroutines, each performing a specific part of the overall task. This makes code easier to understand, test, and maintain. In this guide, we will dive deep into the fundamentals of functions in C, covering everything from declaration and definition to advanced topics like recursion, inline functions, and macros.

1. Declaring and Defining Functions

Functions in C are typically declared and defined separately. The **declaration** tells the compiler about the function's existence, its name, return type, and parameters. This is commonly placed at the beginning of the code or in a header file to allow other functions to reference it.

A **definition**, on the other hand, includes the actual code that performs the function's operations.

Syntax of Function Declaration

return_type function_name(parameter_list);

return_type: The data type of the value returned by the function.

function_name: The identifier for the function.

parameter_list: A comma-separated list of parameters, with their types, that the function accepts.

Example of function declaration:

int add(int a, int b);

Syntax of Function Definition

```
return_type function_name(parameter_list) {
    // Function body
}
```

Example of function definition:

```
int add(int a, int b) {
    return a + b;
}
```

The function add takes two integers as arguments, a and b, and returns their sum as an integer.

2. Function Parameters and Return Types

In C, functions can accept parameters (also called **arguments**) and return a value.

Types of Parameters

Pass by Value: In C, parameters are typically passed by value, meaning the function receives a copy of each argument. Modifications to the parameters do not affect the original arguments.

Pass by Reference: Though C does not natively support passing by reference, it is achieved by passing pointers. This way, changes to the parameter affect the original variable in the calling function.

Example of passing by reference using pointers:

```c
void increment(int *num) {
    (*num)++;
}
```

In the example above, calling increment(&value) will increase value by one.

Return Types

void: A function with a void return type does not return any value.

Primitive Data Types: Functions can return a single value of any primitive data type, such as int, float, or char.

Pointer Return: Functions can return pointers, which is often used to return dynamically allocated memory or modified data.

Example of a function returning a pointer:

```c
int* allocateArray(int size) {
    return (int*) malloc (size * sizeof(int));
}
```

3. Scope and Lifetime of Variables

Understanding variable scope and lifetime is critical in C programming, especially within functions.

Variable Scope

Local Scope: Variables declared inside a function are local to that function. They cannot be accessed outside of the function.

Global Scope: Variables declared outside of any function are global, accessible throughout the entire program.

Example of local and global scope:

```
int globalVar = 10;  // Global scope


void func() {
    int localVar = 5;  // Local scope
}
```

Variable Lifetime

Automatic (Local) Variables: By default, local variables within functions are automatic, meaning they are created each time the function is called and destroyed when it finishes executing.

Static Variables: Variables defined with the static keyword retain their value across function calls.

Example of a static variable:

```
void counter () {
    static int count = 0;
    count++;
    printf("%d ", count);
}
```

Each time counter is called, count retains its value, so subsequent calls increment it.

4. Recursive Functions

Recursion is a technique in which a function calls itself to solve a problem. Recursive functions have two main components:

Base Case: The condition that stops the recursion.
Recursive Case: The part where the function calls itself with a modified argument.

Example of a Recursive Function

Calculating the factorial of a number is a classic example of recursion:

```
int factorial(int n)
{
    if (n == 0) return 1;  // Base case
    return n * factorial(n - 1);  // Recursive case
}
```

The factorial function continues calling itself with decremented values until it reaches the base case (n == 0), at which point it starts returning values back up the recursive chain.

Benefits and Drawbacks of Recursion

Benefits: Recursive functions can be elegant and concise for problems that can be broken down into smaller sub-problems.

Drawbacks: They can be memory-intensive and may lead to stack overflow if the recursion depth is too large.

5. Inline Functions and Macros

In C, **inline functions** and **macros** are two different mechanisms for optimizing function calls.

Inline Functions

Inline functions are defined using the inline keyword. When declared inline, the compiler attempts to replace the function call with the actual code of the function, reducing the overhead of a function call.

Syntax of inline function:

```
inline int square(int x)
{
    return x * x;
}
```

The main advantage of inline functions is faster execution due to reduced function call overhead. However, excessive use of inline functions may increase the program size, leading to code bloat.

Macros

Macros are preprocessor directives defined with the #define keyword. Unlike functions, macros are simply text replacements and do not involve actual function calls.

Example of a macro:

#define SQUARE(x) ((x) * (x))

While macros can be useful, they lack type checking and can introduce unexpected behaviour if not carefully used. Inline functions are generally preferred over macros for complex calculations due to type safety and better debugging support.

Inline Functions vs. Macros

Feature	Inline Functions	Macros
Type Checking	Yes	No
Debugging	Easier to debug	Harder to debug
Code Replacement	Compiler decides	Text replacement by preprocessor

Function is a small program which take some input and give us some output. Function allows a large program to be broken down into a number of smaller self-contained components, each of which has a definite purpose. It avoids rewriting the code over & over. Breaking down of logic into separate functions make the entire process of writing & debugging easier.

Or another hand you can say Function is a self-contained block of statements that is used to perform some tasks. A function is assigned some work once and can be called upon for the task any number of times. Every C program uses some functions, the commonly used functions are printf, scanf, main, etc.

Functions can be library functions or user defined functions. Library functions are those functions which come along with the compiler and are present in the disk. The user defined functions are those which the programmer makes by himself to make his program easier to debug, trace.

Drill Noteprintf (), **scanf(), exit(), pow()** are library functions. Every library function has a header file. **There are a total of 15 header files in C**. main() is a user defined function.

Every program must have a main function. This main function is used to mark the beginning of the execution. It is possible to code any program using only the main program but this leads to many problems. It becomes too large and complex thus difficult to trace, debug and test.

But if the same program is broken into small modulus coded independently and then combined into a single unit then these problems can be solved easily. These modulus are called as functions. Thus, a function can be defined as a small program which takes some input and gives us some output.

Drill Note- I am not going to type header files again and again, so when writing programs please don't forget to start your programs with header files.

Function to calculate the sum of two numbers:

```
int sum(int, int);  /* Function Prototype  or Declaration*/ main()
{
 int a,b,ans;
printf("Enter two numbers: ");
scanf("%d %d", &a,&b ans= sum(a,b);  /*Function Call*/
printf(" sum is %d", ans);

getch();

}
int sum (int x, int y) /*Function Definition or Process*/

{
int z;
z = x + y;
return(z);

}
```

Now let us see some of the features of this program:

The first statement is the declaration of the function which tells the compiler the name of the function and the data type of the arguments passed.

The declaration is also called as prototype.

The declaration of a function is not necessary if the output type is an integer value. In some C compilers declaration is not required for all the function.

The function call is the way of using the function. A function is declared once, defined once but can be used a number of times in the same program.

When the compiler encounters the function call, the control of the program is transferred to the function definition the function is then executed line by line and a value is returned at the end.

At the end of the main program is the definition of the function, which can also be called as process.

The function definition does not terminate with a semicolon.

A function may or may not return any value. Thus, the presence of the return statement is not necessary. When the return statement is encountered, the control is immediately passed back to the calling function.

While it is possible to pass any number of arguments to a function, the called statement returns only one value at a call. The return statement can be used as:

return; or return(value);

The first return without any value, it acts much as the closing of the braces of the function definition.

A function may have more than one return statement. It can be used as:

if (a!=0)
return(a);
else
return(1);

All functions by default return int. But if the function has to return a particular type of data the type specifiers can be used along with the function name.

long int fact(n)

If function main() calls a function sum() then main() is the calling function and sum() is called function.

No arguments and no return values:

Some functions do not receive any value from the calling function. Thus, the function prototype will be as:

prn()

i.e. no arguments will be passed. This can also be achieved as prn(void) And similarly the calling function does not get any value from the function. This is made possible by using the keyword void before the function name.

To illustrate this point let us consider the following program:

void prn(); /*declaration can also be made as void prn(void);*/ main( )
{
prn();

```
prn( );
prn( );
}
void prn()
{
printf("Hello");
}
```

Argument Passing Mechanism

(i) Call by value -

When arguments are passed by value then the copy of the actual parameters is transferred from calling function to the called function definition in formal parameters.

Now any changes made in the formal parameters in called function definition will not be reflected in actual parameters of calling function. Like in the above function to calculate the sum of two numbers the calling statement was written as:

```
ans = sum(a, b);
```

Here the values of variables a, b are passed from the main function to the calling function's definition.

In the definition variables x, y accepts the values of a, b respectively. Here, the variables a, b are called the

actual arguments while x, y will be called the formal arguments.

The scope of the actual and formal arguments is different so any change made in the formal arguments will not be seen in the actual arguments. **e.g:**

```
void swap(int, int); main()
{
int a,b;
printf("Enter 2 numbers");
scanf("%d%d",&a,&b);

swap(a,b);            /*In this call statement a,b are the actual parameters*/

printf("%d\t%d"a,b);

}
void swap(int x,int y)   /*In this function definition x & y are the formal parameters */
```

```
{
int t;
t=x; x=y; y=t;

}
```

Drill Note

In the above e.g.: changes made in x, y will not be reflected in a,b.

(ii) Call by reference

When arguments are passed by reference then the address of the actual parameters are transferred from calling function to the called function definition in formal parameters.

Now any changes made in the formal parameters in called function definition will be reflected in actual parameters of calling function.

Sometimes it is not possible to pass the values of the variables, for example while using an array it will not be possible to pass all the values of the array using call by value.

So, another type of function calling mechanism is used call by reference where the address of the variable is passed.

Here the definition would work by reaching the particular addresses. This method is generally used for the array and pointers.

e.g.:

```
main()
{
int a,b;
printf("Enter 2 numbers");
scanf("%d%d",&a,&b);
swap(&a, &b);              /*In this call statement address of a, b gets transferred*/
printf("%d\t%d"a,b);
}
void swap(int *p1, int *p2)  /*In this function definition p1 & p2 are the pointers which receive the
address of a, b*/
{
int t;
t=*p1;
```

```
*p1=*p2;
*p2=t;
}
```

Drill Note

In the above e.g.: changes made in p1, p2 will be reflected in a, b automatically.

Drill Note

Arrays are also passed by reference. When we pass the name of the array then only the base address is transferred in the function definition.

Type of Functions

1. Library Functions

Functions defined previously in the library are called as library functions.

e.g.

```
#include<math.h>
main()
{
int n, p, ans;
printf("Enter number and its power");
scanf("%d%d",&n,&p);
ans = pow(n,p);
printf("%d",ans);
getch();

}
```

Common Library Functions:

dio.h functions

fclose( )	Closes a stream
fcloseall()	Closes all open streams
feof()	Tests if end-of-file has been reached on a stream
fflush()	Flushes a stream
fgetc()	Gets a character from a stream
fgetpos()	Gets the current file pointer position

fsetpos()	Positions the file pointer of a stream
fgetchar()	Gets a character from stdin
fgets()	Gets a string from a stream
fopen()	Opens a stream
fprintf()	Sends formatted output to stream
fputc()	Outputs a character to a stream
fputs()	Outputs a string to a stream
fread()	Reads data from a stream
fscanf()	Scans and formats input from a stream.
fseek()	Sets the file pointer to a particular position.
ftell()	Returns the current position of the file pointer.
fwrite()	Writes to a stream.
getc()	gets one character.
getchar()	gets a character from stdin.
gets()	Get a string from stdin.
getw()	gets an integer from stream.
printf()	Sends the formatted output to stdin.
putc()	Outputs a character to stdout.
putchar()	Outputs a character on stdout.
puts()	Outputs string and appends a newline character.
putw()	Outputs an integer on a stream
remove()	Removes a file
rename()	Renames a file
Rewind()	Brings the file pointer to stream's beginning

scanf().	Scans and formats input from stdin.

conio.h

clrscr()	Clears text mode window
getch()	gets a character from console but does not echo to the screen
getche()	gets a character from console, and echoes to the screen
putch()	Oututs character to the text window on the screen

cgets()	Reads string from console
getchar()	Inputs a character from stdin.

stdlib.h

itoa()	converts an integer to a string.
atoi()	Converts string of digits to integer.
Random()	Returns a random number between 0 and number – 1
randomize()	initializes random number generator.
exit()	Terminates the program.

min()	Returns the smallest of two numbers.
max()	Returns the largest of two numbers.
ltoa()	converts a long to a string
ultoa()	converts an unsigned long to a string
atof()	converts a string to a floating point
_atold()	converts a string to a long double

math.h

abs()	gets the absolute value of an integer
acos()	Calculates the inverse of cos Accepts the angle value in radians
asin()	Calculates the inverse of sin Accepts the angle value in radians
atan()	Calculates the inverse of tan Accepts the angle value in radians
ceil()	Returns the largest integer in given list.
cos()	Calculates the cosine Accepts the angle value in radians
cosh()	Accepts the angle value in radians
exp()	Calculates the exponent
floor()	Returns the smallest integer in given list.
log()	Calculates the natural logarithm
log10()	Calculates the log of base 10
pow()	Calculates the power of a number
sin()	Calculates the sine value of an angle. Accepts the angle value in radians
sqrt()	Calculates the square root of a number
tan()	Calculates the tangent value of an angle. Accepts the angle tanh() value in radians Calculates the tangent hyperbolic value.

string.h   **string.h**

strcat() Function to concatenate(merge) strings.
strcmp() Function to compare two strings.

strcpy() Function to copy a string to another string
stricmp() Function to compare two strings ignoring their case.

strlen()Function to calculate the length of the string

strlwr() Converts the given string to lowercase
strrev()Function to reverse the given string.
strupr() Converts the given string to uppercase
Strdup() Duplicates a string.

strnicmp() Compares the first n characters of one string to another without being case sensitive.

strncat() Adds the first n characters at the end of second string.
strncpy() Copies the first n characters of a string into another.

strchr() Finds the first occurrence of the character.

strrchr() Finds the last occurrence of the character.

strstr() Finds the first occurrence of string in another string.

strset() Sets all the characters of the string to a given character.

strnset() Sets first n characters of the string to a given character.

2. User Defined Functions

Functions defined by us are known as User Defined Functions. main() function is also user defined function because the definition of main() is defined by us.

e.g.

```
int power(int,
int);
main()
{
int n, p, ans;
printf("Enter number and its power");
scanf("%d%d",&n,&p);
ans = power(n,p);

printf("%d",ans);

getch();
}
int power(int n, int p)
{
in ans=1, i;
(i=1;i<=p;i++)

{
ans = ans * n;
}
return(ans);
}
```

Function whose argument is a two-dim array:

```
void mat_sum(int m1[ ][10], int r1, int c1, int m2[][10], int r2, int c2, int m3[][10])


{
int i,j;
if(r1 != c1 && r2 != c2)
{
printf("Can't sum");
```

```
exit();
}
for(i=0;i<r1;i++)
for(j=0;j<c1;j++)
m3[i][j] = m1[i][j] + m2[i][j];
}
```

The above function can be called from main() as mat_sum(m1,r1,c1,m2,r2,c2,m3);

Recursion

A function is called recursive if a statement within the body of a function calls the same function. Sometimes called as 'circular definition', recursion is a function calling itself in the definition. A recursive function should have two parts recursive statement & a termination condition.

Suppose we want to calculate the factorial of an integer. As we know, the factorial of a number is the product of all the integers between 1 and that number. Factorial of 4 can be expressed as 4! = 4 * 3! Where! stands for factorial. Thus, the factorial of a number can be expressed in the form of itself. Hence this can be programmed using recursion.

e.g.:

```
int fact (int); /*function definition */ main()
{
int n,ans;
printf("Enter a number: ");
scanf("%d",&n);
ans = fact(n);        /*function call */
printf("factorial = %d",ans);
getch();
}
int fact(int n)
{
if(n= =0)              /*terminating condition*/
return (1);
return (n*fact(n-1));        /*recursive statement*/
}
```

Now let us evaluate this program:

Assuming the value of n is 3 when the control of the program is passed from the main() function the function fact. Since n is not equal to 0 so the condition is false and the recursive statement is executed.

3*fact(2)

now fact(2) is the calling function and thus the control of the program again reaches the beginning of the definition. Still the terminating condition is false so the recursive statement is executed.

2*fact(1)

Again fact(1) is the calling function and thus the control of the program again reaches the beginning of the definition. Still the terminating condition is false so the recursive statement is executed.

1 * fact(0)

Now the condition is true so the answer to the calling function(fact(0)) will be 1 and so on. Thus, the sequence of acts will be:

fact(3)=3 * fact(2) fact(2)=2 *
fact(1) fact(1)=1 * fact(0)

When we use a recursive program, a stack is used to organize the data. Stack is a Last In First Out (LIFO) data structure. This means that the last item to be stored (push operation) in the stack will be the first one to come (pop operation) out.

In the above program when the fact(2) is called the value 3 will be stored in the stack. Similarly when fact(1) is called the value 2 will be stored at the top of 3 on the stack.

Now when the fact(0) returns 1. it will be multiplied to the first value in the stack i.e.

1. This result will be multiplied to the second waiting value of the stack i.e. 2 and so on.

When a function in its definition calls another function, it is called chaining. Recursion is a special type of chaining where a function calls itself.

e.g.: main()

```
{
printf("expert\n");
main();
```

}

when executed the program will give the output as:

expert expert

expert

The execution of any recursive function can continue indefinitely so to bring the execution to the end a terminating condition is applied.

Use of recursive functions is to solve the problem where the solution is expressed in terms of successively applying the same solution to subsets of problems.

But there are also some disadvantages of the recursive functions:

These functions are more time consuming, so the execution speed of the program is slow.

More memory space is occupied due to the formation of stack to keep the waiting values.

Conclusion:

Functions are at the core of modular, structured, and efficient programming in C, providing a foundation for tackling complex computational problems in a manageable and systematic way. In this conclusion, we'll revisit key aspects of C functions discussed in this guide, offering insights into their application, benefits, and best practices. This detailed conclusion will encapsulate how functions contribute to flexibility, efficiency, and readability in C programming, preparing developers to write optimal and maintainable code.

1. Importance of Modularity and Reusability

One of the primary advantages of functions is modularity. By breaking down a large task into smaller, well-defined functions, we can create code that is not only easier to understand but also reusable. Each function has a specific purpose and encapsulates a particular logic or task, promoting code organization and reducing redundancy.

For instance, consider a program that performs various arithmetic operations like addition, subtraction, multiplication, and division. By defining each operation as a separate function, we can reuse these functions anywhere in the code without rewriting them, making the program more adaptable to future changes.

Reusability extends beyond a single program. Functions developed in one project can often be adapted and reused in other projects with minimal modification. Libraries and APIs are essentially collections of reusable functions, encapsulating complex functionality that others can use without needing to understand the internal workings. This principle of reusability is foundational in C, as evidenced by its vast standard library filled with pre-written, reusable functions for handling input/output, memory, math, and more.

2. Declarative Approach and Separation of Concerns

Separating function **declaration** and **definition** exemplifies the concept of a declarative approach in C. Declaring a function at the beginning of a program, or in a header file, informs the compiler of the function's existence, its return type, and parameters, while the actual logic (definition) can be placed separately. This separation allows developers to focus on high-level program flow without delving into the details of each function immediately, enhancing code readability.

Furthermore, separation of concerns — the practice of isolating different parts of code with distinct responsibilities — is achieved with functions. When each function has a single, well-defined task, it makes the code less prone to bugs, easier to debug, and allows for more straightforward modifications without unintended side effects. It also facilitates teamwork, as developers can work on different functions independently, minimizing the risk of code conflicts.

3. Parameter Passing and Return Types: Ensuring Flexibility

C functions offer flexible ways of handling data through parameters and return types. Parameters enable functions to operate on various inputs without altering the underlying function code. There are two main methods of passing parameters: by value and by reference.

Pass by Value: Passing by value involves sending a copy of the data to the function. Since the function operates on a copy, the original variable remains unchanged, which is ideal when we need to protect the data from unintended modifications.

Pass by Reference: Passing by reference, achieved using pointers, allows functions to directly modify the original data. This approach is beneficial when working with large data structures or when the function needs to produce multiple outputs. For example, swapping two variables or sorting an array typically requires passing by reference to avoid excessive memory usage.

Return types also contribute to function flexibility, enabling functions to return computed values. This is particularly useful when a function performs calculations or retrieves data, like finding the maximum element in an array. Additionally, functions can return pointers, allowing complex data structures or dynamically allocated memory to be passed between functions seamlessly. C provides complete control over how functions handle data, promoting efficient and flexible programming.

4. Scope and Lifetime of Variables: Avoiding Common Pitfalls

Understanding **scope** and **lifetime** is critical for proper function design in C. Variables declared within a function (local variables) are isolated from the rest of the program, existing only for the function's duration. This localized scope avoids unintended interactions with other parts of the program, reducing the likelihood of bugs. However, it also requires awareness of scope limitations, especially when trying to access variables across functions.

Local Variables: Defined within a function, these variables are destroyed once the function completes. They are ideal for temporary data that only the function requires.

Global Variables: Defined outside any function, these variables can be accessed by any function within the program, making them useful for data shared across functions. However, overusing global variables can lead to unexpected behaviour if multiple functions modify them.

Lifetime also matters, as certain variables need to retain their values across multiple function calls. Using **static variables** enables data persistence within a function, maintaining the variable's value across calls. For example, a function that tracks the number of times it has been called would need a static counter to avoid resetting with each call. This combination of scope and lifetime considerations helps developers write code that is reliable, predictable, and easy to debug.

5. Recursive Functions: Tackling Complex Problems with Elegance

Recursion is a powerful concept in C, allowing functions to call themselves. By breaking down complex problems into smaller sub-problems, recursive functions provide elegant solutions for tasks that involve repetitive operations, such as factorial calculations, Fibonacci series generation, and tree traversals.

However, recursion comes with trade-offs. Each recursive call adds to the **call stack**, and excessive recursion can lead to **stack overflow**. Recursive functions should have a clear **base case** to prevent infinite recursion and should be used judiciously to balance readability and memory efficiency. While recursion is elegant for some problems, understanding its limitations and potential performance costs is essential.

6. Inline Functions and Macros: Optimizing for Speed

C provides mechanisms to optimize performance with **inline functions** and **macros**. Inline functions, marked by the inline keyword, suggest to the compiler to replace function calls with the actual code, reducing function call overhead. This can improve performance, especially for small, frequently used functions.

Macros, defined using #define, also replace code textually before compilation, bypassing the function call entirely.

However, macros have limitations:

They lack type safety, which can lead to bugs if used improperly.

Debugging macros is more challenging than debugging inline functions.

Choosing between inline functions and macros depends on the specific use case, but inline functions are generally preferred for complex operations due to better type safety, debugging support, and readability.

7. Best Practices for Using Functions in C

To harness the full power of functions in C, certain best practices can be applied:

Single Responsibility: Each function should have a single, well-defined purpose. This makes functions easier to understand, test, and reuse.

Descriptive Naming: Function names should clearly convey the task they perform. A function named calculateSum is easier to understand than one named doWork.

Limit Global Variables: While globals are convenient for shared data, excessive use can make code unpredictable. Prefer passing data through parameters whenever possible.

Optimize for Efficiency: Avoid excessive inline or recursive functions if they increase memory use or complexity. Inline functions should only be used for small, frequently called functions.

Document Functions: Brief comments or documentation blocks can describe what a function does, its parameters, and its return type, aiding readability and maintainability.

8. Function Libraries and API Design

Functions are the building blocks for libraries and application programming interfaces (APIs). By encapsulating complex logic within a function library, developers can expose only the necessary functions to other programs while keeping the implementation details hidden. The C standard library itself is an extensive collection of functions that developers can use to manage data, handle I/O, perform math, and more.

When designing function libraries:

Use Modular Design: Break functionality into self-contained modules with distinct tasks.

Ensure Consistency: Follow a consistent naming convention and parameter structure.

Provide Clear Documentation: Explain each function's purpose, parameters, and return values to make the library easy to use.

The standard C library's approach to modular function design exemplifies how well-designed function libraries can drastically enhance productivity and code quality.

Summing Up

Mastering functions in C enables developers to write organized, efficient, and maintainable code. From fundamental concepts like declaration and scope to advanced topics like recursion and inline functions, functions play a pivotal role in structuring code for both small projects and large-scale systems. By leveraging functions thoughtfully, programmers can achieve modularity, reusability, and optimized performance. Adopting best practices and understanding the nuances of parameter passing, variable lifetime, and function scope will ensure that functions work harmoniously, enabling efficient and robust programming in C for 2024 and beyond.

Embracing functions as a core part of programming methodology in C is essential for creating code that is not only efficient but also adaptable, making it possible to tackle a wide range of challenges with confidence. Whether building standalone applications or contributing to shared libraries, the principles outlined here will guide developers in making optimal use of functions to build powerful and reliable software solutions.

6. Arrays and Strings in C

Introduction

In C programming, arrays and strings are fundamental data structures that enable efficient handling and manipulation of data. Arrays store multiple items of the same type in contiguous memory locations, making them useful for scenarios requiring sequential data access, while strings are arrays of characters, used for text handling. Understanding these structures is crucial for solving complex programming tasks.

1. Single-Dimensional Arrays

A single-dimensional array (also known as a one-dimensional array) is a linear structure that stores elements in a contiguous memory block, accessed using an index. Here's a breakdown:

Declaration and Initialization: Arrays in C are declared by specifying the data type and the number of elements.

```
int numbers[5];       // Declares an integer array with 5 elements.
int numbers[5] = {1, 2, 3, 4, 5}; // Initializes the array with values.
```

Accessing Elements: Array elements are accessed using their index, which starts from 0.

```
printf("%d", numbers[2]);  // Outputs 3.
```

Use Cases: Commonly used in situations requiring multiple values of the same type, such as storing test scores, temperatures, or sensor readings.

2. Multi-Dimensional Arrays

Multi-dimensional arrays (usually two-dimensional arrays) represent data in a tabular format, useful for matrices, grids, or any data that has rows and columns.

Declaration and Initialization:

```
int matrix[3][3];  // Declares a 3x3 matrix.
int matrix[2][2] = {{1, 2}, {3, 4}}; // Initializes a 2x2 matrix.
```

Accessing Elements: Elements are accessed by specifying row and column indices.

```
printf("%d", matrix[1][0]);  // Outputs 3.
```

Applications: Often used in game boards, image processing, and scientific computing where two-dimensional data is necessary.

3. Character Arrays and Strings

In C, strings are arrays of characters terminated by a null character \0. Unlike other programming languages, C does not have a dedicated string type; instead, it uses character arrays.

Declaration and Initialization:

char name[6] = "Alice"; // Array size includes space for null character.
char greeting[] = "Hello, World!"; // Size is automatically determined.

Characteristics: Strings in C are mutable (modifiable), and all operations must consider the null terminator.

4. String Manipulation Functions

The C standard library provides various functions for string manipulation, found in <string.h>. Key functions include:

strlen: Returns the length of a string (excluding the null character).

int len = strlen(greeting); // Length of "Hello, World!" is 13.

strcpy: Copies one string to another.

char destination [20];
strcpy(destination, greeting); // Copies greeting to destination.

strcat: Concatenates (appends) one string to the end of another.

char str1[20] = "Hello, ";
char str2[] = "World!";
strcat(str1, str2); // str1 now contains "Hello, World!".

strcmp: Compares two strings lexicographically.

int result = strcmp("apple", "orange"); // Returns a negative value because "apple" < "orange".
These functions are essential for handling and manipulating text data in applications.

5. Handling Strings with Pointers

Pointers offer powerful ways to manipulate strings in C. Instead of using indices, strings can be traversed and manipulated using pointers, providing more flexibility and efficiency in memory management.

Pointer-Based Access:

```c
char str[] = "Hello";
char *ptr = str;
while (*ptr != '\0')
{
    printf("%c", *ptr);  // Prints each character of the string.
    ptr++;
}
```

Dynamic String Handling: With pointers, strings can be managed dynamically using functions like malloc and free, allowing for runtime memory allocation.

Arrays

Luckily, C has arrays. I mean, I know it's considered a low-level language[1] but it does at least have the concept of arrays built-in. And since a great many languages drew inspiration from C's syntax, you're probably already familiar with using [and] for declaring and using arrays.

But C only barely has arrays! As we'll find out later, arrays are just syntactic sugar in C they're actually all pointers and stuff deep down. Freak out! But for now, let's just use them as arrays.

Easy Example

Let's just crank out an example:

```c
#include <stdio.h>
int main(void)
{
int i; float f[4]; // Declare an array of 4 floats
f[0] = 3.14159; // Indexing starts at 0, of course.
f[1] = 1.41421;
f[2] = 1.61803;
f[3] = 2.71828; // Print them all out:
for (i = 0; i < 4; i++)
{
printf("%f\n", f[i]);
```

_____

```
    }
}
```

When you declare an array, you have to give it a size. And the size has to be fixed.

In the above example, we made an array of 4 floats. The value in the square brackets in the declaration lets us know that.

Later on in subsequent lines, we access the values in the array, setting them or getting them, again with square brackets.

Hopefully this looks familiar from languages you already know!

Getting the Length of an Array

You can't...ish. C doesn't record this information. You have to manage it separately in another variable.

When I say "can't", I actually mean there are some circumstances when you can. There is a trick to get the number of elements in an array in the scope in which an array is declared. But, generally speaking, this won't work the way you want if you pass the array to a function.

Let's take a look at this trick. The basic idea is that you take the sizeof the array, and then divide that by the size of each element to get the length. For example, if an int is 4 bytes, and the array is 32 bytes long, there must be room for $\frac{32}{4}$ or 8 ints in there.

```
int x[12]; // 12 ints

printf("%zu\n", sizeof x);       // 48 total bytes
printf("%zu\n", sizeof(int)); // 4 bytes per int
printf("%zu\n", sizeof x / sizeof(int)); // 48/4 = 12 ints!
```

If it's an array of chars, then sizeof the array is the number of elements, since sizeof(char) is defined to be 1. For anything else, you have to divide by the size of each element.

But this trick only works in the scope in which the array was defined. If you pass the array to a function, it doesn't work.

Even if you make it "big" in the function signature:

```
void foo(int x[12])

{
printf("%zu\n", sizeof x);       // 8?! What happened to 48?
printf("%zu\n", sizeof(int)); // 4 bytes per int

printf("%zu\n", sizeof x / sizeof(int)); // 8/4 = 2 ints?? WRONG.
}
```

This is because when you "pass" arrays to functions, you're only passing a pointer to the first element, and that's what sizeof measures. More on this in the Passing Single Dimensional Arrays to Functions section, below.

One more thing you can do with sizeof and arrays is getting the size of an array of a fixed number of elements without declaring the array. This is like how you can get the size of an int with sizeof(int). For example, to see how many bytes would be needed for an array of 48 doubles, you can do this:

```
sizeof(double [48]);
```

Array Initializers

You can initialize an array with constants ahead of time:

```
#include <stdio.h>
int main(void)
{
int i; int a[5] = {22, 37, 3490, 18, 95}; // Initialize with these values
for (i = 0; i < 5; i++)
{
printf("%d\n", a[i]);
}
}
```

Catch: initializer values must be constant terms. Can't throw variables in there. Sorry, Illinois!

You should never have more items in your initializer than there is room for in the array, or the compiler will get cranky:

In function 'main':

```
warning: excess elements in array initializer
int a[5] = {22, 37, 3490, 18, 95, 999};
^~~
```

note: (near initialization for 'a')

But (fun fact!) you can have fewer items in your initializer than there is room for in the array. The remaining elements in the array will be automatically initialized with zero. This is true in general for all types of array initializers: if you have an initializer, anything not explicitly set to a value will be set to zero.

```
int a[5] = {22, 37, 3490}; // is the same as:
```

int a[5] = {22, 37, 3490, 0, 0};

It's a common shortcut to see this in an initializer when you want to set an entire array to zero:

int a[100] = {0};

Which means, "Make the first element zero, and then automatically make the rest zero, as well."

You can set specific array elements in the initializer, as well, by specifying an index for the value! When you do this, C will happily keep initializing subsequent values for you until the initializer runs out, filling everything else with 0.

To do this, put the index in square brackets with an = after, and then set the value.

Here's an example where we build an array:

int a[10] = {0, 11, 22, [5]=55, 66, 77};

Because we listed index 5 as the start for 55, the resulting data in the array is:

0 11 22 0 0 55 66 77 0 0

You can put simple constant expressions in there, as well.

#define COUNT 5

int a[COUNT] = {[COUNT-3]=3, 2, 1}; which gives us:

0 0 3 2 1

Lastly, you can also have C compute the size of the array from the initializer, just by leaving the size off:

int a[3] = {22, 37, 3490}; // is the same as: int a[] = {22, 37, 3490}; // Left the size off!

C doesn't stop you from accessing arrays out of bounds. It might not even warn you.

Let's steal the example from above and keep printing off the end of the array. It only has 5 elements, but let's try to print 10 and see what happens:

```
#include <stdio.h>
int main(void)
{ int i; int a[5] = {22, 37, 3490, 18, 95};
```

```
for (i = 0; i < 10; i++)
{ // BAD NEWS: printing too many elements!
printf("%d\n", a[i]);

}

}
```

Running it on my computer prints:

```
22

37

3490

18

95

32765

1847052032

1780534144

-56487472

21890
```

Yikes! What's that? Well, turns out printing off the end of an array results in what C developers call undefined behavior. We'll talk more about this beast later, but for now it means, "You've done something bad, and anything could happen during your program run."

And by anything, I mean typically things like finding zeroes, finding garbage numbers, or crashing. But really the C spec says in this circumstance the compiler is allowed to emit code that does anything[2].

Short version: don't do anything that causes undefined behavior.

Multidimensional Arrays

You can add as many dimensions as you want to your arrays.

```
int a[10];
int b[2][7];
int c[4][5][6];
```

These are stored in memory in row-major order. This means with a 2D array, the first index listed indicates the row, and the second the column.

You can also use initializers on multidimensional arrays by nesting them:

_____

```c
#include <stdio.h>
int main(void)
{
int row, col;
int a[2][5] =
{           // Initialize a 2D array
{0, 1, 2, 3, 4},
{5, 6, 7, 8, 9}
};
for (row = 0; row < 2; row++)
{
for (col = 0; col < 5; col++)
{
printf("(%d,%d) = %d\n", row, col, a[row][col]);
}
}
}
```

For output of:

```
(0,0) = 0
(0,1) = 1
(0,2) = 2
(0,3) = 3
(0,4) = 4
(1,0) = 5
(1,1) = 6
(1,2) = 7
(1,3) = 8
(1,4) = 9
```

And you can initialize with explicit indexes:

// Make a 3x3 identity matrix

int a[3][3] = {[0][0]=1, [1][1]=1, [2][2]=1}; which builds a 2D array like this:

1 0 0

0 1 0

0 0 1

Arrays and Pointers

[Casually] So… I kind a might have mentioned up there that arrays were pointers, deep down? We should take a shallow dive into that now so that things aren't completely confusing. Later on, we'll look at what the real relationship between arrays and pointers is, but for now I just want to look at passing arrays to functions.

Getting a Pointer to an Array

I want to tell you a secret. Generally speaking, when a C programmer talks about a pointer to an array, they're talking about a pointer to the first element of the array.

So, let's get a pointer to the first element of an array.

```
#include <stdio.h>
int main(void)
{
int a[5] = {11, 22, 33, 44, 55};
int *p; p = &a[0]; // p points to the array // Well, to the first element, actually
printf("%d\n", *p); // Prints "11"
}
```

This is so common to do in C that the language allows us a shorthand:

```
p = &a[0]; // p points to the array // is the same as:
p = a;   // p points to the array, but much nicer-looking!
```

Just referring to the array name in isolation is the same as getting a pointer to the first element of the array! We're going to use this extensively in the upcoming examples.

But hold on a second—isn't p an int*? And *p gives us 11, same as a[0]? Yessss. You're starting to get a glimpse of how arrays and pointers are related in C.

Passing Single Dimensional Arrays to Functions

Let's do an example with a single dimensional array. I'm going to write a couple functions that we can pass the array to that do different things.

Prepare for some mind-blowing function signatures!

```
#include <stdio.h>
// Passing as a pointer to the first element void times2(int *a, int len)
{
```

```c
for (int i = 0; i < len; i++) printf("%d\n", a[i] * 2);
}

// Same thing, but using array notation void times3(int a[], int len)

{

for (int i = 0; i < len; i++) printf("%d\n", a[i] * 3);

}

// Same thing, but using array notation with size void times4(int a[5], int len)

{

for (int i = 0; i < len; i++) printf("%d\n", a[i] * 4);

}

int main(void)

{

int x[5] = {11, 22, 33, 44, 55};

times2(x, 5);
times3(x, 5);
times4(x, 5);

}
```

All those methods of listing the array as a parameter in the function are identical.

void times2(int *a, int len) void times3(int a[], int len)

Arrays and Pointers

void times4(int a[5], int len)

In usage by C regulars, the first is the most common, by far.

And, in fact, in the latter situation, the compiler doesn't even care what number you pass in (other than it has to be greater than zero[3]). It doesn't enforce anything at all.

Now that I've said that, the size of the array in the function declaration actually does matter when you're passing multidimensional arrays into functions, but let's come back to that.

Changing Arrays in Functions

We've said that arrays are just pointers in disguise. This means that if you pass an array to a function, you're likely passing a pointer to the first element in the array.

_____

But if the function has a pointer to the data, it is able to manipulate that data! So, changes that a function makes to an array will be visible back out in the caller.

Here's an example where we pass a pointer to an array to a function, the function manipulates the values in that array, and those changes are visible out in the caller.

```
#include <stdio.h>
void double_array(int *a, int len)
{
// Multiply each element by 2
//
// This doubles the values in x in main() since x and a both point // to the same array in memory!
for (int i = 0; i < len; i++) a[i] *= 2;
}
int main(void)
{
int x[5] = {1, 2, 3, 4, 5};
double_array(x, 5);
for (int i = 0; i < 5; i++)
printf("%d\n", x[i]); // 2, 4, 6, 8, 10!
}
```

Even though we passed the array in as parameter a which is type int*, look at how we access it using array notation with a[i]! Whaaaat. This is totally allowed.

Later when we talk about the equivalence between arrays and pointers, we'll see how this makes a lot more sense. For now, it's enough to know that functions can make changes to arrays that are visible out in the caller.

Passing Multidimensional Arrays to Functions

The story changes a little when we're talking about multidimensional arrays. C needs to know all the dimensions (except the first one) so it has enough information to know where in memory to look to find a value.

Here's an example where we're explicit with all the dimensions:

```
#include <stdio.h>
void print_2D_array (int a[2][3])
{
for (int row = 0; row < 2; row++)
{
```

```
for (int col = 0; col < 3; col++)
printf("%d ", a[row][col]);

printf("\n");

}
}
int main(void)

{
int x[2][3] =
{
{1, 2, 3},

{4, 5, 6}

};

print_2D_array(x);

}
```

But in this case, these two are equivalent:

```
void print_2D_array (int a[2][3]) void print_2D_array(int a[][3])
```

The compiler really only needs the second dimension so it can figure out how far in memory to skip for each increment of the first dimension. In general, it needs to know all the dimensions except the first one.

Also, remember that the compiler does minimal compile-time bounds checking (if you're lucky), and C does zero runtime checking of bounds. No seat belts! Don't crash by accessing array elements out of bounds!

Strings

Finally! Strings! What could be simpler?

Well, turns out strings aren't actually strings in C. That's right! They're pointers! Of course they are! Much like arrays, strings in C barely exist.

But let's check it out—it's not really such a big deal.

String Literals

Before we start, let's talk about string literals in C. These are sequences of characters in double quotes ("). (Single quotes enclose characters, and are a different animal entirely.)

Examples:

"Hello, world!\n"

"This is a test."

"When asked if this string had quotes in it, she replied, \"It does.\"" The first one has a newline at the end—quite a common thing to see.

The last one has quotes embedded within it, but you see each is preceded by (we say "escaped by") a backslash (\) indicating that a literal quote belongs in the string at this point. This is how the C compiler can tell the difference between printing a double quote and the double quote at the end of the string.

String Variables

Now that we know how to make a string literal, let's assign it to a variable so we can do something with it.

char *s = "Hello, world!";

Check out that type: pointer to a char. The string variable s is actually a pointer to the first character in that string, namely the H.

And we can print it with the %s (for "string") format specifier:

char *s = "Hello, world!"; printf("%s\n", s); // "Hello, world!"

String Variables as Arrays

Another option is this, nearly equivalent to the above char* usage:

char s[14] = "Hello, world!";
// or, if we were properly lazy and have the compiler // figure the length for us:
char s[] = "Hello, world!";

This means you can use array notation to access characters in a string. Let's do exactly that to print all the characters in a string on the same line:

```
#include <stdio.h>
int main(void)
{
char s[] = "Hello, world!";
for (int i = 0; i < 13; i++)
printf("%c\n", s[i]);
}
```

Note that we're using the format specifier %c to print a single character.

Also, check this out. The program will still work fine if we change the definition of s to be a char* type:

```c
#include <stdio.h>
int main(void)
{
char *s = "Hello, world!";      // char* here
for (int i = 0; i < 13; i++)
printf("%c\n", s[i]);    // But still use arrays here...?
}
```

And we still can use array notation to get the job done when printing it out! This is surprising, but is still only because we haven't talked about array/pointer equivalence yet. But this is yet another hint that arrays and pointers are the same thing, deep down.

String Initializers

We've already seen some examples with initializing string variables with string literals:

```c
char *s = "Hello, world!"; char t[] = "Hello, again!";
```

But these two are subtly different.

This one is a pointer to a string literal (i.e. a pointer to the first character in a string):

```c
char *s = "Hello, world!";
```

If you try to mutate that string with this:

```c
char *s = "Hello, world!";
s[0] = 'z'; // BAD NEWS: tried to mutate a string literal!
```

The behavior is undefined. Probably, depending on your system, a crash will result.

But declaring it as an array is different. This one is a mutable copy of the string that we can change at will:

```c
char t[] = "Hello, again!"; // t is an array copy of the string t[0] = 'z'; // No problem
```

Getting String Length

```c
printf("%s\n", t); // "zello, again!"
```

So, remember: if you have a pointer to a string literal, don't try to change it! And if you use a string in double quotes to initialize an array, that's not actually a string literal.

You can't, since C doesn't track it for you. And when I say "can't", I actually mean "can"[4]. There's a function in <string.h> called strlen() that can be used to compute the length of any string in bytes.

```
#include <stdio.h> #include <string.h>
int main(void)
{
char *s = "Hello, world!";
printf("The string is %zu bytes long.\n", strlen(s));
}
```

The strlen() function returns type size_t, which is an integer type so you can use it for integer math. We print size_t with %zu.

The above program prints:

The string is 13 bytes long.

Great! So, it is possible to get the string length!

But... if C doesn't track the length of the string anywhere, how does it know how long the string is?

String Termination

C does string a little differently than many programming languages, and in fact differently than almost every modern programming language.

When you're making a new language, you have basically two options for storing a string in memory:

Store the bytes of the string along with a number indicating the length of the string.

Store the bytes of the string, and mark the end of the string with a special byte called the terminator.

If you want strings longer than 255 characters, option 1 requires at least two bytes to store the length. Whereas option 2 only requires one byte to terminate the string. So a bit of savings there.

Of course, these days it seems ridiculous to worry about saving a byte (or 3—lots of languages will happily let you have strings that are 4 gigabytes in length). But back in the day, it was a bigger deal.

So, C took approach #2. In C, a "string" is defined by two basic characteristics:

A pointer to the first character in the string.

_____

A zero-valued byte (or NUL character) somewhere in memory after the pointer that indicates the end of the string.

A NUL character can be written in C code as \0, though you don't often have to do this.

When you include a string in double quotes in your code, the NUL character is automatically, implicitly included.

```
char *s = "Hello!"; // Actually "Hello!\0" behind the scenes
```

So with this in mind, let's write our own strlen() function that counts chars in a string until it finds a NUL.

The procedure is to look down the string for a single NUL character, counting as we go:

```
int my_strlen(char *s)
{
int count = 0;
while (s[count] != '\0') // Single quotes for single char count++;
return count;
}
```

And that's basically how the built-in strlen() gets the job done.

Copying a String

You can't copy a string through the assignment operator (=). All that does is make a copy of the pointer to the first character… so you end up with two pointers to the same string:

```
#include <stdio.h>
int main(void)
{
char s[] = "Hello, world!";
char *t;
// This makes a copy of the pointer, not a copy of the string!
t = s;
// We modify t
t[0] = 'z';
// But printing s shows the modification! // Because t and s point to the same string!
printf("%s\n", s); // "zello, world!"
}
```

If you want to make a copy of a string, you have to copy it a byte at a time—but this is made easier with the strcpy() function.

Before you copy the string, make sure you have room to copy it into, i.e. the destination array that's going to hold the characters needs to be at least as long as the string you're copying.

```c
#include <stdio.h> #include <string.h>

int main(void)

{
char s[] = "Hello, world!";
char t[100]; // Each char is one byte, so plenty of room

// This makes a copy of the string!
strcpy(t, s);

// We modify t
t[0] = 'z';

// And s remains unaffected because it's a different string
printf("%s\n", s); // "Hello, world!"

// But t has been changed
printf("%s\n", t); // "zello, world!"

}
```

Notice with strcpy(), the destination pointer is the first argument, and the source pointer is the second. A mnemonic I use to remember this is that it's the order you would have put t and s if an assignment = worked for strings, with the source on the right and the destination on the left.

Conclusion

In C programming, arrays and strings serve as cornerstones for handling and managing data, representing everything from numeric sequences to text processing. Understanding their intricacies allows programmers to harness C's efficiency, memory control, and low-level capabilities. This conclusion revisits essential points, explores practical applications, and suggests ways to deepen knowledge of arrays and strings, especially in performance-critical contexts like system programming, embedded systems, and data-intensive applications.

Revisiting Core Concepts

Single-Dimensional Arrays: As the simplest form of arrays, single-dimensional arrays provide a contiguous memory structure that stores elements of the same data type. This structure is highly efficient for operations requiring sequential data storage, like lists of numbers or character sequences. In C, array indexing enables direct access to each element, facilitating tasks like summing elements, finding maximum or minimum values, and sorting.

Multi-Dimensional Arrays: Extending beyond one-dimension, multi-dimensional arrays add complexity by arranging data in tables or matrices. This makes them ideal for applications requiring a grid-like structure, such as image processing, matrices in mathematical computations, or tables in data organization. The additional indexing in multi-dimensional arrays allows for clear representation and manipulation of data sets with inherent two-dimensional (or higher) relationships.

Character Arrays and Strings: Strings are indispensable for representing textual information. As arrays of characters, they offer a straightforward way to handle text, while the terminating null character (\0) ensures that functions know where the string ends. The efficiency and simplicity of character arrays make them useful for embedded systems and memory-constrained applications. However, C's lack of a native string type adds complexity to string manipulation, making mastery of string functions critical for effective programming.

String Manipulation Functions: C's standard library provides functions that simplify common string operations, such as determining string length (strlen), copying strings (strcpy), concatenating strings (strcat), and comparing strings (strcmp). These functions enable precise, memory-safe string manipulation, essential for developing programs that process textual data, validate user input, or parse files. Mastery of these functions is necessary for any C programmer dealing with text.

Handling Strings with Pointers: Pointers open up advanced capabilities in C, allowing dynamic memory management, flexible data manipulation, and efficiency in memory usage. For strings, pointers enable traversal, modification, and dynamic resizing, vital in scenarios where memory must be managed efficiently, like in embedded systems. By using pointers, programmers can work directly with memory addresses, facilitating operations on strings without needing traditional indexing.

Practical Applications of Arrays and Strings in C

Understanding how to apply arrays and strings in real-world scenarios is essential. Let's explore some common applications:

Data Storage and Retrieval: Single-dimensional arrays are often used to store lists of items like scores, temperatures, or any data series. These arrays enable rapid access and manipulation, useful in algorithms like sorting and searching. In contrast, multi-dimensional arrays suit applications requiring tabular data, like matrices for linear algebra or images in graphics programming.

Game Development: Multi-dimensional arrays are frequently used in game development to represent grids, maps, or boards. For example, a 2D array can represent a chessboard, where each cell holds information about a piece. Arrays enable quick updates and retrievals, essential for real-time game logic.

Text Processing: Text-based applications rely heavily on strings and string manipulation. For instance, parsing user input, formatting output, and analyzing text (e.g., counting words or identifying patterns) all require efficient string handling. Character arrays and functions like strcpy and strcat are invaluable in applications that process textual data, like command-line interfaces or data parsers.

File I/O and Data Parsing: Many programs involve reading data from files and parsing it for further analysis. In such cases, strings play a crucial role, often combined with arrays to store parsed data. For instance, a program may read a CSV file line-by-line, store each field in an array, and process each row individually, allowing efficient data manipulation.

Scientific and Engineering Computations: Multi-dimensional arrays are fundamental in scientific programming, where they're often used for matrix operations, simulations, and numerical methods. Many algorithms, like matrix multiplication, differential equations, and finite element analysis, heavily rely on multi-dimensional arrays.

Embedded Systems and Low-Level Programming: In embedded systems, efficient memory usage is critical. Single-dimensional arrays are often used to manage sensor data, control signals, or hardware configurations. Arrays also facilitate precise control over data layout, vital in low-level hardware interfacing. Strings, too, are useful in embedded systems for handling text-based communication or logging messages, though often with minimal libraries.

Challenges and Considerations

Working with arrays and strings in C requires an understanding of C's memory model, including pointers, memory allocation, and memory safety. Here are some critical considerations:

Bounds Checking: C does not perform bounds checking on arrays, meaning accessing an element outside the array's declared bounds can lead to undefined behavior. It's the programmer's responsibility to manage these boundaries, as accessing out-of-bounds elements can corrupt memory, causing bugs that are difficult to trace.

String Manipulation Pitfalls: Strings in C require careful handling, especially when using standard library functions. Functions like strcpy can cause buffer overflows if the destination array is not large enough. Buffer overflows can lead to security vulnerabilities, so always ensure that arrays have adequate space for operations involving string manipulation.

Memory Allocation and Deallocation: When dealing with large arrays or dynamically sized data, it's important to allocate memory using malloc and free responsibly. Failure to free memory after it's no longer needed leads to memory leaks, a common issue in C programming, especially in applications that run for extended periods.

Pointer Arithmetic: When handling strings with pointers, pointer arithmetic provides efficiency but requires precision. Mismanagement of pointers can lead to memory access violations, where the program tries to read or write to inaccessible memory, resulting in segmentation faults.

Further Exploration and Advanced Topics

After gaining a foundation in arrays and strings, here are some advanced topics and practical exercises to enhance your understanding:

Dynamic Arrays: Learn how to create and manage dynamic arrays using pointers and the malloc function. Dynamic arrays are useful when array size cannot be determined at compile time. Implement a basic dynamic array data structure that grows as needed, similar to a vector in C++.

String Parsing and Tokenization: Practice parsing and tokenizing strings, useful for reading command-line inputs, configuration files, or structured data formats. Use functions like strtok to break a string into smaller parts based on delimiters.

Multi-dimensional Array Operations: Implement basic matrix operations, such as addition, subtraction, and multiplication. These operations will strengthen your understanding of multi-dimensional arrays and are foundational for fields like data science and machine learning.

Pointer-Based String Functions: Recreate standard string manipulation functions using pointers. Implement functions like strlen, strcpy, strcat, and strcmp from scratch, focusing on pointer manipulation. These exercises provide hands-on experience with pointer arithmetic and memory handling.

Using Arrays in Data Structures: Arrays are the basis for various data structures, like stacks, queues, and hash tables. Implement these structures using arrays to gain insight into how they work. Stacks and queues introduce you to concepts like last-in-first-out (LIFO) and first-in-first-out (FIFO) ordering, while hash tables introduce hashing and collision handling.

Optimizing Memory and Performance: In performance-sensitive applications, such as embedded systems or real-time computing, every byte of memory counts. Explore ways to optimize array usage, such as using smaller data types (like char or short instead of int) when possible, or structuring arrays to reduce memory fragmentation.

Closing Thoughts

Arrays and strings are foundational to C programming, bridging low-level memory management with practical data manipulation capabilities. By mastering these structures, programmers can tackle diverse challenges, from building efficient data-processing applications to developing real-time systems in embedded environments. As you continue exploring these topics, remember that proficiency in C's memory model and a careful approach to array and string handling are key to becoming an expert in the language.

Arrays and strings are not only technical constructs but gateways to deeper understanding in programming. Mastery over these fundamental elements translates into a strong grasp of C's inner workings, paving the way for tackling complex software development tasks, implementing advanced data structures, and optimizing code for real-world performance. Continue practicing, experimenting, and refining your skills, and the knowledge you build here will become invaluable across all realms of programming.

7. Pointers in C

Introduction

Pointers are a foundational concept in C programming, allowing direct memory access and manipulation. They enable dynamic memory management, efficient data structures, and high-level control over hardware resources. In this chapter, we'll explore pointers from the basics to more advanced applications, providing a deep understanding of how pointers work, their syntax, and best practices in C.

1. Pointer Basics and Pointer Arithmetic

Definition and Declaration of Pointers:

Pointers store the memory addresses of other variables, giving direct access to memory locations.

```
int *ptr;      // Declares a pointer to an integer
int variable = 10;
ptr = &variable; // ptr now holds the address of 'variable'
```

Here, ptr is a pointer to an int, and &variable is the address of variable.

Initialization and Dereferencing:

A pointer can be dereferenced to access the value at the memory address it holds. Dereferencing is done with the * operator:

```
int variable = 10;
int *ptr = &variable;
printf("%d", *ptr); // Outputs 10, the value at the address stored in ptr
```

Here, *ptr fetches the value of variable through the pointer.

Pointer Arithmetic:

Pointers can be incremented or decremented to move across contiguous memory locations, making them particularly useful with arrays.

Pointer arithmetic adjusts the pointer by the size of the data type it points to. For example:

```
int arr[] = {10, 20, 30, 40};
int *ptr = arr;
```

```c
printf("%d\n", *ptr);    // Outputs 10
ptr++;
printf("%d\n", *ptr);    // Outputs 20
```

Here, ptr++ moves the pointer to the next int in the array, incrementing by sizeof(int) bytes.

2. Pointers and Arrays

Relationship between Arrays and Pointers:

In C, the name of an array represents a pointer to its first element. Thus, arr and &arr[0] are equivalent.

The notation *(arr + i) is equivalent to arr[i]:

```c
int arr[] = {1, 2, 3, 4};
int *ptr = arr;
printf("%d\n", *(ptr + 2)); // Outputs 3
```

Iterating Arrays with Pointers:

Pointers can be used for efficient array traversal:

```c
int arr[] = {1, 2, 3, 4};
int *ptr = arr;
for (int i = 0; i < 4; i++)
{
printf("%d ", *(ptr + i)); // Outputs each element in arr
}
```

Pointer to Array vs. Array of Pointers:

A **pointer to an array** point to an entire array, whereas an **array of pointers** contains individual pointers to elements.

```c
int arr[3] = {10, 20, 30};
int *ptr[3]; // Array of pointers to integers
ptr[0] = &arr[0];
ptr[1] = &arr[1];
ptr[2] = &arr[2];
```

3. Pointers and Functions

Passing Pointers to Functions:

Pointers are often used to pass large data structures (e.g., arrays) to functions efficiently and to allow the function to modify the original data.

Example with a function to swap values:

```
void swap(int *a, int *b)
{
int temp = *a;
 *a = *b;
 *b = temp;
}
```

Returning Pointers from Functions:

Functions can return pointers, but caution is needed to avoid returning pointers to local variables (which may be deallocated).

Dynamic memory allocation or static storage is recommended:

```
int* createArray(int size) {
    int *arr = malloc(size * sizeof(int));
    if (arr == NULL) return NULL;
    return arr;
}
```

Function Pointers:

Function pointers enable calling a function indirectly, useful for callbacks and runtime function selection.

```
int add(int a, int b)
{
return a + b;
}
int (*funcPtr)(int, int) = add;
printf("%d\n", funcPtr(2, 3)); // Outputs 5
```

4. Dynamic Memory Allocation with malloc, calloc, realloc, and free

Understanding Memory Management:

C provides functions to dynamically allocate memory, allowing memory to be allocated or resized at runtime based on program needs.

malloc and calloc:

malloc allocates uninitialized memory:

```
int *ptr = malloc(5 * sizeof(int)); // Allocates memory for 5 integers
```

calloc allocates zero-initialized memory:

```
int *ptr = calloc(5, sizeof(int)); // Allocates and initializes memory for 5 integers
```

realloc:

realloc resizes previously allocated memory:

```
int *ptr = malloc(2 * sizeof(int));
ptr = realloc(ptr, 4 * sizeof(int)); // Resizes memory for 4 integers
```

Freeing Memory with free:

Always free dynamically allocated memory with free to avoid memory leaks:

```
free(ptr);  // Deallocates memory pointed by ptr
```

5. Null Pointers and Void Pointers

Null Pointers:

Null pointers point to no memory location and are often used as sentinel values.

The value NULL is a standard constant for null pointers:

```
int *ptr = NULL; // A null pointer, indicating no valid memory address
```

Void Pointers:

Void pointers are generic pointers capable of pointing to any data type.

They require casting to a specific type before dereferencing:

```
void *ptr;
int value = 10;
ptr = &value;
printf("%d\n", *(int *)ptr); // Casting to int* for dereferencing
```

6. Pointers to Pointers and Multi-Dimensional Arrays

Pointers to Pointers:

Pointers to pointers allow multi-level indirection, which is useful for dynamic multi-dimensional arrays and complex data structures:

```
int x = 5;
int *ptr1 = &x;
int **ptr2 = &ptr1;
printf("%d\n", **ptr2); // Outputs 5
```

Multi-Dimensional Arrays and Pointers:

Multi-dimensional arrays can be accessed using pointers, with pointers to arrays being essential in dynamic multi-dimensional data structures:

```
int arr[2][3] = {{1, 2, 3}, {4, 5, 6}};
int (*ptr)[3] = arr; // Pointer to an array of 3 integers
printf("%d\n", ptr[1][2]); // Outputs 6
```

Let's start

You can store the address of an object in another object, and this is where we get to *pointers*. A pointer is a variable that stores memory addresses of other objects. You declare a variable to be a pointer by adding an asterisk, *, after the type it points to. If we declare

```
int i = 1; int *pi = &i; int **ppi = &pi;
```

then i is an integer, pi is a pointer to an integer (it has type int *), and ppi is a pointer to a pointer to an integer (it has type int **, so it is a pointer to int *, which is a pointer to an integer). The pi variable stores the address for i (because we assign pi = &i), and the ppi variable stores the address for pi. If we run the code.

```
printf("i = %d, &i = %p\n", i, &i);
printf("pi = %p, &pi = %p\n", pi, &pi);
printf("ppi = %p, &ppi = %p\n", ppi, &ppi);
```

we can see the values the variables hold, and the addresses they sit in. On my computer, I got

i = 1, &i = 0x7ffee283d8fc pi = 0x7ffee283d8fc, &pi = 0x7ffee283d8f0 ppi = 0x7ffee283d8f0, &ppi = 0x7ffee283d8e8

This means that the integer in variable i sits at memory address 0x7ffee283d8fc.

When we assigned &i to pi earlier, it got this address as its value. The value sits at address &pi, which is 0x7ffee283d8f0. The ppi variable holds pi's address, 0x7ffee283d8f0, and sits itself at address 0x7ffee283d8e8; see Figure.

On my machine, the pointers take up 8 bytes (you can check how large they are on your machine using, e.g., sizeof pi), so that is what I have put in the figure. The arrows pointing from pi to i and ppi to pi is the way we typically draw pointers. Later on, it becomes cumbersome to explicitly position values and pointers in memory, and we will represent pointers as arrows to objects instead.

For full disclosure, I have to say that you should not reason the way I just did about the memory layout. There are no guarantees in the C standard about where independent objects sit in memory, and even if the addresses look like they do here would be arranged in this way. Regardless of what the pointer values are, the variables could be arranged in other ways. On my machine, they are arranged this way, but you cannot make assumptions in portable code. It is not important for the example where exactly they sit in memory; however, the structure will be the same. The ppi pointer contains the memory address of the pi pointer that in turn holds the address of the integer i.

Knowing the address of an object is of little use if we cannot also access the object and manipulate the object through the pointer. We can do both by *dereferencing* pointers. If you put an asterisk in front of a pointer, you get the object that it points to. For example, this printf() call will print the value in i because we get what pi points to when we write *pi, and we print the value in pi (i's address) when we get *ppi:

```
printf("i = %d, pi = %p\n", *pi, *ppi);
```

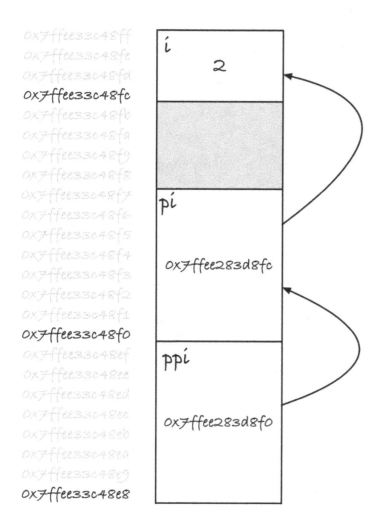

Figure. Memory location and values of i, pi, and ppi

If you want the value in i from ppi, you must dereference twice. Writing *ppi gives you the value in pi, which is i's address, and dereferencing that gives you i, so **ppi refers to i.

If you assign to a dereferenced pointer, you change the object that it is pointing at. If you run this code:

*pi = 2;

printf("i = %d, pi = %p, ppi = %p\n", i, pi, ppi);

**ppi = 3;

printf("i = %d, pi = %p, ppi = %p\n", i, pi, ppi);

you should get output that looks like this (except for the exact addresses):

i = 2, pi = 0x7ffee283d8fc, ppi = 0x7ffee283d8f0 i = 3, pi = 0x7ffee283d8fc, ppi = 0x7ffee283d8f0

In both assignments, we change i because that is what both *pi and **ppi refer to. We do not change pi or ppi. You do not modify a pointer when you modify what it points at. If you want to change the pointer, you must assign to the pointer itself.

Here, for example, we point pi to another integer's address:

int i2 = 42; pi = &i2;

Now, pi holds the address of i2 instead of i. The assignment doesn't change i or any of the other variables, but it changes the value of pi such that it now points elsewhere to the address of i2.

Pointers give us the possibility to refer to the same value through more than one variable. That is one of the purposes of them. When this happens, we call it aliasing.

First, *pi was an alias for i, and when we assigned &i2 to *pi, it became an alias for i2.

Call by Reference

What is the point of having pointers if they only let you alias variables you already have? Not much, but that is not what we use them for. If it were, this would be the end of the book. There are, of course, other uses in contexts that we will cover in detail in the remainder of the book. In this section, I will motivate pointers via so-called call-by- reference function calls, something you cannot do without pointers in C. Then, for the remaining sections in the chapter, I will go through more technical aspects of pointers and pointer types.

In C, functions are call by value. What this means is that when you provide an argument to a function call, that value goes into the local variable that the corresponding function parameter holds.

Consider this function:

```
void doesnt_mutate(int i)
{
i += 42;
}
```

It takes an integer as its single parameter, the argument will be held in the local variable i, and the function then adds 42 to it. This modifies the value stored in i. Now let us imagine that we call the function like this:

int j = 0; doesnt_mutate(j);

What then happens to j? If you have written C functions before, and I assume that you have, then you know that j doesn't change because we call doesnt_mutate() with it. The variable j holds an integer, it is zero since we initialize it as such, and it remains zero after the function call. What we pass to the function is the *value* that j holds, zero, but not the variable itself. Inside the function call, i will get the value zero when we call the function, and then it is updated. But the two integer variables are stored in different places in memory, and nothing connects them; see Figure.

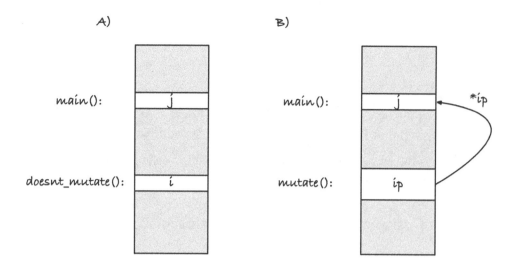

Figure. Pointer arguments to functions

The function call copies the bytes that variable j holds into the memory that contains the parameter i, and it is only the memory in the second location that we modify inside the function call.

If we have a pointer to the address of the function argument, however, we can write values into it; see B). If our function looked like this

```
void mutate(int *ip)
{
  *ip += 42;
}
```

and we called it like this

```
mutate(&j);
```

then the ip variable inside the function call holds the *address* of j, not its value. It is still a local variable; there is still an object sitting on the stack that contains its memory, but the local variable is a pointer to j. If we dereference ip, we look at the memory where j sits, and if we modify the memory there, then we modify the memory that j holds. So, with this function, we *are* changing j. With the pointer, you have access to the memory in the calling function, not just the memory of the variable in the callee. You get a reference to an object instead of its value—that is call by reference.

The function argument, ip, is still a local variable. It resides on the stack in the mutates() call's stack frame. If you change the memory it sits in, say

```
void foo(int *ip)
```

```
{
ip = 0;
}
```

then you have changed the local variable, and you have not affected the caller. If you want to change a pointer, then you need a pointer to a pointer:

```
void bar(int **ipp)
{
  *ipp = 0;
}
```

To change an object, you need a reference to it, which means that you need a pointer to it. A pointer isn't different from other types in this regard; if you want a function to change an argument pointer, then it needs a reference to it, that is, it needs a pointer to it.

If possible, you should avoid writing functions that have side effects through references, but they do have their uses in many places, where they can simplify your code. Mostly, however, you want to use them when you operate on structures that represent more complex types of objects. This is particularly relevant when you build data structures where you want to update different elements throughout your program.

Say we need to write a program that manipulates points and rectangles. This could, for example, be part of a GUI application. It is natural to define a type for points and rectangles and functions for moving them around. The following is an example with somewhat limited functionality that doesn't use pointers:

```
#include <stdio.h>
typedef struct point
{
double x, y;
}
point;

point move_point_horizontally(point p, double amount)

{
p.x += amount;
return p;
}

point move_point_vertically(point p, double amount)

{
p.y += amount;
return p;
}
```

```c
point move_point(point p, double delta_x, double delta_y)
{
p = move_point_horizontally(p, delta_x);
p = move_point_vertically(p, delta_y);
return p;
}

void print_point(point p)
{
  printf("point <%.2f, %.2f>\n", p.x, p.y);
}

typedef struct rectangle
{
point upper_left;
point lower_right;
}
rectangle;

rectangle move_rectangle(rectangle rect, double delta_x, double delta_y)
{
rect.upper_left =  move_point(rect.upper_left, delta_x, delta_y);
rect.lower_right = move_point(rect.lower_right, delta_x, delta_y);
return rect;
}

void print_rectangle(rectangle rect)
{
printf("rectangle:\n");
print_point(rect.upper_left);
print_point(rect.lower_right);
printf("\n");
}

int main(void)
{
point p = { .x = 0.0, .y = 0.0 };
print_point(p);
p = move_point(p, 10, 10);
print_point(p);   printf("\n");

rectangle rect = {
   .upper_left =  { .x =  0.0, .y = 10.0 },
   .lower_right = { .x = 10.0, .y =  0.0 }
  };
  print_rectangle(rect);
  rect = move_rectangle(rect, 10, 10);
print_rectangle(rect);
```

```
return 0;
}
```

It might not be the most realistic code. I probably wouldn't have written functions move_point_horizontally() and move_point_vertically(), or if I did I would not implement move_point() based on them but instead go the other way, but the code illustrates a point (no pun intended). In the code, since we cannot modify our input beyond the local variable for a point or a rectangle we get as an argument, we must return a new object every time we want to modify one, and we need to overwrite the old one. If we assume that both passing an argument and returning one require copying the object—the compiler might be able to optimize something away, but it could be two copies then the move_point() function results in multiple unnecessary copies.

The move_point() function potentially copies a point into the parameter, and it has to return a point, that is, two copies. I say potentially because the compiler might inline functions and save copying, but in the worst case, it needs to copy everything. Each of the function calls in the function body might also copy the object twice. So we could end up with copying the point six times.

```
point move_point(point p /* 1 */, double delta_x, double delta_y)

{

p = move_point_horizontally(p, delta_x); /* 2 copies */

p = move_point_vertically(p, delta_y); /* 2 copies */

return p; /* another copy */

}
```

There is nothing wrong with copying structures as input and output, and for smaller structures, you do not pay much of a performance penalty, but it is wasteful. Sometimes, it is worthwhile because you get cleaner code. For large objects, however, you should prefer to pass a pointer to the object instead of copying it.

With move_rectangle(), it gets worse. Here, we might need to copy two points in and out of the function, and the calls to move_point() inside the function involve the six copies we counted earlier, each.

```
rectangle move_rectangle(rectangle rect, /* 2 */ double delta_x, double delta_y)

{

rect.upper_left = /* 6 */

move_point(rect.upper_left, delta_x, delta_y);

rect.lower_right = /* 6 */

move_point(rect.lower_right, delta_x, delta_y);

return rect; /* 2 */

}
```

The larger the object, and the more components it has, the more you have to copy.

If you want to modify an object, you have to overwrite it every time you call a function. If we write

```
point p = { .x = 0.0, .y = 0.0 };
p = move_point(p, 10, 10);
print_point(p);
```

it is easy to forget the assignment and end up with

```
point p = { .x = 0.0, .y = 0.0 };
move_point(p, 10, 10);
print_point(p);
```

This is valid C code; the compiler won't complain, but you do not get what you want.

If you pass the objects to the functions as pointers, you can modify them without copying them. You still have to copy data, the input pointer, but that is always a relatively small object that is quickly copied (and will be copied in a register in practice which makes it very fast).

A pointer version of move_point_horizontally() will look like this:

```
void move_point_horizontally(point *p, double amount)
{
  p->x += amount;
}
```

The p->x syntax gets the component x from the point structure through a pointer.

It is syntactic sugar for (*p).x. It is a question of taste which of the syntaxes you prefer.

I always use the arrow operator, but I know friends who swear to the dereference syntax. If you are consistent, and your choice matches your collaborators, then you are fine.

The complete rewrite is listed in the following. The main difference, except for passing the points and rectangles as references, is that we do not return an updated object from any of the functions. We do not need to, as we modify the input object where it is.

```
#include <stdio.h>
typedef struct point
{
double x, y;
}
point;
void move_point_horizontally(point *p, double amount)
{
  p->x += amount;
}
```

```c
void move_point_vertically(point *p, double amount)

{

  p->y += amount;
}

void move_point(point *p, double delta_x, double delta_y)

{

move_point_horizontally(p, delta_x);
move_point_vertically(p, delta_y);

}

void print_point(point *p)

{

  printf("point <%.2f, %.2f>\n", p->x, p->y);
}

typedef struct rectangle
{
point upper_left;
point lower_right;
}
rectangle;

void move_rectangle(rectangle *rect, double delta_x, double delta_y)

{

move_point(&rect->upper_left, delta_x, delta_y);
move_point(&rect->lower_right, delta_x, delta_y);
}

void print_rectangle(rectangle *rect)

{

printf("rectangle:\n");
print_point(&rect->upper_left);
print_point(&rect->lower_right);
printf("\n");
}
int main(void)
{

 point p = { .x = 0.0, .y = 0.0 };
print_point(&p);
move_point(&p, 10, 10);
print_point(&p);   printf("\n");
rectangle rect = {

   .upper_left =  { .x =  0.0, .y = 10.0 },

   .lower_right = { .x = 10.0, .y =  0.0 }

 };

 print_rectangle(&rect);
```

```c
  move_rectangle(&rect, 10, 10);
print_rectangle(&rect);

  return 0;
}
```

A separate issue to taking pointers as arguments is returning pointers. You can return pointers from a function as you can return any other type, but you have to be careful with what that pointer contains!

Here is a small example that might not appear dangerous at first sight, except for the BOOOM!!! comment.

```c
#include <math.h>

#include <float.h>
#include <stdio.h>
typedef struct vector
{   double x; double y; double z; }
vector;

void print_vector(vector const *v)

{

double x = v->x, y = v->y, z = v->z;
printf("<%.2f, %.2f, %.2f>\n", x, y, z); }

double vector_length(vector *v)

{

double x = v->x, y = v->y, z = v->z;
return sqrt(x*x + y*y * z*z);

vector *shortest(int n, vector *vectors[n])

{

  vector *shortest = &(vector)

{

    .x = DBL_MAX, y = DBL_MAX, z = DBL_MAX

  };
double shortest_length = vector_length(shortest);
for (int i = 0; i < n; ++i)

{
vector *v = vectors[i];
double length = vector_length(v);
if (length < shortest_length)

{
shortest = v;

shortest_length = length;

    }

  }

return shortest;
}
```

```
int main(void)
{
  vector *vectors[] = {
    &(vector){ .x = 10.0, .y = 13.0, .z = 42.0 },
    &(vector){ .x = -1.0, .y = 32.0, .z = 15.0 },
    &(vector){ .x =  0.0, .y =  3.0, .z =  1.0 }
  };
print_vector(shortest(3, vectors));
print_vector(shortest(2, vectors));
print_vector(shortest(1, vectors));
print_vector(shortest(0, vectors)); // BOOOM!!!
  return 0;
}
```

We have a 3D vector type, and we have a function, shortest(), that finds the shortest vector in an array. When finding the shortest vector, to avoid a special case when the input is an empty sequence, we say that if there are no vectors, then the shortest vector is one with maximal values for all three coordinates.

That is the DBL_MAX defined in <float.h>. The

```
(vector){
  .x = DBL_MAX, .y = DBL_MAX, .z = DBL_MAX
};
```

creates a vector with the initialization from inside the curly brackets, and adding & to it

```
vector *shortest = &(vector){
  .x = DBL_MAX, .y = DBL_MAX, .z = DBL_MAX
};
```

gives us its address. We put that address in the shortest pointer to use as the default value. It will be replaced as soon as we find a smaller value.

However, in the BOOOM!!! line, where we do have an empty sequence, things go sideways. Potentially, anyway, it will depend on your architecture how bad it goes. The shortest() function returns a pointer to the default value we created, but that is a variable *allocated on the stack*, and we have just returned from the function that allocated it. The address for it is still there, and presumably the data is as well, but as soon as we call another function, the data could be overwritten.

The error is especially nefarious in this program because there is a good chance that you do *not* see it in this code. When we call print_vector(), the compiler might not allocate space for its local variables, it can optimize them away and get the values from v, and v might not overwrite the stack location where longest sits. The printf() call might not overwrite it either. And as long as the function calls leave the object alone, you will not see that it doesn't exist any longer. The data is still there, after all. As long as you do not overwrite it, you will not see any problems. So you could test it and observe that everything goes according to plan. And then, one day, you use the function, call a function that overwrites the object, and now you are in trouble. Weeks, months, or years after you tested that everything worked.

We can try to fake this situation with a function that writes to a large part of the stack:

```
void trash_stack(void)
{
  volatile char x[1000];   for (int i = 0; i < 1000; i++) {     x[i] = 0;
  }
}
```

The volatile is there to prevent the optimizer from removing the loop. Without it, it can conclude that we never use x and eliminate it. By making x volatile, we tell the compiler that someone else might be looking at it, so it won't optimize it away. Now call it between getting the longest object and printing it:

```
vector *v = shortest(0, vectors); print_vector(v); trash_stack(); print_vector(v);
```

The first call to print_vector() might give you the expected output, but the second call probably won't. In the second call, you are likely to see that the longest vector is now the shortest: (0,0,0). This is not something that your compiler will catch—not unless it caught that you returned the address of a local variable in the first place—but it will likely break your program. And it could be hard to track down this bug.

Worse, it could still work fine for you, with your compiler and on your development machine, but someday someone else will compile it when your code is rolled out in production, and then BOOOM!!! is too mild a word.

It is safe to pass an address of an object on the stack along to further function calls. The object is alive while those functions execute, and it will not be deallocated until they, and the calling function, return. But you should never point to a local variable that is no longer alive. If you never return the address of a local variable, you will be fine, so be careful when you return pointers to ensure that they cannot point at local variables. If you need to return a pointer from a function, do not allocate it on the stack. If you need to create an object to return the address of, you must use dynamic memory allocation;

We could try to get around the problem by making the default vector static. Then it wouldn't be destroyed when we return from shortest(), but we would get another problem: if we get a pointer to the static default, we can change it, and that would modify the behavior of all future calls to shortest().

We would be better off to choose a different default to return from shortest() when we do not have any elements to choose the shortest from. We need to return an address because that is the return type, but it must be something we cannot confuse for a valid vector. There is a special kind of pointer for this, the NULL pointer.

NULL Pointers

NULL pointers are pointers that hold a unique value that sets them apart from other pointers and indicate that they do not point at anything. This is different from not *actually* pointing at anything. A pointer that isn't initialized, or points at a variable that no longer exists, does not point at anything either. We just cannot recognize that such a pointer refers to memory that it is no longer valid to access. With a NULL pointer, we know that it doesn't refer to anything, and we know that we should refrain from dereferencing it. Most likely, dereferencing a NULL pointer will crash your program, but it is up to the underlying platform, so you cannot rely on it. Nothing good will come of dereferencing a NULL pointer, though you can safely assume that.

You set a pointer of any type to a NULL pointer using the literal 0 or the macro-NULL from <stddef.h>.

int *i_null = 0; // integer NULL pointer double *d_null = NULL; // double NULL pointer

It is a question of taste whether you use 0 or NULL. I will use 0 in this book.

In the comments here, I specified which type of NULL pointer they were, because the standard allows for different NULL pointers for different types. However, if you assign a NULL pointer of one type to another type, you get that type's NULL pointer:

i_null = (int *)d_null; // Still an integer NULL pointer and NULL pointers compare equal
if (i_null == (int *)d_null)   printf("Yep!\n"); if (d_null == (double *)i_null) printf("Also yep!\n");

Comparing any NULL pointer to NULL or 0 also evaluates to true.

if (i_null == NULL) printf("Yep!\n"); if (d_null == 0)   printf("Also yep!\n");

NULL pointers, however, do not compare equal to any other pointer. So int *ip = ...; // any value that is not a NULL pointer if (i_null == ip) printf("This doesn't happen.\n"); if (ip == 0)   printf("Also doesn't happen.\n");

So, there is not much use in thinking about NULL pointers of different types as being different. They are simply allowed to be represented differently, but as the standard does not specify how they must be represented, merely how they should behave, it makes no practical difference.

However, the representation can matter if you try to assign zero to a pointer in some other way.

int zero = 0; int *ip = (int *) zero;

Here, you assign an integer to ip, and you are allowed to do this. You can use it to point to a specific address. For embedded systems, for example, this is useful. It is highly platform dependent, and thus not portable, so it is not something we do in this book, but it is allowed. However, you have given ip the address zero, and NULL is not defined to be zero. The literal 0, when you assign it to a pointer, means the NULL pointer.

The compiler has to give ip the bit pattern it uses for NULL pointers, and it has to implement the rules for NULL pointers. Since NULL pointers typically *are* the zero address, it will likely work, but this potentially has a different semantics than assigning the literal 0. You should not get up to such shenanigan; use 0 or NULL.

If you use a pointer as a Boolean:

```
if (p) {
  // Do something...
}
```

then p evaluates to false if p is a NULL pointer, and otherwise it evaluates to true.

```
if (!p) {
  // We have a NULL pointer
} else {
  // p is not NULL. It points at *something*
  // but it might point at something invalid
}
```

Again, don't rely on any particular representation of a pointer. It is when you use a pointer as a truth value that the NULL pointer rules apply. This might not be the same as testing if p is NULL: int null = 0; int *p = NULL;

```
if (p == (int *)null) // do stuff
```

Here, you should compare with NULL:

```
if (p == NULL) // do stuff
```

or with the literal 0

```
if (p == 0) // do stuff
```

(this will work because both NULL and 0 are NULL pointers here; they have that type when we compare with a pointer), or you should use simply p as a truth value: if (p) // do stuff

Those are the ways you should check if a pointer is NULL. Otherwise, you are entering undefined behavior by relying on the bit representation of NULL pointers.

Pointers are not automatically NULL when they do not point at a valid object. It would require C to keep track of all addresses that you have assigned any pointer to, which would incur appreciable overhead in your programs, nor does C automatically initialize pointers to be NULL. C doesn't initialize automatic, that is, stack-allocated variables in general, and the same holds for pointers. You have to explicitly state that a pointer doesn't point at anything by assigning it 0 or NULL.

It is good practice to initialize pointers to be NULL if you do not have a better value, but it is a question of taste whether you do it if the control flow is simple enough to make it clear that the pointer will be assigned to shortly. I tend to always start out with a NULL pointer unless I have a value to assign it right away.

In the example from the previous section, where we returned a pointer to a stack- allocated object, we can use a NULL pointer instead. If the input to shortest doesn't have at least one element, we return a NULL pointer, and then we let the caller work out what to do about it.

```
vector *shortest(int n, vector *vectors[n])
{
if (n < 1) return 0; // Return a NULL pointer

vector *shortest = vectors[0];
double shortest_length = vector_length(shortest);
for (int i = 1; i < n; ++i)
{
vector *v = vectors[i];
double length = vector_length(v);

if (length < shortest_length)
{
shortest = v;

shortest_length = length;

  }

 }

  return shortest;
}
```

If the caller wants a default, they are responsible for choosing it.

```
vector const longest = {
   .x = DBL_MAX, y = DBL_MAX, z = DBL_MAX
};
vector const *v = shortest(0, vectors); v = v ? v : &longest; print_vector((vector *)v);
```

In v ? v : &longest, we use the return value from shortest() as a truth value. The expression says that if v is not NULL, then we use it, and otherwise we use the longest vector.

This code is far from safe. We create a const object because we do not want to change longest, but we cast the const away. If we wanted a constant longest object, we could have defined a global variable in the first place, but we discarded that solution earlier. We shouldn't use one in shortest() because that makes assumptions about what the caller wants with the shortest vector. Leaving the decision about what to do if there isn't a shortest vector to the caller is better, because they know what they want to do with the vector they get, and they can decide what the appropriate action is.

If we start allowing NULL pointers in our code—and generally we should—then it is a design choice which functions should handle them. Some we might allow assuming that they never get NULL input, while others must be able to handle them.

If we leave the vector_length() function as it is:

```
double vector_length(vector *v)
{
  double x = v->x, y = v->y, z = v->z;   return sqrt(x*x + y*y * z*z);
}
```

Then it cannot handle NULL. The v-> operation dereferences the pointer, and dereferencing NULL pointers is undefined behavior, typically crashing your program. It is reasonable to require that this function cannot handle NULL pointers. It should return the length of a vector, and NULL means we do not have a vector, so what would a natural return value be in that case?

There is nothing in print_vector()'s responsibility that says that it cannot print a NULL vector, so we can update it to do this:

```
void print_vector(vector const *v)
{
if (!v)
{
   printf("NULL\n");
} else
{
double x = v->x, y = v->y, z = v->z;
printf("<%.2f, %.2f, %.2f>\n", x, y, z);
  }
}
```

With dynamic memory management, we use NULL pointers to handle allocation errors, and when we build recursive data structures, they are the go-to value for the base cases in the recursion.

Const and Pointers

If you declare a variable using the const keyword, it tells the compiler that you are declaring a constant, a variable that shouldn't change. It does two things: it will make the compiler complain if you try to change the value of a constant, and it gives the compiler the option of optimizing references to the value because it knows that you promised not to change that value. If you declare an integer, you can make it constant by putting the const keyword before or after the type:

const int i = 42; or int const i = 42; You can read the first as "a constant integer i" and the second as "an integer constant

i." Either formulation works, and both declarations do the same thing. They make it a compilation error to change the value of i.

Early on, I got used to the first variant, and it is the one I instinctively use, but if you are just learning C, I urge you to use the second instead, and I have done my best to only use that variant in this book. If I have messed up in places, I beg your forgiveness. It is hard to change an old habit. The reason that I think the second is better is that it makes it easier to combine pointers and qualifiers such as const, as we shall see in this section.

If we didn't have the first variant, we would have a consistent rule for how to specify which types are constants and which are not; with the first rule, we have a special case for the base type. Special cases too often mess things up, so avoid them if you can. If you get started with the first variant, it is as hard to switch to the second as it is quitting smoking, so don't get started. You should only ever use the second variant.

Back to const variables! If you declare a variable const, then you cannot assign a new value to it later, and that rule is easy to remember. But if you add pointers to the mix, things get muddier. A const variable sits somewhere in memory, at least if the compiler hasn't optimized that away, so you can get a reference to that address. If you get a pointer to that address that you *are* allowed to write through, you could change the "constant." What happens, however, is where it can get complicated.

If you declare a pointer, the type before the * is the type you point at. So, if you declare const int *ip;

(the first variant), you get a pointer to const int. The same, of course, is the case if you declare int const *ip;

(the second variant), which gives you a pointer to int const which is the same qualified integer.

This pointer can point to our int const variable i from before because we have declared that we shouldn't be allowed to change what it points at. We have declared that we don't want to change i, so we shouldn't be able to do it indirectly either. If we say that ip points to a constant, then the compiler will check that we do not change the object we point to, and so we get the same type safety through *ip and i when we do

int const i = 42; int const *ip = &i;

Both variables say that they will not change the value in i. So here, all is well. But you could also write

int const i = 42; int *ip = (int *)&i;

Now you have a pointer through which you can change i, even though you have declared i to be const! You are allowed to do this. You are allowed to cast a qualified type, but are you then allowed to change what ip points at? The compiler will not complain; you have told it that ip points to a non-const integer, but what will happen at runtime?

The answer is an unsatisfactory "we don't know." The standard says that it is undefined behavior to change a variable we defined as const. In practice, however, compilers usually exploit undefined behavior for optimization purposes. If you allow it to do what it wants in a given situation, it might as well try to make the code more efficient. If you run this:

int const i = 42; int *ip = (int *)&i;

```
*ip = 13; // i == 42 or i == 13? printf("i == %d, *ip == %d\n", i, *ip);
```

chances are that i and *ip have different values after you assign to ip. Even though we have declared i as const, it doesn't quite mean that it is a constant the way compile- time constants are. It has an address when you use &, so *ip will point at an address that can contain an integer. This is safe because int const and int are the same underlying type, and they only differ in the qualifier const. So, you can write to *ip, and it gets the value 13, so that is what we will print for that variable in the last line. However, the compiler might recognize that i is the constant 42 and use that in the call to printf().

So, although we are talking about the same memory address, we get two different values after the compiler has optimized the code. Or then again, you might get something completely different. You have invoked undefined behavior, after all.

To make things more complicated (because why not?), it is not undefined behavior when you modify a variable that wasn't declared const, even if the code goes through a pointer to const at some point before modifying it.

Imagine that we have a function such as this:

```
void foo(int const *cip)
{
  int *ip = (int *)cip;
  *ip = 5;
}
```

We take a pointer to int const, we cast it, and then we modify what it points to. We are allowed to do this. Then we run code like this elsewhere in our program:

```
int const i = 42; int j = 13; foo(&i); foo(&j);
printf("i == %d, j == %d\n", i, j);
```

The compiler will likely optimize the generated code, so i remains a 42 after we call foo(&i), but it will *not* optimize for j, even though foo() promised not to change what its input points at. What foo() does is valid, and it should change what its argument points to. You are allowed to change const values this way.

It is confusing, but it is the way it is. It would be easier if it was always illegal to modify a const value. Still, there are many applications where we want to do so, where the const value isn't truly const, for example, because we change some meta- information but conceptually have a const. When you declare a pointer to const, you ask the compiler to help you with remembering that you shouldn't change what it points to, but you are allowed to—you just need to make your intent explicit through a type- cast.

When you define a variable, you allocate the memory for it and you specify whether it can change. If it is const, you shouldn't expect it to change, and the compiler probably won't expect it either. If you do not define it as const, then you are allowed to change it, even if you have a const pointer to it. You can cast the pointer and change the value. If you call a function that promises not to change its input, the compiler doesn't trust it, and neither should you.

Because const doesn't actually mean *constant*, it means that you want the type- checker to remind you to be explicit about your intent before you change the value. If you declare a pointer to a constant integer, either as const int *ip; or int const *ip; you have not declared the *pointer* to be constant. It is the type that the pointer points *at* that is constant—not the pointer. Here is the rule for const (and other qualifiers) and why the second variant is easier to work with:

For any type T, T const is a constant of that type.

Understand "constant" in the context of what we just saw earlier. It might not be constant, but it is something the compiler will yell at you for writing to unless you use an explicit cast. If you also use the first variant for const declaration, you have a special case because a const before the first type makes that type const. Stick with using the second variant.

If you do, you have the same rule for pointers:

For any type T, T * is a pointer to that type. With these two rules, you can work out that int const *icp;

is a pointer to type T (because it has the form T *) and that the type T is a constant type; it has the form U const where the type U is int. So, we have a pointer to a constant int. When you apply these two rules, you will find it easier to read the type declaration from the right and to the left. The * and const in the rules affect the type to the left of them, and we apply the rules recursively—so read it backward.

If we want the *pointer* to be constant, so it always points to the same address, but we want to be able to change what it points at, then we can work out the type declaration from the rules as well. We want a constant, so write const to the right of the type we are declaring. Now the type has the form T const. What do we want T to be? It should be a pointer, so we update T to a pointer U *, and then our type is U * const. We have reached the end of our declaration now if we want a constant pointer to int, because then U must be int, and thus we declare

int i; int * const cip = &i;

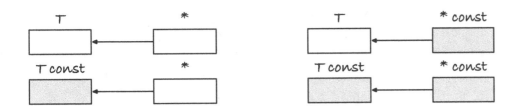

Figure. Constant data and constant pointers

We must initialize the pointer here because it is constant, so we cannot point an address at it later. Here, it points to the variable i, and it always will. We cannot give it another address. But we can change i and *cip to our heart's content.

The four combinations of const/non-const underlying type and const/non-const pointers look like this:

int * i_p   = 0; int const * ic_p = 0; int * const i_pc = 0; int const * const ic_pc = 0;

and I have tried to illustrate the types in Figure where white boxes mean a variable is mutable and gray means that they are const.

You can change both i_p and what it points to because none of those are const. For ic_p, you can change the pointer, but not what it points at. With i_pc, you cannot change the pointer, but you can modify what it points at, and with ic_pc you can modify neither of the two.

We have seen many times by now, and probably earlier in our lives, that we can assign from a const variable to a non-const. Nothing can go wrong with that because we only modify the memory of the non-const variable. The same is, obviously, also true for pointers. You can assign a const pointer to a non-const pointer. Naturally, you can also assign a non-const pointer to a non-const pointer, but there is nothing particularly surprising in that. With pointers, though, we also have to consider what we point *at*.

We could make a rule that you can only assign between pointers to the exact same type, but there is nothing wrong with letting a pointer, which promises not to change its pointed- at value, look at a non-const address. It is not changing anything, so there is no reason to restrict it from doing so. And indeed, we are allowed to assign a pointer to non-const to a pointer to const.

In Figure, I have summarized these two rules in a graphical form. The squiggly boxes mean any type and qualifier as long as the two are the same before and after the assignment. Rule A) is the one we have used many times and rule B) is the same rule, just for pointers. If two pointers point to the same type, then there are no differences between pointer types and other variable types. We can assign a const value to a non- const variable because it cannot change anything except the variable we assign to. The new rule is in C) and says that we can add const-ness to the pointed-at type, but we are not allowed to go the other way and remove const from what we point at. That rule, in a more concise form, is shown in Figure.

In the figure, it says "qualifier" because the rule applies to all qualifiers and not just const. The section is about const because we tend to use it more than the other qualifiers. Still, everything in this section about specifying types and assigning between them also applies to, for example, volatile. You can remove qualifiers from the pointer and add them to the type you point at, but not the reverse.

The rules for declaring types and assigning between pointers are the same as we add more levels of indirection, so I will not go on about it for much longer, but there is a point I want to make so I will take us one more level up and add pointers to the four types we have seen so far.

int ** i_p_p   = 0; int const ** ic_p_p = 0; int * const * i_pc_p = 0;

```
int const * const *    ic_pc_p = 0;
```

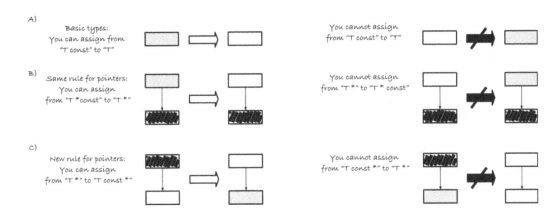

Figure. Rules for const and pointers in assignments

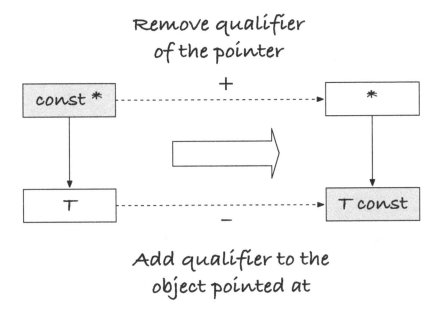

Figure. Adding and removing qualifiers for pointer assignment

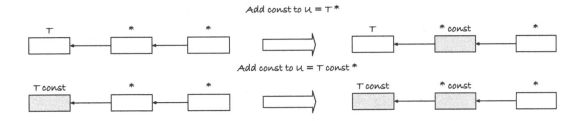

Figure. Assignments between pointers to pointers with and without const

I won't include the corresponding const variables; they will tell us nothing except that we cannot assign to them. In Figure, I have illustrated these four pointers as well, including the two legal assignments between them. You can assign from the unqualified int ** pointer to int * const * and from int const ** to int const * const *, but not between any of the others.

Why? Because that is what the rules say. You can assign from T * to T const * (and other qualifiers besides const), but not between T * and U * for different types T and U. If we peel away the last pointer in the preceding types, we have the two non-const types T = int * and U = int const *.

typedef int * T; typedef int const * U;

```
*      i_p_p  = 0;
*      ic_p_p = 0;
const * i_pc_p  = 0;
const * ic_pc_p = 0;
```

We can assign from i_p_p to i_pc_p because they have type T * and T const *, and we can assign from ic_p_p to ic_pc_p because they have type U * and U const *, respectively.

You might now object that surely there shouldn't be a problem with assigning from, for example, i_p_p to ic_p_p, because you make a non-const value const, so you won't change anything you shouldn't. You restrict what you can do, and that cannot cause problems. The thing is that it can—because you can create a non-const alias to a const object if you were allowed to do this.

Say I have variables

int *p = 0; int const ** q = 0; int const i = 42;

and follow along in Figure. In the figure, boxes and arrows that are dashed do not represent actual objects. We start with p and q as NULL pointers, so they do not point at any existing objects. The dashed boxes are there to show their type and nothing more.

Actual data will be shown in fully drawn boxes.

I can take the address of p, it has type int **, and assign it to q. This is the assignment that isn't allowed, but we do it anyway (and in code, you can explicitly cast it, so you can always do it, even if you shouldn't).

q = (int const **) &p;

Now I have created an alias for p in *q. In the figure, boxes that touch are aliases; they are the same object but represented as different boxes to indicate their types. The pointer q points at the object p, so p and *q are the same objects, and unless we direct q somewhere else, they remain so. This means that anything they might end up pointing at later will be accessible through both of them.

Then we assign &i to *q:

*q = &i;

Both the address of i and *q has type int const *, so this is a perfectly valid assignment. We expect to be able to assign one pointer type to another, so we are not doing anything wrong when doing that.

However, it creates more aliases. Since q points to p and *q now points to i, all three of *p, **q, and i refer to the same object. They differ in type; *p is not const, but the other two are. But because *p is not const, we can change the value of the object through it. The actual object is const; we declared that memory location to be int const, so if we change *p, we enter undefined behavior.

You can try it out yourself with this program. The questionable part is the assignment from &p to q, where the code needs an explicit cast to compile. When I run the program, I get different values for i and *p in the last printf(), because the compiler has optimized reading the const integer. What you get is up to your compiler.

The behavior is undefined.

```
#include <stdio.h>

int main(void)

{
int *p = 0;
int const **q = 0;
int const i = 42;

q = (int const **)&p;   *q = &i;
   // Now I have an int alias to an int const!
printf("&i == %p, *p == %p\n", (void *)&i, (void *)p);

   *p = 5; // DANGER: We are trying to change const int   // This may or may not actually change i.

   // It is up to the C compiler
printf("i == %d / %d\n", i, *p);

   return 0;

}
```

```
int *p = 0;
int const **q = 0;
int const i = 42;
```

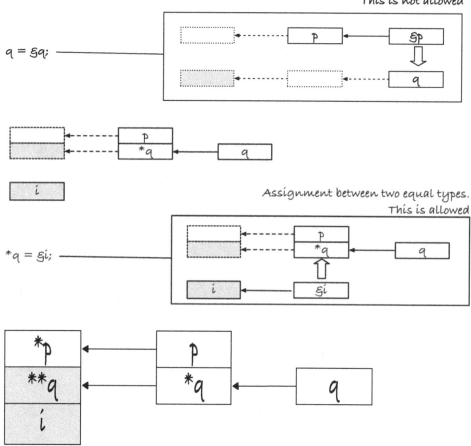

Figure. Creating a non-const alias to a const object

```
int **p = 0;
int const * const **q = 0;
int const i = 42;
int const * const r = &i;
```

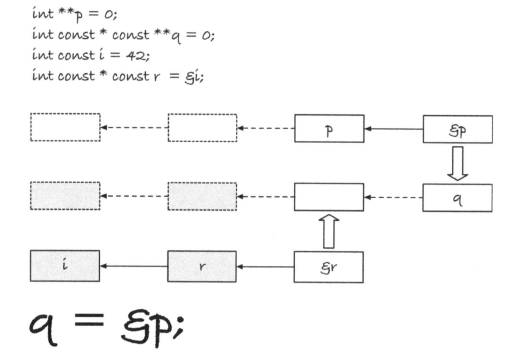

$q = \&p;$

$*q = r;$

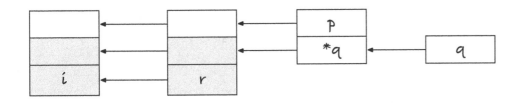

Figure. Creating yet another illegal alias

What about the other types? Do I run into the same problem if I assign from int ** to int const * const? No, here I cannot do the same trick to create an invalid alias, but that is because I consider the types in isolation. If we allow ourselves to add another level of pointers, we are back in the same situation. Consider Figure.

Here, we have an int ** pointer p, we assign its address to an int const * const ** pointer u, and when we then assign the address of an int const * const object, r, into *q, we have created not just one but two illegal aliases.

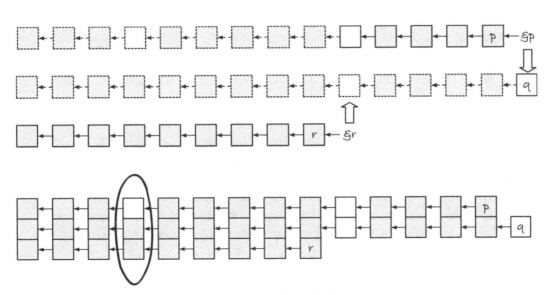

Figure. General setup for smuggling in an illegal alias

Admittedly, here we are not assigning an int ** to an int const * const * when we assign from &p to q. The types are int *** and int const * const **. We do not create a problem if we allowed assignments from int ** to int const * const *, but then we would have to disallow assignments for some cases with more levels of pointers.

In the examples, we have exploited that we can write &p into q and then an object we shouldn't modify into *q, but there can be several levels of references between the two places where we write pointers to create an illegal alias. All it takes is that we have a place where we can write p into a pointer structure that allows us to write another, more restricted type, r, somewhere further down the chain. By "more restricted" I mean that r has an immutable object in its chain of pointers that is allowed to be modified through p.

If there is a non-const link in the type we assign from, to the left of a non-const link in the type we assign to, then we can create an illegal alias this way. This is what the type-checker prevents. If the first link in the first assignment is non-const for p but const for q, we cannot smuggle in the extra assignment to make an illegal alias. That is why we can add a const to the type we point at. If the type except for the const at the immediate level is the same, then we cannot have alias issues either—if the type is the same, then what we can modify with one alias we can also modify through another.

The assignment rules are stricter than they need to be. They prevent entirely safe assignments, like int ** to int const * const, where you cannot smuggle in any false alias—if you tried to put a const object into a chain with the int ** alias, you would have to go through the int const * const type, which doesn't allow you any assignments. You could allow such assignments but at the cost of complicating the type rules. Or make a special case for links of pointers that are all const. C takes the simpler approach and allows you to add const to the object you point to, but otherwise the type must be the same.

Restricted Pointers

When the compiler sees a const variable (but not a pointer to const), it knows that its value doesn't change, so it can optimize the code it generates to exploit this. If it reads the value of a const variable, it can generate code that remembers the constant value instead of fetching it from a variable. Getting a constant is orders of magnitude faster than fetching a value from cache or main memory, so there is much to gain here. The restrict keyword provides a similar optimization opportunity. It is a qualifier to a pointer type (so like with const, you need to put it after the * to modify the pointer and not the underlying type). It tells the compiler that this pointer is not an alias of anything else; the memory it points at is only referenced through the pointer itself. Writing to other pointers will not change the value it points at, and writing through the pointer will not affect what other pointers read.

Before the compiler generates code, it will analyze it to find the optimal machine code. If it can work out where you get data from, and maybe remember it for later instead of fetching it from memory every time you use it, it can generate faster code. The promise you make when you write restrict helps it eliminate the case where it would otherwise have to assume that a value you access could have changed since it fetched data from it last and force it to fetch the data once more. Beware, though, that current compilers are not really good at warning you if you break that promise! If you *actually* modify data through a different pointer, the optimized code will be incorrect.

The following program illustrates the difference:

```
#include <stdio.h>
void abc(int *a, int *b, int *c)
{
  *a += *c;
  *b += *c;
}
void abc_restrict(int *a, int *b, int * restrict c)
{
  *a += *c;
  *b += *c;
}
int main(void)
```

```
{   int x, y;   x = y = 13;

    // No problem here. We haven't made any restrict

    // promises
abc(&x, &y, &x);
printf("%d %d\n", x, y);

    // We break the promise here by passing

    // using &a both as argument a and c in

    // in the function
x = y = 13;

abc_restrict(&x, &y, &x);

printf("%d %d\n", x, y);

    return 0;

}
```

In the function abc(), we add the value that c points at to the integers that a and b point to, and we dereference c twice to do this. We call abc() as abc(&x,&y,&x), so c points to the same integer as x. Consequently, when we update *a, we change the value at *c before we add it to *b.

With abc_restrict(), we have told the compiler that *c doesn't change (unless we write to *c, which we don't). It is, therefore, free to remember *c from the first access, so when it needs *c to add it to *b, it can use the saved value. In this code, I *lied* to the compiler when I told it that *c wouldn't change through other pointers, because both a and c point at the same integer, x, but the compiler is gullible and believed me, and it might have optimized the code accordingly. It is usually not a good idea to lie to your compiler. You will be the one to suffer; it really couldn't care less.

When I run the code without compiler optimization, the result of both function calls is the same:

26 39

26 39

If I turn on optimization, however, I get

26 39

26 26

In the second function, the compiler didn't fetch the value at *c a second time to add it to *b. I have told it that it doesn't change, and it believed me.

The optimization that the compiler can do with restrict is similar to what it can do with const, but you are allowed to change what c points at. The compiler will change the value there, and it will recognize that the value has changed if you dereference the pointer again. The optimization is only there to tell the compiler that the value doesn't change through some other pointer. Then the code that the compiler generates can remember values instead of fetching them again each time you look at the memory at the other end of a restricted pointer.

Pointers and Types

If pointers simply hold memory addresses, why do they have different types? Isn't a memory address just a memory address? Usually, yes, an address is simply an address on a modern architecture, but the language standard doesn't guarantee it. Pointers to different types are allowed to have different representations if the underlying hardware requires it (with a few rules for how you can convert between them), and you should be careful with assuming that they hold the same kinds of addresses.

Even if a pointer merely holds an address, and all addresses are equal, there are still at least three reasons that we want them to have types. First is type-checking. In statically typed languages such as C, the type-checker seeks to eliminate programming errors by analyzing your program and checking if all variables are used in a way consistent with their intended purpose, as specified by their type. Many operations are nonsensical on most types. What does it mean to turn a floating-point number into uppercase? Or divide a string by four? If you attempted to do it in a running program, it would either crash or completely garble up its computation. The type-checker is there to prevent such errors. It is not perfect at catching all errors, which is provably impossible for a program to do, but it identifies many errors that want to catch as early as possible—before your program is running in any critical setting.

Second, types do more than check that you use objects as you intended. They specify how bit patterns and chunks of computer memory should be interpreted. A 64-bit integer and a 64-bit floating-point number are both 64-bit binary words, but we interpret the bit patterns differently. We also interpret a 64-bit and a 32-bit integer differently, when we look at the memory location where we find it. If we are looking for a 64-bit (or 8-byte) integer, we need to look at 8 bytes to get the number; if we are looking at a 32-bit (4-byte) integer, we only need to look at the next 4 bytes at the address. When you dereference a pointer, you want C to interpret what it finds at the address the correct way. The pointer type ensures this. If we only worked with (untyped) addresses, we would need to explicitly specify the interpretation we want of what we point at, each time we dereference.

Pointers, Types, and Data Interpretation

In the following, I will do some things that you shouldn't ever do. I do it to illustrate a point, but I enter a territory that the C standard says the behavior is undefined. The standard uses the term "undefined behavior" frequently. It means that you are allowed to do it, but you won't know what will happen in general. It is not laziness that leaves things undefined; instead, it is giving compilers freedom to optimize their code to the hardware the code will run on. Suppose you specify the behavior of a program too tightly. In that case, the compiler has to generate extra code to adjust the behavior when it deviates from what the underlying hardware would do.

Leaving it undefined frees the compiler to generate optimal code for any platform. The side effect is, of course, that you cannot write portable code if you rely on the behavior that the standard leaves undefined. The following example is not portable to all platforms, because I cast between pointer types that I might not be allowed to. It will probably work for you as well, as most desktop architectures will allow it, but if it doesn't work, read the example and move on to the next section where I explain why that might be.

But back to the example. If pointers are just addresses, we can cast one pointer type to another and make them point to the same address. If we then dereference them, they will look at the same data—it is the data at the same address, after all—but they will interpret the data differently.

Consider this program:

```
#include <stdio.h>
int main(void)
{
printf("sizes: double = %zu, long = %zu, int = %zu, char = %zu\n", sizeof(double), sizeof(long),
sizeof(int), sizeof(char));
double d;
double *dp = &d;
long   *lp = (long *)&d;
int *ip = (int *)&d;
char *cp = (char *)&d;
printf("dp == %p, lp = %p\nip == %p, cp == %p\n\n", dp, lp, ip, cp);
d = 42.0;
printf("*dp == %.20f, *lp == %ld,\n*ip == %d, *cp == %d\n", *dp, *lp, *ip, *cp);
*ip = 4200;
printf("*dp == %.20f, *lp == %ld,\n*ip == %d, *cp == %d\n", *dp, *lp, *ip, *cp);
 *cp = 42;
 printf("*dp == %.20f, *lp == %ld,\n*ip == %d, *cp == %d\n", *dp, *lp, *ip, *cp);
 return 0;
}
```

If you run it, you might get this output:

```
sizes: double = 8, long = 8, int = 4, char = 1 dp == 0x7ffee0d88f0, lp == 0x7ffee0d88f0, ip ==
0x7ffee0d88f0, cp == 0x7ffee0d88f0
*dp == 42.00000000000000000000, *lp == 4631107791820423168,
*ip == 0, *cp == 0
*dp == 42.00000000002984279490, *lp == 4631107791820427368,
*ip == 4200, *cp == 104
*dp == 42.00000000002940225841, *lp == 4631107791820427306,
*ip == 4138, *cp == 42
```

It is unlikely that you get the same addresses; you might not get the exact same sizes, but if you are using an x86-64 architecture, as most personal computers do these days, then the dereferenced values will be the same.

The four pointers all see the same address, and dp and lp know they should look at 8 bytes (their sizeof is 8 sizeof(char) and char on this architecture is a byte). The pointer ip should look at 4 and cp at 1 byte. Thus, it should not surprise that we get different values for ip and cp than we do for the others. That lp and dp interpret what they point at differently is a consequence of how we represent floating-point numbers. I will not go into it in this book but suffice to say that the bits in those 8 bytes are interpreted differently, and that is reflected in the output.

When we assign 42.0 to the double, we set the bit pattern in its 8 bytes such that we have the floating-point representation of 42. This looks very different if we interpret the same bits as a long integer, as we can see. The integer and character pointers see 0, which we can conclude means that the low 4 bytes in the double are all 0 bits.

When we assign to *ip, we change the 4 lower bytes. We go through an integer pointer, so C knows (even though we lied to it) that it is looking at a memory object of 4 bytes, and it overwrites the existing data with the bits that represent the integer 4200. It changes both the double and the long—it changes half their bits, after all—but it is the lower bits, and we do not see a large change. The change is there, though. We also change the char at the first byte because the lower byte in the 4-byte 4200 is no longer 0. We can get the lower byte of a number by taking the division remainder of 256 (think of bytes as base 256, i.e., 2 to the power of 8), and that is the 104 we see. When we assign 42 to *cp, we change the char to 42, and we replace the 104 in the integer with 42.

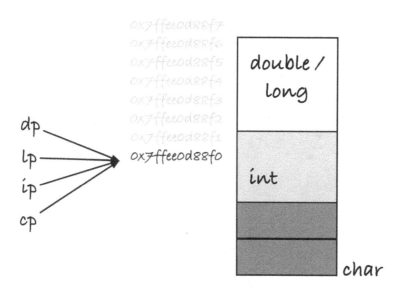

Figure. The same memory, interpreted as a char, an int, and a double

The type we give a pointer tells C how it should handle dereferenced values, that is, how it should treat the memory at the address we point at and how many memory cells starting at that address are part of the object. Since C will look beyond the first address whenever sizeof is greater than one, you also have to be careful here. If you cast the address of a small object to a pointer of a larger type, you can quickly get into trouble.

You can always cast integer values to a larger type, for example:

int i = 42; long l = (long)i; (you do not even need the type-cast here). This is safe because C already has memory set aside for the variables, and you are merely copying bits.

This, however, is not safe:

```
int i = 42; long *lp = (long *)&i;
```

If you dereference lp, C will pick 8 bytes from the memory address where i sits, but there are only four allocated for the integer (on my machine, at least). What happens is anyone's guess, but it probably will be bad.

If you want to put a char, an int, and a double at the same position, then you should use a union. That is what unions are for, after all. You can achieve the same thing with a union, and that is the safe way to do it. You can even get pointers of the different types to the union's address.

The point of the example is not that you cannot put different objects in the same memory, you can, but you need type information to treat the size and the data in the memory correctly. If pointers didn't have types, we would need to provide the type in some other way.

The third reason we want to give pointers types might be less apparent but has to do with how we handle arrays of objects and array-like objects, that is, memory where we have laid out objects of the same type contiguously. The next object's address is exactly one past previous object's last address. Here, the types tell us how far apart two consecutive objects are—objects of type T are sizeof(T) apart—and because the pointers know how large the objects, they point at are, we can use so-called *pointer arithmetic* when we work with arrays. Here, I will give you a taste of how it works.

In the following program, I have defined a to be a sequence of five integers, one to five. This gives me 5 * sizeof(int) consecutive memory addresses. The first integer sits at index 0, the second at offset sizeof(int), and number i sits at offset (i - 1) * sizeof(int). The address just past the array is 5 * sizeof(int).

```
#include <stdio.h>
int main(void)
{
int a[] = { 1, 2, 3, 4, 5 };
int n = sizeof a / sizeof *a;   // get a pointer to the beginning of a
int *ip = a;
char *cp = (char *)a;

for (int i = 0; i < n; i++)
{
printf("a[%d] sits at %p / %p / %p\n", i, (void *)&a[i], (void *)(ip + i), (void *)(cp + i * sizeof *a));
}

  return 0;
}
```

The line int n = sizeof a / sizeof *a; is an idiom for getting the correct number of elements in an array. The first sizeof gives us the size of the array, and the second provides us with the size of one element, what the array "points to," so dividing the first by the second gives us the number of elements. Here, of course, we know that it is five, but we might change the size later and forget to update n. We don't use sizeof(int) for the second number for a similar reason. We don't want to count the wrong number of elements if we change the type of the array later.

When running the program, I got

a[0] sits at 0x7ffeeaa468f0 / 0x7ffeeaa468f0 / 0x7ffeeaa468f0 a[1] sits at 0x7ffeeaa468f4 / 0x7ffeeaa468f4 / 0x7ffeeaa468f4 a[2] sits at 0x7ffeeaa468f8 / 0x7ffeeaa468f8 / 0x7ffeeaa468f8 a[3] sits at 0x7ffeeaa468fc / 0x7ffeeaa468fc / 0x7ffeeaa468fc a[4] sits at 0x7ffeeaa46900 / 0x7ffeeaa46900 / 0x7ffeeaa46900

but you can check for yourself. As you can see, the addresses match. Notice that to get to index i from the integer pointer, we use ip + i. Because of the type, we know that we need to move in jumps of sizeof(int). With the char pointer, we have to explicitly include the size; a character pointer jumps in quantities of the size of char which is always 1. This might look like a fringe case where types are important, but pointer arithmetic is used throughout C programs.

Generally, you do not want to index into the middle of an object, because you do not know how C chooses to represent objects. But it can have its uses. For example, we might want to pick out the individual bytes of an integer. In Chapter, we see how we can sort integers in linear time if we do this, although there we do so without pointing into the integers. Here is a program that runs through the array from before and prints the individual bytes in the elements:

```
#include <stdio.h>

int main(void)
{
int a[] = { 1, 2, 3, 4, 5 };
int n = sizeof a / sizeof *a;
for (int i = 0; i < n; i++)
{
printf("%d = [", a[i]);
char *cp = (char *)(a + i);
for (int j = 0; j < sizeof *a; j++)
{
printf(" %d ", cp[j]);

}
printf("]\n");
}

  return 0;
}
```

We iterate through the integers, and for each integer, we set a char pointer to point to the address of the first byte in that integer. When we write a + i, we use a as a pointer, and we get the address of a[i] (with no ampersand needed because we already get the address from a + i). Now we go through the number of bytes in an integer. If cp is a char pointer, then cp + j is the char that is j addresses higher than it. We can dereference it with *(cp + j), but cp[j] is syntactic sugar for doing exactly this. The types matter for the correct indexing. For the array, a + i is i *integers* past a, but cp + j is j *characters* past cp. The type of the pointer/array determines what the step size is when we add a number to them.

pointers and types

Although I will tell you in the next section that you should be careful with casting from one pointer type to another, this program is actually standard compliant. You can always cast to a character pointer and use it to run through the bytes in an allocated object.

When I run the program, I get the output:

```
=[1000]
=[2000]
=[3000]
=[4000]
=[5000]
```

There are 4 bytes per int (because sizeof(int) is 4 with the compiler I use), and the numbers 0 to 5 sit in the first byte of the integers, with the remaining 3 bytes set to 0. This will not always be the case. C does not guarantee how integers are represented; that is defined by your hardware architecture. In principle, any kind of bit pattern can be used, but in practice, there are two integer representations: *big-endian* and *little-endian*. They differ in which direction the most to least significant bytes sit. Consider a 32-bit integer; see Figure.

Do we put the first (least significant) 8 bits into the first byte in memory and then the rest in the following bytes? Or do we put the eight most significant bits in the first byte? Different architectures (and various file formats and network protocols) make different choices, but if you use an x86-64 chip, like me, then you will have a little- endian architecture, and you will get the same results as I got earlier.

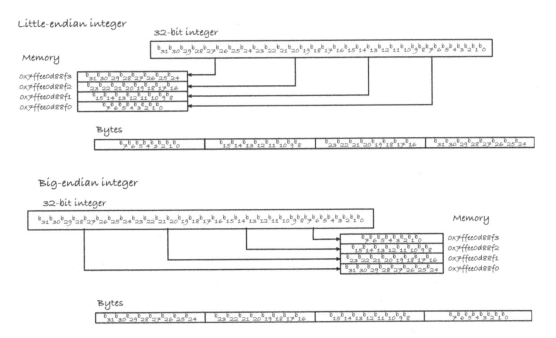

Figure 4-2. *Integer endianness*

You can try this program to check if your integers are one or the other. It computes an integer from its bytes by considering them as base 256 numbers (base 256 because that is the number of digits we have with 8 bits). You already know how the pointer arithmetic for the cp pointer works, and the only difference between the two functions is the order in which we go through the bytes.

```c
#include <stdio.h>

int little_endianess(int i)
{
char *cp = (char *)&i;
int result = 0, coef = 1;
for (int j = 0; j < sizeof i; j++)
{
result += coef * cp[j];
coef *= 256;
}
  return result;
}

int big_endianess(int i)
{
  char *cp = (char *)&i;
int result = 0, coef = 1;
for (int j = sizeof i - 1; j >= 0; j--)
{
result += coef * cp[j];    coef *= 256;
}
  return result;
}

int main(void)
{
  for (int i = 0; i < 10; i++)
{
printf("%d: little = %d, big = %d\n", i, little_endianess(i), big_endianess(i));
}
  return 0;
}
```

In the interest of honesty, I must admit that the program only works for non-negative integers, but the failure has nothing to do with endianness. The two-complement representation of negative numbers, used on practically all hardware, doesn't allow us to consider a 32-bit integer as a four-digit base 256 integer. Looking into the guts of an object only takes us so far, and while we can examine the individual bytes in an integer using a char pointer, there are limits to what we can do with it.

The way our programs interpret data, stored in its raw bit format, depends on the type we give our objects, and the same goes for pointers. At their heart, they are nothing but addresses into the computer's memory, but the type we give them tells the program how to interpret what it finds at the address they store (and what we mean when we want an address a specific offset from the address we point to).

Although I did it myself in this section, I don't want you to cast pointers of one type into another. Do as I say, and not as I do. Casting a pointer of one type to a pointer of another, or addressing the same memory as different types, as I have done, was for educational purposes. If you do it, you easily enter undefined behavior territory. In the next section, I will explain some of the main reasons for this.

Casting Between Pointers of Different Types

A pointer holds an address, but pointers of different types hold pointers to different types—obviously. Does that mean that they are represented the same way, and the type information is only used by the compiler to check that you use them correctly? Often, yes, but this is not guaranteed by the C standard.

Void Pointers

What you are guaranteed is that you can assign a pointer to an object of any type to a void pointer (see later), and if you cast it back, you get the original pointer.

```
int *ip = 0x12345; void *p = ip; int *ip2 = p; assert(ip == ip2);
```

A void pointer is a generic pointer with no underlying type—void is an incomplete type that you cannot otherwise use. You can assign to any data pointer from a void pointer without type-casts. This is an easy way to slip past type-checking, so be careful.

These rules only apply to pointers to data objects. The C standard does not require that pointers to functions and pointers to data are compatible, so assigning a function pointer to a void pointer is not necessarily supported. You can convert between function pointers of different types, though. In the POSIX standard, you can store function pointers in void *, but the C standard leaves the behavior undefined. We return to function pointers in Chapter.

Qualified Types

If you have pointers to the same underlying type, for example, int, but one is qualified,[5] it could be volatile int, and the other is not, then you can assign the nonqualified to the qualified and get the same representation.

```
int i; int *ip = &i; volatile int *ip2 = ip; assert(ip == ip2);
```

You don't need an explicit cast to add a qualifier, but you do need one to remove it if you want to get back to the original type.

You can cast away the const qualifier. This is legal, and you get a pointer to the same object. Be careful, though, because if the object you point to is const, then modifying it invokes undefined behavior.

```
int i = 42;
```

```
int const *ip = &i;   // Adding qualified, fine
int *ip2 = (int *)ip; // Removing it again, fine
*ip2 = 13;            // Changing i, no problem, i isn't const
int const i2 = 13; ip2 = (int *)&i2;    // Removing qualifier, but ok
*ip2 = 42;  // UNDEFINED BEHAVIOUR, i2 is const Unions
```

You are allowed to cast a union to the types that its members have:

```
union U {  int i;  double d; };
union U u; int *ip = (int *)&u;
double *dp = (double *)&u;
```

and you will get the correct pointer if you cast them back again.

```
assert((union U *)ip == &u);
assert((union U *)dp == &u);
```

You are not guaranteed that you can safely cast in the other direction, though, for example, cast an int pointer to a union pointer, just because the union has an int member.

```
int i; union U *up = (union U *)&i;
```

You do not have the guarantee that you can do this, only that if the original address holds the union, then it will be correct. A union U pointer might not be allowed to point to an arbitrary integer. There could be alignment issues, for one thing, and even if not, if you use up to access the double member, the integer object at the address is likely too small to hold the data you write into it. For me, with sizeof(int) == 4 and sizeof(double) == 8, something very bad might happen if I tried.

Struct Pointers

You can assign a pointer to a struct of any type to a pointer to a struct of any type.

```
struct S *s = ...;
struct T *t = (struct T *)s;
assert((struct S *)t == s);
```

If you cast a pointer to one type of structure to a pointer to another kind of structure, and back again, you get the original pointer. This does not mean that it is safe to dereference such a pointer, of course, because the structures can look very different—but one struct pointer can hold the value that another struct pointer can hold.

Character Pointers

You can always cast any pointer to an object to a character type, for example, char or unsigned char, and you get a pointer to the first address of where that object sits.

```
int i;
char *x = (char *)&i;
assert((char *)&i == x);
```

The following sizeof(T) addresses for the type T object we look at, we can access the data, and we can modify the data if the object we are pointing at is mutable, that is, not const.

Arbitrary Types

You are also guaranteed that you can cast from a T * to a U * for any types T and U, but here you are *not* guaranteed that you get the same pointer if you go back again. That depends on the alignment of the referenced type, the type of what you point to. If the types have the same alignment, then you are guaranteed that you get the same object back, but otherwise the behavior is undefined.

```
int i = 42; int *ip = &i; double *dp = (double *)ip; int *ip2 = (int *)dp; // Maybe ip == ip2, or maybe not.
```

This generally means that if you cast to a type that has stricter alignment constraints, like from an int with alignment 4 on my computer to double with alignment 8, then the behavior is undefined. I could get away with casting in the other direction, but when we write code, we do not know what the alignment constraints will be for other architectures, so this is dangerous to make assumptions about.

Don't cast between arbitrary types. You have no idea about what will happen, the standard gives you no guarantees, and in any case, it might be meaningless to dereference a pointer you got this way. Because what happens if you dereference pointers after you have converted them? You cannot dereference a void pointer, so we don't need to worry about that. You can safely dereference a pointer to an object of the pointer's underlying type, even with other qualifiers, but what happens might involve undefined behavior. For example, changing a const object is undefined.

If you cast between some arbitrary types, and their alignment matches so this is a well-defined operation, dereferencing them can still go arbitrarily wrong. We have two aliases to the same object, but with different types, and while there are a few exceptions, this generally involves undefined behavior. This means that the compiler is free to do what it wants with that code. Obviously, if you have an object of one size, and write to it through a pointer to a larger type, you will write outside of the bounds of its memory. Your program might crash, or most likely you will overwrite other variables.

That is an obvious problem. But you are not out of the woods if you write to a large object through a smaller type. The bit patterns used to represent different values mean that writing the smaller object into the larger doesn't necessarily match what you want. A float is typically smaller than a double, and it is always valid to write float f = 1.34; double d = f; but go through pointers and you can get into trouble:

```
double d; float *f = &d; *f = 1.34;
```

We write the value 1.34 to the address *f as a float. What that looks like to a double is up to the compiler (and the computer architecture, of course).

If you aim a pointer of the wrong type at an object, you have an *invalid alias*, and the C standard doesn't give you any guarantees about what happens. It does, however, give the compiler some freedom to optimize. There is a rule, called the *strict alias* rule, that says that whatever pointers of different types point at, it is different objects. Turn on your compiler's optimization, and it will exploit this.

Consider this program:

```
#include <stdio.h>
int f(int *i, long *l)
{
  *i = -1;
  *l = 0;   return *i;
}
int main(void)
{
long x;
int i = f((int *)&x, &x);
printf("%ld %d\n", x, i);   return 0;
}
```

In f(), we have a pointer to an int and to a long. We write -1 to the integer, which sets all its bits to 1 in the two-complement representation. Then we write 0 to the long, which sets all its bits to 0 (for all integer representations that I have ever heard about). In main(), we call f() with two pointers to the same object. So we would expect that *i = -1 wrote 1 bit in some of the bits in the long object x. With the compiler I am using, an int is half the size of a long, so it would set the first half of the bits to 1 and leave the rest the way they were. Not that it matters, because we then write zero bits into the entire object.

Finally, we return the integer that i points to. If we have just set the entire x to zeros, it should point to an integer where all the bits are zero as well, so we expect that f() returns zero. If I compile the program without optimization, that is indeed what I see. If I turn optimization on, however, f() returns -1. Why?

The strict alias rule says that i and l cannot point to the same object, because they do not have compatible types. So when the compiler works out what to return from f(), it can see that we just assigned -1 to *i, and the rule tells it that the assignment to *l cannot have changed that, so it concludes that it can return -1 and that it does not need to fetch *i once more from memory. We lied to the compiler when we pointed an int * at a long, and we shouldn't have done that.

The general rule is that you should never alias objects of different types—you might be able to store the pointer to one type in another, but you shouldn't *use* the object you point to then. The actual rules in the language standard are slightly more complex, but if you do not do this, then you are safe.

With a char pointer, the strict aliasing rule does not apply. Character pointers are special in that they are always allowed to point to any other object, and if the object is mutable, we are allowed to modify the object we point to.

In the following program, j gets the value 0 regardless of optimization:

```c
#include <stdio.h>
int f(int *i, long *l)
{
  *i = -1;
   *l = 0;
return *i;
}
int g(char *c, long *l)
{
  *c = -1;
   *l = 0;
return *c; }

int main(void)
{
long x;
int i = f((int *)&x, &x);
int j = g((char *)&x, &x);
printf("%ld %d %d\n", x, i, j);

return 0;
}
```

Void Pointers

There are cases where we want pointers to "something," where "something" means that we do not care (right now) what it is. The type you use for such pointers is void. If you declare a void pointer, you can point it at anything at all.

```c
int i; char c;
void *p = &i;
p = &c;
```

Here, we point p at an integer and then at a char, and we do so without casting the type. That is acceptable because a void pointer just holds an address. We cannot do much with void pointers. If you dereference them, you get the type void, which isn't a type as such and C will not interpret it in any way. The only thing you can do with a void pointer is to store an address. That sounds pretty useless, but it is how C can implement generic functionality, that is, functionality that works for more than one type.

The qsort() function from the standard library is an example of a generic function. You can use it to sort arrays of any type that you can define an order on—integers, strings, floating points—anything at all that can be ordered. It can sort anything because it is oblivious to the type of the objects it sorts. For qsort(), the data is just a chunk of memory. It knows how many data elements are in the chunk, and it knows how large they are (so it knows how many addresses go between one element and the next), but that is all it knows. It is up to the caller of the function to make sense of the data; you do this by providing the call with a function for comparing elements.

When qsort() sorts the element, and it wants to know if one element is larger than another, all it has is the addresses where the elements are found in memory, referenced by void pointers. It will call the comparison function with these, and the comparison function must then (1) assign the void const * pointers into pointers of the correct type, so it can use them for something, and (2) compare the elements. The function should return a negative integer if the first element is smaller than the second, zero if the two elements are equal, and a positive number if the second element is larger than the first. If you want to sort an array of integers, for example, you must convert the void pointers into int pointers and compare what they point at. That comparison could be subtracting the second element from the first; it will be negative if the second element is larger, positive if it is smaller, and zero if the two values are equal, exactly as it should be. The following function does this; see also Figure.

```
int int_compare(void const *x, void const *y)
{
  // Get the objects, and interpret them as integers
  int const *a = x;
  int const *b = y;
  return *a - *b;
}
```

Functions such as qsort() can operate on any data by delegating the part of the algorithm that requires data knowledge to a parameter function. We will revisit using void pointers as generic data and using functions as arguments—function pointers, as it turns out—several places in the book. For now, I will leave you with the following program that shows how you can use qsort() to sort both integers and strings, by providing the correct comparison function:

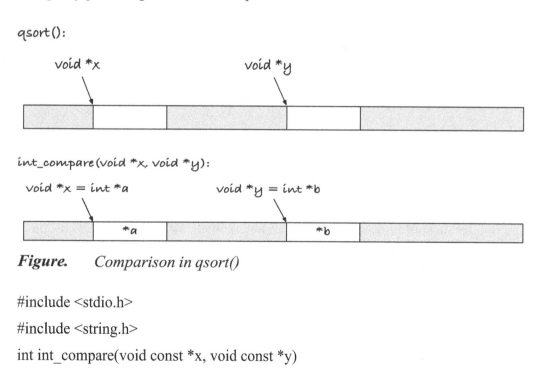

Figure. *Comparison in qsort()*

```
#include <stdio.h>
#include <string.h>
int int_compare(void const *x, void const *y)
{
```

```c
    // Get the objects, and interpret them as integers
int const *a = x;
int const *b = y;
return *a - *b;
}

int string_compare(void const *x, void const *y)

{

    // Get the objects and interpet them as strings
char * const *a = x;
char * const *b = y;
return strcmp(*a, *b);

}

int main(void)

{

  int int_array[] = { 10, 5, 30, 15, 20, 30 };
int int_array_length = sizeof int_array / sizeof *int_array;

qsort(int_array, int_array_length, sizeof *int_array, int_compare);

printf("int_array = ");

for (int i = 0; i < int_array_length; i++)

{

printf("%d, ", int_array[i]);

}
printf("\n");

char *string_array[] = { "foo", "bar", "baz" };
int string_array_length = sizeof string_array / sizeof *string_array;

qsort(string_array, string_array_length, sizeof *string_array, string_compare);
printf("string_array = ");

for (int i = 0; i < string_array_length; i++)

{

printf("%s, ", string_array[i]);

}
 printf("\n");
return 0;
}
```

For the string_compare() function, remember that we get the *address* of the elements in the array. The array consists of strings, that is, char *, but that is not what the function is called with. That is the values in the array. The function is called with pointers to the values, so pointers to strings or pointers to pointers to char, that is, char **. And because it is a const in the parameter, we need to get that added somewhere as well.

The easiest way to work out the type, and get const at the right place, I think is this: In the algorithm, qsort() thinks that we have an array of void—conceptually at least, since it is impossible to have anything of void. We know that we have an array of char *, so we should get the correct type by substituting void for char * everywhere. So, void const *, with void -> char *, becomes char * const *.

It is no different from the integer case, where we have an array of int that qsort() thinks is an array of void, so we get the type by void -> int which gives us void const * to int const *. Still, I have often seen students cast the void pointers to char pointers (or char const *) perhaps because they reason that they are both pointers. With the pointer to pointer, you also get three places to put the const, char const ** (wrong), char * const * (correct), char ** const (wrong). If you always substitute void with the correct type, you will get the correct pointer type.

The arguments to qsort(), besides the comparison function, are the array, which it obviously needs, the number of elements—it needs to know the length of the array— and the size of the data objects. It needs to know how large objects are to know where individual objects are. It needs to know how many bytes two objects are apart, and that is a multiple of the object size in bytes. We return to indexing into arrays in Chapter.

It is not necessary to use an explicit cast to convert void pointers from and to other types.

```
int i = 42;
int *ip = &i;
void *vp = ip;
char *cp = vp;
```

You do not need an explicit cast to convert to and from void and data pointers. This is potentially dangerous since we are implicitly casting between pointer types. However, in many cases, it is convenient that you do not need to cast void pointers because we use them with generic functions. We do not need to cast the preceding input to qsort() to (void *). Similarly, when we have functions that return void pointers. The preceding example circumvents the type-checker and casts an integer pointer to a character pointer without errors or warnings. It is easy to see that this is happening in simple code like this, but it is obviously more challenging in more complicated code. If we want to change the type of a pointer, we should be explicit about it. It should never be by accident. Do be careful when going to and from void pointers.

Conclusion

The journey through pointers in C is often seen as one of the most challenging yet rewarding parts of learning C programming. Pointers are a powerful feature that distinguishes C from many higher-level languages, offering control over memory and performance optimizations that are indispensable in low-level programming. From basic pointer usage to complex applications, mastering pointers can unlock a new level of efficiency and flexibility in your code. Let's revisit each core concept, understand its significance, and explore how these foundational skills empower developers in C programming and beyond.

Pointer Basics and Pointer Arithmetic

Understanding pointer basics is the first step toward appreciating the power of pointers. At its core, a pointer is simply a variable that stores a memory address. But this seemingly simple concept opens up a world of possibilities, enabling direct access to memory, which is essential for tasks such as manipulating data structures, controlling hardware resources, and optimizing performance.

Pointer arithmetic further enhances this capability. Since pointers store memory addresses, arithmetic operations on pointers allow traversal across contiguous memory blocks. This feature is particularly useful when working with arrays and data structures where efficient memory access patterns are needed. Pointer arithmetic essentially translates to moving a cursor across memory, letting you access sequential elements quickly. This is why pointers are widely used in algorithms that require optimized memory access, such as sorting algorithms and data processing applications. The efficiency provided by pointer arithmetic can be the difference between a program that runs adequately and one that performs exceptionally.

Pointers and Arrays

The close relationship between pointers and arrays is another cornerstone of C programming. In C, an array name is a pointer to its first element, which means you can access and manipulate array elements via pointers. This equivalence between arrays and pointers allows you to write highly efficient code, especially when dealing with large datasets or performing bulk data operations.

Using pointers with arrays allows developers to iterate through elements more flexibly, giving them control over how they access and manipulate each item. Pointers also enable passing large arrays to functions without copying them, saving memory and processing time. This is crucial in scenarios like image processing, scientific computing, and data analytics, where large datasets are commonplace. By understanding how pointers and arrays interact, you can write compact, efficient code that leverages memory to its full potential.

Pointers to arrays and arrays of pointers add even more flexibility. With a pointer to an array, you can treat entire arrays as single units, useful in modular programming and multidimensional array manipulation. Arrays of pointers, on the other hand, are essential for managing collections of strings or dynamically allocated data structures. Both techniques contribute to C's reputation as a language that provides fine-grained control over data organization.

Pointers and Functions

Passing pointers to functions is a technique that goes hand in hand with efficient programming in C. By passing a pointer, you allow the function to work directly on the original data rather than a copy, which is both memory- and time-efficient. This practice, known as "passing by reference," is especially important when dealing with large data structures like arrays or structures, as it avoids the overhead of copying.

Functions that return pointers are equally significant. They allow dynamic memory allocation and the creation of data that persists beyond a function's scope. This concept forms the basis of numerous data structures, such as linked lists, trees, and graphs. Understanding when and how to return pointers from functions is key to writing modular and reusable code.

Function pointers add another dimension by enabling dynamic selection of functions at runtime. They are invaluable in implementing callback mechanisms, state machines, and polymorphism in C. With function pointers, you can design flexible and extensible applications, handling tasks like event handling, signal processing, and more. Mastery of function pointers is a significant step toward creating sophisticated C programs that adapt and respond to various conditions.

Dynamic Memory Allocation with malloc, calloc, realloc, and free

Dynamic memory allocation functions (malloc, calloc, realloc) are at the heart of memory management in C. They allow programs to request memory at runtime, a crucial feature for applications where memory requirements change dynamically. In contrast to statically allocated memory, dynamic memory gives your program flexibility, adapting to varying data sizes and conditions as it runs.

The ability to allocate and resize memory during execution is particularly important in applications like databases, real-time systems, and complex data processing. For instance, databases often handle unpredictable amounts of data, and dynamic allocation allows them to manage memory based on real-time needs. Understanding the intricacies of malloc, calloc, and realloc enables you to optimize memory usage effectively.

Equally important is the free function, which deallocates memory to prevent memory leaks—a critical aspect of C programming. Memory leaks can slow down or crash applications, making free an indispensable part of safe memory management. Together, dynamic memory allocation and deallocation make up the backbone of C's memory control, allowing you to use resources efficiently and keep your program's footprint as low as possible.

Null Pointers and Void Pointers

Null pointers serve as a valuable tool for indicating the absence of data, functioning as a safeguard against dereferencing uninitialized or invalid memory addresses. Using null pointers correctly can prevent segmentation faults and unexpected behavior, making them a critical practice for writing robust and stable C programs. A well-placed null pointer check ensures that a function doesn't proceed with an invalid memory reference, making your program more resilient.

Void pointers, on the other hand, offer a high degree of flexibility by acting as generic pointers capable of pointing to any data type. This flexibility is particularly useful in creating generic data structures and functions, such as those used in standard libraries or custom libraries. By leveraging void pointers, you can write code that works with various data types without rewriting functions for each type, a technique that is foundational for implementing flexible APIs and libraries.

The versatility provided by void pointers allows C programmers to create abstraction layers, modularize code, and manage complex data interactions in a clean and manageable way. Mastering null and void pointers is essential for writing versatile and error-resistant code in C.

Pointers to Pointers and Multi-Dimensional Arrays

Pointers to pointers enable a multi-level indirection that is fundamental for handling dynamic data structures, such as two-dimensional arrays, linked lists of linked lists, or complex graphs. By using pointers to pointers, you can create arrays of pointers, manage hierarchical data, and build complex relationships between data elements. This technique is essential in applications where data structures need to be highly flexible, such as operating systems, network programming, and embedded systems.

Multi-dimensional arrays are another area where pointers prove invaluable. They allow for efficient storage and traversal of matrices, tables, and grids. Pointers simplify the process of accessing and modifying elements within multi-dimensional arrays, allowing for concise and efficient code, especially in matrix operations, simulations, and image processing applications.

Using pointers with multi-dimensional arrays also enables you to dynamically allocate and resize structures that otherwise would be limited by static array declarations. By mastering pointers to pointers and multi-dimensional arrays, you can develop highly efficient programs that handle complex data relationships with ease.

Final Thoughts

Pointers are at the core of what makes C a powerful and flexible language. Mastering pointers is not just about understanding syntax but developing a mindset that appreciates low-level memory management and efficient data handling. As a C programmer, pointers give you the ability to control resources in a way that higher-level languages abstract away, providing performance advantages that are critical in fields such as systems programming, embedded systems, game development, and more.

In many ways, pointers are the gateway to understanding how computers manage memory and data at a fundamental level. They encourage a deeper understanding of how data is stored, accessed, and manipulated. By learning pointers, you're building a foundation that will serve you across different programming languages, especially those that offer similar control, such as C++, Rust, and assembly.

While pointers can be challenging, they are also incredibly rewarding. They provide both power and responsibility, making it essential to use them wisely. Practicing pointer usage, studying best practices, and learning from mistakes are all part of the journey to mastering C. Once you're comfortable with pointers, you'll find yourself capable of writing more efficient, flexible, and powerful programs.

Pointers transform C programming from a basic exercise in syntax to an art of memory control and resource management. With pointers, you're not just writing code; you're directly shaping how your program interacts with memory, enabling it to operate at peak efficiency. The skills you gain through mastering pointers will not only make you a proficient C programmer but will also equip you with the knowledge to tackle advanced programming challenges and excel in the broader field of computer science.

8. Structures and Unions in C

Introduction

1. Defining and Using Structures

Structures in C are user-defined data types that group related variables of different data types under a single name. This feature is particularly useful in cases where you need to organize data for complex entities, like storing information about a book, a student, or an employee.

Syntax

```
struct StructureName {
    dataType member1;
    dataType member2;
    ...
};
```

Example

```
struct Book {
    char title[50];
    char author[50];
    int pages;
    float price;
};
```

Here, struct Book is a structure containing a title, author, page count, and price for a book. Once defined, this structure allows you to create instances (variables) of type struct Book.

Usage

To declare and initialize a structure:

```
struct Book myBook = {"C Programming Language", "Brian Kernighan and Dennis Ritchie", 274, 29.99};
```

You can access members of the structure using the dot (.) operator:

```
printf("Title: %s\n", myBook.title);
printf("Author: %s\n", myBook.author);
```

2. Nested Structures

Nested structures are structures within structures. They allow grouping data in hierarchical forms, which is beneficial when entities have multiple layers of attributes.

Syntax and Example

```
struct Address {
    char city[30];
    char state[30];
    int zip;
};

struct Employee {
    char name[50];
    int id;
    struct Address address;
};
```

In this example, struct Employee contains an Address structure. The nested structure allows each employee to have their own address information stored as a sub-structure.

Accessing Nested Members

```
struct Employee emp = {"Alice Johnson", 1001, {"New York", "NY", 10001}};
printf("Employee: %s, City: %s\n", emp.name, emp.address.city);
```

3. Arrays of Structures and Pointers to Structures

Arrays of Structures

An array of structures is an excellent choice when managing lists of structured data. For instance, an array of structures can store information about multiple books or employees in a single collection.

```
struct Book library[100]; // Array of 100 Book structures
```

Using a loop, you can assign or access each Book structure in the library array:

```
for (int i = 0; i < 100; i++) {
    printf("Book Title: %s\n", library[i].title);
```

}

Pointers to Structures

Pointers to structures enable dynamic memory management and are useful in situations like passing structures to functions efficiently.

struct Book *ptr = &myBook;

printf("Book Title: %s\n", ptr->title);

The -> operator allows access to the members of a structure through a pointer.

4. Unions and Their Use Cases

Unions in C are similar to structures but with a critical difference: all members of a union share the same memory location. This unique behavior makes unions memory-efficient but limits the use of members to one at a time.

Syntax

```
union Data {
    int i;
    float f;
    char str[20];
};
```

Example and Explanation

In this union, int, float, and char array members share the same memory. Only one member can hold a valid value at any time.

```
union Data data;
data.i = 10;
printf("data.i: %d\n", data.i);


data.f = 220.5;
printf("data.f: %f\n", data.f);
```

Setting data.f will overwrite data.i due to the shared memory space. This behavior is useful in applications where different types of data need to be stored at different times, optimizing memory usage.

5. Differences Between Structures and Unions

Feature	Structure	Union
Memory Allocation	Each member has its own memory space.	All members share the same memory location.
Usage	Useful for grouping related data with fixed size.	Ideal for saving memory when only one member is needed at a time.
Initialization	All members can be initialized simultaneously.	Only the first member can be reliably initialized.
Access	All members can hold values at once.	Only one member can hold a value at any given time.

Use Cases

Structures are preferred when the data members need to coexist, such as in a database of records.

Unions are beneficial in cases like variant data storage, where only one data type is required at any time (e.g., in embedded systems where memory optimization is critical).

6. Practical Examples and Use Cases

Structures Example: Database Entry

Consider a simple employee database where each employee has a name, ID, and salary:

```
struct Employee {
    char name[50];
    int id;
    float salary;
};
```

Using an array of struct Employee, we can maintain a list of employees, which is essential for applications requiring data storage.

Union Example: Sensor Data

In a sensor monitoring system, only one type of data might be read at a time. A union can be used to store different sensor values while conserving memory:

```
union SensorData
{
```

```
        int temperature;
        float humidity;
        int pressure;
    };
```

With this setup, memory for only one reading is allocated, ideal for memory-constrained environments.

Structures

A structure is a collection of one or more variables, possibly of different types, grouped together under a single name for convenient handling. (Structures are called ``records'' in some languages, notably Pascal.) Structures help to organize complicated data, particularly in large programs, because they permit a group of related variables to be treated as a unit instead of as separate entities.

One traditional example of a structure is the payroll record: an employee is described by a set of attributes such as name, address, social security number, salary, etc. Some of these in turn could be structures: a name has several components, as does an address and even a salary. Another example, more typical for C, comes from graphics: a point is a pair of coordinates, a rectangle is a pair of points, and so on.

The main change made by the ANSI standard is to define structure assignment - structures may be copied and assigned to, passed to functions, and returned by functions. This has been supported by most compilers for many years, but the properties are now precisely defined.

Automatic structures and arrays may now also be initialized.

Basics of Structures

Let us create a few structures suitable for graphics. The basic object is a point, which we will assume has an x coordinate and a y coordinate, both integers.

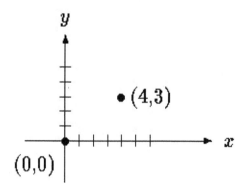

The two components can be placed in a structure declared like this:

```
    struct point
{
int x;
int y;

    };
```

The keyword struct introduces a structure declaration, which is a list of declarations enclosed in braces. An optional name called a structure tag may follow the word struct (as with point here). The tag names this kind of structure, and can be used subsequently as a shorthand for the part of the declaration in braces.

The variables named in a structure are called members. A structure member or tag and an ordinary (i.e., non-member) variable can have the same name without conflict, since they can always be distinguished by context. Furthermore, the same member names may occur in different structures, although as a matter of style one would normally use the same names only for closely related objects.

A struct declaration defines a type. The right brace that terminates the list of members may be followed by a list of variables, just as for any basic type.

That is, struct { ... } x, y, z; is syntactically analogous to int x, y, z; in the sense that each statement declares x, y and z to be variables of the named type and causes space to be set aside for them.

A structure declaration that is not followed by a list of variables reserves no storage; it merely describes a template or shape of a structure. If the declaration is tagged, however, the tag can be used later in definitions of instances of the structure. For example, given the declaration of point above, struct point pt;

defines a variable pt which is a structure of type struct point. A structure can be initialized by following its definition with a list of initializers, each a constant expression, for the members:

struct maxpt = {320, 200};

An automatic structure may also be initialized by assignment or by calling a function that returns a structure of the right type.

A member of a particular structure is referred to in an expression by a construction of the form structure-name.member

The structure member operator ``.'' connects the structure name and the member's name. To print the coordinates of the point pt, for instance, printf("%d,%d", pt.x, pt.y); or to compute the distance from the origin (0,0) to pt, double dist, sqrt(double); dist = sqrt((double)pt.x * pt.x + (double)pt.y * pt.y);

Structures can be nested. One representation of a rectangle is a pair of points that denote the diagonally opposite corners:

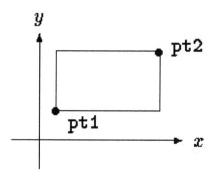

```
struct rect
{
struct point pt1;
struct point pt2;

};
```

The rect structure contains two-point structures. If we declare screen as struct rect screen; then
screen.pt1.x

refers to the x coordinate of the pt1 member of screen.

Structures and Functions

The only legal operations on a structure are copying it or assigning to it as a unit, taking its address with &, and accessing its members. Copy and assignment include passing arguments to functions and returning values from functions as well. Structures may not be compared. A structure may be initialized by a list of constant member values; an automatic structure may also be initialized by an assignment.

Let us investigate structures by writing some functions to manipulate points and rectangles. There are at least three possible approaches: pass components separately, pass an entire structure, or pass a pointer to it.

Each has its good points and bad points.

The first function, makepoint, will take two integers and return a point structure:

```
/* makepoint:  make a point from x and y components */   struct point makepoint(int x, int y)
{
struct point temp;

    temp.x = x;
temp.y = y;
return temp;

}
```

Notice that there is no conflict between the argument name and the member with the same name; indeed, the re-use of the names stresses the relationship. makepoint can now be used to initialize any structure dynamically, or to provide structure arguments to a function:

```
struct rect screen;

struct point middle;
struct point makepoint(int, int);

screen.pt1 = makepoint(0,0);
screen.pt2 = makepoint(XMAX, YMAX);

middle = makepoint((screen.pt1.x + screen.pt2.x)/2, (screen.pt1.y + screen.pt2.y)/2);
```

The next step is a set of functions to do arithmetic on points. For instance,

```
/* addpoints:  add two points */

struct addpoint(struct point p1, struct point p2)

{

        p1.x += p2.x;
        p1.y += p2.y;

        return p1;

}
```

Here both the arguments and the return value are structures. We incremented the components in p1 rather than using an explicit temporary variable to emphasize that structure parameters are passed by value like any others.

As another example, the function ptinrect tests whether a point is inside a rectangle, where we have adopted the convention that a rectangle includes its left and bottom sides but not its top and right sides:

```
/* ptinrect:  return 1 if p in r, 0 if not */   int ptinrect(struct point p, struct rect r)

{

    return p.x >= r.pt1.x && p.x < r.pt2.x  && p.y >= r.pt1.y && p.y < r.pt2.y;

}
```

This assumes that the rectangle is presented in a standard form where the pt1 coordinates are less than the pt2 coordinates. The following function returns a rectangle guaranteed to be in canonical form:

```
#define min(a, b) ((a) < (b) ? (a) : (b))

#define max(a, b) ((a) > (b) ? (a) : (b))

/* canonrect: canonicalize coordinates of rectangle */
struct rect canonrect(struct rect r)

{

struct rect temp;

    temp.pt1.x = min(r.pt1.x, r.pt2.x);
    temp.pt1.y = min(r.pt1.y, r.pt2.y);
    temp.pt2.x = max(r.pt1.x, r.pt2.x);
```

```
        temp.pt2.y = max(r.pt1.y, r.pt2.y);
        return temp;

    }
```

If a large structure is to be passed to a function, it is generally more efficient to pass a pointer than to copy the whole structure. Structure pointers are just like pointers to ordinary variables. The declaration struct point *pp;

says that pp is a pointer to a structure of type struct point. If pp points to a point structure, *pp is the structure, and (*pp).x and (*pp).y are the members. To use pp, we might write, for example,

```
struct point origin, *pp;

    pp = &origin;

    printf("origin is (%d,%d)\n", (*pp).x, (*pp).y);
```

The parentheses are necessary in (*pp).x because the precedence of the structure member operator. is higher then *. The expression *pp.x means *(pp.x), which is illegal here because x is not a pointer.

Pointers to structures are so frequently used that an alternative notation is provided as a shorthand. If p is a pointer to a structure, then p->member-of-structure refers to the particular member. So, we could write instead printf("origin is (%d,%d)\n", pp->x, pp->y);

Both. and -> associate from left to right, so if we have struct rect r, *rp = &; then these four expressions are equivalent:

```
    r.pt1.x   rp->pt1.x (r.pt1).x

    (rp->pt1).x
```

The structure operators. and ->, together with () for function calls and [] for subscripts, are at the top of the precedence hierarchy and thus bind very tightly. For example, given the declaration

```
    struct {
int len;
char *str;

    } *p;
```
then

```
    ++p->len
```

increments len, not p, because the implied parenthesization is ++(p->len). Parentheses can be used to alter binding: (++p)->len increments p before accessing len, and (p++)->len increments p afterward. (This last set of parentheses is unnecessary.)

In the same way, *p->str fetches whatever str points to; *p->str++ increments str after accessing whatever it points to (just like *s++); (*p->str)++ increments whatever str points to; and *p++->str increments p after accessing whatever str points to.

Arrays of Structures

Consider writing a program to count the occurrences of each C keyword. We need an array of character strings to hold the names, and an array of integers for the counts. One possibility is to use two parallel arrays, keyword and keycount, as in

```
char *keyword[NKEYS];   int keycount[NKEYS];
```

But the very fact that the arrays are parallel suggests a different organization, an array of structures. Each keyword is a pair:

```
char *word;
int cout;
```

and there is an array of pairs. The structure declaration

```
    struct key
{
char *word;
int count;
}
keytab[NKEYS];
```

declares a structure type key, defines an array keytab of structures of this type, and sets aside storage for them. Each element of the array is a structure. This could also be written

```
    struct key
{
char *word;
int count;
    };
struct key keytab[NKEYS];
```

Since the structure keytab contains a constant set of names, it is easiest to make it an external variable and initialize it once and for all when it is defined. The structure initialization is analogous to earlier ones - the definition is followed by a list of initializers enclosed in braces:

```
struct key {
char *word;
int count;
}
keytab[] = {"auto", 0,
    "break", 0,
    "case", 0,
```

```
    "char", 0,
    "const", 0,
    "continue", 0,
    "default", 0,
    /* ... */
    "unsigned", 0,
    "void", 0,
    "volatile", 0,
    "while", 0
};
```

The initializers are listed in pairs corresponding to the structure members. It would be more precise to enclose the initializers for each "row" or structure in braces, as in

```
{"auto", 0},
{"break", 0}, {"case", 0}, ...
```

but inner braces are not necessary when the initializers are simple variables or character strings, and when all are present. As usual, the number of entries in the array keytab will be computed if the initializers are present and the [] is left empty.

The keyword counting program begins with the definition of keytab. The main routine reads the input by repeatedly calling a function getword that fetches one word at a time. Each word is looked up in keytab with a version of the binary search function.

The list of keywords must be sorted in increasing order in the table.

```
#include <stdio.h>
#include <ctype.h>
#include <string.h>
#define MAXWORD 100

int getword(char *, int);
int binsearch(char *, struct key *, int); /* count C keywords */
main()
{
int n;
char word[MAXWORD];

while (getword(word, MAXWORD) != EOF) if (isalpha(word[0]))

if ((n = binsearch(word, keytab, NKEYS)) >= 0)
keytab[n].count++;
for (n = 0; n < NKEYS; n++)
if (keytab[n].count > 0)
printf("%4d %s\n", keytab[n].count, keytab[n].word);
```

```
    return 0;
} /* binsearch: find word in tab[0]...tab[n-1] */
int binsearch(char *word, struct key tab[], int n)

{
int cond;
int low, high, mid;

low = 0;
high = n - 1;
while (low <= high)
{
mid = (low+high) / 2;

if ((cond = strcmp(word, tab[mid].word)) < 0)
high = mid - 1;
else if (cond > 0)
low = mid + 1;
else
return mid;

}
return -1;

}
```

We will show the function getword in a moment; for now, it suffices to say that each call to getword finds a word, which is copied into the array named as its first argument.

The quantity NKEYS is the number of keywords in keytab. Although we could count this by hand, it's a lot easier and safer to do it by machine, especially if the list is subject to change. One possibility would be to terminate the list of initializers with a null pointer, then loop along keytab until the end is found.

But this is more than is needed, since the size of the array is completely determined at compile time. The size of the array is the size of one entry times the number of entries, so the number of entries is just size of keytab / size of struct key

C provides a compile-time unary operator called sizeof that can be used to compute the size of any object.

The expressions sizeof object and sizeof (type name) yield an integer equal to the size of the specified object or type in bytes. (Strictly, sizeof produces an unsigned integer value whose type, size_t, is defined in the header <stddef.h>.) An object can be a variable or array or structure. A type name can be the name of a basic type like int or double, or a derived type like a structure or a pointer.

In our case, the number of keywords is the size of the array divided by the size of one element. This computation is used in a #define statement to set the value of NKEYS:

```
    #define NKEYS (sizeof keytab / sizeof(struct key))
```

Another way to write this is to divide the array size by the size of a specific element:

```
#define NKEYS (sizeof keytab / sizeof(keytab[0]))
```

This has the advantage that it does not need to be changed if the type changes.

A sizeof cannot be used in a #if line, because the preprocessor does not parse type names. But the expression in the #define is not evaluated by the preprocessor, so the code here is legal.

Now for the function getword. We have written a more general getword than is necessary for this program, but it is not complicated. getword fetches the next ``word" from the input, where a word is either a string of letters and digits beginning with a letter, or a single nonwhite space character. The function value is the first character of the word, or EOF for end of file, or the character itself if it is not alphabetic.

```
/* getword:  get next word or character from input */

int getword(char *word, int lim)
{
int c, getch(void);
void ungetch(int);

char *w = word;

while (isspace(c = getch()));
if (c != EOF) *w++ = c;
if (!isalpha(c))
{
*w = '\0';
return c;

}
for ( ; --lim > 0; w++)  if (!isalnum(*w = getch()))
{
ungetch(*w);
break;
}
*w = '\0';
return word[0];
}
```

When the collection of an alphanumeric token stops, getword has gone one character too far. The call to ungetch pushes that character back on the input for the next call. getword also uses is space to skip whitespace, isalpha to identify letters, and isalnum to identify letters and digits; all are from the standard header <ctype.h>.

Exercise. Our version of getword does not properly handle underscores, string constants, comments, or preprocessor control lines. Write a better version.

Pointers to Structures

To illustrate some of the considerations involved with pointers to and arrays of structures, let us write the keyword-counting program again, this time using pointers instead of array indices.

The external declaration of keytab need not change, but main and binsearch do need modification.

```
#include <stdio.h>

#include <ctype.h>

#include <string.h>
#define MAXWORD 100

int getword(char *, int);
struct key *binsearch(char *, struct key *, int); /* count C keywords; pointer version */
main()
{
word[MAXWORD];
struct key *p;

while (getword(word, MAXWORD) != EOF) if (isalpha(word[0]))

if ((p=binsearch(word, keytab, NKEYS)) != NULL)
p->count++;

for (p = keytab; p < keytab + NKEYS; p++)
if (p->count > 0)

printf("%4d %s\n", p->count, p->word);
return 0;
} /* binsearch: find word in tab[0]...tab[n-1] */
struct key *binsearch(char *word, struck key *tab, int n)

{
int cond;

struct key *low = &tab[0];
struct key *high = &tab[n];
struct key *mid;

while (low < high)
{
mid = low + (high-low) / 2;

if ((cond = strcmp(word, mid->word)) < 0)
high = mid;
else if (cond > 0)
low = mid + 1;
else

return mid;

}
return NULL;

}
```

There are several things worthy of note here. First, the declaration of binsearch must indicate that it returns a pointer to struct key instead of an integer; this is declared both in the function prototype and in binsearch. If binsearch finds the word, it returns a pointer to it; if it fails, it returns NULL.

Second, the elements of keytab are now accessed by pointers. This requires significant changes in binsearch.

The initializers for low and high are now pointers to the beginning and just past the end of the table.

The computation of the middle element can no longer be simply   mid = (low+high) / 2   /* WRONG */

because the addition of pointers is illegal. Subtraction is legal, however, so high-low is the number of elements, and thus   mid = low + (high-low) / 2 sets mid to the element halfway between low and high.

The most important change is to adjust the algorithm to make sure that it does not generate an illegal pointer or attempt to access an element outside the array. The problem is that &tab[-1] and &tab[n] are both outside the limits of the array tab. The former is strictly illegal, and it is illegal to dereference the latter. The language definition does guarantee, however, that pointer arithmetic that involves the first element beyond the end of an array (that is, &tab[n]) will work correctly.

In main we wrote

for (p = keytab; p < keytab + NKEYS; p++)

If p is a pointer to a structure, arithmetic on p takes into account the size of the structure, so p++ increments p by the correct amount to get the next element of the array of structures, and the test stops the loop at the right time.

Don't assume, however, that the size of a structure is the sum of the sizes of its members. Because of alignment requirements for different objects, there may be unnamed ``holes'' in a structure. Thus, for instance, if a char is one byte and an int four bytes, the structure

```
    struct
{
char c;
int i;
};
```

might well require eight bytes, not five. The sizeof operator returns the proper value. Finally, an aside on program format: when a function returns a complicated type like a structure pointer, as in

struct key *binsearch(char *word, struct key *tab, int n) the function name can be hard to see, and to find with a text editor. Accordingly, an alternate style is sometimes used:

```
    struct key *
    binsearch(char *word, struct key *tab, int n)
```

This is a matter of personal taste; pick the form you like and hold to it.

Self-referential Structures

Suppose we want to handle the more general problem of counting the occurrences of all the words in some input. Since the list of words isn't known in advance, we can't conveniently sort it and use a binary search. Yet we can't do a linear search for each word as it arrives, to see if it's already been seen; the program would take too long. (More precisely, its running time is likely to grow quadratically with the number of input words.) How can we organize the data to copy efficiently with a list or arbitrary words?

One solution is to keep the set of words seen so far sorted at all times, by placing each word into its proper position in the order as it arrives. This shouldn't be done by shifting words in a linear array, though - that also takes too long. Instead, we will use a data structure called a binary tree.

The tree contains one ``node'' per distinct word; each node contains

A pointer to the text of the word,

A count of the number of occurrences,

A pointer to the left child node,

A pointer to the right child node.

No node may have more than two children; it might have only zero or one.

The nodes are maintained so that at any node the left subtree contains only words that are lexicographically less than the word at the node, and the right subtree contains only words that are greater. This is the tree for the sentence ``now is the time for all good men to come to the aid of their party'', as built by inserting each word as it is encountered:

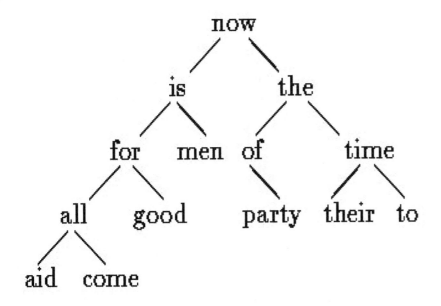

To find out whether a new word is already in the tree, start at the root and compare the new word to the word stored at that node. If they match, the question is answered affirmatively. If the new record is less than the tree word, continue searching at the left child, otherwise at the right child. If there is no child in the required direction, the new word is not in the tree, and in fact the empty slot is the proper place to add the new word. This process is recursive, since the search from any node uses a search from one of its children. Accordingly, recursive routines for insertion and printing will be most natural.

Going back to the description of a node, it is most conveniently represented as a structure with four components:

```
struct tnode
{      /* the tree node: */
char *word;          /* points to the text */
int count;           /* number of occurrences */
struct tnode *left;  /* left child */
struct tnode *right; /* right child */
};
```

This recursive declaration of a node might look chancy, but it's correct. It is illegal for a structure to contain an instance of itself, but struct tnode *left; declares left to be a pointer to a tnode, not a tnode itself.

Occasionally, one needs a variation of self-referential structures: two structures that refer to each other. The way to handle this is:

```
struct t
{
struct s *p;   /* p points to an s */
};
struct s
{
struct t *q;   /* q points to a t */
  };
```

The code for the whole program is surprisingly small, given a handful of supporting routines like getword that we have already written. The main routine reads words with getword and installs them in the tree with addtree.

```
#include <stdio.h>
#include <ctype.h>
#include <string.h>
#define MAXWORD 100
struct tnode *addtree(struct tnode *, char *);
void treeprint(struct tnode *);
int getword(char *, int);
/* word frequency count */
main()
{
```

```
    struct tnode *root;

    char word[MAXWORD];

    root = NULL;

    while (getword(word, MAXWORD) != EOF)  if (isalpha(word[0]))
    root = addtree(root, word);

    treeprint(root);

    return 0;

    }
```

The function addtree is recursive. A word is presented by main to the top level (the root) of the tree. At each stage, that word is compared to the word already stored at the node, and is percolated down to either the left or right subtree by a recursive call to adtree. Eventually, the word either matches something already in the tree (in which case the count is incremented), or a null pointer is encountered, indicating that a node must be created and added to the tree. If a new node is created, addtree returns a pointer to it, which is installed in the parent node.

```
struct tnode *talloc(void);

char *strdup(char *);   /* addtree:  add a node with w, at or below p */

struct treenode *addtree(struct tnode *p, char *w)

{

int cond;

if (p == NULL)

{ /* a new word has arrived */

p = talloc();   /* make a new node */

p->word = strdup(w);

p->count = 1;

p->left = p->right = NULL;

}

else if ((cond = strcmp(w, p->word)) == 0) p->count++;     /* repeated word */

else if (cond < 0)   /* less than into left subtree */

p->left = addtree(p->left, w);

else /* greater than into right subtree */

p->right = addtree(p->right, w);

return p;

}
```

Storage for the new node is fetched by a routine talloc, which returns a pointer to a free space suitable for holding a tree node, and the new word is copied into a hidden space by strdup. (We will discuss these routines in a moment.) The count is initialized, and the two children are made null. This part of the code is executed only at the leaves of the tree, when a new node is being added. We have (unwisely) omitted error checking on the values returned by strdup and talloc.

treeprint prints the tree in sorted order; at each node, it prints the left subtree (all the words less than this word), then the word itself, then the right subtree (all the words greater). If you feel shaky about how recursion works, simulate treeprint as it operates on the tree shown above.

```
/* treeprint:  in-order print of tree p */   void treeprint(struct tnode *p)
{
    if (p != NULL) {
    treeprint(p->left);
    printf("%4d %s\n", p->count, p->word);
    treeprint(p->right);
    }
}
```

A practical note: if the tree becomes ``unbalanced'' because the words don't arrive in random order, the running time of the program can grow too much. As a worst case, if the words are already in order, this program does an expensive simulation of linear search. There are generalizations of the binary tree that do not suffer from this worst-case behavior, but we will not describe them here.

Before leaving this example, it is also worth a brief digression on a problem related to storage allocators. Clearly, it's desirable that there be only one storage allocator in a program, even though it allocates different kinds of objects. But if one allocator is to process requests for, say, pointers to chars and pointers to struct tnodes, two questions arise. First, how does it meet the requirement of most real machines that objects of certain types must satisfy alignment restrictions (for example, integers often must be located at even addresses)? Second, what declarations can cope with the fact that an allocator must necessarily return different kinds of pointers?

Alignment requirements can generally be satisfied easily, at the cost of some wasted space, by ensuring that the allocator always returns a pointer that meets all alignment restrictions. The question of the type declaration for a function like malloc is a vexing one for any language that takes its type-checking seriously. In C, the proper method is to declare that malloc returns a pointer to void, then explicitly coerce the pointer into the desired type with a cast. malloc and related routines are declared in the standard header <stdlib.h>.

Thus, talloc can be written as

```
#include <stdlib.h> /* talloc:  make a tnode */
struct tnode *talloc(void)
{
    return (struct tnode *) malloc(sizeof(struct tnode));
}
```

strdup merely copies the string given by its argument into a safe place, obtained by a call on malloc:

```
char *strdup(char *s)    /* make a duplicate of s */
{
char *p;
p = (char *) malloc(strlen(s)+1); /* +1 for '\0' */
 if (p != NULL)
 strcpy(p, s);
 return p;
}
```

malloc returns NULL if no space is available; strdup passes that value on, leaving errorhandling to its caller.

Storage obtained by calling malloc may be freed for re-use by calling free;

Exercise. Write a program that reads a C program and prints in alphabetical order each group of variable names that are identical in the first 6 characters, but different somewhere thereafter. Don't count words within strings and comments. Make 6 a parameter that can be set from the command line.

Exercise. Write a cross-reference that prints a list of all words in a document, and for each word, a list of the line numbers on which it occurs. Remove noise words like ``the,'' ``and,'' and so on.

Exercise. Write a program that prints the distinct words in its input sorted into decreasing order of frequency of occurrence. Precede each word by its count.

Table Lookup

In this section we will write the innards of a table-lookup package, to illustrate more aspects of structures. This code is typical of what might be found in the symbol table management routines of a macro processor or a compiler. For example, consider the #define statement.

When a line like   #define IN 1 is encountered, the name IN and the replacement text 1 are stored in a table. Later, when the name IN appears in a statement like   state = IN; it must be replaced by 1.

There are two routines that manipulate the names and replacement texts. install(s,t) records the name s and the replacement text t in a table; s and t are just character strings. lookup(s) searches for s in the table, and returns a pointer to the place where it was found, or NULL if it wasn't there.

The algorithm is a hash-search - the incoming name is converted into a small non-negative integer, which is then used to index into an array of pointers. An array element points to the beginning of a linked list of blocks describing names that have that hash value. It is NULL if no names have hashed to that value.

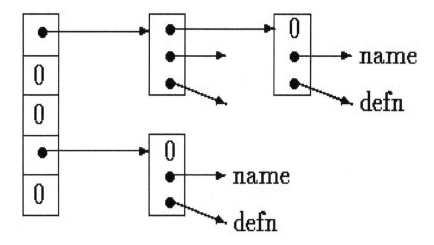

A block in the list is a structure containing pointers to the name, the replacement text, and the next block in the list. A null next-pointer marks the end of the list.

struct nlist

{
/* table entry: */

struct nlist *next;
/* next entry in chain */
char *name;   /* defined name */
char *defn;   /* replacement text */   };

The pointer array is just

#define HASHSIZE 101   static struct nlist *hashtab[HASHSIZE]; /* pointer table */

The hashing function, which is used by both lookup and install, adds each character value in the string to a scrambled combination of the previous ones and returns the remainder modulo the array size. This is not the best possible hash function, but it is short and effective.


```
   /* hash:  form hash value for string s */
unsigned hash(char *s)

{
unsigned hashval;

for (hashval = 0; *s != '\0'; s++)
hashval = *s + 31 * hashval;
return hashval % HASHSIZE;

}
```


Unsigned arithmetic ensures that the hash value is non-negative.

The hashing process produces a starting index in the array hashtab; if the string is to be found anywhere, it will be in the list of blocks beginning there. The search is performed by lookup. If lookup finds the entry already present, it returns a pointer to it; if not, it returns NULL.

```
    /* lookup:  look for s in hashtab */
struct nlist *lookup(char *s)

{
struct nlist *np;
for (np = hashtab[hash(s)];
np != NULL; np = np->next)
if (strcmp(s, np->name) == 0)
return np;     /* found */
return NULL;         /* not found */

}
```

The for loop in lookup is the standard idiom for walking along a linked list:

```
    for (ptr = head; ptr != NULL; ptr = ptr->next)    ...
```

install uses lookup to determine whether the name being installed is already present; if so, the new definition will supersede the old one. Otherwise, a new entry is created. install returns NULL if for any reason there is no room for a new entry.

```
struct nlist *lookup(char *);
char *strdup(char *);

    /* install:  put (name, defn) in hashtab */
struct nlist *install(char *name, char *defn)
{
struct nlist *np;
unsigned hashval;

if ((np = lookup(name)) == NULL) { /* not found */
np = (struct nlist *) malloc(sizeof(*np));
if (np == NULL || (np->name = strdup(name)) == NULL)
return NULL;
hashval = hash(name);
np->next = hashtab[hashval];
hashtab[hashval] = np;
} else      /* already there */

free((void *) np->defn);   /*free previous defn */
if ((np->defn = strdup(defn)) == NULL)
return NULL;
return np;

}
```

Exercise. Write a function undef that will remove a name and definition from the table maintained by lookup and install.

Exercise. Implement a simple version of the #define processor (i.e., no arguments) suitable for use with C programs, based on the routines of this section. You may also find getch and ungetch helpful.

Typedef

C provides a facility called typedef for creating new data type names. For example, the declaration typedef int Length; makes the name Length a synonym for int. The type Length can be used in declarations, casts, etc., in exactly the same ways that the int type can be:

```
Length len, maxlen;
Length *lengths[];
```

Similarly, the declaration

```
typedef char *String;
```

makes String a synonym for char * or character pointer, which may then be used in declarations and casts:

```
String p, lineptr[MAXLINES], alloc(int);    int strcmp(String, String);    p = (String) malloc(100);
```

Notice that the type being declared in a typedef appears in the position of a variable name, not right after the word typedef. Syntactically, typedef is like the storage classes extern, static, etc. We have used capitalized names for typedefs, to make them stand out.

As a more complicated example, we could make typedefs for the tree nodes shown earlier in this chapter:

```
typedef struct tnode *Treeptr;

typedef struct tnode
{ /* the tree node: */
char *word; /* points to the text */
int count;          /* number of occurrences */
struct tnode *left;   /* left child */

struct tnode *right;  /* right child */

}
Treenode;
```

This creates two new type keywords called Treenode (a structure) and Treeptr (a pointer to the structure). Then the routine talloc could become

```
Treeptr talloc(void)

{

    return (Treeptr) malloc(sizeof(Treenode));
}
```

It must be emphasized that a typedef declaration does not create a new type in any sense; it merely adds a new name for some existing type. Nor are there any new semantics: variables declared this way have exactly the same properties as variables whose declarations are spelled out explicitly. In effect, typedef is like #define, except that since it is interpreted by the compiler, it can cope with textual substitutions that are beyond the capabilities of the preprocessor.

For example,

typedef int (*PFI)(char *, char *);

creates the type PFI, for ``pointer to function (of two char * arguments) returning int," which can be used in contexts like PFI strcmp, numcmp; in the sort program.

Besides purely aesthetic issues, there are two main reasons for using typedefs. The first is to parameterize a program against portability problems. If typedefs are used for data types that may be machine-dependent, only the typedefs need change when the program is moved. One common situation is to use typedef names for various integer quantities, then make an appropriate set of choices of short, int, and long for each host machine. Types like size_t and ptrdiff_t from the standard library are examples.

The second purpose of typedefs is to provide better documentation for a program - a type called Treeptr may be easier to understand than one declared only as a pointer to a complicated structure.

Unions

A union is a variable that may hold (at different times) objects of different types and sizes, with the compiler keeping track of size and alignment requirements. Unions provide a way to manipulate different kinds of data in a single area of storage, without embedding any machine dependent information in the program. They are analogous to variant records in pascal.

As an example, such as might be found in a compiler symbol table manager, suppose that a constant may be an int, a float, or a character pointer. The value of a particular constant must be stored in a variable of the proper type, yet it is most convenient for table management if the value occupies the same amount of storage and is stored in the same place regardless of its type. This is the purpose of a union - a single variable that can legitimately hold any of one of several types.

The syntax is based on structures:

```
  union u_tag
{
int ival;
float fval;
char *sval;
  } u;
```

The variable u will be large enough to hold the largest of the three types; the specific size is implementation-dependent. Any of these types may be assigned to u and then used in expressions, so long as the usage is consistent: the type retrieved must be the type most recently stored. It is the programmer's responsibility to keep track of which type is currently stored in a union; the results are implementation-dependent if something is stored as one type and extracted as another.

Syntactically, members of a union are accessed as   union-name.member or union-pointer->member

just as for structures. If the variable utype is used to keep track of the current type stored in u, then one might see code such as

```
if (utype == INT)  printf("%d\n", u.ival);
if (utype == FLOAT)      printf("%f\n", u.fval);
if (utype == STRING)      printf("%s\n", u.sval);
else
```

printf("bad type %d in utype\n", utype);

Unions may occur within structures and arrays, and vice versa. The notation for accessing a member of a union in a structure (or vice versa) is identical to that for nested structures. For example, in the structure array defined by

```
struct {char *name;
int flags;  int utype;
union {int ival;
float fval;
char *sval;
}
u;
} symtab[NSYM];
```

the member ival is referred to as symtab[i].u.ival and the first character of the string sval by either of
*symtab[i].u.sval   symtab[i].u.sval[0]

In effect, a union is a structure in which all members have offset zero from the base, the structure is big enough to hold the ``widest'' member, and the alignment is appropriate for all of the types in the union. The same operations are permitted on unions as on structures: assignment to or copying as a unit, taking the address, and accessing a member.

A union may only be initialized with a value of the type of its first member; thus, union u described above can only be initialized with an integer value.

The storage allocator shows how a union can be used to force a variable to be aligned on a particular kind of storage boundary.

Bit-fields

When storage space is at a premium, it may be necessary to pack several objects into a single machine word; one common use is a set of single-bit flags in applications like compiler symbol tables. Externally-imposed data formats, such as interfaces to hardware devices, also often require the ability to get at pieces of a word.

Imagine a fragment of a compiler that manipulates a symbol table. Each identifier in a program has certain information associated with it, for example, whether or not it is a keyword, whether or not it is external and/or static, and so on. The most compact way to encode such information is a set of one-bit flags in a single char or int.

The usual way this is done is to define a set of ``masks'' corresponding to the relevant bit positions, as in

```
#define KEYWORD  01

#define EXTRENAL 02
#define STATIC   04
```

or

```
enum {KEYWORD = 01, EXTERNAL = 02, STATIC = 04};
```

The numbers must be powers of two. Then accessing the bits becomes a matter of ``bitfiddling'' with the shifting, masking, and complementing operators that were described.

Certain idioms appear frequently: flags |= EXTERNAL | STATIC; turns on the EXTERNAL and STATIC bits in flags, while flags &= ~(EXTERNAL | STATIC); turns them off, and if ((flags & (EXTERNAL | STATIC)) == 0) ... is true if both bits are off.

Although these idioms are readily mastered, as an alternative C offers the capability of defining and accessing fields within a word directly rather than by bitwise logical operators. A bit-field, or field for short, is a set of adjacent bits within a single implementation-defined storage unit that we will call a ``word.'' For example, the symbol table #defines above could be replaced by the definition of three fields:

```
struct {
    unsigned int is_keyword: 1;     unsigned int is_extern : 1;     unsigned int is_static : 1;
} flags;
```

This defines a variable table called flags that contains three 1-bit fields. The number following the colon represents the field width in bits. The fields are declared unsigned int to ensure that they are unsigned quantities.

Individual fields are referenced in the same way as other structure members: flags.is_keyword, flags.is_extern, etc. Fields behave like small integers, and may participate in arithmetic expressions just like other integers. Thus, the previous examples may be written more naturally as

```
flags.is_extern = flags.is_static = 1;
```

to turn the bits on;

```
flags.is_extern = flags.is_static = 0;
```

to turn them off; and

```
if (flags.is_extern == 0 && flags.is_static == 0)        ... to test them.
```

Almost everything about fields is implementation-dependent. Whether a field may overlap a word boundary is implementation-defined. Fields need not be names; unnamed fields (a colon and width only) are used for padding. The special width 0 may be used to force alignment at the next word boundary.

Fields are assigned left to right on some machines and right to left on others. This means that although fields are useful for maintaining internally-defined data structures, the question of which end comes first has to be carefully considered when picking apart externally-defined data; programs that depend on such things are not portable. Fields may be declared only as ints; for portability, specify signed or unsigned explicitly. They are not arrays and they do not have addresses, so the & operator cannot be applied on them.

Conclusion

In C programming, understanding and effectively using structures and unions is fundamental to mastering data organization, memory management, and efficient program design. Both constructs provide tools to group multiple related variables, but they cater to distinct needs and behaviors, serving as complementary options in various programming scenarios.

Recap of Structures

Structures (struct) in C enable the grouping of variables of diverse data types under a single name, allowing developers to define complex entities that mirror real-world objects. For instance, a structure can represent an employee by including name, ID, and salary as fields, each holding different data types. This unified format allows developers to model complex data relationships more naturally and intuitively.

Organized Data Representation: Structures bring order to data by encapsulating related information in one organized block. This is especially valuable when handling multiple entities of the same type, such as an array of Employee structures for a company's personnel records.

Improved Readability and Maintenance: By defining data in a structured format, code readability and maintenance improve significantly. A developer can intuitively understand the nature of data within a structure, which enhances collaboration in team environments and makes debugging more manageable.

Efficient Access and Modification: Using the dot (.) operator, members of structures can be accessed or modified effortlessly. Arrays of structures or pointers to structures further increase flexibility, allowing structures to scale to more extensive data collections or pass efficiently into functions by reference rather than by value.

Support for Complex Relationships: Nested structures allow developers to create hierarchical relationships among data, which is essential when building data models with multiple layers. For example, an employee structure containing an Address structure allows each employee to be associated with their address details, simulating a real-world hierarchy within a program's data model.

Recap of Unions

Unions, in contrast, are a specialized data type where all members share the same memory location, making unions particularly memory-efficient but limited to storing only one member's data at a time. Unions serve scenarios where only one type of data is active at any given time, thus avoiding unnecessary memory allocation.

Memory Optimization: Because a union's members occupy the same memory space, it saves memory, making unions ideal for constrained environments like embedded systems. Only the largest member's size dictates the union's memory footprint, which can lead to significant savings when dealing with variant data.

Single Value Representation: In scenarios where a variable may represent different types of values but never at the same time, unions are the preferred choice. For instance, a union might represent sensor data where only one type of reading—temperature, humidity, or pressure—is needed at any point. This structure prevents wastage of memory resources by reusing the same memory location for each reading.

Simplifying Variant Data Handling: Unions are also helpful in contexts like protocol implementations or variant-based applications where multiple types can represent a single entity based on changing needs. A union, for instance, may be used in a network packet parser to interpret different packet formats by switching between member types depending on the packet type.

Choosing Between Structures and Unions

Knowing when to use structures versus unions is a skill that greatly benefits program design:

Structures for Multi-Value Entities: If an entity needs to store multiple values simultaneously, structures are the logical choice. For example, representing an employee requires both an ID and a name to coexist; thus, a structure is necessary.

Unions for Single-Value Variants: When a single piece of data out of a set is sufficient at any one time, unions are ideal due to their memory efficiency. Applications that require different forms of data depending on the state—such as a command processor that parses only one data type per command— can efficiently use unions.

Real-World Applications and Practical Significance

Database Management Systems: Structures are heavily used in database applications to represent records, facilitating organized and accessible data storage. For example, a database row could be mapped to a structure with multiple fields representing columns.

Networking and Protocol Design: Unions are essential in networking, where protocols might represent data in multiple formats. By using unions, memory usage is minimized as packets are parsed and handled efficiently depending on their type.

Embedded Systems and Low-Level Programming: In embedded systems, memory constraints are often strict. Unions provide a mechanism to optimize memory, enabling resource-efficient program designs. A union can be used to hold sensor data from multiple sensors, with only one active reading at any time, thereby conserving limited memory space.

Graphical Applications and Game Development: Structures are common in game development, where entities (characters, objects, levels) each require several properties like position, dimensions, and status. By storing these attributes within structures, the codebase remains organized, making it easier to manage and manipulate game entities. Meanwhile, unions might be used for memory-intensive graphical data where only a single data format is necessary at a time.

Device Drivers and OS Kernels: Device drivers and operating system kernels frequently use structures and unions due to their performance implications and memory constraints. For instance, a union might represent different registers in hardware access, switching between types as needed without excessive memory overhead.

Advantages and Limitations

Structures - Advantages and Limitations:

Advantages: Provide well-organized data storage, improve code readability, and allow complex data representation.

Limitations: Structures occupy more memory than unions because each member has its dedicated space, which may lead to higher memory usage in memory-sensitive applications.

Unions - Advantages and Limitations:

Advantages: Memory-efficient by sharing space among all members, suitable for applications where data variants are needed one at a time.

Limitations: Only one member holds valid data at any given time, and improper use may lead to data overwrites, requiring careful management to prevent errors.

Strategic Usage Tips for Structures and Unions

Use Structures for Complex Entities: When representing entities with multiple attributes, structures should be the default choice. Organizing related information in a structure makes the code manageable and logical.

Use Unions for Memory Optimization: In applications with restricted memory, such as embedded systems, unions offer memory savings without sacrificing functionality. Consider unions for cases with mutually exclusive data needs to leverage efficient memory use.

Combine Structures and Unions for Flexibility: Often, structures and unions can be combined to maximize functionality. For instance, a structure may contain both regular variables and a union to handle variant data types, providing both flexibility and memory efficiency.

Be Cautious with Unions in Complex Applications: Unions, while memory-efficient, can introduce complexity. When using unions, ensure that all accesses and modifications are carefully managed to prevent data corruption. This is especially critical in multi-threaded environments or shared-memory applications.

Looking Forward: The Role of Structures and Unions in Modern C Development

As C remains a primary choice for systems programming, embedded development, and performance-critical applications, structures and unions continue to play a vital role in modern programming. Advanced compilers and optimizers leverage structures and unions to enhance performance and reduce memory footprints, making these constructs just as relevant today as in the early days of C.

In emerging fields such as IoT and high-performance computing, where resource efficiency is paramount, structures and unions will likely continue to be indispensable tools. Developers aiming to optimize their applications must have a solid grasp of when and how to apply these constructs.

Conclusion Summary

Structures and unions are foundational constructs in C, offering two distinct approaches to managing data complexity and memory efficiency:

Structures: Ideal for grouping multiple values under one entity, they provide clarity and ease of access in complex programs.

Unions: Memory-saving constructs, unions allow flexible data handling where only one active value is required.

By mastering structures and unions, developers can create robust, efficient C programs that handle data elegantly while maximizing memory utilization. Whether building databases, embedded systems, or complex applications, the strategic use of structures and unions elevates program efficiency, making them essential tools for any proficient C programmer. Understanding their nuances empowers developers to tackle real-world challenges with greater confidence and control, ensuring that they not only write functional code but also optimized and maintainable code in the long term.

9. Mastering File Manipulation in C

Introduction

File manipulation in C is essential for handling data storage and retrieval in applications. Whether creating log files, storing structured data, or simply reading configuration files, C provides robust functions in the stdio.h library for handling files. This guide covers the types of files, modes of file operations, common file handling functions, error handling, and practical applications.

1. Understanding File Types in C

In C, files can primarily be categorized into:

Text Files: These files store data in a readable text format, generally organized line by line. Text files use character encoding, which makes them platform-dependent, as newline characters may vary between operating systems (e.g., \n in UNIX vs. \r\n in Windows).

Binary Files: Binary files contain data in a binary format, allowing for compact storage and faster I/O operations since data is written exactly as it appears in memory. Binary files are ideal for non-text data, such as images or complex data structures, though they are less readable by humans.

2. File Modes and Access Types

Opening a file requires specifying a mode, which determines the intended operation. Here's a breakdown of the commonly used file modes:

"r": Opens an existing file for reading. If the file doesn't exist, the operation fails.

"w": Opens a file for writing. If the file exists, it's truncated (cleared). If not, a new file is created.

"a": Opens a file for appending. If the file exists, data is written at the end of the file without truncating. If it doesn't exist, a new file is created.

"r+": Opens an existing file for both reading and writing.

"w+": Opens a file for reading and writing. If the file exists, it's truncated. If not, a new file is created.

"a+": Opens a file for both reading and appending. If the file doesn't exist, it's created.

Example:

```
FILE *file;
file = fopen("example.txt", "w+"); // Open for reading and writing, truncate if exists.
if (file == NULL) {
    perror("Error opening file");
```

}

3. Opening and Closing Files

File pointers are the primary means for file manipulation in C. They're created with fopen() and closed with fclose().

fopen():

FILE *fopen(const char *filename, const char *mode);
It returns a FILE* on success and NULL on failure.

fclose():

int fclose(FILE *file_pointer);

Always close files to release resources and ensure all data is written to disk.

Example:

```
FILE *file = fopen("example.txt", "w");
if (file == NULL) {
   perror("Error opening file");
   return 1;
}
fclose(file);
```

4. Reading and Writing Files

The C standard library provides several functions for reading and writing files:

Character-based Functions

fgetc(): Reads the next character from a file.

int ch = fgetc(file);

fputc(): Writes a character to a file.

fputc('A', file);

String-based Functions

fgets(): Reads a line or specified number of characters from a file.

```
char buffer[100];
fgets(buffer, sizeof(buffer), file);
```

fputs(): Writes a string to a file.

```
fputs("Hello, World!", file);
```

Formatted Input/Output Functions

fscanf() and **fprintf()**: Used for formatted data. They work like scanf() and printf() but operate on files.

```
int num;
fscanf(file, "%d", &num); // Reading integer
fprintf(file, "Number: %d\n", num); // Writing integer
```

5. Binary File Operations

Binary operations are essential for applications requiring efficient storage and high precision:

fread():

```
size_t fread(void *ptr, size_t size, size_t count, FILE *stream);
```
Reads binary data into a buffer.

fwrite():

```
size_t fwrite(const void *ptr, size_t size, size_t count, FILE *stream);
```
Writes binary data from a buffer to a file.

Example of Binary Writing:

```
struct Data {
    int id;
    char name[20];
};

FILE *file = fopen("data.bin", "wb");
```

```
struct Data data = {1, "Example"};
fwrite(&data, sizeof(struct Data), 1, file);
fclose(file);
```

6. File Positioning Functions

For greater control, C provides functions to move the file pointer:

ftell(): Gets the current position of the file pointer.
```
long position = ftell(file);
```

fseek(): Moves the file pointer to a specific location.

```
fseek(file, offset, SEEK_SET);
```

rewind(): Moves the pointer back to the start of the file.

Example:

```
fseek(file, 0, SEEK_END); // Move to end
long fileSize = ftell(file); // Get file size
rewind(file); // Move back to start
```

7. Error Handling in File Operations

Error handling ensures program robustness:

ferror():

```
int ferror(FILE *file_pointer);
```
Checks for an error in file operations.

clearerr():

```
void clearerr(FILE *file_pointer);
```
Clears any errors for a file.

EOF: Indicates the end of a file, often used in a loop:

```
while (fgetc(file) != EOF) { ... }
```

8. Working with File Directories

On UNIX-based systems, the <dirent.h> library provides functions for handling directories. It includes DIR, opendir(), readdir(), and closedir() functions.

Example (Directory Traversal):

```
#include <dirent.h>
DIR *dir = opendir("/path/to/directory");
struct dirent *entry;
while ((entry = readdir(dir)) != NULL) {
    printf("%s\n", entry->d_name);
}
closedir(dir);
```

9. Practical Examples

Example 1: Reading and Writing Text Files

A program that reads names from names.txt, adds "Mr./Ms." before each name, and writes the updated names to updated_names.txt.

```
FILE *input = fopen("names.txt", "r");
FILE *output = fopen("updated_names.txt", "w");

char name[50];
while (fgets(name, sizeof(name), input)) {
    fprintf(output, "Mr./Ms. %s", name);
}

fclose(input);
fclose(output);
```

Example 2: Working with Binary Files

A program that saves and loads a list of records (e.g., employees) from a binary file.

```
struct Employee {
    int id;
    char name[30];
```

```c
};

void saveEmployee(FILE *file, struct Employee emp) {
    fwrite(&emp, sizeof(struct Employee), 1, file);
}

void loadEmployees(FILE *file) {
    struct Employee emp;
    while (fread(&emp, sizeof(struct Employee), 1, file) == 1) {
        printf("ID: %d, Name: %s\n", emp.id, emp.name);
    }
}

int main() {
    FILE *file = fopen("employees.bin", "wb+");
    struct Employee emp1 = {1, "Alice"};
    struct Employee emp2 = {2, "Bob"};
    saveEmployee(file, emp1);
    saveEmployee(file, emp2);
    rewind(file);
    loadEmployees(file);
    fclose(file);
    return 0;
}
```

Until now we have studied console input and output functions for input and output and written a number of programs with the help of these functions. However, in real life applications data volumes to be handled are very large and console input/output does not become a convenient method. This is where we make use of files to store data on disks and read it from the disks whenever required. Thus, a file is a place on a disk where related data is stored. C has a number of standard library functions to perform basic file operations.

Functions to perform input/output operations on files are broadly classified as:

Low level File I/O functions also called as System Input/Output functions.

High Level File I/O functions also called as standard or stream Input/Output functions. The standard I/O library of C has a number of functions to perform high level file I/O. High level I/O functions are much easier to use than low level disk I/O. However low-level disk I/O functions are much more efficient in terms of operation and amount of memory used by the program.

The high-level disk input/output operations are further classified as text and binary. The basic difference between these two modes lies in the way in which a file is opened. In both these modes we have both the formatted and unformatted functions. Text and binary files handle the following areas in different ways:

- How new lines are handled
- How end of file is represented
- How numbers are stored
- Handling of new lines

In this chapter our primary focus will be on high level disk input/output operations in the text mode.

High Level Input/Output Functions

Before we study the high-level input/output functions on files in detail, let us first know a few things related to opening, closing and purpose of opening the file.

Opening a File:

Before reading from a file or writing to it the first thing to be accomplished is to open the file. Once a file is opened a link is established between the operating system and the program. The operating system has to know certain things about the file viz:

File name: File name is a string which makes a valid filename depending upon the operating system, eg. hello.c, abc.out etc.

Data Structure: The data structure of the file is defined as FILE in the standard I/O function definition. This structure has been defined in the header file stdio.h (standard input/output header file). This header file is always required to be included in our programs when we wish to perform operations on files. All files should therefore be declared of type FILE before they are used. FILE is a defined data type.

Purpose: When we open the file, we have to mention the purpose of opening the file i.e whether we want to read a file, write to an already existing file, append new contents at the end of a file etc.

Declaring and Opening a File:

Every file which we open has its own FILE structure which contains information about the file like its size, its current location in memory etc. The FILE structure contains a character pointer which points to the first character that is about to be read.

The format for declaring and opening a file is:

FILE *fp;

fp = fopen("filename", "mode");

fp is declared to be a pointer to the data type FILE. fp contains the address of the structure FILE which has been defined in the standard I/O header file stdio.h. The second statement opens the file whose name is filename. Note that both the filename and mode are strings and therefore enclosed in double quotes. The mode indicates the purpose of opening the file.

The mode can be one of the following:

"r" searches for the file. If it exists, it is loaded in memory and the pointer is set to the first character in the file. If the file does not exist it returns NULL. reading from file is possible.

"w" searches for the file. If it exists, its contents are overwritten. If the file does not exist, a new file is created. If the file cannot be opened returns NULL. Writing to the file can be done.

"a" searches a file. If it exists, it is loaded in memory and a pointer is set to point to the first character in the file. If it does not exist, a new file is created. If unable to open a file returns NULL appending new contents at the end of the file is possible.

"r+" Searches for the file. If it exists it is loaded into memory and a pointer is set to point to the first character in the file. If the file does not exist returns NULL.

It is possible to read, write new contents, modify existing contents "w+" Searches for file. If found its contents are destroyed. If the file is not found a new file is created. If unable to open file returns NULL.

writing new contents, reading them back, and modifying existing contents is possible "a+" Searches for file. If it exists it gets loaded into memory and a pointer is set to point to the first character in the file. If it does not exist, a new file is created. Returns NULL if unable to open the file. Reading existing contents, appending new contents is possible. Cannot modify existing contents.

Multiple files can be opened and used at a given time. The exact number however is dependent on the system which we are using.

Closing a File:

When we have finished the operations on a file, the file must be closed. This ensures that all the outstanding information associated with the file is removed from the buffers and all links to the file are broken. There are a number of other reasons for which the file has to be closed. They include:

- Misuse of the file is prevented.
- We might also be required to close a file in order to open it in some other mode - There is a limit to the number of files that can be kept open at a particular time.

In such cases, unwanted files may be closed.

The function to close a file is:

fclose(filepointer);

This function will close the file associated with the FILE Pointer file pointer. Closing a file deactivate the file and the file is no longer accessible. As soon as a file is closed, the file pointer associated with it may be used for another file.

Unformatted High Level File Input Output (Text Mode):

fgetc and fputc functions:

The simplest file Input/Output functions from the standard I/O routines are fgetc and fputc. These functions can handle one character at a time.

If a file is opened in the "r" mode with the file pointer fp, then fgetc(fp); reads a character from the file whose pointer is fp.

If a file is opened in the "w" mode, with the file pointer fp, then fputc(ch, fp); will write the character contained in ch to the file associated with FILE pointer fp.

fgetc and fputc make the file pointer move ahead by one character for every operation. The reading of the file should be stopped when the EOF (end of file is encountered).

Let us write a program to open a file and display its contents on the monitor to illustrate the use of the fgetc.

Example : To read a file and display its contents

```
#include "stdarg.h"
#include "stdio.h"
main()

{
FILE *fp; char i; fp = fopen("array1.c", "r");
if(fp == NULL)

{
printf("Cannot open source file");
exit();

}
i = fgetc(fp);
while((i = fgetc(fp)) != (char)EOF)
printf("%c", i);

printf("%c", i);
fclose(fp);

}
```

In the above example, if the file cannot be opened successfully print the message "Cannot open-source file" is printed and the program is exited. If the file has been successfully opened the data in the file will be read character by character till end of file is encountered. Every time we read a character we display it on the screen. Once the entire file has been read, the file should be closed with fclose.

fgetc and fputc can be used together in order to copy contents of one file to another. The following example will illustrate the use of the fgetc and fputc to read characters from a file and write them to a new file.

Example: To read a file and copy its contents to another file

```
#include "stdarg.h"
#include "stdio.h" main()

{

FILE *fp, *fp1;
char ch; fp = fopen("myfile", "r");
fp1 = fopen("copyfile", "w") if(fp == NULL)

{ printf("Cannot open source file"); exit();

}

if(fp1 == NULL)

{ printf("Cannot open target file"); exit();

}

ch = fgetc(fp); while((ch = fgetc(fp)) != (char)EOF)

{
fputc(ch, fp1);

}
fclose(fp);
fclose(fp1);
printf("File copying successful!");

}
```

In this example, we have opened myfile in the read mode to copy its contents to the copyfile. Remember that copyfile is to be opened in the w mode. If the source file (myfile in our case) is not found it returns NULL. Once the file has been successfully openend the contents of myfile are copied to copyfile character by character till EOF of myfile occurs. Remember that when copyfile is opened in w mode, if the file does not exist a new file is created to write, but if the file does exist its contents are overwritten.

The getw and putw functions:

getw and putw are similar to fgetc and fputc. They are used to read integer values. These functions are useful when you are dealing with only integer data. The general form of putw is:

putw(integer, fp);

to put an integer into the file and getw(fp); to read an integer from the file.

Example: To illustrate getw and putw

```c
#include "stdarg.h"
#include "stdio.h"
main()

{
int i;

FILE *fp; fp = fopen("Intfile", "w");
if (fp == NULL)

{
printf("Unable to open file");
exit(1);

}
printf("Enter integer values to file (-1) to finish :\n");
whi!e(i!=-1)

        {       scanf("%d", &i);

putw(i.fp);

}
fclose(fp);
fp = fopen("Intfile","r");
while((i = getw(fp)) != EOF)
printf("%d\t",i);

fclose(fp);

}
```

The program reads in integer values till you enter -1 to indicate end of data entry and prints them again on the screen by retrieving them from the Intfile using getw.

String I/O in Files:

In this section, let us study the functions that are capable of handling strings. The functions to read and write strings from and to a file are fgets() and fputs().

Let us write a program to write strings to a file by making use of the functionfputs() and to display them on the screen by opening the file and using fgets().

Example: To write strings to a file and read them back

```c
#include "stdarg.h"
#include "stdio.h"
main()

{
FILE *fp; char str1[80];
fp = fopen("Sample.txt", "w");
if (fp == NULL)

{
```

```
printf("\nUnable to open file");

exit();

}

printf("\nEnter strings for file :\n");
while(strlen(gets(str1)) >0)

{
fputs(str1, fp); fputs("\n", fp);

}
fclose(fp);

printf("\nLet us write strings back from the file :\n");
fp = fopen("Sample.txt", "r"); while(fgets(str1,79,fp) != NULL)
printf("%s",str1);

fclose(fp);

}
```

A sample output:

Enter strings for file:

Mary had a little lamb

Its fleece was white as snow

Let us write strings back from the file:

Mary had a little lamb

Its fleece was white as snow

There are a number of things to note in this program. str1 is defined as an array of characters i.e. a string of size 80 (width of the screen). The function fputs() writes the contents of str1 to the file pointed to by fp. The file is opened in the "w" mode to write. Once again note that "w" will create a new file if it does not exist and will overwrite the file if it does exist. fputs() does not automatically insert a new line character at the end of the line. Therefore, the second fputs() is used to enter a newline character to the file after every string input. When inputting strings, each string input is terminated by pressing the Enter key. In order to terminate entering strings press Enter as the first character on a new line. This implies that the string is of zero length and the condition strlen(gets(str1) >0) will become false. The file is then closed.

The second part of the program now opens the file in the read mode to read its contents and display them. For this purpose we make use of the fgets() function. fgets() takes three arguments, the first is the address where the string is stored, second the maximum length of the string and third is the pointer to the structure FILE. A NULL will be returned by fgets() when all the lines have been read and the program will end.

Formatted Disk I/O Functions:

The two functions for formatted disk I/O to write characters, strings, integers, floats are the fscanf() and the fprintf(). fscanf() and fprintf() are identical to printf and scanf except that they work on files.

The general form of the fprintf() is :

fprintf(fp, "control string", list);

Here fp is the file pointer associated with the file to which we are writing. The control string contains the output specifications for the items in the list as in the case of printf. The list can include variables, constants and strings.

The general form of fscanf() is fscanf(fp, "control string", list);

where fp is the file pointer associated to the file from which we are reading. The control string contains the specifications for reading the items from the list.

Let us see how to make use of the formatted disk I/O functions with the help of the following program:

Example: To use fscanf() and fprintf() for formatted file Input/Output

```
#include "stdarg.h"
#include "stdio.h"
main()
{
FILE *fp;
char name[20], email[20];
long unsigned ph; char more;
fp = fopen("Person", "w") if (fp== NULL)
{ printf("Cannot open file");
exit();
}
more = 'y'; while (more == 'y')
{
printf("Enter name, email, phone:\n");
scanf("%s %s %lu", name, email, &ph) fprintf(fp, "%s\n%s\n%lu\n", name, email, ph);
printf("\nEnter more data :");
fflush(stdin);
scanf("%c", &more);
}
fclose(fp);
fp = fopen("Person", "r");
```

while(fscanf(fp, "%s %s %lu", name, email, &ph) != EOF) printf("%s %s %lu\n", name, email, ph);

fclose(fp);

}

In this program we have made use of the fflush() function. The fflush() function removes any data remaining in the buffer. The argument that fflush() takes is the buffer which we want to flush out. Here our buffer is the stdin which is the buffer related to the standard input device which in this case is the keyboard.

The fflush() is required in this program, because you prompt the user with the statement "Enter more data :" But the user has typed the Enter key after completing his entries of the previous name, email and ph and the program takes the Enter key as an answer to Enter more data ? and hence will stop reading further. To avoid this, we first empty the buffer and then ask the user whether he wishes to enter more data.

This program has been used to write and read dissimilar data types to a file. Therefore, we can make efficient use of structures while reading and writing such records to a file. This program illustrates how to make use of structures for formatted file I/O.

Example:

```
#include "stdarg.h" #include "stdio.h" main()
{
FILE *fp; struct per
{
char name[20]; char email[20];
long unsigned ph;
};
struct per person; char more = 'Y';
fp = fopen("Person.dat", "w"); if(fp == NULL)
{
printf("\nCannot open file"); exit();
}
while(more == 'Y')
{
printf("\nEnter name, email and phone :\n");
scanf("%s %s %lu", person.name, person.email, &person.ph);
fprintf(fp, "%s\n%s\n%lu\n", person.name, person.email, person.ph);
printf("\nEnter another record (Y/N) ?");
fflush(stdin); more = getche();
}
```

```
printf("\n"); fclose(fp);
fp = fopen("person.dat", "r");
if(fp == NULL)
{
printf("\nCannot open file\n");
exit();
}
while(fscanf(fp, "%s %s %lu", person.name, person.email, person.ph)
!= EOF) printf("%s %s %lu\n", person.name, person.email, person.ph);
fclose(fp);
}
```

Random File Access

In our above discussion we have seen the various methods by which we can access data sequentially for reading and writing. However, in practical usage there are numerous situations when we are interested in accessing a particular part of a file and not the other parts. The standard C library provides functions for such random access. These functions are fseek, ftell and rewind.

ftell: This function takes a file pointer as its argument. It returns a long integer value which corresponds to the current position in the file. This function is useful to save current position of the file for later use. The ftell takes the following form:

n = ftell(fp);

where n is a long integer, n gives the relative offset from the current position (in bytes) which implies that n bytes have been read (or written) so far.

rewind: rewind takes the file pointer as its argument and resets the position to the start of the file. eg. rewind(fp); will set the file position to the beginning of the file. The first byte in the file is numbered 0, the second 1 and so on. We can use rewind to read or write to file again, without having to close and reopen it. fseek is a function which is used to move the file position to the required location. The form of fseek is:

fseek(filepointer, offset, position);

where filepointer is a pointer to the file, offset is the value of type long and the position is an integer. The offset specifies the number of bytes to be moved from the location specified in position. Position can take one of the following three values:

Position	Value
0	Beginning of file
1	Current position

If the offset is positive, the position is moved forward, if it is negative, the position is moved backward. eg.

fseek(fp, m, 1);   will move the position forward by m bytes from current position

fseek(fp, -m, 2);   will move the position backward by m bytes from end of file

fseekfp, m, 0)   will move forward by m bytes starting from beginning of file.

If the operation is successful fseek returns a zero. In the event that we attempt to read beyond the limits of the file, fseek returns a value -1 and an error occurs. Always be sure to check for errors when using fseek.

Let us create a file in a sample program to make use of these functions:

Example:

```
#include "stdarg.h"
#include "stdio.h"
main()

{
int ch;
FILE *fp;

fp = fopen("charfile", "w");
printf("\nEnter characters for file ");
while ((ch = getche()) != 'Z')

{
fputc(ch, fp);
printf("%c", ch);

}
fclose(fp);
fp = fopen(charfile", "r");
fseek(fp,2,0);
printf("\nPosition of character : %ld\tCharacter is : %c", ftell(fp), fgetc(fp));
fseek(fp, -6, 2);
printf("\nPosition of character : %ld\tCharacter is : %c", ftell(fp), fgetc(fp));
printf("\nCurrent position %ld", ftell(fp));
rewind(fp);

printf("\nThe first position is %ld\tCharacter is :&c", ftell(fp), fgetc(fp));

}
```

The program uses the random file access function to determine the character at various positions by going forward, rewinding etc. Follow the program carefully and try to seek more characters using the random file access functions.

Command Line Arguments

A command line argument is a parameter which is supplied to a program when the particular program is invoked eg. it may be a filename of a file which is to be processed by that command.

Let us understand command line arguments by using the example of creating a file to copy the source file to the target file. So, if you want to copy a file named source to a file named target then we may use a command like: C>flcopy source target where flcopy is the program which is the executable file (An executable file is one which has the .exe extension and can be executed as the DOS prompt).

How do we send the source and target filenames as parameters to flcopy? It is possible for us to pass the source filename and the target filename to main() to make these parameters available to the program. Up till now, we have been using main() in all our programs and this is the place where our program execution starts. However, we have not yet passed any parameters to main(). Actually main() can take two parameters argc and argv. Information contained in the command line is passed to the program through these two arguments argc and argv whenever main() is invoked.

argc is an int which counts the number of arguments on the command line. argv is an array of pointers to strings(which are the command line arguments). Thus argc is an integer whose value is equal to the number of strings to which argv points. When the program is executed, the strings on the command line are passed to main(). argv is an array called the argument vector. It is an array of character pointers that points to the command line arguments. Thus, in our example flcopy source target the value of argc is 3 (which is the number of arguments on the command line) and the array of character pointers to strings (argv) is:

argv[0]contains the base address of the string "flcopy" argv[1] contains the base address of the string "source" argv[2] contains the base address of the string "target"

When the command line arguments are to be passed to main(), we have to declare the main() function as follows :

main(argc, argv) int argc; char *argv[]; or

main(int argc, char *argv[]);

Note the order of arguments in passing them to main(). It is is argc and then argv. The first parameter in the command line is always the program name. This implies that argv[0] is always the name of the program.

Having understood this, let us make use of the command line arguments to write a program to copy the source file to the target file.

Example: Use command line arguments to copy source to target.

```
#include "stdarg.h"

#include "stdio.h"
main(int argc, char *argv[])
```

```c
{
int i;

FILE *fs, *ft;
if(argc !=3)

{
printf("Incorrect arguments");
exit();

}
fs = fopen(argv[1], "r");
if (fs == NULL)

{
printf("Unable to open source file");
exit();

}
ft = fopen(argv[2], "w");
if (ft == NULL)

{
printf("Unabkle to open target file");
exit();

}

while (i = fgetc(fs)) != EOF)

fputc(i,ft);

fclose(fs);
fclose(ft);

}
```

Here we have used the same logic of copying source to target as in our previous program. Save this file with the name flcopy.c. After successful compilation the exe file flcopy.exe will be generated. This file can now be executed at the command prompt.

Now you can run the flcopy file at the command prompt as:

c> flcopy myfile yourfile

This program will copy the contents of myfile to yourfile. You have now successfully created a program that will copy the source file to the target file at the DOS prompt.

Advantages of using argc and argv:

The advantages of using argc and argv are:

We can execute this program at the command prompt, there is no need to compile the program every time we want to run it.

In our previous program we had to either specify the filename of source and target in the program itself or prompt the user every time to enter the filenames during execution.

Conclusion: Mastering File Manipulation in C

File manipulation is a cornerstone of programming in C, enabling developers to store, retrieve, and manage data persistently. Mastering file handling ensures that programs can work seamlessly with both text and binary data, opening up possibilities for a range of applications, from simple data logs to complex data storage solutions. By handling files correctly, developers can create software that not only interacts with data efficiently but also provides reliable data management and retrieval mechanisms—essentials for real-world software applications.

Key Concepts Revisited

In this guide, we've covered a broad spectrum of topics related to file manipulation in C. Each topic builds upon the last, forming a cohesive understanding of how files are managed in this language. Revisiting these key concepts will cement our understanding of each.

File Types: We first looked at text and binary files, each serving different purposes based on their structure and intended use. Text files are readable and human-friendly, while binary files are compact and efficient for storage and retrieval, making them ideal for high-performance applications.

File Modes and Access Types: We discussed different modes in which files can be opened—read, write, and append modes—as well as their variations when combined with reading and writing access. Each mode is suited to specific needs, and understanding these distinctions allows programmers to avoid common pitfalls like unintentional file truncation or attempting operations on read-only files.

Opening and Closing Files: Managing file resources effectively is crucial in C programming. Using fopen() and fclose() correctly avoids memory leaks and ensures that files are not left in an open state, which can cause data corruption and wasted system resources.

Reading and Writing Files: C provides several powerful functions for reading and writing. From basic character-level I/O (using fgetc() and fputc()) to line-based I/O with fgets() and fputs(), and even formatted I/O with fscanf() and fprintf(), each method serves different needs depending on the data and application requirements.

Binary File Operations: We also explored binary file handling with fread() and fwrite(). Working with binary files unlocks the ability to handle non-text data, such as images, sound files, and complex data structures. Binary file handling requires precision and attention to data types, as improper handling can lead to data misinterpretation.

File Positioning Functions: By using ftell(), fseek(), and rewind(), developers gain control over the file pointer, which allows for non-linear access within files. This is particularly useful for applications where data retrieval speed is critical or when specific sections of a file need to be accessed without reading the entire file.

Error Handling: Effective error handling is crucial for robust file manipulation. Functions like ferror() and clearerr() allow programmers to check and manage file I/O errors, providing a layer of reliability to applications. Furthermore, recognizing the end-of-file indicator (EOF) is essential for avoiding endless loops and unexpected behavior during file reading operations.

Directory Management: For applications requiring multiple files or dealing with file hierarchies, directory management becomes essential. With libraries like <dirent.h> on UNIX-based systems, developers can explore directories, opening up possibilities for more complex file-handling applications such as file management tools, file searching, and organizing systems.

The Importance of File Manipulation in Software Development

File manipulation in C is not just a matter of reading and writing data; it represents the foundation for developing more advanced data-driven applications. By understanding file handling, C developers can create programs that persist data beyond runtime, which is invaluable for everything from configuration files and log files to databases and multimedia files.

The importance of file handling also extends to data security, integrity, and performance:

Data Security: Proper file handling ensures that sensitive data is handled securely. Files can be opened in specific modes to prevent unauthorized reading or writing, and file pointers provide a controlled way to access and manage data.

Data Integrity: By following correct file manipulation techniques, developers ensure that data remains accurate and consistent. For instance, closing files properly prevents data corruption, while error checking during file I/O prevents misinterpretation of data.

Performance Optimization: Binary file handling, buffer management, and efficient file positioning can significantly enhance program performance, especially when working with large files or in resource-constrained environments.

Applications and Use Cases of File Manipulation

Mastery of file manipulation in C is essential for many fields and applications. Below are some key areas where this knowledge is indispensable:

Embedded Systems: In embedded systems, efficient data handling is critical due to limited memory. Binary file handling allows for compact data storage, which is essential in devices with minimal storage and processing capabilities.

Database Management: Many custom databases are implemented using binary files in C. Understanding file manipulation is vital for implementing low-level database functionalities, such as indexing, search algorithms, and data retrieval optimization.

Configuration Management: Many programs rely on configuration files (often text files) to store settings that persist between runs. Proper file manipulation allows these files to be read at startup, modified, and saved as needed, making software more adaptable and user-configurable.

Logging and Auditing: File manipulation is essential for logging errors, events, and operations in an application. By writing logs to a file, developers provide a traceable record of the program's execution, which is invaluable for debugging, performance analysis, and compliance.

Data Serialization: Applications that need to save the state of objects or data structures for later retrieval benefit from file manipulation, particularly with binary files. Serialization is widely used in applications that require saving game states, application data, or checkpoints in simulations.

Media and File Processing: Handling binary files enables the manipulation of various media files, such as images, audio, and video. Programs that edit, compress, or analyze media content rely heavily on efficient file I/O to handle large volumes of data.

Challenges and Best Practices in File Manipulation

While file handling in C is powerful, it comes with its own set of challenges. These challenges include ensuring portability, managing system resources, and avoiding memory leaks. Here are some best practices to address these issues:

Always Check File Open Status: Before performing any operations on a file, check that fopen() succeeded. Attempting to read or write to a file that didn't open correctly can lead to undefined behavior.

Close Files Properly: Every file opened with fopen() should be closed with fclose(). Not closing files can lead to memory leaks, especially in long-running applications or applications that open multiple files.

Handle Errors Gracefully: Use ferror() and clearerr() to detect and handle file errors. Handling errors ensures that the application doesn't crash unexpectedly and that users are informed of any issues.

Use Binary Files for Structured Data: When working with structured data (e.g., arrays, structs), binary files are preferable as they store data in a compact form and are faster to read and write.

Seek and Tell with Caution: Use fseek() and ftell() carefully, especially in text files, as newline characters can vary between systems. This is less of an issue in binary files but should be considered in cross-platform applications.

Use Buffers for Large Files: For large file operations, consider using buffers to manage data in chunks. This approach reduces memory usage and speeds up I/O operations by minimizing disk access.

Future of File Manipulation in C

As technology advances, C continues to play a crucial role in systems programming, embedded software, and performance-critical applications. File manipulation remains relevant, especially as the need for data handling becomes more sophisticated in areas like IoT, AI, and big data. C programmers can expect file handling techniques to remain a critical skill, especially in contexts where efficiency, control, and precision are paramount.

Closing Thoughts

File manipulation in C represents a powerful set of tools for any programmer. By mastering these techniques, developers unlock the potential to create robust, data-driven applications that interact with files efficiently and effectively. Whether you're developing an embedded system, managing application settings, or building a custom database, the knowledge of file handling in C will serve as an invaluable asset. With practice and a deep understanding of these concepts, programmers can wield the power of file manipulation to create applications that are not only functional but also optimized for performance and reliability.

Mastery of file manipulation in C lays the foundation for becoming a proficient systems programmer, capable of developing applications that meet today's demands for data integrity, security, and efficiency. As the scope of C programming continues to grow, so does the relevance of file handling, ensuring it remains a vital part of every C programmer's toolkit.

10. Memory Management in C

1. Introduction

Definition and Importance: Memory management in C is the technique of allocating, managing, and deallocating memory for program operations. C provides low-level access to memory, which offers developers powerful control over how memory is used, making memory management an essential skill for any C programmer.

Memory Segments in C:

Code Segment: Stores the compiled code of the program. It's read-only to prevent accidental modifications to the code during runtime.

Data Segment: Contains initialized global and static variables. This segment persists for the duration of the program's execution.

Stack Segment: Allocates memory automatically for function calls and local variables. When a function is called, its local variables are stored in the stack, and they are released once the function exits.

Heap Segment: Memory in the heap is allocated dynamically during runtime, allowing for flexibility. Heap memory must be manually managed by the programmer.

Why Memory Management Matters in C: Unlike languages with automatic garbage collection (like Java or Python), C requires explicit memory management. This allows more efficient memory use but also increases the risk of memory leaks and segmentation faults if mismanaged.

2. Static vs. Dynamic Memory

Static Memory Allocation:

Definition: Memory is allocated at compile time, making the memory space fixed throughout the program's lifecycle.

Example: Declaring an array as int arr[10]; allocates a fixed size of memory for 10 integers at compile-time.

Pros:

Memory is automatically managed (released when the program exits).

Faster access due to its predictability and fixed memory location.

Cons:

Limited flexibility; memory size cannot be changed during runtime.

May lead to wasted memory if allocated space is underutilized.

Dynamic Memory Allocation:

Definition: Memory is allocated at runtime, allowing programs to adjust memory usage as needed.

Example: Using malloc or calloc to allocate memory based on user input, enabling more efficient use of memory.

Pros:

Allows flexible memory usage, resizing as necessary.
Useful in cases where memory requirements are unpredictable.

Cons:

Requires manual deallocation (using free), making it prone to memory leaks and dangling pointers.

3. Memory Allocation Functions

malloc (Memory Allocation):

Purpose: Allocates a specified number of bytes on the heap and returns a pointer to the allocated memory.

Syntax: void* malloc(size_t size); where size is the number of bytes needed.

Example: int* ptr = (int*) malloc(10 * sizeof(int)); allocates space for 10 integers.

Characteristics:

Uninitialized memory: The allocated block contains garbage values initially.

Can return NULL if memory allocation fails (e.g., if the system runs out of memory).

Common Issues:

Forgetting to check if malloc returned NULL, leading to undefined behavior if accessed.

Misinterpreting size: Using the wrong size_t calculation (e.g., malloc(10) instead of malloc(10 * sizeof(int))).

calloc (Contiguous Allocation):

Purpose: Allocates memory for an array of elements, initializing all bytes to zero.

Syntax: void* calloc(size_t num_elements, size_t element_size);

Example: int* ptr = (int*) calloc(10, sizeof(int)); allocates and zeroes space for 10 integers.

Differences from malloc: Initializes memory to zero, making it useful when zero-initialization is needed.

Common Issues:

Allocating fewer elements than required, leading to out-of-bounds errors.

realloc (Resize Allocation):

Purpose: Changes the size of an existing memory block, either expanding or shrinking it.

Syntax: void* realloc(void* ptr, size_t new_size);

Example: ptr = (int*) realloc(ptr, 20 * sizeof(int)); resizes the existing memory block to fit 20 integers.

Advantages:

Retains existing data in the original memory block (if resized smaller) and moves data if a larger block is required.

Common Issues:

Potential data loss if realloc returns NULL and the old pointer is overwritten.
Not compatible with statically allocated memory.

free (Deallocate Memory):

Purpose: Releases memory allocated by malloc, calloc, or realloc.

Syntax: void free(void* ptr);

Usage Tips:

After freeing, set the pointer to NULL to prevent dangling pointers.

Common Issues:

Double Free: Freeing the same pointer twice, which can lead to undefined behavior.

Invalid Free: Freeing memory not dynamically allocated.

4. Memory Leaks and Handling Memory Errors

Memory Leaks:

Definition: Occur when allocated memory is not freed, creating inaccessible memory that persists until the program exits.

Examples:

Allocating memory in a loop without freeing it each time.
Losing the reference to dynamically allocated memory.

Consequences: Unreleased memory accumulates, potentially exhausting available memory and leading to crashes.

Prevention:

Keep track of all allocated memory and ensure each allocation has a corresponding free.
Structure code to allocate and free memory in the same scope.

Memory Errors:

Dangling Pointers: Point to freed memory, leading to undefined behavior if accessed.

Invalid Free: Attempting to free a pointer that was never dynamically allocated or has already been freed.

Buffer Overflow: Writing beyond allocated memory, causing potential crashes or vulnerabilities.

Avoiding Memory Errors:

Initialize pointers to NULL and check their status before freeing.
Use bounds checks to avoid overflow errors.

Allocate only what's necessary to minimize wasted memory and potential errors.

5. Using Valgrind or Similar Tools for Memory Management

Introduction to Valgrind:

Overview: Valgrind is a memory profiling tool that detects memory leaks, invalid accesses, and other memory-related errors in C programs.

Benefits: Essential for debugging and ensuring robust memory management, especially in complex programs.

Installation and Basic Commands:

Install Valgrind on Linux: sudo apt install valgrind.
Basic command to check memory issues: valgrind ./program_name.

Common Flags:

--leak-check=yes: Ensures a detailed report on memory leaks.
--track-origins=yes: Shows where uninitialized values originate.

How Valgrind Detects Memory Leaks and Errors:

Tracks all allocations and frees, providing warnings if memory is not released.
Sample Output: For example, "Invalid read of size 4" indicates a pointer accessing freed memory.

Example Workflow:

Run the program with valgrind ./program_name.

Interpret output: Look for "definitely lost" memory as a direct sign of leaks, while "possibly lost" indicates potential leaks.

Improving Program Based on Valgrind Results: Modify code based on errors detected to prevent memory misuse.

Alternative Tools:

AddressSanitizer: Available in GCC/Clang compilers, detects memory errors like buffer overflows, invalid frees, and use-after-free.

Dr. Memory: Similar to Valgrind but available on Windows, provides similar insights into memory usage.

Memory Manipulation

Every value or complex data type exists in memory. Here, we explore various ways to create and manipulate memory. We also explore the life cycle of different kinds of memory structures.

Understanding Memory Allocation and Lifetime

Every instance of a value—be it a literal, an intrinsic data type, or a complex data type—exists in memory. Here, we will explore various ways in which memory is allocated. The different mechanisms for memory allocation are called **storage classes**. In this chapter, we will review the storage class we've been using thus far, that of automatic storage, as well as introducing the static storage class. We will also explore the lifetime of each storage class, as well as introduce the scope of a storage class—internal versus external storage.

After exploring automatic and static storage classes, this chapter paves the way for a special and extremely flexible storage class—that of dynamic memory allocation. Dynamic memory allocation is so powerful and flexible that it will be introduced and discussed in more, Using Dynamic Memory Allocation, with the creation and manipulation of a dynamic data structure called a linked list.

Each storage class also has a specific scope or visibility to other parts of the program; the scope of both variables and functions will be explored, Understanding Scope.

The following topics will be covered in this chapter:

Defining storage classes

Understanding automatic versus dynamic storage classes

Understanding internal versus external storage classes

Exploring the **static** storage class Exploring the lifetime of each storage class

Defining storage classes

C provides a number of storage classes. These fall into the following two general categories:

Fixed storage allocation: Fixed storage allocation means that memory is allocated in the location where it is declared. All fixed storage is named; we have called these variables identifiers, or just variables. Fixed storage includes both the automatic storage class and the static storage class. We have been using automatic storage for every variable thus far. When you declare a variable and—optionally—initialize it, you are using automatic storage. We will introduce static storage later in this chapter.

Dynamic storage allocation: Dynamic storage allocation means that memory is allocated upon demand and is only referenced via a pointer. The pointer may be a fixed, named pointer variable, or it may be a part of another dynamic structure.

Two properties of storage classes are their visibility—or scope—within a program or statement block, and their lifetime, or how long that memory exists as the program runs.

Within the general category of fixed storage, there are the following two subcategories:

Internal storage allocation: Internal storage is storage that is declared within the context of a function block or compound statement—in other words, declared between {and}. Internal storage has both a limited scope and a limited lifetime.

External storage allocation: External storage is storage that is declared outside of any function block. It has a much broader scope and a lifetime greater than that of internal storage. We'll address each of these categories in turn.

Understanding automatic versus dynamic storage classes

In all the preceding chapters, we have been using a fixed or named storage allocation. That is, whenever we declared a variable or a structure, we gave that memory location a data type and a name. This was fixed in position in our program's main routine and functions. Once that named memory was created, we could access it directly via its name, or indirectly with a pointer to that named location. In this chapter, we will specifically explore the fixed storage classes in greater detail.

Likewise, whenever we declare a literal value—say, 52 or 13—the compiler interprets this value and puts it directly into the code, fixing it in the place where it has been declared. The memory that it occupies is part of the program itself.

In contrast, dynamic storage allocation is unnamed; it can only be accessed via pointers.

Dynamic memory allocation will be introduced and explored in the next chapter.

Automatic storage

Automatic storage means that memory is allocated by the compiler at precisely the point when a literal value, variable, array, or structure is declared. A less obvious but well-defined point is when a formal parameter to a function is declared. That memory is automatically deallocated at specific and other well-known points within the program.

In all cases except literal values, when this storage class is allocated, it is given a name—its variable name—along with its data type. Even a pointer to another, already allocated memory location is given a name. When that memory is an element of an array, it is the array name and its offset in the array. For example, the memory name of the third element of **anArray** is **anArray[2]**.

Dynamic storage

In comparison to fixed storage, dynamic storage is memory that is unnamed but is accessed solely indirectly via pointers. There are special library functions to allocate and deallocate dynamic memory. As we will see in the next chapter, we must take extra care to keep track of unnamed allocated memory.

Understanding internal versus external storage classes

In the storage class of fixed or named memory, C has explicit mechanisms to allocate that memory.

These correlate to the following four C keywords:

auto static register extern

Note that the **auto** keyword represents the automatic storage class, and the static keyword specifies the **static** storage class. We are currently interested in only the first two of these mechanisms. These keywords precede a variable specification, as follows:

<storage class> [const] <data type> <name> [= <initial value>]; In this specification, the following applies:

<storage class> is one of these four keywords: **auto, static, register**, and **extern**.

[const] is an optional keyword to indicate whether the named memory can be changed after initialization.

If **const** is present, an initial value must be supplied.

<data type> is an intrinsic or custom data type.

<name> is the variable or constant name for the value and data type.

[= <initial value>] is an optional initial value or values to be assigned to the named memory location.

If **const** is present, the value in that memory cannot be changed; otherwise, it can be reassigned another value.

When **<storage class>** is omitted, the **auto** keyword is assumed. So, all of our programs up to this point have been using **auto** memory variables by default. Function parameters are also **auto** memory variables and have all the same properties as those we explicitly declare in the body of functions or in compound statements.

The **register** keyword was used in older versions of C to signal to the compiler to store a value in one of the registers of the **central processing unit** (**CPU**) for very quick access to that value. Compilers have become so much more sophisticated that this keyword is ignored, except in some very specialized C compilers.

The **extern** keyword has to do with the scope of external variables declared in other files.

Internal or local storage classes

Not only have we been using automatic, fixed storage in all the preceding chapters, but we have also been using the subclass of internal storage. Internal storage is memory that is allocated either with a compound statement (between {and}) or as a function parameter.

Internal memory includes loop variables that are allocated when the loop is entered and deallocated when the loop is exited or completed.

Internal memory variables are only accessible within the compound statement where they've been declared, and any sub compound statement is declared within that compound statement. Their scope is limited to their enclosing {and}. They are not accessible from any other function or any function that calls them. Therefore, they are often referred to as local memory because they are strictly local to the code block within which they are declared. We will see exactly how these are stored in the next chapter.

Consider the following function:

```
double doSomething (double aReal, int aNumber )
{
double d1 = aReal;
double d2 = 0.0 ;
int   n1 = aNumber;
int   n2 = aNumber * 10 ;
for( int i = 1; i < n1 , i++ )
{
for( int j = 1; j < n2 ; j++  )
{
d1 = i / j;
d2 + = d1;
}
}
return d2;
```

This function consists of two function parameters and a return value. It also contains within its function body four local variables and two looping variables. This function might be called with the following statement: double aSum = doSomething (2.25, 10);

When the function is called, the **aReal** and **aNumber** automatic local variables are allocated and assigned (copied) the values of **2.25** and **10**, respectively. These variables can then be used throughout the function body. Within the function body, the **d1, d2, n1**, and **n2** variables are automatic local variables. They, too, can be used throughout the function body.

Lastly, we create the loop with the **i** loop-local variable, where i is only accessible within its loop block. Within that block is another loop with the j loop-local variable, where both j and i, and all other function-local variables, are accessible. Finally, the function returns the value of **d2**.

In the calling statement, the function assigns the value of the **d2** function-local variable to the **aSum** automatic variable. At the completion of **doSomething()**, all of the memory allocated by that function is no longer accessible.

External or global storage classes

External storage is memory that is declared outside of any function body, including **main()**. Such variables can potentially be accessed from any part of the program. These are more often called **global variables** because they are globally accessible from within the file where they are declared.

Historical Note

In versions of C before C90, a global variable in one file (compilation unit) was accessible to all other files. This is no longer true. And so, the global storage class, without any other directives in other files, can only be accessed from the file where they are declared. Yet they can be accessed by any function within that file.

One advantage of global variables is their ease of accessibility. However, this is also their disadvantage. When a variable can be accessed from anywhere, it becomes increasingly difficult as a program grows in size and complexity to know when that variable changed and what changed it. Global variables should be used sparingly and with great care.

The lifetime of automatic storage

When we consider the various storage classes, not only do we consider when they are created and accessed, but we must also consider when they are deallocated or destroyed. This is their lifetime—from creation to destruction.

Automatic, internal variables are created when the variable is declared either in the body of a compound statement or in a function's formal parameter list. Internal variables are destroyed and no longer accessible when that compound statement or function is exited.

Consider the **doSomething()** function. The **aReal, aNumber, d1, d2, n1**, and **n2** variables are created when the function is called. All of them are destroyed after the function returns its $d2$ value. The i loop variable is created when we enter the loop and is destroyed when we exit that outer loop. The j variable is created at each iteration of the outer loop, controlled by i, and destroyed at the completion of the inner loop, controlled by **j**.

Local variables have a lifetime that is only as long as the compound statement in which they are declared.

Automatic, external variables are created when the program is loaded into memory. They exist for the lifetime of the program. When the program exits (the **main()** function block returns), they are destroyed.

Now that we have covered the various characteristics of memory, we can explore one of the storage classes, **static**.

Exploring the static storage class

Sometimes, it is desirable to allocate memory in such a way that it can hold a value beyond the lifetime of automatic memory variables. An example of this might be a routine that could be called from anywhere within a program that returns a continuously increasing value each time it is called, such as a page number or a unique record identifier. Furthermore, we might want to give such a function a starting value and increment the sequence of numbers from that point. We will see how to do each of these.

Neither of these can be achieved easily with automatic storage classes. For this, there is the **static** storage class. As with the automatic storage class, it can exist as both internal and external storage.

Internal static storage

When a variable is declared within a function block with the **static** keyword, that variable is accessible only from within that function block when the function is called. The initial value of the static value is assigned at compile time and is not re-evaluated at runtime. Therefore, the value assigned to the static variable must be known at compile time and cannot be an expression or variable.

Consider the following program:

```
#include <stdio.h>

void printPage( const char* aHeading );
int main( void )  {   printPage( "Title Page" );
printPage( "Chapter 1 " );
printPage( "          " );
printPage( "          " );
printPage( "Chapter 2 " );
printPage( "          " );
printPage( "Conclusion" ); }

void printPage( const char* aHeading )
{
static int pageNo = 1;
printf( "--------------------\n"          "| %10s      |\n" , aHeading );
printf( "|              |\n"       "|   Page Content  |\n"
      "|   Goes Here   |\n"      "|              |\n");
printf( "|        Page %1d |\n"        "--------------------\n" , pageNo );
pageNo++;
}
```

The **printPage()** function contains the **pageNo** static variable. **pageNo** has **1** as its initial value when the program is started. When **printPage()** is called, the given heading string is printed along with the current page number value. **pageNo** is then incremented in preparation for the next call to it.

This program also demonstrates how to concatenate multiple string literals together into a single string literal. Such concatenation can also be done when a string array is initialized. Note that there is no comma between the two string literals. This is useful for printing multiple lines of text such that the text of each can be easily aligned.

Create a file called **pageCounter.c** and enter the preceding program. Compile and run this program. You should see the following output:

```
> cc pageCounter.c -o pageCounter -Wall -Werror -std=c17
> ./pageCounter
----------------------
| Title Page          |
|                     |
|    Page Content     |
|    Goes Here        |
|                     |
|            Page 1   |
----------------------
----------------------
| Chapter 1           |
|                     |
|    Page Content     |
|    Goes Here        |
|                     |
|            Page 2   |
----------------------
----------------------
|                     |
|                     |
|    Page Content     |
|    Goes Here        |
|                     |
|            Page 3   |
----------------------
----------------------
| Chapter 2           |
|                     |
|    Page Content     |
|    Goes Here        |
|                     |
|            Page 4   |
----------------------
----------------------
| Conclusion          |
|                     |
|    Page Content     |
|    Goes Here        |
|                     |
|            Page 5   |
----------------------
```

Figure – Screenshot of pageCount.c using a static variable

The value of the static memory is incremented and preserved even after the function exits.

Now, consider what would happen if the **static** keyword was removed. Do that—remove the **static** keyword.

Compile and run the program.

You should see the following output:

```
> cc pageCounter.c -o pageCounter -Wall -Werror -std=c17
> ./pageCounter
```

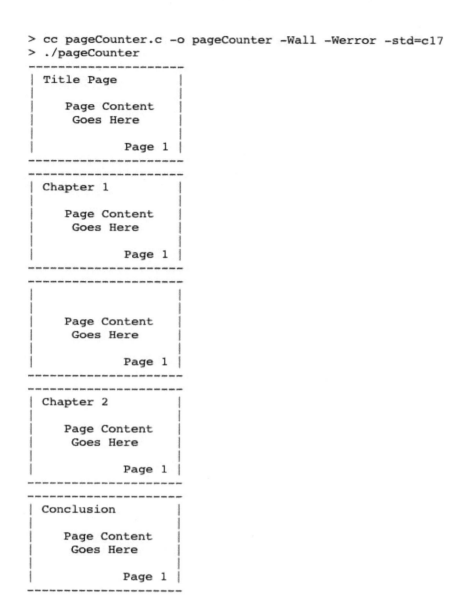

Figure – Screenshot of pageCount.c using an automatic variable

In this case, the automatic variable is initialized each time the function is called, and we never see the incremented value because it is destroyed when the function exits.

External static storage

Because an internal static variable can only be initialized by the compiler, we need another mechanism to safely store a value that we might want to initialize, or seed, ourselves. For this, we can use an external static variable.

External static variables can only be accessible by any other variable or code block, including function blocks, within the file where they are declared. The **static** attribute prevents them from having external visibility outside of the file where they are declared. Ideally, then, the code for the external static variable and the function that accesses it should be in a single, separate **.c** file, as follows:

```
// seriesGenerator
```

```c
static int seriesNumber = 100; // default seed value
void seriesStart( int seed )
{
seriesNumber = seed;
}
int series( void )
{
  return seriesNumber++;
}
```

To use these functions, we would need to include a header file with function prototypes for it, as follows:

```c
// seriesGenerator.h void seriesStart( int seed ); int  series( void );
```

We would create the **seriesGenerator.c** and **seriesGenerator.h** files with these functions and prototypes. We would also have to add **#include <seriesGenerator.h>** to any file that calls these functions. We would then compile these files, along with our other source files, into a single executable file.

This series generator, when compiled into the main program, would be initialized, or seeded, with

a call to **seriesStart()** with some known integer value. After that, each call to **series()** would generate the next number in the series.

This pattern may seem familiar from the last chapter, Chapter 16, Creating and Using More Complex Structures. There, we used **srand()** to seed our **pseudorandom number generator** (**PRNG**), and then subsequently called **rand()** to get the next number in the random sequence. You can now more clearly imagine how **srand()** and **rand()** would be implemented using static external memory allocation.

The lifetime of static storage

The lifetimes for both internal and external static memory are the same. Static memory is allocated when the program is loaded before any statements are executed. Static memory is only destroyed when the program completes or exits. Therefore, the lifetime of static memory is the same as the lifetime of the program.

Using Dynamic Memory Allocation

Not all data can be allocated statically or automatically. Sometimes, the number of items to be manipulated is not known beforehand; that number can only be known at runtime and may vary from run to run, depending on external inputs (such as user input and files). In the preceding chapter, we examined automatic and static memory allocation. We now stand on the threshold of an incredibly powerful feature of C – dynamic memory allocation and manipulation. Once we pass this threshold, many flexible dynamic data manipulations will be available to us. We will briefly introduce many of these data structures and their uses in this chapter.

As mentioned in the preceding chapter, dynamic memory is unnamed, so it can only be manipulated via pointers.

Furthermore, dynamic memory has a different lifetime than either automatic or static memory.

The following topics will be covered in this chapter:

Acquiring an introductory understanding of the power and flexibility of dynamic memory allocation

Learning how to allocate and release dynamic memory

Implementing a simple linked list dynamic data structure

Creating and using a dynamic function pointer

Becoming aware of various special considerations when using dynamic memory

Learning about some other important dynamic data structures

Let's get started!

Introducing dynamic memory

Do we always know exactly how many objects we will need to manipulate and allocate memory for in a program? The answer is a resounding no!

Not every situation or program can be efficiently addressed using just automatic or static memory. The number of objects may vary widely over the runtime of the program and from one run to another of the same program.

Furthermore, some problems cannot be easily solved with simple automatic or static memory. These types of problems include sorting algorithms, efficient searching and lookup of large amounts of data, and many geometric and graph theory optimization techniques. All of these are advanced programming topics.

Dynamic memory opens the doors to these fascinating and powerful algorithms.

Before we dive into dynamic memory allocation, let's examine the way C allocates all types of memory in a program's memory space.

A brief tour of C's memory layout

It is now time to gain a cursory understanding of how C organizes memory when a program is loaded and run. When a program is invoked to be run, the system first performs a number of steps before **main()** is called.

A rough outline of this process is as follows:

The operating system creates a new process and allocates memory space for the process.

System device addresses and system executables are mapped into the memory space.

The program code is loaded into the memory space.

Global variables, static variables, and string constants are loaded into memory. These addresses won't change over the life of the program.

Other required initializations occur. This includes setting the starting heap address and the starting stack address.

main() is called and the execution of the program begins.

Consider the following diagram:

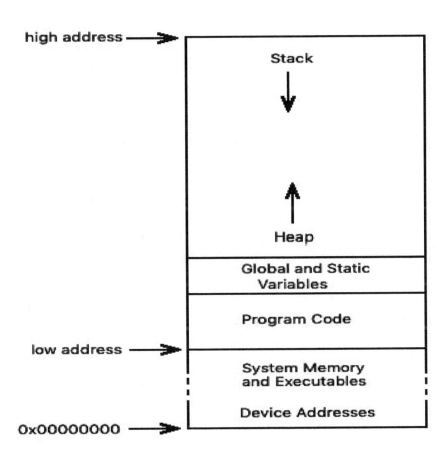

Figure– Simplified map of program memory

This is a very simple conceptual view of a program's memory space. The operating system provides this space to the program when it is loaded and ready to be run. The C runtime then divvies up the memory given to it into segments, each for a specific use.

It consists of the following segments:

• **System memory**: This consists of system memory and system programs, as well as the addresses for all of the devices on the computer. This segment is mapped for all running programs so that there is only ever one copy of the system code in the overall system memory space. The system exclusively manages this memory.

- **Program code**: This is where the compiled program is loaded and executed. Function definitions—the executable part of each function—are located here.

- **Global and static memory**: After the program is loaded, global and static variables are allocated and initialized, as well as string literals.

- **The call stack**: When your program makes a function call, its parameters, any automatic variables declared within it, and its return value are allocated in this segment or pushed onto the stack. The call stack grows from high memory to lower memory, and then to the heap space, as one function calls another and that function calls yet another. When a function returns, its memory is popped off the stack (deallocated). Think of a stack of plates —you put a plate on top of the stack one after the other; then, you take them off the stack one at a time in the reverse order they were placed on the stack.

- **The heap**: When your program allocates dynamic memory, it is allocated from this segment. Heap space grows from low memory to higher memory, toward the stack space. Most allocations here are done somewhat randomly using the best fit allocation scheme. That is, the lowest available space is allocated, if possible. When that memory is deallocated, it becomes available for other allocations of the same or smaller size.

Each program lives in its own memory space. The system space is common to all programs. After your program has been loaded into this memory space and the global and static variables have been allocated, the system calls the **main()** function and begins execution. When you call a function, execution jumps to the memory address of that function and pushes its parameters, automatic variables, and return values onto the call stack. When the function completes, it pops its memory off the stack and returns execution to the location in the program space where it was called.

All dynamic memory allocations are made from within the heap segment of the program memory space. Now, we will explore the mechanisms we can use to allocate and release dynamic memory.

Allocating and releasing dynamic memory

Dynamic memory is allocated and released (deallocated) only at very explicit points by a program. It doesn't happen automatically; it doesn't happen by accident or by chance. You make this happen when you call specific C Standard Library calls to allocate and release dynamic memory.

Allocating dynamic memory

Memory allocation routines are declared in **stdlib.h** and are a part of the C runtime library. There are two very similar allocation routines, **malloc()** and **calloc()**, which are used to allocate a new block of memory from the heap. The main difference between **malloc()** and **calloc()** is that **calloc()** clears the memory block it allocates, whereas **malloc()** only does allocation. There is a third routine, **realloc()**, which is used to resize an existing block of heap memory.

These functions have the following prototypes:

```
void* malloc( size_t size );
```

void* calloc(size_t count , size_t size);
void* realloc(void *ptr , size_t size); **size_t** is defined somewhere in **stdlib.h**, as follows: type unsigned int size_t;

Each of these functions returns a **void*** pointer to a block of memory in the heap space. Recall that **void*** is a pointer type that is of an unknown or generic type; a pointer of the **void*** type must be cast to the required pointer type before you can use that pointer. Notice that **malloc()** takes a single **size** parameter, while **calloc()** takes the **count** and **size** parameters. The total amount of memory allocated for **malloc()** is **size**. The total amount of memory allocated for **calloc()** is **count** multiplied by **size**. Very often **count** is **1** and **size** is the total memory to allocate.

If neither function can find memory in the heap space, the returned pointer will be **NULL**. It is a good practice to check whether these routines were successful.

The following code shows how each allocates memory for a single **Card** structure:

```
Card* pCard1 = (Card*)malloc( sizeof( Card ) );

if( NULL == pCard1 ) ...            // out of memory error
Card* pCard2 = (Card*)calloc( 1 , sizeof( Card ) );

if( NULL == pCard2 ) ...            // out of memory error
```

If we wanted to allocate memory for, say, five cards, we would use the following code:

```
Card* pHand1 = (Card)malloc( 5 * sizeof( Card ) ); if( NULL == pHand1 ) ... // out of memory error
Card* pHand2 = (Card*)calloc( 5 , sizeof( Card ) ); if( NULL == pHand2 ) ... // out of memory error
```

In this second example, we are allocating space for five cards contiguously in dynamic memory. This sounds like an array, doesn't it? Well, in fact, it is. Instead of an automatic array declared with **Card hand1[5]** and **Card hand2[5]**, both of which allocate blocks of memory to hold five cards on the stack, **pHand1** and **pHand2** both point to contiguous blocks of memory in the heap space.

Recall how array names and pointers to arrays are interchangeable. With these allocations, we can now refer to individual cards in the heap space (allocated previously) with **pHand1[3]** and **pHand2[i]**. This is simply astounding! We can access arrays in either the stack space or the heap space using array notation or pointer notation. Examples of how to do this are provided in the Accessing dynamic memory section.

In both examples, each call to allocate memory using **calloc()** or **malloc()** appears to be interchangeable. So, why use one function over the other? Is one of these preferred over the other? Before we can answer that, we need to know that **calloc()** both allocates memory and initializes it to all zeros, while **malloc()** simply allocates the memory and leaves initialization up to us. So, the simple answer is to prefer **calloc()** over **malloc()**.

The **realloc()** function changes the size of the memory that's pointed to by **ptr** to the given **size**, which may be larger or smaller than the original memory allocation. If **size** is larger, the original contents are copied and the extra space is uninitialized. If **size** is smaller, the original contents are truncated. If **ptr** is

NULL, then **realloc()** behaves exactly like **malloc()**. As with **malloc()** and **calloc()**, the pointer returned by **realloc()** must be cast to the required type before it can be used.

Releasing dynamic memory

When we are done with the heap memory we've allocated, we release it with a call to **free()**. The **free()** function returns the allocated memory to the available heap pool of memory. This call does not have to occur within the same function where the memory was allocated.

The prototype in **stdlib.h** for **free()** is as follows:

```
void  free( void* ptr );
```

The pointer that's passed to **free()** must contain a value that originated from one of the calls to **malloc()**, **calloc()**, or **realloc()**. There is no need to cast the **void*** pointer argument. If **ptr** is **NULL**, then **free()** does nothing.

We would release the memory that was allocated in the previous subsection as follows:

```
free( pCard1 ); free( pCard2 ); free( pHand1 ); free( pHand2 );
```

These four statements release each block of memory that we allocated earlier. Allocated dynamic memory can be freed in any order; it does not have to be freed in the same order it was allocated.

Accessing dynamic memory

Once we've allocated dynamic memory, we can access it via the pointer that's returned by the allocation functions, as we would with any other pointer. With each of the previous examples, we could use that dynamic memory as follows:

```
InitializeCard( pCard1 , spade , ace , kNotWild );
InitializeCard( pCard2 , heart , queen , kNotWild );
```

pCard1 and **pCard2** are pointers to individual **Card** structures. Therefore, we can use them just like we used the pointers in **carddeck.c** using automatic variables.

However, consider the following:

```
pHand1[3].suit = diamond;
pHand1[3].face = two;
for( int i = 0 ; i < kCardsInHand , i++ )
{
PrintCard( &(pHand[i]) );

}
```

Both **pHand1** and **pHand2** point to a contiguous block of memory that is equivalent to the size of five **Card** structures. Using array notation, we set the **suit** and **face** structure members of the fourth element via **pHand1**. The **PrintCard()** function takes a pointer to a **Card** structure, while **pHand2** points to a block of **Card** structures. Array notation gives us the individual cards in the block; we must then get the address of that card element and pass it **PrintCard()**.

Rather than using arrays in heap memory, it is far more common to manipulate structures individually, as we shall see when we explore the linked list dynamic structure in the next section.

The lifetime of dynamic memory

Heap memory has a lifetime that begins when the memory is allocated. Once allocated, that memory exists until the **free()** function is called to release that memory. Allocating and releasing memory is also called **memory management** within a program.

Alternatively, all memory is deallocated when the program exits, both in terms of fixed memory and dynamic memory. It is generally considered a sloppy practice to ignore memory management of dynamic memory, especially for large, complex programs or for programs that are likely to run for a very long time.

Knowing the lifetime of heap memory, let's now consider some of the situations involved with managing heap memory. These will be common considerations. Unfortunately, they will not be all possible situations.

Special considerations for dynamic allocation

Dynamic memory allocation does not come without a cost. In this case, the cost is typically conceptual complexity. This cost also takes the form of added management of heap memory and awareness of the pitfalls of potential memory leaks.

To be honest, I should add that it may take some time to get your head around some of these concepts. For me, some of them took me quite a while to grasp. The best way, I've found, is to take a working program and alter it, see how it behaves, and then understand why it did what it did. Assume nothing. Or, start with a minimal working program that uses the mind-bending feature and then build upon it. Interact with your code; play with it. No matter how you do it, you can't just think about it. You have to twist, poke, prod, and cajole your code until you understand what it is doing. Otherwise, it is just guesswork.

Heap memory management

The amount or degree of heap memory management required in a program is a consideration that depends on the complexity and expected runtime duration of that program.

When heap memory is initialized at the start of a program and remains largely unchanged after it is initialized, little heap management will be required. It may be acceptable to simply let heap memory exist until the program exits.

The **free()** function may never be called in such a program.

On the other hand, for programs whose complexity is large, or where heap memory is heavily used, or where the runtime duration is hours, days, months, or even years, heap management is essential. A program that controls, say, a banking system, a fighter jet, or a petroleum refinery might have catastrophic consequences if the heap for that program is not properly managed, causing the program to terminate abnormally. The bank may suddenly show a pile of money in your account or take it all away from you; the fighter jet may lose control while in flight and crash; the petroleum refinery may suddenly react chaotically and explode. The discipline of software engineering exists primarily to make such software systems both maintainable by various levels of programmers and extremely reliable over the long lifespan of such systems.

For some data structures, such as a linked list, which we will explore in depth later in this chapter, memory management is relatively straightforward. However, for others, memory management may not be obvious. Each data structure and algorithm has its own set of memory considerations to be addressed. When we ignore memory management or do not address it fully, we might encounter a common dynamic memory problem known as **memory leaks**.

Memory leaks

One of the main challenges of heap management is to prevent memory leaks. A memory leak is when a block of memory is allocated and the pointer to it is lost so that it cannot be released until the program quits.

The following is a simple example of a memory leak:

Card* pCard = (Card*)calloc(1 , sizeof(Card)); ... pCard = (Card*)calloc(1 , sizeof(Card)); // <-- Leak!

In this example, **pCard** first points to one block of heap memory. Later, **pCard** is assigned to another block of heap memory. The first block of memory is allocated but has not been freed. After **pCard** is given another address, there is nothing pointing to the first block of heap memory. Without a pointer to it, it cannot be accessed nor can it be freed; the first block of heap memory is leaked.

To correct this error, first call **free()** before reassigning **pCard**, as follows:

Card* pCard = (Card*)calloc(1 , sizeof(Card)); ...

free(pCard);

pCard = (Card*)calloc(1 , sizeof(Card)); A more subtle leak is as follows:

struct Thing1 { int size; struct Thing2* pThing2 }

struct Thing1* pThing1 = (struct Thing1*)calloc(1,sizeof(Thing1)); Thing1->pThing2 = (struct Thing2*)calloc(1,sizeof(Thing2)); ... free(pThing1); // <-- Leak!

In this example, we create the **Thing1** structure, which contains a pointer to another dynamically allocated **Thing2** structure. We allocate heap memory for **Thing1**, which is pointed to by **pThing1**. We then allocate heap memory for **Thing2**, which is pointed to by the **pThing2** pointer element of **Thing1**.

So far, so good, and we go on our merry way.

Later, we release **pThing1**. Uh oh! What happened to the pointer to **pThing2**? It's gone. That means that whatever **pThing2** pointed to cannot be accessed again. We just leaked the memory of **pThing2**.

The correct way to release all of the memory of **pThing1** is as follows:

free(pThing1->pThing2); free(pThing1);

First, the **free()** function is called on **pThing1->pThing2**, which is the pointer element of **pThing2**. Then, and only then, can we release the memory of **pThing1**.

A third, equally subtle leak is as follows:

```
Card* CreateCard( ... ) {   Card* pCard = (Card*) calloc( 1 , sizeof( Card ) );   InitializeCard( pCard ,
... );   return pCard;
}
```

In the **CreateCard()** function, memory for **Card** is allocated in the heap space, initialized, and the pointer to it is returned. This is all fine and dandy.

Now, consider how this function might be called, as follows:

```
Card* aCard = CreateCard( ... ); PrintCard( aCard ); aCard = CreateCard( ... );  // <-- Leak! PrintCard(
aCard );
```

This is similar, but less obvious than the first memory leak example. Each time the **CreateCard()** function is called, it allocates more heap memory. However, when it is called multiple times, the pointer to the allocated memory may be overwritten as it is in the sequence of **CreateCard()** and **PrintCard()**. The **CreateCard()** function has added the burden on the caller of being responsible for either calling **free()** before reusing **aCard**, or to somehow keep track of the various pointer values that are returned, as follows:

```
Card* aCard = CreateCard( ... );
PrintCard( aCard ); free( aCard ); aCard = CreateCard( ... );
PrintCard( aCard );
free( aCard ) Card* pHand = (Card*)calloc( 5 , sizeof( Card* ) );
for( int i = 0 ; i<5 ; i++ )  {   pHand[i] = CreateCard( ... );
PrintCard( pHand[i] );

}
for( int i = 0 ; i<5 ; i++ )   free( pHand[i] );
free( pHand );
```

In the first group of statements, **free()** is called before **aCard** is assigned a new pointer to the heap memory.

In the second group of statements, an array of five pointers to **Card** is allocated. Note that this is not the same as allocating memory for five **Card** structures; **CreateCard()** does the allocation for a **Card** one at a time in a loop. Using a loop, five cards are created in the heap space and printed. Later, a loop is used to properly release the **Card** memory allocated in **CreateCard()**, which is pointed to by each element of **pHand**. Finally, **pHand** (a block of five pointers) is released.

Simply being aware of possible memory leaks and what might cause them goes a long way when it comes to recognizing and preventing them from happening in the first place.

We will now explore a general, yet very useful, dynamic structure.

The linked list dynamic data structure

The most basic dynamic data structure is the **linked list**. A linked list is the basis for other dynamic structures, such as stacks, queues, and deques. A stack conforms to the rules that each new element must be added to the front of the list, and that each element can only be removed from the front of the list. A queue conforms to the rules that each new element must be added to the back of the list, and that each element can only be removed from the front of the list. A deque is a generalized form of both a stack and queue and has the operations of both of them.

We will implement a simple linked list and then test it from within the **main()** function.

Create a file called **linklisttester.c.** It is in this single file that we will create our linked list structure, operations, and test code. Before we begin, consider the following diagram of the linked list we will create:

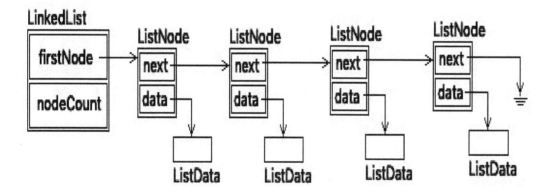

Figure– Linked list

A linked list consists of a header structure that contains information about the list, as well as a link to the first element, or **list node**. Any link that is **NULL** signifies that it is the last list node in the list. If the head structure has a **NULL** link, the list is empty. In the preceding diagram, the linked list contains the link list header with four list nodes. Each node contains a pointer to the next list node and a pointer to a data element. We must ensure that each node has a non-null data pointer; otherwise, the node is not valid. The data element could be a simple variable or a complex structure.

Notice how this list structure has a backbone of **ListNode** instances, and the actual data for each **ListNode** instance is a separate, dynamically allocated variable or structure, or even an array. This makes this implementation of a link list rather generic. We could replace our **ListData** with different data types and still use the same operations on the linked list. Using File Input and File Output, but the **ListData** will be a string instead of a structure.

Also, note that this is just one implementation of a singly-linked list. There are many variations of linked list implementations. Nonetheless, the operations on a linked list are fairly standard regardless of the details of the implementation.

Linked list structures

It should be no surprise given our diagram of a linked list in Figure 18.2 that we need two structures—a linked list header structure and a list node structure.

They are defined as follows:

typedef struct _Node ListNode; typedef struct _Node {   ListNode* pNext;

ListData* pData; } ListNode; typedef struct {   ListNode* pFirstNode;   int nodeCount; } LinkedList;

First, we define an arbitrary tag, **struct _Node**, as a **ListNode** structure. This is a naming mechanism so that we can use the name **ListNode** in the following structure definition with the members of **struct _Node**. The **struct _Node** tag contains a **ListNode** pointer and a **ListData** pointer, both of which will be known henceforth as simple **ListNode** custom types. We won't need to use **struct _Node** again. Our list will consist of zero or more **ListNode** structures.

Next, we define a heading for our linked list, **LinkedList**, which consists of a **ListNode** pointer and an **int** element to keep track of the number of elements in our list. Note that we don't need a temporary tag name after **struct**; this structure will only be known as **LinkedList**.

Note that the data portion of **ListNode** is a pointer to something called **ListData**. We will redefine **ListData** as an **int** element, as follows: typedef int ListData;

We're doing this so that we don't get bogged down in the unnecessary details of **ListData**. Later, when we complete and validate our linked list code, we will change **ListData** for our revised **carddeck.c** program so that it looks as follows:

typedef Card ListData;

This linked list code will work the same for pointers to **int**, as well as pointers to **Card**, or as a pointer to any other structure that we want our list to contain. This is the power (or confusion, depending on your perspective) of using **typedef**.

Declaring operations on a linked list

Now that we have the required data structures defined, we can declare operations on those data structures. A data structure is defined by both the data it contains or represents and the operations that can be performed on it. The operations we will need to perform in order to manipulate a general linked list mechanism independently of the specific data contents of the list are as follows:

Create a new **LinkedList** header that allocates and properly initializes the header record.

Create a new **ListNode** element that allocates and properly initializes the node element. Once created, the node still isn't part of the list.

Delete a node. This doesn't involve the list; typically, this will be done after a node is removed from the list.

Insert a node either into the front or back of the list.

Remove a node, either from the front or back of the list, and return that node to the caller.

Get the node from either the front or back of the list; this only observes the node data – it does not change the list in any way.

Determine whether the list is empty.

Determine the size of the list.

Print the list. This involves traversing the list and printing each node.

Print an individual node. This involves printing the **ListData** element of the node. The function to print **ListData** needs to be specific to the type of **ListData**. We will need a way to pass a **print** function as a parameter to this operation.

These operations lead to the following function prototypes:

```
LinkedList* CreateLinkedList();
bool IsEmpty(   LinkedList* pList );

int Size(LinkedList* pList );

void     InsertNodeToFront(LinkedList* pList , ListNode* pNode );

void     InsertNodeToBack(   LinkedList* pList , ListNode* pNode );

ListNode* RemoveNodeFromFront( LinkedList* pList );

ListNode* RemoveNodeFromBack( LinkedList* pList );

ListNode* GetNode(LinkedList* pList , int pos );

ListNode* CreateNode( ListData* pData );

void DeleteNode( ListNode* pNode );

void PrintList(  LinkedList* pList ,
```

```
         void (*printData)(ListData* pData ) ); void      PrintNode( ListNode* pNode ,
         void (*printData)(ListData* pData ) ); void      OutOfStorage( void );
```

As we go through the definitions of each of these operations, you may find it helpful to refer to the diagram of the linked list. Try to identify how each pointer in the list is manipulated in each function.

Here, we will add a **CreateData()** operation. It will be deferred to the final implementation where the specific **ListData** type is known. At that point, we'll also define the **printListData** function.

Notice the **OutOfStorage()** function. We don't know whether we'll ever need this function. We will need it if the **CreateXXX()** function fails to allocate memory.

It is generally a good practice to provide some feedback when a program fails, as follows:

```
void OutOfStorage (void)
{
  fprintf(stderr,"### FATAL RUNTIME ERROR ### No Memory Available" );
  exit( EXIT_FAILURE );
}
```

This is a simple function that does the following:

Prints an error message to a special output stream, **stderr**.

Exits the program with a non-zero exit value. The program exits immediately and no further program execution is done. Using File Input and File Output.

We can now see how each operation is defined.

A new **LinkedList** header can be created as follows:

```
LinkedList*  CreateLinkedList()
{
LinkedList* pLL = (LinkedList*) calloc( 1 , sizeof( LinkedList ) );
if( NULL == pLL ) OutOfStorage();
return pLL;
}
```

The **calloc()** function is used to allocate memory for the **LinkedList** header and initialize all the values in the structure to **0**; a pointer to that memory is returned unless **calloc()** fails, in which case, **OutOfStorage()** is called and the program stops.

The **IsEmpty()** and **Size()** functions are as follows:

```
bool  IsEmpty( LinkedList* pList )
{
```

```
return( 0 == pList->nodeCount );
}

int  Size( LinkedList* pList )
{
return pList->nodeCount;
}
```

The **IsEmpty()** utility function returns **true** if the list is empty, and **false** otherwise.

The **Size()** utility function simply returns the value of **nodeCount**. We use a function to get this value rather than access it directly because the structure of **LinkedList** may need to be changed. This approach encapsulates the size information, regardless of how it might be implemented later.

The next two functions define how a **ListNode** structure can be inserted into the list, as follows:

```
void  InsertNodeToFront( LinkedList* pList , ListNode* pNode )
{
ListNode* pNext   = pList->pFirstNode;
pList->pFirstNode = pNode;
pNode->pNext      = pNext;
pList->nodeCount++;
}
```

The following is the second function:

```
void InsertNodeToBack (LinkedList* pList , ListNode* pNode )
{
if( IsEmpty( pList ) )
{
pList->pFirstNode = pNode;
} else
{
ListNode* pCurr = pList->pFirstNode ;
while( NULL != pCurr->pNext )
{
pCurr = pCurr->pNext;
}

pCurr->pNext  = pNode;
}

pList->nodeCount++;

}
```

To insert a **ListNode** structure into the front of the list, we only need to adjust two pointers, **pList->pFirstNode** (saving it before we change it) and the new node's **pNode->pNext** pointer. If the list is empty, **pList>pFirstNode** will be **NULL** anyway, so this code properly handles all cases. Finally, the node count is incremented.

Let's see what inserting a new node at the front of the list looks like. The following diagram illustrates the list when this function is entered:

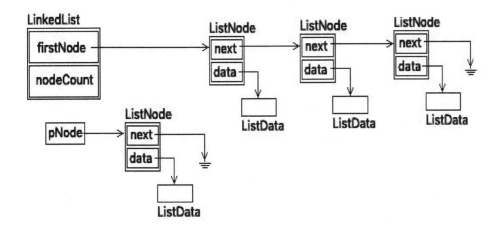

Figure – Linked list before inserting a new item at the front

After the two pointers have been adjusted, the list will look as follows:

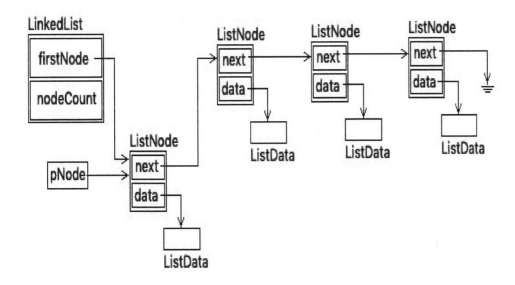

Figure – Linked list after inserting a new item at the front

Notice that the **pNode** pointer is no longer needed since **pList->pFirstNode** also points to the new node.

To insert a **ListNode** structure at the back of the list, we first have to see if the list is empty; if so, we only need to set **pList->pFirstNode**. Otherwise, we have to traverse the list to the last entry. This is done by first setting a temporary pointer, **pCurr**, to the first item in the list. When **pCurr->pNext** is **NULL**, then **pCurr** is pointing to the last item in the list. We only need to set **pCurr->pNext** to the new node; its **pNext** pointer is already **NULL**. Finally, the node count is incremented.

Now, let's see what inserting a new node at the back of the list looks like. The following diagram illustrates the list when this function is entered:

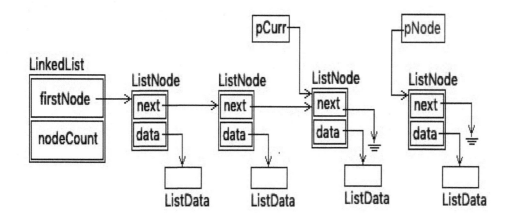

Figure – Linked list before inserting a new item at the back After the **next** final pointer is adjusted, the list will look as follows:

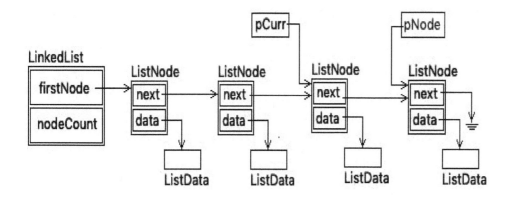

Figure – Linked list after inserting a new item at the back

Once **pCurr->next** points to our new node, both the **pCurr** and **pNode** pointers are no longer needed.

Like the **insert** functions, the next two functions define how a **ListNode** structure can be removed from the list, as follows:

```
ListNode*  RemoveNodeFromFront( LinkedList* pList )
{
if( IsEmpty( pList )) return NULL;
ListNode* pCurr   = pList->pFirstNode;
pList->pFirstNode = pList->pFirstNode->pNext;
pList->nodeCount--;
return pCurr;
}
```

The following is the second function:

```
ListNode* RemoveNodeFromBack(LinkedList* pList )
{   if( IsEmpty( pList ) )
```

```
{
return NULL;
} else
{
ListNode* pCurr = pList->pFirstNode ;
ListNode* pPrev = NULL;
while( NULL != pCurr->pNext )
{
pPrev = pCurr;
pCurr = pCurr->pNext;
}

pPrev->pNext = NULL;
pList->nodeCount--;
return pCurr;   }

}
```

To remove a **ListNode** structure from the front of the list, we need to check whether the list is empty and return **NULL** if it is. Otherwise, we set the node to be returned by **pCurr** to **pList->pFirstNode**, and then we set the next node after **pList->pFirstNode**, which is being pointed to by **pList->pFirstNode->pNext**, as the first node. The node count is decremented and returns **pCurr**.

Let's see what deleting a node from the front of the list looks like. The following diagram illustrates the list when this function is entered:

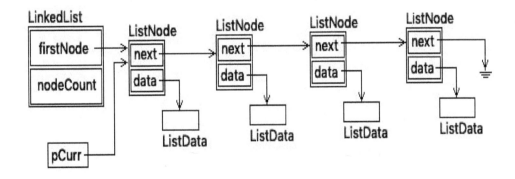

Figure – Linked list before removing list item from the front

Notice that **pCurr** also points to **pList->pFirstNode**. After the two pointers have been adjusted, the list will look as follows:

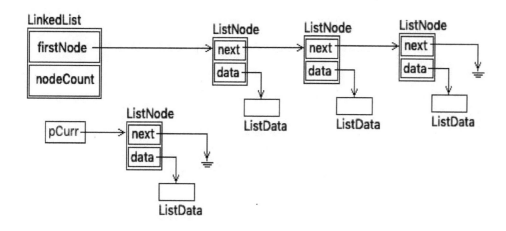

Figure – Linked list after removing list item from the front

Notice that **pCurr** is the only pointer pointing to the node to be deleted and that the first node in the list pointed to by **pList->pFirstNode** now points to the new first node.

To remove a **ListNode** item from the back of the list, we have to see if the list is empty; if so, we return **NULL**. Otherwise, we have to traverse the list to the last entry. This is done by setting a temporary pointer, **pCurr**, to the first item in the list. We need another temporary pointer, **pPrev**, which points to the node before the node we want to remove. Both are adjusted as the list is traversed. When **pCurr->pNext** is **NULL**, then **pCurr** is pointing to the last item in the list – the node we want to remove. But we also need to set **pPrev->pNext** to **NULL** to indicate it is the last item in the list. The node count is decremented and **pCurr** is returned.

Now, let's see what deleting a node from the back of the list looks like. The following diagram illustrates the list when this function is entered:

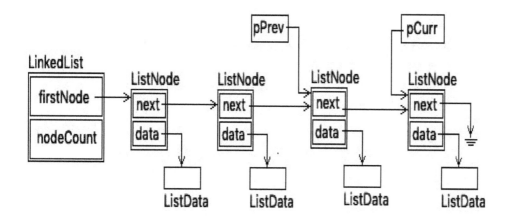

Figure – Linked list before removing list item from the back

After the final **next** pointer is adjusted, the list will look as follows:

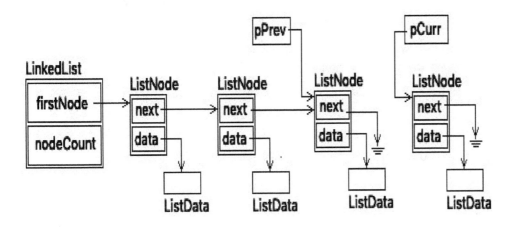

Figure – Linked list after removing list item from the back

Once **pCurr->next** points to our new node, the **pCurr** and **pNode** pointers are no longer needed.

The **GetNode()** function inspects a node's data without removing it from the list, as follows:

```
ListNode*  GetNode( LinkedList* pList , int pos )
{
ListNode* pCurr = pList->pFirstNode;
if( NULL == pCurr )
{
return pList->pFirstNode;
} else if ( pos == 0 )
{
return pList->pFirstNode;
} else
{
int i = 0;

while (NULL!= pCurr->pNext )
{
if( i == pos ) return pCurr;
i++;

pCurr = pCurr->pNext;
}
return pCurr;
}

}
```

Before traversing the list, **GetNode()** first checks to see whether the list is empty, and then checks to see whether the 0th position (a magic number indicating the front of the list) is requested. If so, the **pFirstNode** pointer is returned. Otherwise, the list is traversed, adjusting **pCurr** in order to check for both the end of the list and whether the current node count is the node we are looking for. This will be either a pointer to the node we are requesting or a pointer to the last node that was returned. The list remains unchanged.

The **CreateNode()** function simply creates a new node structure, as follows:

```
ListNode* CreateNode( ListData* pData )
{
ListNode* pNewNode = (ListNode*) calloc( 1 , sizeof( ListNode ) );
if( NULL == pNewNode ) OutOfStorage();
pNewNode->pData = pData;
return pNewNode;
}
```

The **calloc()** function is used to allocate memory for a **ListNode** structure and initialize all the values in it to **0**; a pointer to that memory is returned unless **calloc()** fails, in which case, **OutOfStorage()** is called and the program stops. Note that the linked list is not involved; this function only creates the node and correctly initializes it with the **ListData** pointer, which itself needs to have been created before we call this routine.

When items are removed from the list, they are not deleted until **DeleteNode()** is called, as follows:

```
void DeleteNode( ListNode* pNode )
{
free( pNode->pData );
free( pNode );
}
```

Notice that in order to prevent a subtle memory leak, **DeleteNode()** frees both the **ListData** structure (pointed to by **pNode->pData**) and the **ListNode** structure (pointed to by **pNode**).

To print the list, **PrintList()** is called, as follows:

```
void PrintList( LinkedList* pList , void (*printData)(ListData* pData ) )
{
printf( "List has %2d entries: [" , Size( pList ) );

ListNode* pCurr = pList->pFirstNode;

while( NULL != pCurr )
{
PrintNode( pCurr , printData );
pCurr = pCurr->pNext;
}

printf ("] \n");
}
```

The **PrintList()** function takes two parameters—the first should be familiar to you, while the second deserves some explanation. Recall from our memory layout diagram earlier in this chapter that a function is a named location in memory where program execution jumps to and returns back to the location it was called from. Most of the time, we've simply used the function name. In this case, we don't know the function name because the **ListData** type could change. The **print** function for **ListData** will need to change to reflect its actual type. Therefore, we need to pass a pointer to that function so that we can simply call it by using a pointer to it at some later time.

Pointers to functions

When we declare a pointer to a function, we need more than just the pointer value – we need to specify both the return type of the function and the parameter list of the function being pointed to.

Let's break this apparent syntactical gobbledygook down into understandable parts. It consists of three parts:

The return type of the function; in this case, **void**.

The name of the pointer to the function; in this case, **(*printData)**. This indicates that **printData** is the name pointer to a function; the function itself may have a completely different name. Given the first item, we know that the function returns **void**.

 The function we'll implement via this pointer to it has a parameter list, in this case, **(ListData* pData)**.

Given these three parts, compare the function pointer declaration to the function's prototype, in this case, **PrintInt()**: void (*printData)(ListData* pData); // function pointer void PrintInt(ListData* pData); // function prototype void PrintInt(ListData* pData) { // function definition ...

}

Notice how, except for the declaration of a function pointer, the other elements of a function call are present—the return type and the function parameter list. A function pointer cannot point to just any function. It must be declared with the same return type and parameter list as the function it will be used to call.

In the function body of **PrintList()**, we do not call the function using the function pointer named **printData**; instead, we pass that pointer value to the function that will call it, that is, **PrintNode()**.

To print the list, we print some information about the list and then iterate through it, updating the temporary pointer, **pCurr**, all while visiting each node in the list. At each iteration, **PrintNode()** is called with the current node pointer and the pointer to the function to print the data.

To print an individual node's data, **PrintNode()** is called, as follows:

```
void PrintNode( ListNode* pNode , void(*printData)( ListData* pData ) )
{
printData( pNode->pData );
}
```

The parameter list for **PrintNode()** consists of a pointer to a node and the same function pointer specification (you may still call this syntactical gobbledygook). But notice that here, in the function body, the **printData** pointer is used as if it were a function name (it's just a pointer) with the appropriate parameter list. We'll see the definition of **PrintInt()**, the function this will call, very shortly.

Now would be a good time to enter all of the function prototypes, the functions themselves, a dummy **main()** function, and the following **#include** files in **linkedlisttester.c** before going any further:

```
#include <stdio.h>        // for printf() and fprintf()
#include <stdlib.h>       // for calloc() and free()
#include <stdbool.h>      // for bool, true, false
```

Compile the program. You should receive no errors. This will serve as a simple checkpoint. Address any compiler errors. Most likely, they will be typos or omissions of simple things. Do not proceed until you get a clean compile.

More complex operations on a linked list

Our list provides a useful but minimal set of operations. It contains both stack and queue operations so that we can use it for either a stack or a queue, as needed. There are other list operations you might want to try to implement yourself.

Some of them might include the following function prototypes:

```
ListNode* InsertNodeAt( LinkedList* pList , ListNode* pNode );
ListNode* RemoveNodeAt( LinkedList* pList , ListNode* pNode );
void SortList ( LinkedList* pList , eSortOrder order );
void ConcatenateList( LinkedList* pList1 , LinkedList* pList2 );
```

We will not implement these functions right now. We will, however, implement some of them when we revisit our **carddeck.c** program.

A program to test our linked list structure

OK, so we implemented a linked list in C, or so we think. We wrote a lot of code that we compiled for errors as we wrote it; however, we can't know for certain until we test it. We need to test it thoroughly and get all the results we expect. The testing and verification part of programming is just as important— sometimes even more important— than just writing code that compiles. Writing and verifying the code you write distinguishes a novice programmer from an expert.

Before we can continue, we need two functions specific to our **ListData** type. The first is as follows:

```
void PrintInt( int* i )
{
printf( "%2d ", *i );
}
```

The second is as follows:

```
ListData* CreateData( ListData d )
{
```

```
ListData* pD = (ListData*)calloc( 1 , sizeof( ListData ) );
if( pD == NULL )  OutOfStorage();   *pD = d;
return pD;
}
```

The **PrintInt()** function simply prints the integer value passed to it by calling **printf()**. If we were to use a different **ListData** type, we would need to provide an appropriate **PrintData()** routine for it. We'll see how this function is called in **main()** with the **PrintList()** function calls.

The **CreateData()** function calls **calloc()** to allocate memory for a **ListData** structure and initializes all the values in the structure to **0**; a pointer to that memory is returned unless **calloc()** fails, in which case, **OutOfStorage()** is called and the program stops. This function will be used in our test functions to exercise our linked list. By creating a **ListData** structure and putting data into it, we can then insert this data element into our list as needed.

To facilitate testing, we will first declare the following enumerated values:

```
typedef enum  {  eFront = 0 ,  eBack } eWhere;
typedef enum  {  eLook = 0 ,  eInsert ,  eDelete }
eAction;
```

We can now start with the **main()** function and work backward. The test code in **main()** is as follows:

```
int main( void )

{
LinkedList* pLL = CreateLinkedList();

printf( "Input or operation          "         "Current state of linked list\n"

       "========================== "
"====================================="); printf( "\nUsing input{ 1  2  3  4 } " );
PrintList( pLL , PrintInt );
int data1[] = { 1 , 2 , 3 , 4 };
for( int i = 0 ; i < 4 ; i++) {
TestPrintOperation( pLL , eInsert , data1[i] , eFront );

}
TestPrintOperation( pLL , eLook  , 0  , eFront );
TestPrintOperation( pLL , eDelete , 0  , eBack );
printf( "\nUsing input{ 31 32 33 }   " );
PrintList( pLL , PrintInt );
int data2[] = { 31 , 32 , 33 };
for( int i = 0 ; i < 3 ; i++)
{
TestPrintOperation( pLL , eInsert , data2[i] , eBack );

}
TestPrintOperation (pLL, eLook, 0, eBack );
```

```
int count = pLL->nodeCount;
for( int i = 0 ; i < count ; i++)
{
TestPrintOperation( pLL , eDelete, 0 , eFront );

}

}
```

In **main()**, we are exercising all of the features of our linked list. This test consists of the following operations:

Create a new linked list.

Print it out, showing that it is empty.

Insert four nodes, each into the front of the list. Each time a node is inserted, the action is described and the current list is printed.

Look at the first node.

Delete a node from the back. Each time a node is inserted, the action is described and the current list is printed.

Insert three nodes, each into the back of it.

Look at the last node.

Delete each node from the front of the list until it is empty. Each time a node is deleted, the action is described and the current list is printed.

At each operation, we print some information about what happened and the current state of the list. Most of the test work occurs in **TestPrintOperation()**, as follows:

```
void TestPrintOperation( LinkedList* pLL , eAction action , ListData data   , eWhere  where )
{
switch( action ) {
case eLook:

data = TestExamineNode( pLL , where );
printf( "Get %s node, see [%2d]. " , where==eFront ? "front" : " back" , data );
break;
case eInsert:

printf( "Insert [%2d] to %s.    ", data , where==eFront ? "front" : " back" );
TestCreateNodeAndInsert( pLL , data , where );
break;
case eDelete:

data = TestRemoveNodeAndFree( pLL , where );
printf( "Remove [%2d] from %s.  " , data , where==eFront ? "front" : " back" );
break;
default:
printf( "::ERROR:: unknown action\n" );
break;

}
```

```
PrintList( pLL , TestPrintInt );

}
```

For testing purposes, some enumerations are defined, that is, **eAction { eLook , eInsert, eDelete }** and **eWhere {eFront , eBack }**, to enable a central test routine, **TestPrintOperation()**, to be called. For each possible **eAction**, we use a switch to print information about the action, as well as call either **TestExamineNode()**,

TestCreateNodeAndInsert(), or **TestRemoveNodeAndFree()**.

Before returning, the current list is printed for inspection. Three action functions are implemented. The first is as follows:

```
void TestCreateNodeAndInsert( LinkedList* pLL , ListData data , eWhere where )

{
ListData* pData = CreateData( data );
ListNode* pNode = CreateNode( pData );
switch( where )
{

case eFront:
InsertNodeToFront( pLL , pNode );
break;
case eBack:
InsertNodeToBack( pLL , pNode );
break;
}

}
```

The second is as follows:

```
ListData TestExamineNode( LinkedList* pLL , eWhere where )
{
ListNode * pNode;
switch( where )
{
case eFront: pNode = GetNode( pLL , 0 );
break;
case eBack:
pNode = GetNode( pLL , pLL->nodeCount ); break;
}
ListData data = *(pNode->pData);
return data;
}
```

The third is as follows:

```
ListData TestRemoveNodeAndFree( LinkedList* pLL , eWhere where )
{
ListNode * pNode;
switch( where ) {
case eFront:
pNode = RemoveNodeFromFront( pLL );
break;
case eBack:
pNode = RemoveNodeFromBack( pLL );
break;
}

ListData data = *(pNode->pData);
DeleteNode( pNode );
return data;
}
```

Enter each of these test routines after all of the linked list code but before **main()**. Then, enter the **main()** routine. Save the file and then compile and run this program. Because there is quite a bit of code, you may have to edit and compile your version several times until you get a clean compilation.

When you run the program, you should see the following output:

```
> cc linkedlisttester.c -o linkedlisttester -Wall -Werror -std=c17
> ./linkedlisttester
Input or operation        Current state of linked list
========================  ===================================
Using input{ 1  2  3  4 }. List has  0 entries: []
Insert [ 1] to front.     List has  1 entries: [ 1 ]
Insert [ 2] to front.     List has  2 entries: [ 2  1 ]
Insert [ 3] to front.     List has  3 entries: [ 3  2  1 ]
Insert [ 4] to front.     List has  4 entries: [ 4  3  2  1 ]
Get front node, see [ 4]. List has  4 entries: [ 4  3  2  1 ]
Remove [ 1] from  back.   List has  3 entries: [ 4  3  2 ]

Using input{ 31 32 33 }.  List has  3 entries: [ 4  3  2 ]
Insert [31] to  back.     List has  4 entries: [ 4  3  2 31 ]
Insert [32] to  back.     List has  5 entries: [ 4  3  2 31 32 ]
Insert [33] to  back.     List has  6 entries: [ 4  3  2 31 32 33 ]
Get  back node, see [33]. List has  6 entries: [ 4  3  2 31 32 33 ]
Remove [ 4] from front.   List has  5 entries: [ 3  2 31 32 33 ]
Remove [ 3] from front.   List has  4 entries: [ 2 31 32 33 ]
Remove [ 2] from front.   List has  3 entries: [31 32 33 ]
Remove [31] from front.   List has  2 entries: [32 33 ]
Remove [32] from front.   List has  1 entries: [33 ]
Remove [33] from front.   List has  0 entries: []
>
```

Figure – Screenshot of the linkedlisttester.c output

Notice how each line of the program corresponds to the test outline given previously. Carefully compare the action taken to the impact resulting in the state of the list. When this validation passes, we can feel confident in using this code in other, more useful scenarios.

You may have noticed that writing test code is nearly as much work as writing the code itself. This is very often the case. Writing concise, complete, and correct test code is hard. From my years of experience, I would argue that writing such test code is as worthwhile as writing the code, for several reasons:

When your tests fail, you invariably learn something.

You gain a very high level of confidence that the body of code works as intended.

You can make changes to the code and verify that the code still works as expected.

There tends to be much less reworking and debugging with tested code.

Often, as a professional programmer, you may be pushed and cajoled to omit testing. Don't do it, largely for the reasons given here, as well as to preserve your own sanity.

Other dynamic data structures

In this chapter, we have created a program that implements a singly-linked list where we can add and remove list elements, or list nodes, from the front or back of the list. This is a fairly general, minimal list implementation that leaves out a few other possibly useful operations, such as **listConcatenate()** to join two lists, **listSplit()** to break a list into two given criteria, **listSort()** to order the elements of the list in various ways, and **listReverse()** to reverse the elements of a list. We may also want to enhance our **insert** and **remove** operations so that we can add and remove nodes from anywhere in the list. Because of space limitations, we will not do so here.

The following is a brief, annotated list of other useful, possibly mind-bending, data structures:

● **Doubly-linked list**: A linked list that contains not only a single pointer to the next list node, but also another pointer that points to the preceding list node. The list may be traversed easily from front to back, as well as from back to front.

● **Stack**: A linked list where each list node is added only to the front of the list (pushed onto the stack). Subsequently, each list node is only removed from the front of the list (popped off the stack). This is also known as a **Last In First Out (LIFO)** list.

● **Queue**: A linked list where each list node is added only to the back of the list (enqueued). Subsequently, each list node is only removed from the front of the list (dequeued). This is also known as a **First In First Out (FIFO)** list.

● **Deque**: A generalized list that combines the properties of both a stack and a queue. Elements can be added or removed from anywhere in the list. Our implementation of a linked list is very close to that of a deque.

● **Priority queue**: A list where each list node also has a given priority. List nodes are added to the list in order of priority and removed from the list according to a priority scheduling scheme.

● **Set**: A collection of unique elements, in no particular order. Sometimes, they are implemented using other dynamic data structures, such as trees or hash tables.

- **Map**: A collection of key-value pairs, where the key is unique and is used to look up a value associated with that key. This can also be called an associative array, symbol table, or dictionary.

- **Tree**: A tree simulates a hierarchical tree structure, with a single root node from which child nodes form branches. Like branches in a real tree, child nodes can only contain sub children and cannot be linked to other branches.

- **Graph**: A collection of nodes connected via links. A graph is more of a general form of a tree in that it may have cycles (where a node from one branch may link to the root or a node in another branch).

Studying these data structures and implementing them yourself is beyond the scope of this book. However, such a study would be extremely worthwhile and should be one of the next steps in your journey to becoming an expert C programmer.

Conclusion:

Memory management in C is not only foundational for understanding how programs interact with computer memory but also essential for writing robust, efficient, and safe software. With C's manual approach to memory handling, developers gain a powerful advantage in control but must exercise caution to avoid common pitfalls like memory leaks, dangling pointers, and buffer overflows.

Recap of Memory Management Concepts

Understanding Memory Segments:

C programs use four primary memory segments: code, data, stack, and heap. This segmentation helps efficiently organize memory, especially with large programs or those that require substantial resources. Each segment serves a distinct purpose, with the heap being particularly critical due to its role in dynamic memory allocation.

Heap and Stack Comparison: The stack, which manages local variables and function calls, benefits from its automatic memory management, where memory is automatically freed after use. The heap, in contrast, demands manual memory handling to ensure that memory is allocated only when necessary and released when no longer in use.

Static vs. Dynamic Allocation:

Static memory allocation, often used for small and predictable data structures, contrasts with dynamic allocation, which allows for flexible memory usage at runtime. Understanding the trade-offs between these two methods (predictability vs. flexibility) is essential for writing scalable programs.

Pros and Cons Revisited: Static allocation is simple and safe, but it may not efficiently use memory. Dynamic memory allocation provides flexibility but also introduces risk and requires responsible handling to avoid memory waste or program instability.

Core Memory Allocation Functions:

The functions malloc, calloc, realloc, and free provide essential tools for dynamic memory handling in C. Each function serves a unique purpose, from basic memory allocation (malloc) to zero-initialization (calloc) and resizing (realloc).

Using malloc, calloc, and realloc Safely: It's crucial to check the return values of these functions for NULL, indicating that memory could not be allocated. Additionally, setting pointers to NULL after freeing memory prevents accidental reuse, which is a best practice for avoiding segmentation faults.

Common Memory Issues:

The three main categories of memory errors are memory leaks, dangling pointers, and buffer overflows. These issues not only lead to performance degradation and increased memory consumption but also create vulnerabilities that can compromise program security.

Avoiding Memory Leaks: Memory leaks occur when memory is allocated but not freed. These leaks may accumulate over time, eventually exhausting the system's available memory. Best practices to avoid leaks include pairing every malloc or calloc with a corresponding free, maintaining consistent memory allocation patterns, and avoiding reassigning pointers before freeing their memory.

Using Tools Like Valgrind for Effective Debugging:

Valgrind is invaluable for debugging complex memory issues, as it checks for memory leaks, invalid accesses, and more. By running a C program through Valgrind, developers gain a clear view of how memory is used, where it's misused, and any areas for improvement.

Benefits of Memory Management Tools: Valgrind is complemented by tools like AddressSanitizer and Dr. Memory, which help in identifying common memory issues and ensuring that programs run efficiently and securely. These tools give immediate feedback on memory-related errors, which can be difficult to trace manually.

Best Practices for Memory Management

Consistent Allocation and Deallocation:

Consistency in memory management is essential. Developing a pattern or habit of always freeing memory within the same scope or module where it was allocated can prevent accidental memory leaks.

Modularize Memory Allocation and Deallocation: For complex programs, it's helpful to create dedicated functions for memory allocation and deallocation. This modular approach simplifies memory management, reduces redundancy, and clarifies where each block of memory is allocated and freed.

NULL Check After Allocation:

Always check if malloc, calloc, or realloc returned NULL before using the pointer, as memory allocation can fail, particularly in environments with limited memory or high demands on resources.

NULL After Freeing: After freeing memory, setting the pointer to NULL is a defensive programming technique that helps prevent dangling pointers, reducing the chance of segmentation faults or unpredictable behavior.

Avoiding Double-Free and Invalid Free:

Freeing memory more than once, known as double-freeing, can destabilize a program. Similarly, freeing memory that was not dynamically allocated or has already been freed (invalid free) can lead to memory corruption.

Reference Tracking: For complex applications, consider maintaining a list or structure to track dynamically allocated memory blocks. This practice can help prevent accidental double-freeing or invalid access.

Avoid Buffer Overflows:

Writing beyond the bounds of allocated memory is a common but dangerous error. Buffer overflows can cause crashes, data corruption, or even security vulnerabilities.

Bounds Checking: Always check array and pointer bounds before accessing memory, especially when working with user input or large data structures.

Regular Use of Debugging Tools:

Tools like Valgrind should be an integral part of the development process, especially when finalizing or optimizing a program. Routine checks for memory leaks and validation errors can catch issues early, before they become critical.

Build Configurations for Testing: Use debug builds with additional flags for memory error detection during development. These settings can be turned off in the production build to reduce overhead.

The Bigger Picture: The Importance of Memory Management

C's power comes with the responsibility of managing memory manually. Unlike high-level languages that handle memory automatically, C leaves the details to the developer. This low-level memory access enables efficient programming and fine-tuned performance, which is why C remains widely used in system-level and performance-critical applications like operating systems, embedded systems, and real-time processing.

1. Efficiency: Effective memory management leads to efficient programs. Proper memory usage reduces system load, speeds up program execution, and ensures that resources are available for other processes. This efficiency is critical in systems with limited memory or those requiring high performance.

2. Stability: Memory leaks and errors cause crashes and unexpected behavior, which could be catastrophic in applications like aerospace, healthcare, or finance. Ensuring memory stability in these fields is essential to maintain reliability, making memory management a priority for safety-critical applications.

3. Security: Poor memory management often leads to vulnerabilities, which malicious users can exploit. Buffer overflows and use-after-free errors are common attack vectors for gaining unauthorized access or executing arbitrary code. By managing memory carefully, developers can create secure programs resilient to such attacks.

In conclusion, mastering memory management in C is about balancing control with responsibility. It requires vigilance, consistent habits, and effective use of tools to ensure that memory is allocated efficiently, used effectively, and released responsibly. While it may seem daunting, especially for beginners, the discipline of memory management builds a deeper understanding of computer architecture and software efficiency that is invaluable to any developer.

By following the principles and practices discussed, developers can not only avoid common errors but also harness the full power of C to write fast, stable, and secure software. As new tools and techniques emerge, the fundamentals of memory management will remain central to reliable C programming, reinforcing C's role in building the systems that underpin modern computing.

11. Standard Library in C

1. Introduction to the C Standard Library

The C Standard Library is a collection of pre-written code that provides essential functions, helping programmers avoid writing code from scratch for basic tasks. These libraries simplify tasks such as input/output operations, string handling, memory management, and math operations, improving efficiency and readability. Key headers like stdio.h, stdlib.h, string.h, and math.h are indispensable for most C programs.

2. stdio.h - Standard Input/Output Functions

The stdio.h library provides tools for handling input and output, both for terminal interaction and file management.

Important Functions

printf: Outputs formatted data to the console. It uses format specifiers like %d (for integers), %f (for floating-point numbers), %c (for characters), and %s (for strings) to format different data types.

For example:

```
int num = 5;
printf("The number is %d\n", num); // Output: The number is 5
```

scanf: Reads formatted input from standard input (keyboard). Like printf, it uses format specifiers and requires the address of the variables (using &) where the input should be stored.

```
int age;
printf("Enter your age: ");
scanf("%d", &age);
```

File I/O:

fopen and fclose: Used to open and close files. fopen takes a file name and mode ("r" for read, "w" for write, etc.) and returns a FILE pointer.

```
FILE *file = fopen("example.txt", "w");
if (file == NULL) {
  perror("Error opening file");
}
```

fprintf and fscanf: These functions work like printf and scanf but operate on files.

fgets and fputs: For reading and writing strings to files. fgets is safer than gets for reading strings as it prevents buffer overflow by limiting the number of characters read.

3. stdlib.h - General Utilities

The stdlib.h library provides functions for memory allocation, process control, and data conversions.

Memory Management

malloc, calloc, realloc, free:

malloc allocates a specified number of bytes and returns a pointer to the allocated memory, but does not initialize the memory.

calloc allocates and initializes the memory to zero, making it safer for certain use cases.

realloc resizes previously allocated memory.

free deallocates memory previously allocated by malloc, calloc, or realloc, preventing memory leaks.

```
int *arr = (int*)malloc(10 * sizeof(int));
if (arr == NULL) {
  perror("Memory allocation failed");
}
free(arr);
```

Conversion Functions

atoi, atof, strtol, strtod: These functions convert strings to integers, floating-point numbers, and other types. For instance, atoi converts a string to an integer, while strtol provides more flexibility, including error handling.

```
char str[] = "1234";
int num = atoi(str);
```

Process Control

exit, abort, system: exit terminates the program and can return a status code. system allows executing system commands, which is powerful but can introduce security risks, so it should be used with caution.

Random Number Generation

rand and srand: rand generate pseudo-random numbers, typically seeded by srand to produce a different sequence each run.

```
srand(time(NULL));  // Seed the random number generator
int randomNum = rand() % 100;  // Random number between 0 and 99
```

4. string.h - String Manipulation

string.h provides functions for string operations, crucial for text handling in C.

Important Functions

String Manipulation:

strcpy and strncpy: Copy strings. strncpy is safer, allowing you to specify the number of characters to copy.

```
char dest[10];
strncpy(dest, "Hello", sizeof(dest) - 1);
```

String Comparison:

strcmp and strncmp: Compare strings lexicographically.

```
if (strcmp("apple", "banana") < 0) {
  printf("Apple comes before banana");
}
```

String Length and Search:

strlen returns the length of a string, excluding the null character.
strchr and strstr: Locate a character or substring within a string.

5. math.h - Mathematical Functions

The math.h library provides a variety of mathematical functions for scientific and engineering applications.

Common Functions

Basic Arithmetic:

pow and sqrt: Compute powers and square roots.

```
double root = sqrt(25.0);  // 5.0
```

Trigonometry:

sin, cos, tan: Calculate sine, cosine, and tangent for radian angles.

```
double angle = M_PI / 4;
double result = sin(angle);  // 0.7071
```

Logarithmic and Exponential Functions:

log (natural log), exp (exponentiation): Useful for scientific calculations.

Rounding and Remainder: ceil and floor round up or down, and fmod finds the remainder of division.

6. Error Handling in C Standard Library

Error handling in C requires checking return values and using specific error-handling functions.

Key Functions

errno: A global variable set by some functions when an error occurs.

perror: Prints an error message based on the current errno value.

strerror: Returns a string representation of an error code.

```
FILE *file = fopen("nonexistent.txt", "r");
if (file == NULL) {
  perror("File open error");
}
```

7. Random Number Generation in C

Random numbers are useful in simulations, games, and testing. The C library provides rand for generating pseudo-random numbers.

Usage

Seeding with srand: srand(time(NULL)) seeds the generator to get different results each time.

Generating Numbers in a Range:

```
int randomNum = rand() % 100;  // Between 0 and 99
```

Let's Start

The C compiler is accompanied by a number of useful functions and macros called the C standard library. These functions are defined in standard-library header files. To use the C standard-library functions, we simply include the appropriate header into our program.

Here are some of the C standard-library headers:

Available in all C standards:

<assert.h>	Assertion macros
<ctype.h>	Utils for individual characters
<errno.h>	Macros reporting error conditions
<float.h>	Floating type limits
<limits.h>	Sizes of basic types
<locale.h>	Localization utils
<math.h>	Math functions
<setjmp.h>	Jumps
<signal.h>	Signal functions
<stdarg.h>	Variable arguments
<stddef.h>	Common macros
<stdio.h>	Input and output functions
<stdlib.h>	General utilities for memory, string and program flow
<string.h>	String manipulation functions
<time.h>	Time and date
<wchar.h>	Multibyte and wide characters utilities
<wctype.h>	Wide character types
<iso646.h>	Macros for alternative operator spellings

Available   since   C99:

<complex.h> Complex number arithmetic

<fenv.h> Floating-point environment

<inttypes.h> Format conversion of integer types

<stdbool.h> Type bool

<stdint.h>   Fixed-width integer types
<tgmath.h>   Generic math and complex macros

Available   since   C11:

<threads.h> Thread library

<stdalign.h> alignas and alignof macros

<stdatomic.h> Atomic types

<stdnoreturn.h> noreturn macros

<uchar.h>UTF-16 and UTF-32 utils

The following sections describe some of the most used functions inside the library.

String Manipulation

Here we describe a couple of useful functions we use to manipulate our character arrays (strings).

Strlen

The strlen function returns the number of characters inside a null-terminated character array, excluding the null-terminating character.

The function is of the following signature:

sizet_t strlen (const char* str);

To use this function, we include the <string.h> header and supply a character array as an argument.

Example:
```
#include <stdio.h>
#include <string.h>

int main(void)
{
const char str[] = "How many characters here?";
size_t myStrLength = strlen(str);

printf("The string contains %zu characters.\n", myStrLength);
}
```

Output:

The string contains 25 characters.

We could rewrite the above example to use a const char *p pointer to a character string:

```
#include <stdio.h>
#include <string.h>
int main(void)
```

```c
{
const char *p = "How many characters here?";
size_t myStrLength = strlen(p);
printf("The string contains %zu characters.\n", myStrLength);
}
```

Output:

The string contains 25 characters.

Strcmp

The strcmp function compares two strings. If strings are equal, the function returns the value of 0. If strings are not equal, the function returns a value of either < 0 or > 0. The function compares strings one character at a time. When a character from the left-hand string does not match the character from the right-hand-side string, the function can either:

Return a value less than 0 if unmatched left-hand side character comes before the right-hand side character in lexicographical order

Return a value greater than 0 if unmatched left-hand side character comes after the right-hand side character in lexicographical order

For the most part, we will be checking if two strings are equal. Example:

```c
#include <stdio.h>
#include <string.h>
int main(void)
{
const char *str1 = "Hello World!";
const char *str2 = "Hello World!";
if (strcmp(str1, str2) == 0)
    {
        printf("The strings are equal.\n");
    }else
    {
        printf("The strings are not equal.\n");
    }
}
```

Output:

The strings are equal.

Strcat

The strcat function concatenates two strings. It appends the source_str string to the destination_str string. The function is of the following signature:

char *strcat(char *destination_str, const char *source_str);

To concatenate two strings, we write:

```
#include <stdio.h>
#include <string.h>
int main(void)
{
char destination_str[30] = "Hello ";
char source_str[30] = "World!";
strcat(destination_str, source_str);
printf("The concatenated string is: %s\n", destination_str);

}
```

Output:

The concatenated string is: Hello World!

The destination string array must be large enough to accept the concatenated string.

strcpy

The strcpy function copies one string to another. It copies the characters from the source_str string to the destination_str string. The function signature is:

char *strcpy(char *destination_str, const char *source_str);

To copy one string to another, we write:

```
#include <stdio.h>
#include <string.h>
int main(void)
{
char destination_str[30];
char source_str[30] = "Hello World!";
strcpy(destination_str, source_str);
printf("The copied string is: %s\n", destination_str);

}
```

Output:

The copied string is: Hello World!

The destination array must be large enough to accommodate the copied characters, including the (invisible) null terminating character.

Strstr

The strstr function searches for a substring inside a string. It returns the first position at which the substring is found. The function is of the following signature:

char *strstr(const char* string, const char* substring);

To search for a substring within a string, we write:

```
#include <stdio.h>

#include <string.h>

int main(void)

{

char myString[] = "Hello World!";

char mySubstring[] = "World";

    if (strstr(myString, mySubstring))

    {

        printf("Substring found.\n");

    }else

    {

        printf("Substring not found.\n");

    }

}
```

Output:

Substring found.

To print out the position at which the substring was found, we subtract the original string's address from the strstr's function return value as in posFound - myString. Remember, array names get converted to pointers when used as function arguments.

Subtracting pointers gives us a position of a substring:

```
#include <stdio.h>

#include <string.h>

int main(void)

{

char myString[] = "Hello World!";

char mySubstring[] = "World";
```

```c
char *posFound = strstr(myString, mySubstring);
if (posFound)
    {
        printf("Substring found at position: %ld.\n", posFound myString);
    }else
    {
        printf("Substring not found.\n");
    }
}
```

Output:

Substring found at position: 6.

Memory Manipulation Functions

The C standard library provides several functions that allow us to work with bytes inside memory blocks. For example, these functions allow us to set the values of the entire memory block, copy bytes from one memory block to another, compare memory blocks, and more. Note that type unsigned char can be used to represent a single byte.

Memset

The memory obtained through malloc is not initialized. The allocated memory blocks hold no meaningful values. Trying to read uninitialized memory will result in undefined behavior. Earlier, we have used the calloc function to allocate and initialize the memory blocks to zero.

Another way to initialize the memory is through a memset function declared inside the <string.h> header file. The function has the following signature:

```c
void *memset(void *destination, int value, size_t N);
```

The function accepts a pointer to allocated memory here called destination, the value to fill the allocated bytes, and the memory block's size in bytes, here named N.

To allocate space for five integers and then fill the entire memory block/all the bytes in the allocated memory with zeros, we write:

```c
#include <stdio.h>
#include <stdlib.h>
#include <string.h>

int main(void)
{
    int *p = malloc(5 * sizeof(int));
if (p)
    {
```

```
        memset(p, 0, 5 * sizeof(int));
for (int i = 0; i < 5; i++)
        {
                printf("%d ", p[i]);
        }
    }
free(p);

}
```

Output:

0 0 0 0 0

Memcpy

The memcpy function copies N bytes/characters from a memory location/block pointed to by source, to a memory area pointed to by destination. The function is of the following signature:

void* memcpy(void *destination, const void *source, size_t N);

The function interprets memory bytes as unsigned char. The function is defined inside the

<string.h> header. For example, to copy 5 bytes from one string array to another string array, we write:

```
#include <stdio.h>
#include <string.h>
int main(void)
{
char source[] = "Hello World.";
char destination[5];
memcpy(destination, source, sizeof destination);
printf("The source is: %s\n", source);
printf("The destination after copying 5 characters is:\n");      // write a character, one by
one using putchar() function
for (size_t i = 0; i < sizeof destination; i++)
    {
        putchar(destination[i]);
    }
}
```

Output:

The source is: Hello World.

The destination after copying 5 characters is:

Hello

This example copies five characters from a source array to a destination array and uses the putchar() function to print out the destination characters one by one.

To copy an array of elements into a dynamically allocated memory block, we write:

```c
#include <stdio.h>
#include <stdlib.h>
#include <string.h>

int main(void)

{
int myArr[] = {10, 20, 30, 40, 50}; // allocate space for 5 integers
int *p = malloc(5 * sizeof(int)); // copy bytes from an array to an allocated space
memcpy(p, myArr, 5 * sizeof(int));

printf("Copied bytes from an array to an allocated space. The values are:\n");

    for (int i = 0; i < 5; i++)

    {

        printf("%d ", p[i]);

    }
free(p);

}
```

Output:

Copied bytes from an array to an allocated space. The values are:

10 20 30 40 50

To copy a struct data object into another struct object, we write:

```c
#include <stdio.h>

#include <string.h>

typedef struct

{
char c;      int x;
double d; } MyStruct;

int main(void)

{
MyStruct source, destination;

source.c = 'a'; source.x = 123; source.d = 456.789;

memcpy(&destination, &source, sizeof(destination));

printf("The result after copying bytes from source to destination:\n");
printf("Member destination.c has a value of: %c\n", destination.c);
```

```
printf("Member destination.x has a value of: %d\n", destination.x);
printf("Member destination.d has a value of: %f\n", destination.d);
}
```

Output:

The result after copying bytes from source to destination:

Member destination.c has a value of: a

Member destination.x has a value of: 123

Member destination.d has a value of: 456.789000

Here, we declared two variables of type MyStruct, called source and destination. We populate the data of the source struct and then copy individual bytes of source into destination using memcpy function. Since the memcpy function accepts pointers, we use our structs' addresses: &destination and &source. Now both structs have identical data.

Memcmp

The memcmp function compares the first N bytes from the memory block pointed by p1 to the first N bytes pointed to by p2. The function returns 0 if the byte values match.

The function has the following signature:

```
int memcmp( const void* p1, const void* p2, size_t N );
```

To compare two arrays byte by byte using memcmp, we write:

```
#include <stdio.h>
#include <string.h>
int main(void)
{
int arr1[] = {10, 20, 30, 40, 50};
int arr2[] = {10, 20, 20, 40, 50};
int myResult = memcmp(arr1, arr2, 5 * sizeof(int));
if (myResult == 0)
    {
        printf("The arrays values match.\n");
    }else
    {
        printf("The arrays values do not match.\n");
    }
}
```

Output:

The arrays values do not match.

This example compares the individual bytes of arr1 and arr2. It compares the first 20 bytes of both arrays. Remember, the size of int is 4, times 5 elements, equals 20 bytes in total, the number calculated using the 5 * sizeof(int) expression. Since the arrays are not equal, the function returns a value other than 0.

If the bytes do not match, the memcmp function can return one of the following: a.

<0, if the first byte that does not match has a lower value in p1 than in p2 b.

>0, if the first byte that does not match has a higher value in p1 than in p2

The memcmp function is a convenient way to compare two data objects in memory, byte by byte.

Memchr

The memchr function searches for a particular byte c in the initial N characters within a memory block pointed to by p. The function is declared inside the <string.h> header and is of the following signature:

void* memchr(const void* p, int c, size_t N);

The function searches for the first occurrence of c, and if the byte/char is found, the function returns a pointer to the location of c. If the byte value is not found, the function returns a NULL. Internally, the c byte is interpreted as unsigned char. The following example searches for a byte with a value of 'W' inside a "Hello World!" character array:

```
#include <stdio.h>
#include <string.h>
int main(void)
{
    char mystr[] = "Hello World!";
    char *pfound = memchr(mystr, 'W', strlen(mystr)); if (pfound != NULL)
    {
        printf("Character/byte found at: %s\n", pfound);
    }else
    {
        printf("Character/byte not found: %s\n", pfound);
    }
}
```

Output:

Character/byte found at: World!

Mathematical Functions

The C standard library provides a set of useful mathematical functions. The functions are defined inside different header files. Here we discuss some of the most widely used ones.

abs

The abs function returns an absolute value of an integer argument. The function is defined inside the <stdlib.h> header.

Example:

```
#include <stdlib.h>

#include <stdio.h>

int main(void)

{
    int x = -123; int y = 456;

    printf("The absolute value of x is: %d\n", abs(x));
    printf("The absolute value of y is: %d\n", abs(y));
}
```

Output:

The absolute value of x is: 123

The absolute value of y is: 456

There are also labs and labs functions that return absolute values of long and long long arguments, respectively.

Fabs

The fabs function returns an absolute value of a double argument. The function is defined inside the <math.h> header.

Example:

```
#include <math.h>

#include <stdio.h>

int main(void)

{
    double x = -123.456; double y = 789.101;

    printf("The absolute value of x is: %f\n", fabs(x));
    printf("The absolute value of y is: %f\n", fabs(y));
}
```

Output:

The absolute value of x is: 123.456000

The absolute value of y is: 789.101000

There are also fabsf and fabsl versions that return absolute values of float and long double arguments, respectively.

Pow

The pow function returns the value of base raised to the power of the exponent. The function has the following syntax:

double pow(double base, double exponent);

The function is declared inside the <math.h> header file. Example:

```
#include <math.h>
#include <stdio.h>

int main(void)
{
    printf("The value of 2 to the power of 10 is: %f\n", pow(2, 10));
    printf("The value of 2 to the power of 20 is: %f\n", pow(2, 20));
}
```

Output:

The value of 2 to the power of 10 is: 1024.000000

The value of 2 to the power of 20 is: 1048576.000000

There are also powf and powl variants that accept float and long double arguments.

Round

The round returns the result of rounding the floating-point argument to the nearest integer, rounding halfway away from 0. The function is declared inside the <math.h> header file and has the following syntax:

double round(double argument);

Example:

```
#include <stdio.h>
#include <math.h>

int main(void)
{
    double d = 1.5;
    printf("The result of rounding the %f is: %f\n", d, round(d)); d = 1.49;
    printf("The result of rounding the %f is: %f\n", d, round(d)); }
```

Output:

The result of rounding the 1.500000 is: 2.000000

The result of rounding the 1.490000 is: 1.000000

To run this example on Linux, we also need to link with the math library by supplying the -lm flag to our compilation string.

There are also roundf and roundl versions that accept float and long double arguments.

To have a rounding function that will return an integral type, we use the lround function.

Example:

```
#include <stdio.h>
#include <math.h>

int main(void)
{
    double d = 1.5;
    printf("The result of rounding the %f is: %ld\n", d, lround(d));
d = 1.49;
    printf("The result of rounding the %f is: %ld\n", d, lround(d)); }
```

Output:

The result of rounding the 1.500000 is: 2

The result of rounding the 1.490000 is: 1

Sqrt

The sqrt function returns the square root of an argument. This function is declared inside the <math.h> header and has the following syntax:

```
double sqrt(double argument);
```

Example:

```
#include <stdio.h>
#include <math.h>

int main(void)
{
    double d = 64.;
    printf("The square root of %f is: %f\n", d, sqrt(d));
    d = 256.00;
    printf("The square root of %f is: %f\n", d, sqrt(d));
}
```

Output:

The square root of 64.000000 is: 8.000000

The square root of 256.000000 is: 16.000000

We use the sqrtf variant for the type float and sqrtl for the type long double.

String Conversion Functions

There are functions in the C standard library that allow us to convert a string to a number and vice versa. Here we discuss the strtol for converting a string to a number and snprintf for converting a number to a string.

Strtol

The strtol function allows us to convert a string to a long int number. The function is defined inside the <stdlib.h> header and has the following syntax:

long strtol(const char *restrict str, char **restrict str_end, int base);

The strtol function takes as many characters as possible from str to form an integer number of base base. The base represents the base of the interpreted integer and can have values from 2 to 36.

The function can also set the pointer pointed to by str_end to point at the one past the last character interpreted. We can also ignore this pointer by passing it a null pointer. To convert a string to a base 10 integer, where we ignore the str_end pointer, we write:

```c
#include <stdio.h>

#include <stdlib.h>

int main(void)

{
const char * str = "123 to a number.";
long result = strtol(str, NULL, 10);
printf("The result is: %ld\n", result);
}
```

Output:

The result is: 123

To convert a string to an integer and get the remainder of the string that could not be converted, we write:

```c
#include <stdio.h>

#include <stdlib.h>

int main(void)

{
    const char * str = "123 to a number.";
    char* str_end;

    long result = strtol(str, &str_end, 10);
    printf("The result is: %ld\n", result);

    printf("The remainder of the string is: %s\n", str_end);
}
```

Output:

The result is: 123 The remainder of the string is: to a number.

Snprintf

The snprintf function allows us to convert a number to a formatted string. Whereas the printf writes to standard output, the snprintf writes to a character array. The function is declared inside the <stdio.h> header and has the following syntax:

int snprintf(char *restrict str_buffer, size_t buffer_size, const char *restrict format, ...);

The function writes the result into a string buffer pointed to by str_buffer. The buffer_size is the maximum number of characters to be written. The function writes at most buffer-size - 1 characters, plus the automatically added null-terminating character. To convert a single integer x to a string buffer pointed to by strbuffer, without checking for the return value, we write:

```
#include <stdio.h>

#include <stdlib.h>

int main(void)

{
    int x = 123;
    char strbuffer [100];

    snprintf(strbuffer, sizeof strbuffer, "%d", x);
    printf("The result is: %s\n", strbuffer);

}
```

Output:

The result is: 123

If successful, the snprintf function returns a number of characters written minus the null terminator. If the conversion was unsuccessful, the function returns a negative number. To convert a single integer to a string and check how many characters were written, we use:

```
#include <stdio.h>

#include <stdlib.h>

int main(void)

{
    int x = 123;
    char strbuffer [100];

    int nc = snprintf(strbuffer, sizeof strbuffer, "%d", x);
    printf("The result is: %s\n", strbuffer);

    printf("The number of characters written is: %d\n", nc);
}
```

Output:

The result is: 123

The number of characters written is: 3

To form a more descriptive string out of int and double values, we use the string constant with format specifiers. We also pass in the comma-separated list of numbers. Example:

```c
#include <stdio.h>
#include <stdlib.h> int main(void)
{
    int x = 123;
    double d = 456.789;
    char strbuffer[100];

    int nc = snprintf(strbuffer, sizeof strbuffer, "int: %d, double: %g", x, d);

    printf("%s\n", strbuffer);

    printf("The number of characters written is: %d\n", nc);
}
```

Output:

int: 123, double: 456.789

The number of characters written is: 25

Conclusion: Mastering the C Standard Library – A Path to Proficiency

The C Standard Library is more than a collection of functions; it is a fundamental toolkit that shapes how developers interact with the language. This library encapsulates decades of knowledge, providing tools that bring efficiency, precision, and robustness to C programming. Mastering these functions not only simplifies development but also opens doors to optimized, error-free, and maintainable code. Let's revisit what makes this library indispensable and explore how it enhances C programming through its core libraries.

1. Revisiting stdio.h - The Input/Output Backbone

The stdio.h library forms the backbone of most C programs. Input and output operations are central to program interaction, making printf, scanf, and file I/O functions crucial for tasks ranging from simple data display to complex file handling.

The power of printf and scanf lies in their ability to handle diverse data types through format specifiers, turning the console into an interactive interface. More than just displaying data, printf allows precise control over output formatting, making it invaluable for applications that require structured data presentation, such as tables or graphs. Meanwhile, file operations (fopen, fclose, fprintf, and fscanf) enable programs to interact with external data sources, a capability essential for data processing and storage.

Incorporating best practices, such as checking for successful file opening and handling scanf errors, ensures robustness. By mastering stdio.h, programmers gain the tools to build interactive applications and manage data efficiently.

2. stdlib.h - Essential Utilities for Dynamic Memory and Process Control

stdlib.h introduces several vital utilities that underpin core programming tasks, especially dynamic memory management and conversions. Memory allocation with malloc, calloc, realloc, and free is a critical skill in C, as it allows efficient use of memory resources based on program needs. By allocating memory at runtime, developers can create flexible data structures like linked lists, dynamically sized arrays, and trees, which are foundational to data manipulation in C.

Conversion functions (atoi, atof, strtol, etc.) further extend C's capabilities by simplifying data type conversions. For instance, these functions are particularly useful in data parsing applications where input might be in string form but needs to be processed numerically.

The random number generation feature in stdlib.h, achieved through rand and srand, proves valuable for simulations, statistical calculations, and gaming applications. Seeding the random number generator ensures variability in program output, enhancing simulation accuracy.

3. string.h - Building Blocks for Text Manipulation

In C, strings are arrays of characters, and string.h provides tools to work with them efficiently. Functions like strcpy, strncpy, strcmp, and strlen help in manipulating and analyzing strings, which is foundational for any text processing. Proper handling of strings is essential for applications in fields such as natural language processing, data parsing, and user interface design, where text plays a central role.

The ability to safely handle strings using functions like strncpy prevents common vulnerabilities like buffer overflow, which can lead to security risks. By understanding string.h, programmers gain the knowledge needed to build robust, secure applications that handle text reliably, even with user input.

4. math.h - Enabling Complex Calculations with Ease

math.h extends C's capabilities by providing access to complex mathematical operations, including powers, roots, trigonometric functions, and logarithmic calculations. This library is invaluable for scientific computing, engineering applications, and any software that requires calculations beyond basic arithmetic.

For instance, functions like pow, sqrt, sin, and cos are the building blocks for simulations, physics engines, and financial modeling. Moreover, rounding and modulus functions (ceil, floor, fmod) provide precise control over numerical data, making them essential for algorithms that demand accuracy.

Mastering math.h enables C programmers to tackle complex computational tasks, making C a preferred choice for scientific and technical applications.

5. Error Handling - Building Reliable Programs

Error handling is a key component of robust software design, and the C Standard Library provides mechanisms like errno, perror, and strerror to help developers manage errors gracefully. In a language like C, where memory management and low-level operations are common, errors can occur frequently, and handling them proactively prevents crashes and data loss.

Using errno and related functions allows developers to diagnose issues precisely, which is especially helpful in large programs with complex dependencies. By implementing reliable error handling practices, such as validating return values and providing informative messages, C programmers create applications that are more resilient to unexpected inputs and system failures.

6. Random Number Generation - Adding Unpredictability

Random number generation, managed by rand and srand, is a simple yet powerful feature, especially in applications that require unpredictability. From games and simulations to cryptographic applications, randomness is essential for realism and security.

However, understanding the limitations of pseudo-random numbers in C is important. Since rand generates predictable sequences without a unique seed, seeding with srand(time(NULL)) ensures different results across program runs. Mastering random number generation lays the groundwork for applications in fields as varied as gaming, statistics, and algorithm testing.

7. The Importance of Best Practices in Using the C Standard Library

In C, where low-level operations are common, following best practices is not merely beneficial—it is essential. Ensuring proper memory allocation and deallocation, verifying function return values, managing strings safely, and handling errors effectively all contribute to the stability and security of C programs.

For instance, failing to free allocated memory can lead to memory leaks, which can degrade performance over time. Likewise, overlooking error handling in functions like scanf or fopen can lead to undefined behavior or program crashes, particularly in production environments where robustness is crucial. By embracing these best practices, C programmers ensure that their code is both efficient and reliable.

8. Expanding Horizons with the C Standard Library

Mastery of the C Standard Library provides a solid foundation for advanced programming and system-level development. With the understanding of fundamental libraries like stdio.h, stdlib.h, string.h, and math.h, developers can confidently tackle a wide array of programming challenges, from developing command-line tools to creating memory-efficient data structures.

Furthermore, this knowledge is transferable to other languages that offer similar libraries or functions, making it valuable even outside the realm of C programming. Proficiency in the C Standard Library also equips developers with a mindset for resource efficiency and error management, traits that are invaluable across all programming languages.

9. The Role of the C Standard Library in Modern Software Development

Although modern programming languages have emerged with extensive libraries and simplified syntax, C remains relevant due to its efficiency and control over hardware. Mastery of the C Standard Library enables programmers to write lean, performant code, which is critical in embedded systems, real-time applications, and performance-intensive software.

The C Standard Library is a testament to the language's enduring design philosophy—providing programmers with the tools they need to work close to the hardware while maintaining portability and efficiency. Whether in operating systems, compilers, or network applications, knowledge of the C Standard Library is a valuable asset that continues to drive technological innovation.

10. Final Thoughts: Embracing the Power of C with the Standard Library

In conclusion, the C Standard Library is both a starting point and a cornerstone for any C programmer. It offers a comprehensive set of functions that support almost every conceivable operation, from basic input/output and memory management to complex mathematical computations. Through diligent study and application of these libraries, C developers gain the skills to write code that is not only efficient but also maintainable and resilient.

The journey to mastering the C Standard Library is one of continual learning and refinement. Each function, whether a simple printf or a complex malloc, teaches valuable lessons about low-level computing, efficiency, and precision. Embracing these tools and practices, programmers are better prepared to contribute to diverse fields, build innovative solutions, and push the boundaries of what's possible with C.

In essence, the C Standard Library is more than a set of functions—it's a gateway to mastering the art and science of programming. By mastering these fundamental libraries, C developers set themselves on a path to proficiency and pave the way for a career grounded in solid technical expertise, capable of tackling the most demanding computing challenges of today and tomorrow.

12. Preprocessor Directives in C

1. Introduction

The C preprocessor is a tool that processes code before actual compilation. Preprocessor directives begin with a # symbol and include commands to control the inclusion of files, define constants or macros, and conditionally compile code. This process is essential in writing modular and efficient code.

Types of Preprocessor Directives:

File Inclusion: #include is used to insert the contents of a file into the program, primarily header files.

Macro Definition: #define creates symbolic constants and macros.

Undefining Macros: #undef removes a macro definition.

Conditional Compilation: Directives like #ifdef, #ifndef, #if, and #endif control which code segments are compiled.

Pragmas: #pragma provides special instructions to the compiler and is often compiler-specific.

Preprocessor directives play a critical role in making code more adaptable, allowing for different configurations, managing dependencies, and ensuring code reusability.

2. Macros and Constants

Defining Macros: The #define directive allows the creation of symbolic names or macros. A macro replaces text in the code before compilation, offering a powerful way to use constants and simplify repetitive tasks.

```
#define PI 3.14159
#define MAX(a, b) ((a) > (b) ? (a) : (b))
```

PI is a constant, substituting the value 3.14159 wherever PI appears.

MAX(a, b) is a function-like macro that returns the larger of two values.

Advantages of Macros for Constants:

Code Clarity: Names like PI make code more readable.

Easier Maintenance: Changing #define PI 3.14 to 3.14159 updates all occurrences without modifying multiple lines.

No Memory Overhead: Unlike variables, macros don't occupy memory, as they're simple text substitutions.

Drawbacks of Macros:

Lack of Type Safety: Macros don't enforce type checks, leading to potential bugs.

Complex Expression Handling: Macros are text substitutions, so complex expressions can yield unexpected results without careful parentheses.

3. Conditional Compilation

Conditional compilation directives allow you to compile code selectively, which is especially useful for managing platform-specific or debug code. The main directives used in conditional compilation are #ifdef, #ifndef, #if, #elif, and #endif.

#ifdef and #ifndef:

#ifdef checks if a macro is defined, and if it is, the code block following it is compiled.

#ifndef does the opposite, compiling the code if the macro is not defined.

```
#define DEBUG_MODE
```

```
#ifdef DEBUG_MODE
printf("Debug mode is enabled.\n");
#endif
```

In this example, the message is printed only if DEBUG_MODE is defined. This is useful for toggling debug-related code without modifying multiple code sections.

Using #if, #elif, and #endif: The #if directive checks a condition, similar to an if statement in regular code. You can also use #elif and #else for multiple conditions.

```
#define VERSION 2
```

```
#if VERSION >= 3
printf("Version 3 or higher features enabled.\n");
#elif VERSION == 2
printf("Version 2 features enabled.\n");
#else
printf("Basic version enabled.\n");
```

#endif

This example allows code to adapt based on the value of VERSION.

Practical Applications:

Platform-Specific Code: Write sections that only compile on certain operating systems (e.g., #ifdef _WIN32 for Windows).

Feature Toggles: Enable or disable specific features for different builds.

4. Including Files (#include)

File inclusion is critical for modular programming in C. By separating code into header files and implementation files, you can write more organized and maintainable programs.

Syntax:

System Headers: #include <stdio.h> includes standard library files.

User-Defined Headers: #include "myheader.h" includes user-defined files, typically searched in the current directory before system directories.

Example:

```
#include <stdio.h>
#include "myheader.h"

int main() {
    printf("Hello, world!\n");
    return 0;
}
```

Header Guards: To prevent multiple inclusions, use header guards in your custom header files. This prevents redefinition errors when a file is included multiple times.

```
#ifndef MYHEADER_H
#define MYHEADER_H

void myFunction();
```

```
#endif
```

Benefits of Header Guards:

Efficiency: Speeds up compilation by avoiding redundant processing.

Avoids Conflicts: Prevents issues from multiple inclusions.

5. Defining Functions as Macros

Macros can also be used to define small functions, particularly for simple, frequently called operations where inline expansion (no function call overhead) is beneficial. A common example is a macro for squaring a number:

```
#define SQUARE(x) ((x) * (x))
```

Advantages:

In-line Code Expansion: Macros avoid the overhead of function calls, which can be beneficial in performance-critical code.

Parameter Flexibility: They can take arguments, which enables writing reusable code snippets.

Disadvantages:

Lack of Type Safety: Macros don't check argument types, increasing the risk of unintended behavior.

Side Effects: If SQUARE(x++) is used, x++ will be incremented twice, leading to unexpected results.

Before your program gets compiled, it actually runs through a phase called preprocessing. It's almost like there's a language on top of the C language that runs first. And it outputs the C code, which then gets compiled.

We've already seen this to an extent with #include! That's the C Preprocessor! Where it sees that directive, it includes the named file right there, just as if you'd typed it in there. And then the compiler builds the whole thing.

But it turns out it's a lot more powerful than just being able to include things. You can define macros that are substituted… and even macros that take arguments!

```
#include
```

Let's start with the one we've already seen a bunch. This is, of course, a way to include other sources in your source. Very commonly used with header files.

While the spec allows for all kinds of behavior with #include, we're going to take a more pragmatic approach and talk about the way it works on every system I've ever seen.

We can split header files into two categories: system and local. Things that are built-in, like stdio.h, stdlib.h, math.h, and so on, you can include with angle brackets:

```
#include <stdio.h>
#include <stdlib.h>
```

The angle brackets tell C, "Hey, don't look in the current directory for this header file—look in the systemwide include directory instead."

Which, of course, implies that there must be a way to include local files from the current directory. And there is: with double quotes:

```
#include "myheader.h"
```

Or you can very probably look in relative directories using forward slashes and dots, like this:

```
#include "mydir/myheader.h"
#include "../someheader.py"
```

Don't use a backslash (\) for your path separators in your #include! It's undefined behavior! Use forward slash (/) only, even on Windows.

In summary, used angle brackets (< and >) for the system includes, and use double quotes (") for your personal includes.

Simple Macros

A macro is an identifier that gets expanded to another piece of code before the compiler even sees it. Think of it like a placeholder—when the preprocessor sees one of those identifiers, it replaces it with another value that you've defined.

We do this with #define (often read "pound define"). Here's an example:

```
#include <stdio.h>
#define HELLO "Hello, world"
#define PI 3.14159

int main(void)
```

```
    {
    printf("%s, %f\n", HELLO, PI);
    }
```

On lines 3 and 4 we defined a couple macros. Wherever these appear elsewhere in the code (line 8), they'll be substituted with the defined values.

From the C compiler's perspective, it's exactly as if we'd written this, instead:

```
#include <stdio.h>
int main(void)
{
printf("%s, %f\n", "Hello, world", 3.14159);
}
```

See how HELLO was replaced with "Hello, world" and PI was replaced with 3.14159? From the compiler's perspective, it's just like those values had appeared right there in the code.

Note that the macros don't have a specific type, per se. Really all that happens is they get replaced wholesale with whatever they're #defined as. If the resulting C code is invalid, the compiler will puke.

You can also define a macro with no value:

```
#define EXTRA_HAPPY
```

In that case, the macro exists and is defined, but is defined to be nothing. So anyplace it occurs in the text will just be replaced with nothing. We'll see a use for this later.

It's conventional to write macro names in ALL_CAPS even though that's not technically required.

Overall, this gives you a way to define constant values that are effectively global and can be used any place.

Even in those places where a const variable won't work, e.g. in switch cases and fixed array lengths.

That said, the debate rages online whether a typed const variable is better than #define macro in the general case.

It can also be used to replace or modify keywords, a concept completely foreign to const, though this practice should be used sparingly.

Conditional Compilation

It's possible to get the preprocessor to decide whether or not to present certain blocks of code to the compiler, or just remove them entirely before compilation.

We do that by basically wrapping up the code in conditional blocks, similar to if-else statements.

If defined, #ifdef and #endif

First of all, let's try to compile specific code depending on whether or not a macro is even defined.

Conditional Compilation

```
#include <stdio.h> #define EXTRA_HAPPY
int main(void) {
#ifdef EXTRA_HAPPY
printf("I'm extra happy!\n");
#endif
printf("OK!\n");
}
```

In that example, we define EXTRA_HAPPY (to be nothing, but it is defined), then on line 8 we check to see if it is defined with an #ifdef directive. If it is defined, the subsequent code will be included up until the #endif.

So, because it is defined, the code will be included for compilation and the output will be:

```
I'm extra happy!
OK!
```

If we were to comment out the #define, like so:

```
//#define EXTRA_HAPPY
```

then it wouldn't be defined, and the code wouldn't be included in compilation. And the output would just be:
```
OK!
```

It's important to remember that these decisions happen at compile time! The code actually gets compiled or removed depending on the condition. This is in contrast to a standard if statement that gets evaluated while the program is running.

If Not Defined, #ifndef

There's also the negative sense of "if defined": "if not defined", or #ifndef. We could change the previous example to output different things based on whether or not something was defined:

```
#ifdef EXTRA_HAPPY printf("I'm extra happy!\n");
#endif
#ifndef EXTRA_HAPPY printf("I'm just regular\n");
#endif
```

We'll see a cleaner way to do that in the next section.

Tying it all back in to header files, we've seen how we can cause header files to only be included one time by wrapping them in preprocessor directives like this:

```
#ifndef MYHEADER_H // First line of myheader.h
#define MYHEADER_H
int x = 12;
#endif // Last line of myheader.h
```

This demonstrates how a macro persists across files and multiple #includes. If it's not yet defined, let's define it and compile the whole header file.

But the next time it's included, we see that MYHEADER_H is defined, so we don't send the header file to the compiler—it gets effectively removed.

#else

But that's not all we can do! There's also an #else that we can throw in the mix.

Let's mod the previous example:

```
#ifdef EXTRA_HAPPY printf("I'm extra happy!\n");
#else printf("I'm just regular\n");
#endif
```

Now if EXTRA_HAPPY is not defined, it'll hit the #else clause and print:

I'm just regular

General Conditional: #if, #elif

This works very much like the #ifdef and #ifndef directives in that you can also have an #else and the whole thing wraps up with #endif.

The only difference is that the constant expression after the #if must evaluate to true (non-zero) for the code in the #if to be compiled. So instead of whether or not something is defined, we want an expression that evaluates to true.

```
#include <stdio.h> #define HAPPY_FACTOR 1
int main(void) {
#if HAPPY_FACTOR == 0 printf("I'm not happy!\n");
#elif HAPPY_FACTOR == 1 printf("I'm just regular\n");
#else printf("I'm extra happy!\n");
#endif
printf("OK!\n");
}
```

Again, for the unmatched #if clauses, the compiler won't even see those lines. For the above code, after the preprocessor gets finished with it, all the compiler sees is:

```
#include <stdio.h>
int main(void)
{
printf("I'm just regular\n");
printf("OK!\n");
}
```

One hackish thing this is used for is to comment out large numbers of lines quickly.

Conditional Compilation

If you put an #if 0 ("if false") at the front of the block to be commented out and an #endif at the end, you can get this effect:

```
#if 0 printf("All this code"); /* is effectively */
printf("commented out"); // by the #if 0
#endif
```

You might have noticed that there's no #elifdef or #elifndef directives. How can we get the same effect with #if? That is, what if I wanted this:

```
#ifdef FOO x = 2;
#elifdef BAR // ERROR: Not supported by standard C x = 3;
```

```
#endif
```

How could I do it?

Turns out there's a preprocessor operator called defined that we can use with an #if statement.

These are equivalent:

```
#ifdef FOO
#if defined FOO
#if defined(FOO)        // Parentheses optional
```
As are these:
```
#ifndef FOO
#if !defined FOO
#if !defined(FOO)       // Parentheses optional
```

Notice how we can use the standard logical NOT operator (!) for "not defined".

So now we're back in #if land and we can use #elif with impunity!

This broken code:

```
#ifdef FOO x = 2;
#elifdef BAR // ERROR: Not supported by standard C x = 3;
#endif can be replaced with:
#if defined FOO x = 2;
#elif defined BAR x = 3;
#endif
```

Losing a Macro: #undef

If you've defined something but you don't need it any longer, you can undefine it with #undef.

```
#include <stdio.h>
int main(void) {
#define GOATS
#ifdef GOATS printf("Goats detected!\n"); // prints #endif
#undef GOATS // Make GOATS no longer defined
#ifdef GOATS printf("Goats detected, again!\n"); // doesn't print
#endif
```

}

Built-in Macros

The standard defines a lot of built-in macros that you can test and use for conditional compilation. Let's look at those here.

Mandatory Macros

These are all defined:

Macro	Description
__DATE__	The date of compilation—like when you're compiling this file—in Mmm dd yyyy format
__TIME__	The time of compilation in hh:mm:ss format
__FILE__	A string containing this file's name
__LINE__	The line number of the file this macro appears on
__func__	The name of the function this appears in, as a string[6]
__STDC__	Defined with 1 if this is a standard C compiler
__STDC_HOSTED__	This will be 1 if the compiler is a hosted implementation[7], otherwise 0
__STDC_VERSION__	This version of C, a constant long int in the form yyyymmL, e.g. 201710L

Let's put these together.

```
#include <stdio.h>

int main(void)
{
printf("This function: %s\n", __func__);
printf("This file: %s\n", __FILE__);
printf("This line: %d\n", __LINE__);
printf("Compiled on: %s %s\n", __DATE__, __TIME__);
printf("C Version: %ld\n", __STDC_VERSION__);
}
```

The output on my system is:

This function: main

This file: foo.c

This line: 7

Compiled on: Nov 23 2020 17:16:27

C Version: 201710

Built-in Macros

__FILE__, __func__ and __LINE__ are particularly useful to report error conditions in messages to developers. The assert() macro in <assert.h> uses these to call out where in the code the assertion failed.

STDC_VERSION__s

In case you're wondering, here are the version numbers for different major releases of the C Language Spec:

Release	ISO/IEC version	__STDC_VERSION__
C89	ISO/IEC 9899:1990	undefined
C89	ISO/IEC 9899:1990/Amd.1:1995	199409L
C99	ISO/IEC 9899:1999	199901L
C11	ISO/IEC 9899:2011/Amd.1:2012	201112L

Note the macro did not exist originally in C89.

Also note that the plan is that the version numbers will strictly increase, so you could always check for, say, "at least C99" with:

#if __STDC_VERSION__ >= 1999901L

Optional Macros

Your implementation might define these, as well. Or it might not.

Macro	Description
__STDC_ISO_10646__	If defined, wchar_t holds Unicode values, otherwise something else
__STDC_MB_MIGHT_NEQ_WC__	A 1 indicates that the values in multibyte characters might not map equally to values in wide characters
__STDC_UTF_16__	A 1 indicates that the system uses UTF-16 encoding in type char16_t
__STDC_UTF_32__	A 1 indicates that the system uses UTF-32 encoding in type char32_t

`__STDC_ANALYZABLE__`	A 1 indicates the code is analyzable[8]
`__STDC_IEC_559__`	1 if IEEE-754 (aka IEC 60559) floating point is supported
`__STDC_IEC_559_COMPLEX__`	1 if IEC 60559 complex floating point is supported
`__STDC_LIB_EXT1__`	1 if this implementation supports a variety of "safe" alternate standard library functions (they have _s suffixes on the name)
`__STDC_NO_ATOMICS__`	1 if this implementation does **not** support _Atomic or <stdatomic.h>
`__STDC_NO_COMPLEX__`	1 if this implementation does **not** support complex types or <complex.h>
`__STDC_NO_THREADS__`	1 if this implementation does **not** support <threads.h>
`__STDC_NO_VLA__`	1 if this implementation does **not** support variable-length arrays

Macros with Arguments

Macros are more powerful than simple substitution, though. You can set them up to take arguments that are substituted in, as well.

A question often arises for when to use parameterized macros versus functions. Short answer: use functions. But you'll see lots of macros in the wild and in the standard library. People tend to use them for short, mathy things, and also for features that might change from platform to platform. You can define different keywords for one platform or another.

Macros with One Argument

Let's start with a simple one that squares a number:

```
#include <stdio.h>
#define SQR(x) x * x // Not quite right, but bear with me
int main(void)
{ printf("%d\n", SQR(12)); // 144
}
```

What that's saying is "everywhere you see SQR with some value, replace it with that value times itself".

_____

So, line 7 will be changed to:

```
printf("%d\n", 12 * 12); // 144 which C comfortably converts to 144.
```

But we've made an elementary error in that macro, one that we need to avoid.

Let's check it out. What if we wanted to compute SQR(3 + 4)? Well, 3 + 4 = 7, so we must want to compute $7^2 = 49$. That's it; 49—final answer.

Let's drop it in our code and see that we get... 19?

```
printf("%d\n", SQR(3 + 4)); // 19!!??
```

What happened?

If we follow the macro expansion, we get

```
printf("%d\n", 3 + 4 * 3 + 4); // 19!
```

Oops! Since multiplication takes precedence, we do the 4×3 = 12 first, and get 3+12+4 = 19. Not what we were after.

So, we have to fix this to make it right.

This is so common that you should automatically do it every time you make a parameterized math macro!

The fix is easy: just add some parentheses!

```
#define SQR(x) (x) * (x)        // Better... but still not quite good enough!
```

And now our macro expands to:

```
printf("%d\n", (3 + 4) * (3 + 4)); // 49! Woo hoo!
```

But we actually still have the same problem which might manifest if we have a higher-precedence operator than multiply (*) nearby.

So, the safe, proper way to put the macro together is to wrap the whole thing in additional parentheses, like so:

```
#define SQR(x) ((x) * (x))      // Good!
```

Macros with Arguments

Just make it a habit to do that when you make a math macro and you can't go wrong.

Macros with More than One Argument

You can stack these things up as much as you want:

#define TRIANGLE_AREA (w, h) (0.5 * (w) * (h))

Let's do some macros that solve for x using the quadratic formula. Just in case you don't have it on the top of your head, it says for equations of the form:

$$ax^2 + bx + c = 0$$

you can solve for x with the quadratic formula:

$$x = \frac{-b \pm \sqrt{b^2 - 4ac}}{2a}$$

Which is crazy. Also notice the plus-or-minus ($\pm$) in there, indicating that there are actually two solutions.

So, let's make macros for both:

#define QUADP(a, b, c) ((-(b) + sqrt((b) * (b) - 4 * (a) * (c))) / (2 * (a)))
#define QUADM(a, b, c) ((-(b) - sqrt((b) * (b) - 4 * (a) * (c))) / (2 * (a)))

So that gets us some math. But let's define one more that we can use as arguments to printf() to print both answers.

Macro replacement

#define QUAD(a, b, c) QUADP(a, b, c), QUADM(a, b, c)

That's just a couple values separated by a comma—and we can use that as a "combined" argument of sorts to printf() like this:

printf("x = %f or x = %f\n", QUAD(2, 10, 5));

Let's put it together into some code:

#include <stdio.h>

```c
#include <math.h> // For sqrt()
#define QUADP(a, b, c) ((-(b) + sqrt((b) * (b) - 4 * (a) * (c))) / (2 * (a)))
#define QUADM(a, b, c) ((-(b) - sqrt((b) * (b) - 4 * (a) * (c))) / (2 * (a)))
#define QUAD(a, b, c) QUADP(a, b, c), QUADM(a, b, c)
int main(void)
{
printf("2*x^2 + 10*x + 5 = 0\n");
printf("x = %f or x = %f\n", QUAD(2, 10, 5));
}
```

And this gives us the output:

2*x^2 + 10*x + 5 = 0 x = -0.563508 or x = -4.436492

Plugging in either of those values gives us roughly zero (a bit off because the numbers aren't exact):

$2 \times -0.563508^2 + 10 \times -0.563508 + 5 \approx 0.000003$

Macros with Variable Arguments

There's also a way to have a variable number of arguments passed to a macro, using ellipses (...) after the known, named arguments. When the macro is expanded, all of the extra arguments will be in a comma separated list in the __VA_ARGS__ macro, and can be replaced from there:

```c
#include <stdio.h>
// Combine the first two arguments to a single number, // then have a comma list of the rest of them:
#define X(a, b, ...) (10*(a) + 20*(b)), __VA_ARGS__
int main(void)
{
printf("%d %f %s %d\n", X(5, 4, 3.14, "Hi!", 12));
}
```

The substitution that takes place on line 10 would be:

```c
printf("%d %f %s %d\n", (10*(5) + 20*(4)), 3.14, "Hi!", 12);
```

for output:

130 3.140000 Hi! 12

You can also "stringify" __VA_ARGS__ by putting a # in front of it:

```
#define X(...) #__VA_ARGS__ printf("%s\n", X(1,2,3)); // Prints "1, 2, 3"
```

Stringification

Already mentioned, just above, you can turn any argument into a string by preceding it with a # in the replacement text.

For example, we could print anything as a string with this macro and printf():

```
#define STR(x) #x
```

```
printf("%s\n", STR(3.14159)); In that case, the substitution leads to:
```

```
printf("%s\n", "3.14159");
```

Let's see if we can use this to greater effect so that we can pass any int variable name into a macro, and have it print out it's name and value.

```
#include <stdio.h>
#define PRINT_INT_VAL(x) printf("%s = %d\n", #x, x)
int main(void)
{
int a = 5;
PRINT_INT_VAL(a); // prints "a = 5"
}
```

On line 9, we get the following macro replacement:

```
printf("%s = %d\n", "a", 5);
```

Concatenation

We can concatenate two arguments together with ##, as well. Fun times!
```
#define CAT(a, b) a ## b
printf("%f\n", CAT(3.14, 1592));      // 3.141592
```

Multiline Macros

It's possible to continue a macro to multiple lines if you escape the newline with a backslash (\).

Let's write a multiline macro that prints numbers from 0 to the product of the two arguments passed in.

```
#include <stdio.h>
```

```
#define PRINT_NUMS_TO_PRODUCT(a, b) do { \ int product = (a) * (b); \ for (int i = 0; i < product;
i++) { \ printf("%d\n", i); \
} \
} while(0)
int main(void)
{
PRINT_NUMS_TO_PRODUCT(2, 4); // Outputs numbers from 0 to 7
}
```

A couple things to note there:

Escapes at the end of every line except the last one to indicate that the macro continues.

The whole thing is wrapped in a do-while(0) loop with squirrely braces.

The latter point might be a little weird, but it's all about absorbing the trailing; the coder drops after the macro.

At first, I thought that just using squirrely braces would be enough, but there's a case where it fails if the coder puts a semicolon after the macro. Here's that case:

```
#include <stdio.h>
#define FOO(x)
{
(x)++;
}
int main(void)
{
int i = 0;
if (i == 0)
FOO(i); else printf(":-(\n");
printf("%d\n", i);
}
```

Looks simple enough, but it won't build without a syntax error:

foo.c:11:5: error: 'else' without a previous 'if'

Do you see it?

Let's look at the expansion:

```
if (i == 0) {
```

```
(i)++;
};        // <-- Trouble with a capital-T!
else
printf(":-(\n");
```

The ; puts an end to the if statement, so the else is just floating out there illegally.

So wrap that multiline macro with a do-while(0).

Example: An Assert Macro

Adding asserts to your code is a good way to catch conditions that you think shouldn't happen. C provides assert() functionality. It checks a condition, and if it's false, the program bombs out telling you the file and line number on which the assertion failed.

But this is wanting.

First of all, you can't specify an additional message with the assert.

Secondly, there's no easy on-off switch for all the asserts.

We can address the first with macros.

Basically, when I have this code:

```
ASSERT(x < 20, "x must be under 20");
```

I want something like this to happen (assuming the ASSERT() is on line 220 of foo.c):

```
if (!(x < 20)) {
fprintf(stderr, "foo.c:220: assertion x < 20 failed: ");
fprintf(stderr, "x must be under 20\n"); exit(1);

}
```

We can get the filename out of the __FILE__ macro, and the line number from __LINE__. The message is already a string, but x < 20 is not, so we'll have to stringify it with #. We can make a multiline macro by using backslash escapes at the end of the line.

```
#define ASSERT(c, m) \ do { \ if (!(c)) { \ fprintf(stderr, __FILE__ ":%d: assertion %s failed: %s\n", \
__LINE__, #c, m); \
exit(1); \
} \
} while(0)
```

(It looks a little weird with __FILE__ out front like that, but remember it is a string literal, and string literals next to each other are automagically concatenated. __LINE__ on the other hand, it's just an int.)

And that works! If I run this:

```
int x = 30;
ASSERT(x < 20, "x must be under 20");
```

I get this output:

```
foo.c:23: assertion x < 20 failed: x must be under 20
```
Very nice!

The only thing left is a way to turn it on and off, and we could do that with conditional compilation.

Here's the complete example:

```
#include <stdio.h>
#include <stdlib.h>
#define ASSERT_ENABLED
```

The #error Directive

```
#if ASSERT_ENABLED #define ASSERT(c, m) \ do { \ if (!(c)) { \ fprintf(stderr, __FILE__ ":%d:
assertion %s failed: %s\n", \
    __LINE__, #c, m); \
exit(1); \
} \
} while(0)
#else
#define ASSERT(c, m) // Empty macro if not enabled
#endif
int main(void)
{
int x = 30;
ASSERT(x < 20, "x must be under 20");
}
```

This has the output:

```
foo.c:23: assertion x < 20 failed: x must be under 20
```

The #error Directive

This directive causes the compiler to error out as soon as it sees it.

Commonly, this is used inside a conditional to prevent compilation unless some prerequisites are met:

```
#ifndef __STDC_IEC_559__
#error I really need IEEE-754 floating point to compile. Sorry!
#endif
```

Some compilers have a non-standard complementary #warning directive that will output a warning but not stop compilation, but this is not in the C11 spec.

The #pragma Directive

This is one funky directive, short for "pragmatic". You can use it to do… well, anything your compiler supports you doing with it.

Basically, the only time you're going to add this to your code is if some documentation tells you to do so.

Non-Standard Pragmas

Here's one non-standard example of using #pragma to cause the compiler to execute a for loop in parallel with multiple threads (if the compiler supports the OpenMP[9] extension):

```
#pragma omp parallel for for (int i = 0; i < 10; i++) {
}
```

There are all kinds of #pragma directives documented across all four corners of the globe.

All unrecognized #pragmas are ignored by the compiler.

Standard Pragmas

There are also a few standard ones, and these start with STDC, and follow the same form:

```
#pragma STDC pragma_name on-off
```
The on-off portion can be either ON, OFF, or DEFAULT.

And the pragma_name can be one of these:

————————————————

Pragma Name	Description
FP_CONTRACT	Allow floating point expressions to be contracted into a single operation to avoid rounding errors that might occur from multiple operations.
FENV_ACCESS	Set to ON if you plan to access the floating-point status flags. If OFF, the compiler might perform optimizations that cause the values in the flags to be inconsistent or invalid.
CX_LIMITED_RANGE	Set to ON to allow the compiler to skip overflow checks when performing complex arithmetic. Defaults to OFF.

For example:

#pragma STDC FP_CONTRACT OFF

#pragma STDC CX_LIMITED_RANGE ON

As for CX_LIMITED_RANGE, the spec points out:

The purpose of the pragma is to allow the implementation to use the formulas:

$$(x + iy) \times (u + iv) = (xu - yv) + i(yu + xv)$$
$$(x + iy)/(u + iv) = [(xu + yv) + i(yu - xv)]/(u^2 + v^2)$$

$|x + iy| = \sqrt{x^2 + y^2}$ where the programmer can determine they are safe.

Pragma Operator

This is another way to declare a pragma that you could use in a macro.

These are equivalent:

#pragma "Unnecessary" quotes

_Pragma ("\"Unnecessary\" quotes") This can be used in a macro, if need be:

#define PRAGMA(x) _Pragma(#x)

The #line Directive

This allows you to override the values for __LINE__ and __FILE__. If you want.

I've never wanted to do this, but in K&R2, they write:

For the benefit of other preprocessors that generate C programs [...]
So maybe there's that.

To override the line number to, say 300:

#line 300

The Null Directive

and __LINE__ will keep counting up from there.

To override the line number and the filename:

#line 300 "newfilename"

The Null Directive

A # on a line by itself is ignored by the preprocessor. Now, to be entirely honest, I don't know what the use case is for this.

I've seen examples like this:

#ifdef FOO #
#else printf("Something");

#endif which is just cosmetic; the line with the solitary # can be deleted with no ill effect.

Or maybe for cosmetic consistency, like this:
#
#ifdef FOO x = 2;
#endif
#
#if BAR == 17 x = 12;
#endif
#
But, with respect to cosmetics, that's just ugly.

Another post mentions elimination of comments—that in GCC, a comment after a # will not be seen by the compiler. Which I don't doubt, but the specification doesn't seem to say this is standard behavior.

Conclusion

In the C programming language, preprocessor directives are foundational elements that allow for flexible, powerful, and efficient code management. From creating reusable macros to managing code compilation conditions, these directives help maintain code organization, improve performance, and adapt the program to different environments and use cases. Let's review and discuss the overarching significance of each concept, along with the trade-offs, best practices, and potential pitfalls.

1. Importance of Preprocessor Directives

Preprocessor directives, which include #include, #define, #ifdef, #ifndef, #if, and #endif, are not part of the C language itself but serve as a layer above the core language syntax. They instruct the preprocessor to make substitutions and configure the code in ways that align with project requirements before actual compilation.

These directives allow developers to:

Organize Code Modularly: By allowing separate compilation of header files and source files, preprocessor directives keep code modular and organized. This enables developers to group similar functionalities into headers and implementation files, promoting cleaner, more maintainable code.

Create Constants and Code Abstractions: With #define, developers can introduce constants and macros that make the code easier to read and maintain, reducing hardcoded values and repetitive code.

Optimize Code for Specific Scenarios: Conditional compilation directives (#ifdef, #ifndef, #if, etc.) allow developers to write adaptable code. This is critical for building software that can target multiple platforms, compile in both debug and release configurations, and even include or exclude experimental features without modifying multiple code files.

Control Compilation Behavior: The preprocessor allows developers to adjust the program for specific scenarios without changing the core source files, enabling more flexibility for feature toggles, environment configurations, or debugging aids.

2. The Dual Role of Macros and Constants

Macros, defined with the #define directive, offer a powerful, flexible way to create reusable constants and simple, inline code snippets. Constants, typically defined as symbolic literals, make code both readable and easy to modify. For example, #define MAX_LENGTH 100 allows developers to replace a literal 100 everywhere in the program with MAX_LENGTH, making it easier to understand and manage if the value needs adjustment.

Benefits of Macros and Constants:

Code Readability and Maintainability: By abstracting values and small code snippets, macros and constants make code more readable. MAX_LENGTH is self-explanatory, while 100 could mean anything.

Memory Efficiency: Unlike global variables, macros don't take up memory, as they're simply substituted into the code during preprocessing. This makes macros particularly useful for defining constants and common small calculations without extra memory overhead.

Challenges with Macros:

Lack of Type Safety: Macros don't enforce data types, which can lead to unexpected results. For instance, #define SQUARE(x) ((x) * (x)) could behave unpredictably if x is a complex expression, as it will expand without concern for types or side effects.

Complex Expressions: Macros require careful handling of complex expressions. For example, if the macro SQUARE(x) is invoked as SQUARE (a + b), it will expand to (a + b) * (a + b), potentially causing unintended results or slower execution if the expression isn't optimized.

To mitigate these issues, best practices suggest enclosing macro parameters and expressions in parentheses and considering inline functions (available in C99 and later) for type-safe alternatives. Inline functions provide similar benefits to macros but with the advantage of type-checking and safer handling of expressions.

3. Strategic Use of Conditional Compilation

Conditional compilation is indispensable for writing adaptable code that responds to different environments, configurations, and requirements. With directives like #ifdef, #ifndef, and #if, developers can selectively include or exclude sections of code based on defined conditions.

Use Cases for Conditional Compilation:

Platform-Specific Code: Conditional directives allow developers to write code that works on multiple operating systems. For instance, using #ifdef _WIN32 helps identify Windows-specific code, while #ifdef __linux__ does the same for Linux.

Debugging and Release Builds: With conditional compilation, developers can create code that behaves differently in debug and release modes. For instance, logging and error-checking code can be enabled in debug mode but excluded in release mode to improve performance.

Feature Toggling: Feature toggling allows experimental or optional features to be compiled only when necessary. This can help in maintaining a single codebase that can adapt to multiple configurations, improving maintainability.

Drawbacks:

Complexity in Large Codebases: Conditional compilation can make code harder to read and understand, especially if many conditions are nested. Developers must document and use conditions sparingly to avoid "spaghetti code."

Compiler-Specific Conditions: Some conditions rely on compiler-specific macros (e.g., _WIN32), which means that changing compilers might require adjusting these definitions.

A best practice is to use conditional directives as judiciously as possible, aiming for a clear and maintainable codebase. Using well-defined macros (e.g., DEBUG, VERSION) and guarding conditions (such as #ifndef guards for headers) ensures efficient conditional compilation.

4. File Inclusion and Header Guards

The #include directive is crucial in C for creating modular programs, enabling developers to write, reuse, and share functions and definitions in different parts of a program. By including standard libraries or custom headers, #include simplifies code management.

System vs. User-Defined Headers:

System Headers (#include <...>): These headers are used for standard libraries and are included with angle brackets. The compiler searches for these headers in standard locations.

User-Defined Headers (#include "..."): These are included with quotes and are typically searched for in the current project directory. User-defined headers often contain function prototypes, data types, and constants specific to the project.

Header Guards: To prevent multiple inclusions of the same header file, header guards (e.g., #ifndef, #define, and #endif) are used. Without them, re-including a header can lead to compilation errors and excessive code generation.

```
#ifndef MY_HEADER_H
#define MY_HEADER_H
```

```
// Function declarations, data types, and constants
```

```
#endif
```

Benefits:

Prevents Redefinitions: Header guards prevent issues related to including the same file multiple times.

Enhances Code Organization: By separating function declarations and definitions, header files promote better organization.

Using header guards and clear file inclusion strategies helps maintain a well-structured project, particularly in larger codebases where multiple files and dependencies are common.

5. Defining Functions as Macros

Function-like macros provide a way to create reusable code blocks without the overhead of function calls. By defining functions as macros (e.g., #define SQUARE(x) ((x) * (x))), developers can create in-line code that executes faster due to the lack of function call overhead. However, function-like macros come with risks and limitations.

Advantages of Function-like Macros:

Performance: Because macros are expanded in-line, there is no function call, making execution faster for simple expressions.

Flexibility: Macros can be defined without concern for data types, making them flexible for different data values.

Pitfalls:

No Type Checking: Since macros aren't functions, they bypass type-checking, which can lead to bugs.

Side Effects: A macro like SQUARE(x++) expands to ((x++) * (x++)), resulting in unexpected behavior due to multiple evaluations of x++.

Difficulty in Debugging: Since macros are expanded in-line, debugging can be challenging, as errors may not clearly show the source macro.

When to Use Inline Functions Instead: For C99 and later standards, inline functions are often preferred to macros for function-like behavior. Inline functions offer the benefit of type-checking while still allowing the compiler to optimize away function call overhead in many cases.

```
inline int square(int x) {
    return x * x;
}
```

This approach combines the readability and safety of regular functions with performance optimizations, making it a recommended alternative to complex function-like macros.

Summary of Best Practices

In conclusion, while preprocessor directives, macros, and conditional compilation are essential tools in C, they come with trade-offs. Here's a summary of best practices for using these tools effectively:

Use Macros for Constants, but Prefer const Variables When Type Safety is Needed: While macros are memory-efficient, const variables provide additional type safety.

Use Conditional Compilation Sparingly and Document Conditional Code: Complex conditions can lead to unreadable code; document and organize conditional sections carefully.

Use Header Guards to Avoid Redefinitions: Header guards prevent issues related to multiple file inclusions and are a best practice in modern C programming.

Consider Inline Functions Over Complex Macros: For cases where function-like behavior is needed, prefer inline functions for type-safe, efficient code.

By adhering to these practices, developers can maximize the power and flexibility of the preprocessor while avoiding common pitfalls. The strategic use of these elements ultimately leads to more readable, maintainable, and efficient C programs.

13. Input & Output and The UNIX System Interface in C

Input and Output in C

1. Overview of Standard Input and Output

In C programming, input and output (I/O) operations are fundamental for interacting with the system and user. These operations typically involve reading from or writing to various sources like the keyboard, files, or other devices.

The **C Standard Library** provides a set of functions in the <stdio.h> library to perform standard I/O operations. These functions are device-independent, meaning they can be used across different environments, including UNIX.

2. Types of Standard I/O Streams

C programs typically use three standard I/O streams, initialized automatically at runtime:

Standard Input (stdin): Used for reading input, typically from the keyboard.

Standard Output (stdout): Used for displaying output, usually to the screen.

Standard Error (stderr): Used for error messages, sent separately from standard output to make debugging easier.

3. Basic I/O Functions

Here are some common I/O functions in C that handle various input and output operations:

printf(): Used to print formatted output to stdout.

```
printf("Hello, World!\n");
```
scanf(): Used to read formatted input from stdin.

```
int num;
scanf("%d", &num);
```

getchar() and putchar(): Used for single-character I/O.

```
char c = getchar();  // Reads a character from stdin
```

```
putchar(c);        // Writes a character to stdout
```

fgets() and fputs(): Used for string I/O.

```
char buffer[100];
fgets(buffer, 100, stdin);  // Reads a line of text from stdin
fputs(buffer, stdout);      // Writes a string to stdout
```

fread() and fwrite(): Used for binary I/O on files.

```
FILE *file = fopen("example.bin", "rb");
fread(buffer, sizeof(char), 100, file);
fclose(file);
```

4. File Handling and I/O Functions

The FILE structure in <stdio.h> is used to manage file operations, allowing for more complex I/O with files beyond standard input and output.

Opening and Closing Files:

```
FILE *file = fopen("filename.txt", "r");  // Open a file in read mode
fclose(file); // Close the file
```

Reading and Writing Files:

fscanf() and fprintf() can read and write formatted data.

fgetc() and fputc() handle character-level I/O.

fread() and fwrite() handle block I/O for binary data.

5. Error Handling in I/O Operations

Error handling in C I/O is essential, as operations can fail due to issues like unavailable files or invalid permissions. Commonly used methods include:

Return Value Checks: Most I/O functions return a status that can be checked for errors. For example, fopen() returns NULL if the file cannot be opened.

perror() and strerror() Functions: Provide human-readable error messages.

The UNIX System Interface in C

1. Introduction to UNIX System Calls

System calls provide an interface between a C program and the UNIX operating system. These low-level functions, unlike standard library I/O functions, interact directly with the OS kernel, allowing for more control over files, processes, and other system resources.

Some key categories of UNIX system calls are:

File Management: Opening, reading, writing, and closing files.

Process Control: Creating and managing processes.

Inter-Process Communication (IPC): Pipes, shared memory, and message passing.

The <unistd.h> library provides many of these essential system calls for UNIX systems.

2. File I/O with UNIX System Calls

UNIX system calls offer a direct way to manage files, which can be more efficient than using C standard I/O functions for certain applications.

open(): Opens a file, returning a file descriptor.

int fd = open("file.txt", O_RDONLY);

read() and write(): Used for reading from and writing to files using file descriptors.

char buffer[100];
read(fd, buffer, 100); // Reads up to 100 bytes from the file
write(fd, buffer, 100); // Writes 100 bytes to the file

close(): Closes a file.
close(fd);

3. Understanding File Descriptors

File descriptors are integers that uniquely identify open files or I/O resources in a process. The UNIX system reserves the following file descriptors:

0 for stdin
1 for stdout
2 for stderr

File descriptors allow C programs to use UNIX I/O functions like read() and write().

4. File Control and Manipulation

The fcntl function provides advanced control over file descriptors and enables actions like duplicating file descriptors or setting file access modes.

fcntl(): Modifies file descriptor properties.

```
int flags = fcntl(fd, F_GETFL);
fcntl(fd, F_SETFL, flags | O_APPEND); // Set append mode
```

5. Process Management and UNIX System Interface

UNIX systems provide system calls to create and manage processes. A process is an instance of a running program, and process management is fundamental in UNIX.

fork(): Creates a new process, duplicating the parent process.

```
pid_t pid = fork();
if (pid == 0) {
    // Child process code
} else if (pid > 0) {
    // Parent process code
}
```

exec(): Replaces the current process image with a new program, often used after fork() to execute a different program.

```
execl("/bin/ls", "ls", "-l", NULL);  // Execute the "ls -l" command
```

wait(): Makes the parent process wait for the child process to finish.

```
int status;
wait(&status);
```

6. Inter-Process Communication (IPC)

IPC mechanisms allow processes to communicate and synchronize. Common methods include:

Pipes: A unidirectional data channel between two processes.

```
int pipefd[2];
pipe(pipefd);
write(pipefd[1], "data", strlen("data"));
read(pipefd[0], buffer, sizeof(buffer));
```

Shared Memory: Enables multiple processes to access a common memory space.

Shared memory is usually created using shmget(), attached with shmat(), and detached with shmdt().

Message Queues and Semaphores: Offer more controlled synchronization for complex IPC.

7. Error Handling in UNIX System Calls

Handling errors in UNIX system calls is essential since many operations involve permissions, resources, and processes that may fail unexpectedly.

Return Value Checks: Most system calls return -1 on failure.

errno Variable: Stores the error code, which can be converted to readable messages using perror() or strerror().

8. Summary and Comparison with Standard I/O

The main differences between standard I/O and UNIX system calls are:

Buffered vs. Unbuffered: Standard I/O is buffered (aggregates data), while system calls are unbuffered (direct).

Control and Performance: System calls provide lower-level control and can be more efficient in certain cases, though they are less portable than standard I/O functions.

Input and Output

Input and output are not part of the C language itself, so we have not emphasized them in our presentation thus far. Nonetheless, programs interact with their environment in much more complicated ways than those we have shown before. In this chapter we will describe the standard library, a set of functions that provide input and output, string handling, storage management, mathematical routines, and a variety of other services for C programs. We will concentrate on input and output.

The ANSI standard defines these library functions precisely, so that they can exist in compatible form on any system where C exists. Programs that confine their system interactions to facilities provided by the standard library can be moved from one system to another without change.

The properties of library functions are specified in more than a dozen headers; we have already seen several of these, including <stdio.h>, <string.h>, and <ctype.h>. We will not present the entire library here, since we are more interested in writing C programs that use it.

Standard Input and Output

As we said, the library implements a simple model of text input and output. A text stream consists of a sequence of lines; each line ends with a newline character. If the system doesn't operate that way, the library does whatever necessary to make it appear as if it does. For instance, the library might convert carriage return and linefeed to newline on input and back again on output.

The simplest input mechanism is to read one character at a time from the standard input, normally the keyboard, with getchar:

int getchar(void)

getchar returns the next input character each time it is called, or EOF when it encounters end of file. The symbolic constant EOF is defined in <stdio.h>. The value is typically -1, bus tests should be written in terms of EOF so as to be independent of the specific value.

In many environments, a file may be substituted for the keyboard by using the < convention for input redirection: if a program prog uses getchar, then the command line   prog <infile causes prog to read characters from infile instead. The switching of the input is done in such a way that prog itself is oblivious to the change; in particular, the string ``<infile'' is not included in the command-line arguments in argv.

Input switching is also invisible if the input comes from another program via a pipe mechanism: on some systems, the command line otherprog | prog runs the two programs otherprog and prog, and pipes the standard output of otherprog into the standard input for prog.

The function   int putchar(int) is used for output: putchar(c) puts the character c on the standard output, which is by default the screen. putchar returns the character written, or EOF is an error occurs. Again, output can usually be directed to a file with >filename: if prog uses putchar, prog >outfile will write the standard output to outfile instead.

If pipes are supported, prog | anotherprog puts the standard output of prog into the standard input of anotherprog.

Output produced by printf also finds its way to the standard output. Calls to putchar and printf may be interleaved - output happens in the order in which the calls are made.

Each source file that refers to an input/output library function must contain the line #include <stdio.h>

before the first reference. When the name is bracketed by < and > a search is made for the header in a standard set of places (for example, on UNIX systems, typically in the directory /usr/include).

Many programs read only one input stream and write only one output stream; for such programs, input and output with getchar, putchar, and printf may be entirely adequate, and is certainly enough to get started. This is particularly true if redirection is used to connect the output of one program to the input of the next. For example, consider the program lower, which converts its input to lower case:

```
#include <stdio.h>
#include <ctype.h>

main() /* lower: convert input to lower case*/
{
int c

while ((c = getchar()) != EOF)
putchar(tolower(c));
return 0;

}
```

The function tolower is defined in <ctype.h>; it converts an upper-case letter to lower case, and returns other characters untouched. As we mentioned earlier, ``functions'' like getchar and putchar in <stdio.h> and tolower in <ctype.h> are often macros, thus avoiding the overhead of a function call per character.

Regardless of how the <ctype.h> functions are implemented on a given machine, programs that use them are shielded from knowledge of the character set.

Formatted Output – printf

The output function printf translates internal values to characters. We have used printf informally in previous chapters. The description here covers most typical uses but is not complete;

```
int printf(char *format, arg1, arg2, ...);
```

printf converts, formats, and prints its arguments on the standard output under control of the format. It returns the number of characters printed.

The format string contains two types of objects: ordinary characters, which are copied to the output stream, and conversion specifications, each of which causes conversion and printing of the next successive argument to printf. Each conversion specification begins with a % and ends with a conversion character.

Between the % and the conversion character there may be, in order:

A minus sign, which specifies left adjustment of the converted argument.

A number that specifies the minimum field width. The converted argument will be printed in a field at least this wide. If necessary, it will be padded on the left (or right, if left adjustment is called for) to make up the field width.

A period, which separates the field width from the precision.

A number, the precision, that specifies the maximum number of characters to be printed from a string, or the number of digits after the decimal point of a floating-point value, or the minimum number of digits for an integer.

An h if the integer is to be printed as a short, or l (letter ell) if as a long.

Conversion characters are shown in Table. If the character after the % is not a conversion specification, the behavior is undefined.

Table Basic Printf Conversions

Character	Argument type; Printed As
d,i	int; decimal number
o	int; unsigned octal number (without a leading zero)
x,X	int; unsigned hexadecimal number (without a leading 0x or 0X), using abcdef or ABCDEF for 10, ...,15.
u	int; unsigned decimal number
c	int; single character
s	char *; print characters from the string until a '\0' or the number of characters given by the precision.
f	double; [-]m.dddddd, where the number of d's is given by the precision (default 6).
e,E	double; [-]m.dddddde+/-xx or [-]m.ddddddE+/-xx, where the number of d's is given by the precision (default 6).
g,G	double; use %e or %E if the exponent is less than -4 or greater than or equal to the precision; otherwise use %f. Trailing zeros and a trailing decimal point are not printed.
p	void *; pointer (implementation-dependent representation).
%	no argument is converted; print a %

A width or precision may be specified as *, in which case the value is computed by converting the next argument (which must be an int). For example, to print at most max characters from a string s,

printf("%.*s", max, s);

Most of the format conversions have been illustrated in earlier chapters. One exception is the precision as it relates to strings. The following table shows the effect of a variety of specifications in printing ``hello, world'' (12 characters). We have put colons around each field so you can see it extent.

```
:%s:        :hello, world:
:%10s:      :hello, world:
:%.10s:     :hello, wor:
:%-10s:     :hello, world:
:%.15s:     :hello, world:
:%-15s:     :hello, world   :
:%15.10s:  :hello, wor:
:%-15.10s:  :hello, wor    :
```

A warning: printf uses its first argument to decide how many arguments follow and what their type is. It will get confused, and you will get wrong answers, if there are not enough arguments of if they are the wrong type. You should also be aware of the difference between these two calls:

```
printf(s);      /* FAILS if s contains % */

printf("%s", s);  /* SAFE */
```

The function sprintf does the same conversions as printf does, but stores the output in a string:

```
int sprintf(char *string, char *format, arg1, arg2, ...);
```

sprintf formats the arguments in arg1, arg2, etc., according to format as before, but places the result in string instead of the standard output; string must be big enough to receive the result.

Variable-length Argument Lists

This section contains an implementation of a minimal version of printf, to show how to write a function that processes a variable-length argument list in a portable way. Since we are mainly interested in the argument processing, minprintf will process the format string and arguments but will call the real printf to do the format conversions. The proper declaration for printf is   int printf(char *fmt, ...) where the declaration ... means that the number and types of these arguments may vary. The declaration ... can only appear at the end of an argument list. Our minprintf is declared as void minprintf(char *fmt, ...) since we will not return the character count that printf does.

The tricky bit is how minprintf walks along the argument list when the list doesn't even have a name. The standard header <stdarg.h> contains a set of macro definitions that define how to step through an argument list. The implementation of this header will vary from machine to machine, but the interface it presents is uniform.

The type va_list is used to declare a variable that will refer to each argument in turn; in minprintf, this variable is called ap, for ``argument pointer." The macro va_start initializes ap to point to the first unnamed argument. It must be called once before ap is used. There must be at least one named argument; the final named argument is used by va_start to get started.

Each call of va_arg returns one argument and steps ap to the next; va_arg uses a type name to determine what type to return and how big a step to take. Finally, va_end does whatever cleanup is necessary. It must be called before the program returns.

These properties form the basis of our simplified printf:

```
#include <stdarg.h>

   /* minprintf: minimal printf with variable argument list */
void minprintf(char *fmt, ...)
{
```

```
va_list ap; /* points to each unnamed arg in turn */
char *p, *sval;

int ival;
double dval;

va_start(ap, fmt); /* make ap point to 1st unnamed arg */
for (p = fmt; *p; p++) {
if (*p != '%') {
putchar(*p);
continue;
}
switch (*++p) {
case 'd':
ival = va_arg(ap, int);
printf("%d", ival);
break;
case 'f':
dval = va_arg(ap, double);
printf("%f", dval);
break;
case 's':
for (sval = va_arg(ap, char *); *sval; sval++)
putchar(*sval);
break;
default:
putchar(*p);
break;

}
}

va_end(ap); /* clean up when done */

}
```

Formatted Input – Scanf

The function scanf is the input analog of printf, providing many of the same conversion facilities in the opposite direction.

```
int scanf(char *format, ...)
```

scanf reads characters from the standard input, interprets them according to the specification in format, and stores the results through the remaining arguments. The format argument is described below; the other arguments, each of which must be a pointer, indicate where the corresponding converted input should be stored. As with printf, this section is a summary of the most useful features, not an exhaustive list.

scanf stops when it exhausts its format string, or when some input fails to match the control specification. It returns as its value the number of successfully matched and assigned input items. This can be used to decide how many items were found. On the end of file, EOF is returned; note that this is different from 0, which means that the next input character does not match the first specification in the format string. The next call to scanf resumes searching immediately after the last character already converted.

There is also a function sscanf that reads from a string instead of the standard input:

  int sscanf(char *string, char *format, arg1, arg2, ...)

It scans the string according to the format in format and stores the resulting values through arg1, arg2, etc. These arguments must be pointers.

The format string usually contains conversion specifications, which are used to control conversion of input.

The format string may contain:

Blanks or tabs, which are not ignored.

Ordinary characters (not %), which are expected to match the next non-white space character of the input stream.

Conversion specifications, consisting of the character %, an optional assignment suppression character *, an optional number specifying a maximum field width, an optional h, l or L indicating the width of the target, and a conversion character.

A conversion specification directs the conversion of the next input field. Normally the result is places in the variable pointed to by the corresponding argument. If assignment suppression is indicated by the * character, however, the input field is skipped; no assignment is made. An input field is defined as a string of non-white space characters; it extends either to the next white space character or until the field width, is specified, is exhausted. This implies that scanf will read across boundaries to find its input, since newlines are white space. (White space characters are blank, tab, newline, carriage return, vertical tab, and form feed.)

The conversion character indicates the interpretation of the input field. The corresponding argument must be a pointer, as required by the call-by-value semantics of C. Conversion characters are shown in Table.

Table Basic Scanf Conversions

Character	Input Data; Argument type
d	decimal integer; int *
i	integer; int *. The integer may be in octal (leading 0) or hexadecimal (leading 0x or 0X).
o	octal integer (with or without leading zero); int *
u	unsigned decimal integer; unsigned int *

x	hexadecimal integer (with or without leading 0x or 0X); int *
c	characters; char *. The next input characters (default 1) are placed at the indicated spot. The normal skip-over white space is suppressed; to read the next non-white space character, use %1s
s	character string (not quoted); char *, pointing to an array of characters long enough for the string and a terminating '\0' that will be added.
e,f,g	floating-point number with optional sign, optional decimal point and optional exponent; float *
%	literal %; no assignment is made.

The conversion characters d, i, o, u, and x may be preceded by h to indicate that a pointer to short rather than int appears in the argument list, or by l (letter ell) to indicate that a pointer to long appears in the argument list.

As a first example, the rudimentary calculator can be written with scanf to do the input conversion:

```
#include <stdio.h>

main()  /* rudimentary calculator */
{
double sum, v;

sum = 0;

while (scanf("%lf", &v) == 1)
printf("\t%.2f\n", sum += v);
return 0;
}
```

Suppose we want to read input lines that contain dates of the form

25 Dec 1988

The scanf statement is

```
int day, year;
char monthname[20];
scanf("%d %s %d", &day, monthname, &year);
```

No & is used with monthname, since an array name is a pointer.

Literal characters can appear in the scanf format string; they must match the same characters in the input.

So, we could read dates of the form mm/dd/yy with the scanf statement:

int day, month, year; scanf("%d/%d/%d", &month, &day, &year); scanf ignores blanks and tabs in its format string. Furthermore, it skips over white space (blanks, tabs, newlines, etc.) as it looks for input values. To read input whose format is not fixed, it is often best to read a line at a time, then pick it apart with scanf. For example, suppose we want to read lines that might contain a date in either of the forms above.

Then we could write

```
while (getline(line, sizeof(line)) > 0) {
if (sscanf(line, "%d %s %d", &day, monthname, &year) == 3)
printf("valid: %s\n", line); /* 25 Dec 1988 form */
else if (sscanf(line, "%d/%d/%d", &month, &day, &year) == 3)
printf("valid: %s\n", line); /* mm/dd/yy form */
else
        printf("invalid: %s\n", line); /* invalid form */
}
```

Calls to scanf can be mixed with calls to other input functions. The next call to any input function will begin by reading the first character not read by scanf.

A final warning: the arguments to scanf and sscanf must be pointers. By far the most common error is writing scanf("%d", n); instead of scanf("%d", &n);

This error is not generally detected at compile time.

File Access

The examples so far have all read the standard input and written the standard output, which are automatically defined for a program by the local operating system.

The next step is to write a program that accesses a file that is not already connected to the program. One program that illustrates the need for such operations is cat, which concatenates a set of named files into the standard output. cat is used for printing files on the screen, and as a general-purpose input collector for programs that do not have the capability of accessing files by name. For example, the command   cat x.c y.c

prints the contents of the files x.c and y.c (and nothing else) on the standard output.

The question is how to arrange for the named files to be read - that is, how to connect the external names that a user thinks of to the statements that read the data.

The rules are simple. Before it can be read or written, a file has to be opened by the library function fopen. fopen takes an external name like x.c or y.c, does some housekeeping and negotiation with the operating system (details of which needn't concern us), and returns a pointer to be used in subsequent reads or writes of the file.

This pointer, called the file pointer, points to a structure that contains information about the file, such as the location of a buffer, the current character position in the buffer, whether the file is being read or written, and whether errors or end of file have occurred. Users don't need to know the details, because the definitions obtained from <stdio.h> include a structure declaration called FILE. The only declaration needed for a file pointer is exemplified by

```
FILE *fp;
FILE *fopen(char *name, char *mode);
```

This says that fp is a pointer to a FILE, and fopen returns a pointer to a FILE. Notice that FILE is a type name, like int, not a structure tag; it is defined with a typedef. The call to fopen in a program is

```
fp = fopen(name, mode);
```

The first argument of fopen is a character string containing the name of the file. The second argument is the mode, also a character string, which indicates how one intends to use the file. Allowable modes include read ("r"), write ("w"), and append ("a"). Some systems distinguish between text and binary files; for the latter, a "b" must be appended to the mode string.

If a file that does not exist is opened for writing or appending, it is created if possible. Opening an existing file for writing causes the old contents to be discarded, while opening for appending preserves them. Trying to read a file that does not exist is an error, and there may be other causes of error as well, like trying to read a file when you don't have permission. If there is any error, fopen will return NULL.

The next thing needed is a way to read or write the file once it is open. getc returns the next character from a file; it needs the file pointer to tell it which file.

```
int getc(FILE *fp)
```

getc returns the next character from the stream referred to by fp; it returns EOF for end of file or error. putc is an output function:

```
int putc(int c, FILE *fp)
```

putc writes the character c to the file fp and returns the character written, or EOF if an error occurs. Like getchar and putchar, getc and putc may be macros instead of functions.

When a C program is started, the operating system environment is responsible for opening three files and providing pointers for them. These files are the standard input, the standard output, and the standard error; the corresponding file pointers are called stdin, stdout, and stderr, and are declared in <stdio.h>. Normally stdin is connected to the keyboard and stdout and stderr are connected to the screen, but stdin and stdout may be redirected to files or pipes as described in Section.

getchar and putchar can be defined in terms of getc, putc, stdin, and stdout as follows:

```
#define getchar()   getc(stdin)
```

```
#define putchar(c)   putc((c), stdout)
```

For formatted input or output of files, the functions fscanf and fprintf may be used. These are identical to scanf and printf, except that the first argument is a file pointer that specifies the file to be read or written; the format string is the second argument.

```
int fscanf(FILE *fp, char *format, ...)   int fprintf(FILE *fp, char *format, ...)
```

With these preliminaries out of the way, we are now in a position to write the program cat to concatenate files. The design is one that has been found convenient for many programs. If there are command-line arguments, they are interpreted as filenames, and processed in order. If there are no arguments, the standard input is processed.

```c
#include <stdio.h>
   /* cat:  concatenate files, version 1 */
main(int argc, char *argv[])
{
FILE *fp;
void filecopy(FILE *, FILE *)

if (argc == 1) /* no args; copy standard input */
filecopy(stdin, stdout);
else

while(--argc > 0)

if ((fp = fopen(*++argv, "r")) == NULL)
{
printf("cat: can't open %s\n, *argv);
return 1;
} else
{
filecopy(fp, stdout);
fclose(fp);
}
return 0;
}

   /* filecopy:  copy file ifp to file ofp */
void filecopy(FILE *ifp, FILE *ofp)
{
int c;

while ((c = getc(ifp)) != EOF)
putc(c, ofp);
}
```

The file pointers stdin and stdout are objects of type FILE *. They are constants, however, not variables, so it is not possible to assign to them. The function   int fclose(FILE *fp) is the inverse of fopen, it breaks the connection between the file pointer and the external name that was established by fopen, freeing the file pointer for another file. Since most operating systems have some limit on the number of files that a program may have open simultaneously, it's a good idea to free the file pointers when they are no longer needed, as we did in cat. There is also another reason for fclose on an output file - it flushes the buffer in which putc is collecting output. fclose is called automatically for each open file when a program terminates normally. (You can close stdin and stdout if they are not needed. They can also be reassigned by the library function freopen.)

Error Handling - Stderr and Exit

The treatment of errors in cat is not ideal. The trouble is that if one of the files can't be accessed for some reason, the diagnostic is printed at the end of the concatenated output. That might be acceptable if the output is going to a screen, but not if it's going into a file or into another program via a pipeline.

To handle this situation better, a second output stream, called stderr, is assigned to a program in the same way that stdin and stdout are. Output written on stderr normally appears on the screen even if the standard output is redirected.

Let us revise cat to write its error messages on the standard error.

```
#include <stdio.h>

    /* cat:  concatenate files, version 2 */
main(int argc, char *argv[])
{
FILE *fp;

void filecopy(FILE *, FILE *);
char *prog = argv[0];  /* program name for errors */

if (argc == 1 ) /* no args; copy standard input */
filecopy(stdin, stdout);
else

while (--argc > 0)

if ((fp = fopen(*++argv, "r")) == NULL)
{
fprintf(stderr, "%s: can't open %s\n", prog, *argv);
exit(1);
} else
{

filecopy(fp, stdout);
fclose(fp);

}
if (ferror(stdout))
{

fprintf(stderr, "%s: error writing stdout\n", prog);
exit(2);

}
exit(0);
```

}

The program signals errors in two ways. First, the diagnostic output produced by fprintf goes to stderr, so it finds its way to the screen instead of disappearing down a pipeline or into an output file. We included the program name, from argv[0], in the message, so if this program is used with others, the source of an error is identified.

Second, the program uses the standard library function exit, which terminates program execution when it is called. The argument of exit is available to whatever process called this one, so the success or failure of the program can be tested by another program that uses this one as a sub-process. Conventionally, a return value of 0 signals that all is well; non-zero values usually signal abnormal situations. exit calls fclose for each open output file, to flush out any buffered output.

Within main, return expr is equivalent to exit(expr). exit has the advantage that it can be called from other functions, and that calls to it can be found with a pattern-searching program.

The function ferror returns non-zero if an error occurred on the stream fp.   int ferror(FILE *fp)

Although output errors are rare, they do occur (for example, if a disk fills up), so a production program should check this as well.

The function feof(FILE *) is analogous to ferror; it returns non-zero if end of file has occurred on the specified file.

int feof(FILE *fp)

We have generally not worried about exit status in our small illustrative programs, but any serious program should take care to return sensible, useful status values.

Line Input and Output

The standard library provides an input and output routine fgets that is similar to the getline function that we have used in earlier chapters:

char *fgets(char *line, int maxline, FILE *fp)

fgets reads the next input line (including the newline) from file fp into the character array line; at most maxline-1 characters will be read. The resulting line is terminated with '\0'. Normally fgets returns line; on end of file or error it returns NULL. (Our getline returns the line length, which is a more useful value; zero means end of file.)

For output, the function fputs writes a string (which need not contain a newline) to a file:

int fputs(char *line, FILE *fp)

It returns EOF if an error occurs, and non-negative otherwise.

The library functions gets and puts are similar to fgets and fputs, but operate on stdin and stdout.

Confusingly, gets deletes the terminating '\n', and puts adds it.

To show that there is nothing special about functions like fgets and fputs, here they are, copied from the standard library on our system:

```
    /* fgets:  get at most n chars from iop */
char *fgets(char *s, int n, FILE *iop)

{

register int c;
register char *cs;

cs = s;

while (--n > 0 && (c = getc(iop)) != EOF)
if ((*cs++ = c) == '\n')
break;
*cs = '\0';

return (c == EOF && cs == s) ? NULL : s;
}
    /* fputs:  put string s on file iop */
int fputs(char *s, FILE *iop)
{
int c;

while (c = *s++)
putc(c, iop);

return ferror(iop) ? EOF: 0;
}
```

For no obvious reason, the standard specifies different return values for ferror and fputs.

It is easy to implement our getline from fgets:

```
    /* getline:  read a line, return length */
int getline(char *line, int max)

    {

        if (fgets(line, max, stdin) == NULL)
        return 0;       else

        return strlen(line);

    }
```

Miscellaneous Functions

The standard library provides a wide variety of functions. This section is a brief synopsis of the most useful.

String Operations

We have already mentioned the string functions strlen, strcpy, strcat, and strcmp, found in <string.h>. In the following, s and t are char *'s, and c and n are ints.

strcat(s,t)   concatenate t to end of s

strncat(s,t,n)   concatenate n characters of t to end of s

strcmp(s,t)   return negative, zero, or positive for s < t, s == t, s > t

strncmp(s,t,n) same as strcmp but only in first n characters

strcpy(s,t)   copy t to s

strncpy(s,t,n) copy at most n characters of t to s

strlen(s)   return length of s

strchr(s,c)   return pointer to first c in s, or NULL if not present
strrchr(s,c)   return pointer to last c in s, or NULL if not present

Character Class Testing and Conversion

Several functions from <ctype.h> perform character tests and conversions. In the following, c is an int that can be represented as an unsigned char or EOF. The function returns int.

isalpha(c) non-zero if c is alphabetic, 0 if not
isupper(c) non-zero if c is upper case, 0 if not
islower(c) non-zero if c is lower case, 0 if not
isdigit(c) non-zero if c is digit, 0 if not

isalnum(c) non-zero if isalpha(c) or isdigit(c), 0 if not

isspace(c) non-zero if c is blank, tab, newline, return, formfeed, vertical tab

toupper(c) return c converted to upper case
tolower(c) return c converted to lower case

Ungetc

The standard library provides a rather restricted version of the function ungetch it is called ungetc.

int ungetc(int c, FILE *fp)

pushes the character c back onto file fp, and returns either c, or EOF for an error. Only one character of pushback is guaranteed per file. ungetc may be used with any of the input functions like scanf, getc, or getchar.

Command Execution

The function system(char *s) executes the command contained in the character string s, then resumes execution of the current program. The contents of s depend strongly on the local operating system.

As a trivial example, on UNIX systems, the statement system("date");

causes the program date to be run; it prints the date and time of day on the standard output. system returns a system-dependent integer status from the command executed. In the UNIX system, the status return is the value returned by exit.

Storage Management

The functions malloc and calloc obtain blocks of memory dynamically. void *malloc(size_t n) returns a pointer to n bytes of uninitialized storage, or NULL if the request cannot be satisfied.

void *calloc(size_t n, size_t size)

returns a pointer to enough free space for an array of n objects of the specified size, or NULL if the request cannot be satisfied. The storage is initialized to zero.

The pointer returned by malloc or calloc has the proper alignment for the object in question, but it must be cast into the appropriate type, as in

```
int *ip;
ip = (int *) calloc(n, sizeof(int));
```

free(p) frees the space pointed to by p, where p was originally obtained by a call to malloc or calloc. There are no restrictions on the order in which space is freed, but it is a ghastly error to free something not obtained by calling malloc or calloc.

It is also an error to use something after it has been freed. A typical but incorrect piece of code is this loop that frees items from a list:

```
for (p = head; p != NULL; p = p->next) /* WRONG */
free(p);
```

The right way is to save whatever is needed before freeing:

```
for (p = head; p != NULL; p = q)
{
q = p->next;
free(p);

}
```

Mathematical Functions

There are more than twenty mathematical functions declared in <math.h>; here are some of the more frequently used. Each takes one or two double arguments and returns a double.

sin(x) sine of x, x in radians cos(x) cosine of x, x in radians atan2(y,x) arctangent of y/x, in radians

exp(x)	exponential function e^x
log(x)	natural (base e) logarithm of x (x>0)
log10(x)	common (base 10) logarithm of x (x>0)
pow(x,y)	xy
sqrt(x)	square root of x (x>0)
fabs(x)	absolute value of x

Random Number generation

The function rand() computes a sequence of pseudo-random integers in the range zero to

RAND_MAX, which is defined in <stdlib.h>. One way to produce random floating-point numbers greater than or equal to zero but less than one is

#define frand() ((double) rand() / (RAND_MAX+1.0))

(If your library already provides a function for floating-point random numbers, it is likely to have better statistical properties than this one.)

The UNIX System Interface

The UNIX operating system provides its services through a set of system calls, which are in effect functions within the operating system that may be called by user programs. This chapter describes how to use some of the most important system calls from C programs. If you use UNIX, this should be directly helpful, for it is sometimes necessary to employ system calls for maximum efficiency, or to access some facility that is not in the library. Even if you use C on a different operating system, however, you should be able to glean insight into C programming from studying these examples; although details vary, similar code will be found on any system. Since the ANSI C library is in many cases modeled on UNIX facilities, this code may help your understanding of the library as well.

This chapter is divided into three major parts: input/output, file system, and storage allocation. The first two parts assume a modest familiarity with the external characteristics of UNIX systems.

It was concerned with an input/output interface that is uniform across operating systems. On any particular system the routines of the standard library have to be written in terms of the facilities provided by the host system. In the next few sections, we will describe the UNIX system calls for input and output, and show how parts of the standard library can be implemented with them.

File Descriptors

In the UNIX operating system, all input and output are done by reading or writing files, because all peripheral devices, even keyboard and screen, are files in the file system. This means that a single homogeneous interface handles all communication between a program and peripheral devices.

In the most general case, before you read and write a file, you must inform the system of your intent to do so, a process called opening the file. If you are going to write on a file it may also be necessary to create it or to discard its previous contents. The system checks your right to do so (Does the file exist? Do you have permission to access it?) and if all is well, returns to the program a small non-negative integer called a file descriptor. Whenever input or output is to be done on the file, the file descriptor is used instead of the name to identify the file. (A file descriptor is analogous to the file pointer used by the standard library, or to the file handle of MS-DOS.) All information about an open file is maintained by the system; the user program refers to the file only by the file descriptor.

Since input and output involving keyboard and screen is so common, special arrangements exist to make this convenient. When the command interpreter (the ``shell'') runs a program, three files are open, with file descriptors 0, 1, and 2, called the standard input, the standard output, and the standard error. If a program reads 0 and writes 1 and 2, it can do input and output without worrying about opening files.

The user of a program can redirect I/O to and from files with < and >:

prog <infile >outfile

In this case, the shell changes the default assignments for the file descriptors 0 and 1 to the named files. Normally file descriptor 2 remains attached to the screen, so error messages can go there. Similar observations hold for input or output associated with a pipe. In all cases, the file assignments are changed by the shell, not by the program. The program does not know where its input comes from nor where its output goes, so long as it uses file 0 for input and 1 and 2 for output.

Low Level I/O - Read and Write

Input and output use the read and write system calls, which are accessed from C programs through two functions called read and write. For both, the first argument is a file descriptor. The second argument is a character array in your program where the data is to go to or to come from. The third argument is the number is the number of bytes to be transferred.

```
int n_read = read(int fd, char *buf, int n);
int n_written = write(int fd, char *buf, int n);
```

Each call returns a count of the number of bytes transferred. On reading, the number of bytes returned may be less than the number requested. A return value of zero bytes implies end of file, and -1 indicates an error of some sort. For writing, the return value is the number of bytes written; an error has occurred if this isn't equal to the number requested.

Any number of bytes can be read or written in one call. The most common values are 1, which means one character at a time (``unbuffered''), and a number like 1024 or 4096 that corresponds to a physical block size on a peripheral device. Larger sizes will be more efficient because fewer system calls will be made.

Putting these facts together, we can write a simple program to copy its input to its output, the equivalent of the file copying program. This program will copy anything to anything, since the input and output can be redirected to any file or device.

```c
#include "syscalls.h"
main()  /* copy input to output */
{
    char buf[BUFSIZ];
    int n;

    while ((n = read(0, buf, BUFSIZ)) > 0)
    write(1, buf, n);

    return 0;
}
```

We have collected function prototypes for the system calls into a file called syscalls.h so we can include it in the programs of this chapter. This name is not standard, however.

The parameter BUFSIZ is also defined in syscalls.h; its value is a good size for the local system. If the file size is not a multiple of BUFSIZ, some read will return a smaller number of bytes to be written by write; the next call to read after that will return zero.

It is instructive to see how read and write can be used to construct higher-level routines like getchar, putchar, etc. For example, here is a version of getchar that does unbuffered input, by reading the standard input one character at a time.

```c
#include "syscalls.h"
   /* getchar:  unbuffered single character input */
int getchar(void)
{
char c;

return (read(0, &c, 1) == 1) ? (unsigned char) c: EOF;

}
```

c must be a char, because read needs a character pointer. Casting c to unsigned char in the return statement eliminates any problem of sign extension.

The second version of getchar does input in big chunks, and hands out the characters one at a time.

```c
#include "syscalls.h"
```

```
   /* getchar:  simple buffered version */
int getchar(void)

{

static char buf[BUFSIZ];
static char *bufp = buf;
static int n = 0;

if (n == 0) {  /* buffer is empty */
n = read(0, buf, sizeof buf);
bufp = buf;

}
return (--n >= 0) ? (unsigned char) *bufp++: EOF;
}
```

If these versions of getchar were to be compiled with <stdio.h> included, it would be necessary to #undef the name getchar in case it is implemented as a macro.

Open, Creat, Close, Unlink

Other than the default standard input, output and error, you must explicitly open files in order to read or write them. There are two system calls for this, open and creat [sic], except that instead of returning a file pointer, it returns a file descriptor, which is just an int. open returns -1 if any error occurs.

```
#include <fcntl.h>

int fd;
int open(char *name, int flags, int perms);
fd = open(name, flags, perms);
```

As with fopen, the name argument is a character string containing the filename. The second argument, flags, is an int that specifies how the file is to be opened; the main values are

O_RDONLY open for reading only

O_WRONLY open for writing only

O_RDWR open for both reading and writing

These constants are defined in <fcntl.h> on System V UNIX systems, and in <sys/file.h> on Berkeley (BSD) versions.

To open an existing file for reading,

```
fd = open(name, O_RDONLY,0);
```

The perms argument is always zero for the uses of open that we will discuss.

It is an error to try to open a file that does not exist. The system call creat is provided to create new files, or to re-write old ones.

```
int creat(char *name, int perms);
fd = creat(name, perms);
```

returns a file descriptor if it was able to create the file, and -1 if not. If the file already exists, creat will truncate it to zero length, thereby discarding its previous contents; it is not an error to creat a file that already exists.

If the file does not already exist, creat creates it with the permissions specified by the perms argument. In the UNIX file system, there are nine bits of permission information associated with a file that control read, write and execute access for the owner of the file, for the owner's group, and for all others. Thus, a three-digit octal number is convenient for specifying the permissions. For example, 0775 specifies read, write and execute permission for the owner, and read and execute permission for the group and everyone else.

To illustrate, here is a simplified version of the UNIX program cp, which copies one file to another. Our version copies only one file, it does not permit the second argument to be a directory, and it invents permissions instead of copying them.

```
#include <stdio.h>

#include <fcntl.h>

#include "syscalls.h"

#define PERMS 0666     /* RW for owner, group, others */
void error(char *, ...);

   /* cp:  copy f1 to f2 */
main(int argc, char *argv[])
{
int f1, f2, n;
char buf[BUFSIZ];

if (argc != 3)
error("Usage: cp from to");

if ((f1 = open(argv[1], O_RDONLY, 0)) == -1)

error("cp: can't open %s", argv[1]);

if ((f2 = creat(argv[2], PERMS)) == -1)

error("cp: can't create %s, mode %03o", argv[2], PERMS);

while ((n = read(f1, buf, BUFSIZ)) > 0) if (write(f2, buf, n) != n)

error("cp: write error on file %s", argv[2]);

return 0;

}
```

This program creates the output file with fixed permissions of 0666. With the stat system call, we can determine the mode of an existing file and thus give the same mode to the copy.

Notice that the function error is called with variable argument lists much like printf. The implementation of error illustrates how to use another member of the printf family. The standard library function vprintf is like printf except that the variable argument list is replaced by a single argument that has been initialized by calling the va_start macro.

Similarly, vfprintf and vsprintf match fprintf and sprintf.

```
#include <stdio.h>
#include <stdarg.h>
/* error:  print an error message and die */
void error(char *fmt, ...)
{
va_list args;
va_start(args, fmt);
fprintf(stderr, "error: ");
vprintf(stderr, fmt, args);
fprintf(stderr, "\n");
va_end(args);
exit(1);
}
```

There is a limit (often about 20) on the number of files that a program may open simultaneously. Accordingly, any program that intends to process many files must be prepared to re-use file descriptors. The function close(int fd) breaks the connection between a file descriptor and an open file, and frees the file descriptor for use with some other file; it corresponds to fclose in the standard library except that there is no buffer to flush.

Termination of a program via exit or return from the main program closes all open files.

The function unlink(char *name) removes the file name from the file system. It corresponds to the standard library function remove.

Random Access – Lseek

Input and output are normally sequential: each read or write takes place at a position in the file right after the previous one. When necessary, however, a file can be read or written in any arbitrary order. The system call lseek provides a way to move around in a file without reading or writing any data:

long lseek(int fd, long offset, int origin);

sets the current position in the file whose descriptor is fd to offset, which is taken relative to the location specified by origin. Subsequent reading or writing will begin at that position. origin can be 0, 1, or 2 to specify that offset is to be measured from the beginning, from the current position, or from the end of the file respectively. For example, to append to a file (the redirection >> in the UNIX shell, or "a" for fopen), seek to the end before writing:

```
lseek(fd, 0L, 2);
```

To get back to the beginning (``rewind"),

```
lseek(fd, 0L, 0);
```

Notice the 0L argument; it could also be written as (long) 0 or just as 0 if lseek is properly declared.

With lseek, it is possible to treat files more or less like arrays, at the price of slower access. For example, the following function reads any number of bytes from any arbitrary place in a file. It returns the number read, or -1 on error.

```
#include "syscalls.h"
    /*get:  read n bytes from position pos */
int get(int fd, long pos, char *buf, int n)
    {
        if (lseek(fd, pos, 0) >= 0) /* get to pos */        return read(fd, buf, n);
        else        return -1;
    }
```

The return value from lseek is a long that gives the new position in the file, or -1 if an error occurs. The standard library function fseek is similar to lseek except that the first argument is a FILE * and the return is non-zero if an error occurred.

Conclusion

The topics of **Input & Output (I/O)** and **The UNIX System Interface in C** are foundational in C programming, especially when developing software for UNIX-like environments. By exploring the details of these interfaces, we gain insight into how C applications interact with users, files, and the operating system at a lower level. This conclusion will consolidate the essential concepts, discuss practical applications, and highlight best practices to consider when working with I/O and system interfaces.

1. The Role of Standard I/O in C Programming

Standard I/O functions, provided in the C Standard Library through <stdio.h>, form the backbone of user interaction and file manipulation in most C programs. These functions, such as printf(), scanf(), fopen(), fclose(), fread(), and fwrite(), allow developers to read from and write to files or standard input and output in a device-independent way.

The abstraction offered by standard I/O functions enhances portability, making it easy to write code that can run on different operating systems without modification. For example, printf() and scanf() provide robust, formatted output and input capabilities across platforms. Additionally, buffered I/O in the C Standard Library optimizes performance by aggregating data before writing it to or reading it from a device, reducing the number of I/O operations and improving speed.

2. Limitations of Standard I/O and the Need for UNIX System Calls

While the standard I/O library is effective for general-purpose programming, it has limitations when developers need precise control over file handling, process management, or low-level system interactions. This is where UNIX system calls, found in <unistd.h> and other related libraries, become essential. System calls like open(), read(), write(), close(), and fork() provide unbuffered, direct access to the operating system, enabling functionalities beyond standard I/O's scope.

For instance, using open() to access files via file descriptors allows control over specific file permissions, non-blocking modes, and file locks. The fork() system call, which creates a new process, and exec() family of calls, which replaces the current process image with a new program, are critical for managing multi-process applications and achieving concurrency in UNIX-based systems. These low-level operations allow developers to build high-performance applications that leverage the full capabilities of the UNIX environment.

3. File Descriptors and Resource Management

A key concept in UNIX system programming is the use of file descriptors, which are unique integer values assigned to open files, devices, sockets, or other I/O resources within a process. By default, UNIX reserves file descriptors 0, 1, and 2 for standard input, standard output, and standard error, respectively.

Understanding how file descriptors work allows developers to perform advanced operations such as duplicating descriptors with dup() or redirecting output in shell-like applications.

Resource management is another essential aspect when working with file descriptors and system resources. Each open file descriptor consumes system resources, so it is crucial to close descriptors using close() when they are no longer needed. This practice prevents resource leaks and ensures efficient use of available resources, a common requirement in multi-user, multi-tasking environments like UNIX.

4. Process Control and Management

The UNIX process model allows each program to execute as an independent process, with its memory space and system resources. System calls like fork() and exec() are essential for process management, particularly in building applications that require parallel execution, such as web servers, compilers, or any multi-threaded applications. By using fork(), a process can create a child process that inherits its code and data segments. The exec() system calls enable replacing this new process with an entirely different program, making it possible to run multiple programs within the same application.

Process control includes synchronizing between parent and child processes, often achieved with system calls like wait(), which makes the parent process wait for the child to complete. This synchronization is crucial in applications that rely on the child's results or need to ensure proper order of execution. Effective process management is fundamental for building robust applications that make optimal use of the CPU and system resources in UNIX environments.

5. Inter-Process Communication (IPC) and Data Exchange

Inter-Process Communication (IPC) in UNIX systems allows separate processes to share data and coordinate their actions, making it vital for complex applications that involve multiple interacting processes. IPC mechanisms like pipes, shared memory, message queues, and semaphores each serve different use cases:

Pipes provide a unidirectional communication channel, enabling data flow from one process to another in a producer-consumer pattern.

Shared Memory allows multiple processes to access the same memory space, which can be faster than other IPC methods for large data exchange.

Message Queues and Semaphores offer synchronization capabilities, controlling access to resources in multi-process applications.

Efficiently using IPC mechanisms can reduce bottlenecks and improve the performance of applications with multiple interacting processes, such as network servers or database management systems.

6. Error Handling and Best Practices in System Calls

Handling errors is a crucial aspect of robust C programming, especially with system calls that depend on the operating system's current state and resources. For instance, a call to open() might fail if a file does not exist or if permissions are insufficient, while fork() might fail if there are too many processes running.

Error handling in system calls typically involves checking return values and using the errno variable, which stores error codes set by failed system calls. Functions like perror() and strerror() help convert these codes into human-readable messages, making it easier to diagnose issues and implement corrective actions.

Some best practices for error handling and system call usage include:

Checking Return Values: Always validate system call outcomes. For example, check if open() returns -1 (indicating failure) and handle the error appropriately.

Resource Cleanup: Close file descriptors and release memory to avoid leaks. In long-running programs, resource mismanagement can lead to performance degradation and crashes.

Using Signals and Signal Handling: Signals in UNIX can interrupt processes to handle events like interrupts or termination requests. Understanding signal handling with functions like signal() and sigaction() allows programs to respond gracefully to external interruptions.

7. Real-World Applications and Relevance

Understanding and leveraging I/O and system calls is essential for developing applications that need to interact closely with the UNIX system. Several practical applications benefit from these capabilities:

Network Servers and Client Applications: These applications require handling multiple connections, often through processes or threads. Using fork() for each incoming connection or employing IPC for communication between processes can help manage concurrent connections efficiently.

Database Management Systems: Databases perform extensive file operations to read, write, and modify data. Efficient file I/O, file locking, and process management are critical to ensure data consistency and performance.

Compilers and Interpreters: These programs often spawn multiple processes, read and write files, and communicate between components. Utilizing low-level I/O operations and managing processes directly improves performance and resource utilization.

Shells and Command-Line Tools: Many UNIX command-line tools rely on direct system calls to provide powerful text processing, file management, and user interaction capabilities.

8. Future of C Programming with UNIX Interfaces

Although higher-level programming languages have become more popular, C remains indispensable for system programming due to its close relationship with hardware and operating systems. The UNIX system interface, especially when combined with C's flexibility and performance, continues to be a foundation for many low-level and high-performance applications.

As modern UNIX-like systems evolve, C developers are likely to see enhancements in libraries and tools that make low-level system programming more accessible. Concepts like memory safety, type safety, and better debugging tools may continue to improve, but the core knowledge of UNIX system calls and I/O will remain invaluable for those aiming to write efficient, reliable, and performant code.

Final Thoughts

The **Input & Output** and **UNIX System Interface** capabilities in C enable developers to go beyond basic programming, providing powerful tools to interact directly with the operating system. These concepts are essential not only for building standalone applications but also for creating the underlying infrastructure that supports modern computing environments.

Mastering these interfaces allows C programmers to build complex, high-performance software that fully utilizes the system's resources. Whether it's handling files, managing processes, or creating network applications, a solid understanding of I/O and UNIX system calls is a gateway to efficient and versatile software engineering.

As you continue learning, practical experience through building projects, experimenting with system calls, and exploring UNIX-specific programming paradigms will solidify these skills, giving you a strong foundation for both current and future projects.

14. Modern C Standards

Introduction to C11 Standard

The C11 standard, published in 2011, introduced significant advancements in the C programming language, catering to the needs of modern computing environments. After the C99 standard, C11 focused on enhancing safety, portability, and concurrency, aligning C with the demands of high-performance computing, multi-core processors, and real-time systems. This guide delves into the essential C11 features, including multi-threading, atomics, memory model updates, and generic functions. These features collectively strengthen C's reliability, flexibility, and performance, making it a versatile choice for systems programming and beyond.

Overview of C11 Features

C11's features aim to modernize the C language by addressing long-standing issues and introducing new functionalities to streamline programming. Key features include:

Standardized Multi-threading: C11 introduces native support for threading, previously unavailable in standard C.

Atomics and Memory Model: To facilitate safe concurrency, C11 provides a memory model and atomic operations.

Generic Functions and Types: C11's _Generic keyword brings type-generic programming to C, allowing functions to work with multiple data types.

Enhanced Error Handling and Bounds Checking: Optional bounds-checking functions improve safety in array handling and memory operations.

Static Assertions: With static_assert, developers can enforce compile-time conditions, increasing code safety and correctness.

The following sections expand on each of these significant features.

1. Multi-threading with C11 Threads

Multi-threading is a cornerstone of modern computing, especially with the rise of multi-core processors. While libraries like POSIX Threads (pthreads) provided threading capabilities, these were non-standard and not cross-platform. C11 resolves this by introducing stdatomic.h and threads.h, which bring native thread support directly to the C language.

Key Components of C11 multi-threading

Threads: The thrd_t type represents a thread in C11, and functions like thrd_create, thrd_join, and thrd_exit manage thread lifecycle.

Mutexes: The mtx_t type provides mutual exclusion locks, using functions like mtx_init, mtx_lock, and mtx_unlock for critical sections.

Condition Variables: C11 includes condition variables (cnd_t type) for synchronizing thread access to shared data.

Thread Local Storage: C11 allows thread-local variables using thread_local, enabling each thread to maintain its own copy of a variable.

Example of Multi-threading in C11

Here's a simple example demonstrating thread creation and joining in C11:

```c
#include <threads.h>
#include <stdio.h>

int thread_function(void *arg) {
    int *num = (int*)arg;
    printf("Hello from thread: %d\n", *num);
    return 0;
}

int main() {
    thrd_t thread;
    int thread_arg = 42;

    if (thrd_create(&thread, thread_function, &thread_arg) == thrd_success) {
        thrd_join(thread, NULL);
        printf("Thread joined successfully.\n");
    } else {
        printf("Failed to create thread.\n");
    }

    return 0;
}
```

This code creates a thread that executes thread_function, passing thread_arg as an argument. thrd_join waits for the thread to complete before proceeding.

2. Atomics and Memory Model Updates

Concurrency introduces complexity in data sharing, as multiple threads might try to access and modify shared variables simultaneously. C11 addresses this with an enhanced memory model and atomic operations to ensure data integrity.

C11 Memory Model

The C11 memory model provides rules and constraints for memory operations across threads, introducing several memory ordering options to control data visibility:

Relaxed Ordering: Allows operations to be reordered but ensures atomicity.

Acquire and Release Semantics: Ensures visibility of operations before or after a specific atomic operation.

Sequential Consistency: Enforces strict ordering, preserving the expected sequence of operations.

Atomic Types and Operations

The stdatomic.h header offers atomic types (atomic_int, atomic_long, etc.) and functions (atomic_load, atomic_store, etc.) to perform lock-free, thread-safe operations.

Example of Atomic Operation in C11

The following example demonstrates an atomic counter increment in a multi-threaded environment:

```
#include <stdatomic.h>
#include <threads.h>
#include <stdio.h>

atomic_int counter = 0;

int increment_counter(void *arg) {
    for (int i = 0; i < 1000; i++) {
        atomic_fetch_add(&counter, 1);
    }
    return 0;
```

```c
}

int main() {
    thrd_t threads[10];

    for (int i = 0; i < 10; i++) {
        thrd_create(&threads[i], increment_counter, NULL);
    }

    for (int i = 0; i < 10; i++) {
        thrd_join(threads[i], NULL);
    }

    printf("Counter: %d\n", counter);
    return 0;
}
```

In this example, each thread increments the counter variable 1000 times. Using atomic_fetch_add ensures the operation is atomic, avoiding race conditions.

3. Generic Functions and Types

Type-generic programming in C has historically been challenging due to its statically-typed nature. C11 introduces _Generic, a feature that allows functions to operate on different types without explicit function overloading.

The _Generic Keyword

The _Generic keyword enables type selection at compile-time, allowing developers to implement type-safe functions that adapt based on the data type passed.

Example of a Generic Macro for Absolute Value

The following example demonstrates a type-generic macro for an absolute value function:

```c
#include <stdio.h>
#define abs_generic(x) _Generic((x), \
    int: abs_int, \
    double: abs_double, \
    float: abs_float \
```

```
)(x)

int abs_int(int x) {
   return x < 0 ? -x : x;
}

double abs_double(double x) {
   return x < 0 ? -x : x;
}

float abs_float(float x) {
   return x < 0 ? -x : x;
}

int main() {
   int i = -10;
   double d = -10.5;
   float f = -2.3f;

   printf("Absolute value of %d is %d\n", i, abs_generic(i));
   printf("Absolute value of %.2f is %.2f\n", d, abs_generic(d));
   printf("Absolute value of %.2f is %.2f\n", f, abs_generic(f));

   return 0;
}
```

This macro uses _Generic to select the correct absolute value function based on the type of argument passed, ensuring type-safe, type-generic code.

4. Additional C11 Features

Alongside threading, atomics, and generic programming, C11 includes several additional enhancements:

Static Assertions: static_assert enables compile-time assertions, allowing checks that certain conditions are met during compilation, aiding in debugging and ensuring code validity.

Bounds-checking Interfaces: C11 introduces optional bounds-checking functions (e.g., gets_s, memcpy_s) that aim to prevent buffer overflows and other memory-related issues. These are particularly useful in applications where safety is paramount, though they remain optional and may not be available in all environments.

Let's start

The C11 standard, formally known as ISO/IEC 9899:2011, was a C standard adopted in late 2011. The C11 standard replaced the C99 standard and was superseded by C17. C11 introduces new features to the C language and C standard library and modifies a few existing ones. Here, we discuss some of the notable features.

Static_assert

The _Static_assert performs assertion during compile time before our program starts. The static assertion has the following syntax:

_Static_assert(expression, message);

The static assertion evaluates the constant expression during compile time. If the expression is evaluated to 0(false), a message is displayed, and the compilation fails. If the expression does not evaluate to 0, no message is displayed, and nothing happens. For example, let us check if the size of type int is equal to 8 using static assertion. Chances are the size of our int is equal to 4 and the assertion will fail.

Example:

```
int main(void)
{
    _Static_assert(sizeof(int) == 8, "The size of int is not 8.\n");
}
```

If we used long instead of int, chances are there will be no error message and the compilation will continue.

Example:

```
int main(void)
{
    _Static_assert(sizeof(long) == 8, "The size of long is not 8.\n");
}
```

The _Static_assert keyword can be replaced by a static_assert macro declared inside the <assert.h> header.

Example:

```
#include <assert.h> int main(void)
{
    static_assert(sizeof(int) == 8, "The size of int is not 8.\n");
}
```

In short, static assertions are a convenient way to enforce assertions and catch errors during compile time.

The Noreturn Function Specifier

The _Noreturn function specifier, when applied to a function declaration, specifies that the function does not return. More precisely, it specifies that the function does not return by

- Executing a return statement
- Hitting the end of the function block marked by the closing brace (})

Having the _Noreturn specifier suppresses some of the spurious warnings and further optimizes the code.

Example:

```
#include <stdlib.h>
#include <stdio.h>
_Noreturn void justExit()
{
    printf("This function does not return. Exiting...\n");
exit(0);
}
int main(void)
{
    justExit();
}
```

The specifier can be replaced by the equivalent noreturn macro declared inside the <stdnoreturn.h> header.

Example:

```
#include <stdlib.h>
#include <stdio.h>
#include <stdnoreturn.h>
```

```
noreturn void justExit()
{
    printf("This function does not return. Exiting...\n");
    exit(0);
}
int main(void)
{
    justExit();
}
```

Type Generic Macros Using Generic

The use of _Generic provides a way to select one of several expressions during compile time, based on a type of a given controlling expression.

The blueprint for a generic expression/macro is:

_Generic (controlling_expression, list_of_associations)

The controlling expression is an expression whose type will be compared to types listed in the association list.

The association list is a comma-separated list of the following content:

type1 : expression1, type2 : expression2, default : default_expression

The type of the controlling expression is compared to the types in the list. If it matches one of them, the generic selection becomes the expression after the colon.

Let us assume we had several functions that accept different types of parameters. We then want to choose the appropriate function based on a type of argument while using a single generic macro name. In that case, we utilize the _Generic selection in the following way:

```
#include <stdio.h>
#define myfn(X) _Generic((X), \
int : myfn_i, \
float : myfn_f, \
double : myfn_d, \
default : myfn_ld \
)(X) void myfn_i(int x)
{
```

```c
    printf("Printing int: %d\n", x); }
void myfn_f(float x)
{
    printf("Printing float: %f\n", x); }
void myfn_d(double x)
{
    printf("Printing double: %f\n", x); }
void myfn_ld(long double x)
{
    printf("Printing long double: %Lf\n", x); }
int main(void)
{
int x = 123; float f = 456.789f; double d = 101.112; long double ld = 134.456l; myfn(x); myfn(f);
myfn(d); myfn(ld);
}
```

Output:

Printing int: 123

Printing float: 456.789001

Printing double: 101.112000

Printing long double: 134.456000

This example expands the myfn macro to the appropriate expression based on the type of X. If no type can be matched in the association list, the macro expands to the default expression. The default expression, in our case, is the myfn_ld function. This approach closely matches the function overloading concept found in other languages.

The Alignof Operator

The _Alignof operator returns the alignment requirements of the type. Let us assume we have two data objects in memory of the same type, positioned in successive memory addresses. The alignment requirement is the property of an object that says how many bytes there must be between these two addresses in order to store the objects successfully. The _Alignof operator gets this number for us and has the following blueprint:
_Alignof(type_name)

Example:

```c
#include <stdio.h>
struct S1
{char c; char d;};
```

```c
struct S2
{char c; int x;};
int main(void)
{
printf("The alignment of char: %zu\n", _Alignof(char));
printf("The alignment of int: %zu\n", _Alignof(int));
printf("The alignment of struct S1: %zu\n", _Alignof(struct S1));
printf("The alignment of struct S2: %zu\n", _Alignof(struct S2));
}
```

Output:

The alignment of char: 1

The alignment of int: 4

The alignment of struct S1: 1

The alignment of struct S2: 4

There is also a convenience macro called alignof inside the <stdalign.h> header that expands to our _Alignof operator.

The Alignas Specifier

The _Alignas specifier modifies the alignment requirement when declaring an object. The _Alignas specifier has two syntaxes, one in which it accepts an expression that evaluates to the number of bytes and one in which it accepts a type name:

_Alignas (constant_int_expression)

_Alignas (type_name)

The alignment expression must be a positive power of 2. For example, if we want to enforce a specific alignment of our structure, we write:

```c
#include <stdio.h>
struct MyStruct
{
  _Alignas(16) int x[4];
};
int main(void)
{
printf("The alignment of MyStruct is: %zu bytes\n", _Alignof(struct
MyStruct));
```

}

Output:

The alignment of MyStruct is: 16 bytes

In this example, every object of type struct MyStruct will be aligned to a 16-byte boundary. We can also use the alignas macro defined inside the <stdalign.h> header. The compiler will issue an error if,

The value is not 0 or a positive power of 2

The value exceeds the maximum allowed alignment

The value is less than the physically possible minimum alignment

Anonymous Structures and Unions

Structures (or unions) without a name are called anonymous structures. They come in handy when we want to nest a structure (or a union) inside another structure (or a union).

Example:

```
#include <stdio.h>
struct MyStruct
{
int a;
    struct // anonymous structure
{
int b;
int c;
};
};
int main(void)
{
    struct MyStruct s;
    s.a = 123;
    s.b = 456;
    s.c = 789;
printf("Field a: %d\n", s.a);
printf("Inner field b: %d\n", s.b);
printf("Inner field c: %d\n", s.c);
}
```

Output:

Field a: 123

Inner field b: 456

Inner field c: 789

In this example, we used a structure and called it MyStruct. Inside that structure, there is one integer field called a and a nested, anonymous structure having two fields, b and c. To access these fields, we simply use the s.b and s.c syntax as anonymous struct members are members of the enclosing struct.

Aligned Memory Allocation: aligned_alloc

The C11 standard introduces an aligned_alloc function, which allocates a memory block with a specified alignment.

The syntax is:

void *aligned_alloc(size_t alignment, size_t size);

The function is defined inside the <stdlib.h> header. The memory is not initialized and must be freed with free or deallocated with realloc. The size in bytes must be a multiple of alignment.

Example:

```
#include <stdio.h>
#include <stdlib.h>
int main(void)
{
int *p = aligned_alloc(512, 512 * sizeof *p);
printf("Allocated a 512-byte aligned memory block.\n");
printf("The address is: %p\n", (void *)p);
free(p);
}
```

Output:

Allocated a 512-byte aligned memory block.

The address is: 0x55ca95945200

Unicode Support for UTF-16 and UTF-32

The C11 standard provides types for storing UTF-16 and UTF-32 encoded strings. They are char16_t and char32_t. Both types and the Unicode conversion functions are declared in a <uchar.h> header file.

Example:

```
#include <uchar.h>
int main(void)
{
char16_t arr16[] = u"Our 16-bit wide characters here.\n";
char32_t arr32[] = U"Our 32-bit wide characters here.\n";
}
```

We use the u prefix for the char16_t character array and the U prefix for the char32_t character array.

The width of the type char16_t can be larger than 16 bits, but the size of the value stored will be exactly 16 bits wide. Similarly, for a char32_t type, the size of the char32_t type itself can be larger than 32 bits, but the value stored inside this type will be exactly 32 bits wide.

Bounds Checking and Threads Overview

While the detailed analysis of the following features is out of scope for this book, we will briefly mention two additional things introduced in the C11 standard. They are bounds-checking (safe) functions and a thread support   library.

Bounds-Checking Functions

A few string and I/O functions can cause a buffer overflow. The C11 standard offers an optional extension containing the so-called bounds-checking functions that rectify this problem. These functions are also referred to as safety functions and carry the _s suffix. Some of them are gets_s, fopen_s, printf_s, scanf_s, strcpy_s, and wcscpy_s. The compiler might not provide these, and they are only available if the __STD_LIB_EXT1__ macro is defined.

Threads Support

The C11 standard offers an optional thread support library. The functions are defined inside the <threads.h> header. These functions bring the native thread support to the C language. They allow for creating and joining threads, creating mutexes, synchronizing access, working with conditional variables, and more.

The following example creates a thread that executes a code from a function which accepts one argument:

```
#include <threads.h>
#include <stdio.h>
int dowork(void *arg)
{
thrd_t mythreadid = thrd_current();
```

```c
for (int i = 0; i < 5; i++)
{
printf("Thread id: %lu, counter: %d, code: %s\n", mythreadid, i, (char *)arg);
}
return 0;
}

int main(void)

{

thrd_t mythread;

    // create a thread that executes a function code

if (thrd_success != thrd_create(&mythread, dowork, "Hello from a thread!"))

{

printf("Could not create a thread.\n");
return 1;
}

    // join a thread to the main thread
thrd_join(mythread, NULL);
}
```

Output:

Thread id: 140647017862912, counter: 0, code: Hello from a thread!

Thread id: 140647017862912, counter: 1, code: Hello from a thread!

Thread id: 140647017862912, counter: 2, code: Hello from a thread!

Thread id: 140647017862912, counter: 3, code: Hello from a thread!

Thread id: 140647017862912, counter: 4, code: Hello from a thread!

This example defines a function that will be executed by our thread. In the main program, we create/spawn the thread by calling the thrd_create function, to which we pass the address of our local mythread variable, the name of the function to be executed, dowork, and a string representing the function argument. Inside the user-defined function dowork, we also print out the current thread ID obtained through a thrd_current() function call.

When compiling a multithreaded application on Linux, we need to add the -pthread flag to the compilation string:

gcc -Wall source.c -std=c11 -pedantic -pthread

Note that <threads.h> support is optional and might not be fully implemented in GCC.

The C17 Standard

At the time of writing, the C17 standard, officially named ISO/IEC 9899:2018, is the last published C standard. It replaces the C11 standard, does not introduce new features, and fixes defects reported for C11. The __STDC_VERSION__ macro for this standard has the value of 201710L. To compile for a C17 standard, we include the -stdc=17 flag.

The Upcoming C23 Standard

At the time of writing, there is a new C standard in the making, informally referred to as the C23 or C2X. The standard will probably be published in 2024, with a working draft now available. Currently, we can install gcc version 13 or higher to try out some of the C23 features. We need to include the -std=c2x flag in the compilation string when targeting the C23 standard.

Constexpr

Starting with C23, objects marked with constexpr are constants whose value is determined during the compilation time. The constexpr object must be fully initialized at the point of declaration. Although constexpr objects occupy memory and have an address, they are read-only.

The following example uses the constexpr storage specifier applied to several different objects:

```
#include <stdio.h>
int main(void)
{
constexpr int x = 123;
constexpr unsigned u = 456u;
constexpr char mystring[] = {"Hello."};
printf("The value of x is: %d\n", x);
printf("The value of u is: %u\n", u);
printf("The value of mystring is: %s\n", mystring);
}
```

Output:

The value of x is: 123

The value of u is: 456 The value of mystring is: Hello.

The constexpr object can also be used as an initializer in other constant expressions.

Example:

```
#include <stdio.h>
int main(void)
{
constexpr int x = 10;
enum
```

```
{
FIRST = x, SECOND, THIRD
};
constexpr int y = x;
static int myvar = x + 20;
int myarray[x]; // valid, not a variable length array
printf("The value of x is: %d\n.", x);
printf("The value of y is: %d\n.", y);
printf("The value of myvar is: %d\n.", myvar);

printf("Declared an array of %d elements. Valid, not a VLA.\n", x);
}
```

Output:

The value of x is: 10

The value of y is: 10

The value of myvar is: 30

Declared an array of 10 elements. Valid, not a VLA.

This example uses the constexpr object to initialize an enumerator, another constexpr object, a static variable, and inside an array declaration. Unlike regular constants whose value is determined during runtime, the constexpr object's value is determined during compilation time, and they can safely be used to declare the size of the array without participating in the creation of the variable length array.

Binary Integer Constants

The C23 standard introduces binary integer constants. The binary constant starts with the 0b or 0B sequence, followed by binary digits 1 and/or 0. This allows us to write down the value of an integer variable using the binary representation.

Example:

```
#include <stdio.h>

int main(void)

{
int x = 0b1010;
printf("The value of the integer variable x is: %d\n", x);
}
```

Output:

The value of the integer variable x is 10

The 0b1010 integer constant is a binary representation of a decimal number 10. As with previous standards, we can also add integer suffixes to our binary constant if needed. Let us rewrite the preceding example to use the unsigned type instead:

```
#include <stdio.h>

int main(void)
{
unsigned x = 0b1010u;

printf("The value of the unsigned variable x is: %u\n", x);
}
```

Output:

```
The value of the unsigned variable x is: 10
```

We have added the u suffix to our integer constant to avoid implicit conversion from int to unsigned. Let us now write an example that uses decimal, hexadecimal, octal, and binary integer constants to represent the same value of 100:

```
#include <stdio.h>

int main(void)
{
int x1 = 100; // decimal
int x2 = 0x64; // hexadecimal
int x3 = 0144; // decimal
int x4 = 0b01100100; // binary

printf("The value of the variable x1 is: %d\n", x1);
printf("The value of the variable x2 is: %d\n", x2);
printf("The value of the variable x3 is: %d\n", x3);
printf("The value of the variable x4 is: %d\n", x4);
}
```

Output:

```
The value of the variable x1 is: 100
The value of the variable x2 is: 100
The value of the variable x3 is: 100
The value of the variable x4 is: 100
```

True and false

Starting with C23, we do not have to include any particular header to define bool variables to which we can assign true or false values. These predefined true and false constants are now keywords in C23.

Example:

```c
#include <stdio.h>
int main(void)
{
    bool condition = true;    if (condition)
    {
        printf("The condition is true.\n");
    }    else
    {
        printf("The condition is false.\n");
    }
}
```

Output:

The condition is true

Prior to C23, we had to include the <stdbool.h> header file to be able to use the bool type.

Nullptr

C23 introduces a new keyword, nullptr, representing a null pointer constant. This value is a predefined constant of the underlying nullptr_t type. The type is defined inside a <stddef.h> header file. Prior to C23, we had to use NULL, (void*), or 0 to set the pointer to null pointer constant.

Depending on the implementation, this could potentially cause problems as NULL is a macro. Starting with C23, we can initialize our pointers to a null pointer constant using the keyword nullptr.

Example:

```c
#include <stdio.h>
#include <stddef.h>
int main(void)
{
int *p1 = nullptr;
double *p2 = nullptr;
struct MyStruct *p3 = nullptr;

printf("The value of the p1 pointer is: %p.\n", (void*)p1);
printf("The value of the p2 pointer is: %p.\n", (void*)p2);
printf("The value of the p3 pointer is: %p.\n", (void*)p3);
```

```
}
```

Output:

The value of the p1 pointer is: (nil).

The value of the p2 pointer is: (nil).

The value of the p3 pointer is: (nil).

Empty initializer = {}

We can utilize an empty initializer in C23 for variables, arrays, and structs using the = {} syntax instead of a = {0} one. When we explicitly initialize an object using the empty initializer, the underlying values are zeroed, and we do not have to use the memset function.

Example:

```
#include <stdio.h>
int main(void)
{
int x = {};
struct MyStruct

{
int a;
double b;
}
s = {};
int arr[5] = {};

printf("The value of x is: %d.\n", x);
printf("The value of s.a is: %d.\n", s.a);
printf("The value of s.b is: %f.\n", s.b);

printf("The array values are: ");
for (int i = 0; i < 5; i++)

{
printf("%d ", arr[i]);

}
}
```

Output:

The value of x is: 0.

The value of s.a is: 0.

The value of s.b is: 0.000000.

The array values are: 0 0 0 0 0

#embed

The #embed preprocessor directive is used to include the binary resource in our program/build.

To initialize a single variable with the content of some external somefile.dat file, using the #embed directive, we write:

```
int main(void)
{
int x = {
#embed "somefile.dat"
};
}
```

The preceding example is valid only if somefile.dat produces only one value. To initialize a structure using somefile.dat, we write:

```
#include <stdio.h>
int main(void)
{
struct MyStruct
{
int x;
double d;
};
struct MyStruct s = {
    // initializes each field with
    // comma-delimited integer constant-expressions
#embed "somefile.dat"
    };
}
```

In this example, we used the #embed preprocessor directive to initialize a structure since the directive can produce one of the following:

Comma-separated list of integer constant expressions

A single integer constant expression

Nothing (none of the above)

To initialize a fixed-width unsigned integer array with the content of a binary resource, such as an external image, we write:

```
#include <stdint.h>
#include <stdio.h>
int main(void)
{
const uint8_t arr[] = {
#embed "somefile.jpg"
    };
}
```

To initialize a character array with the content of a textual file, we type:

```
#include <stdint.h>
#include <stdio.h>
int main(void)
{
const char arr[] = {
#embed "myfile.txt"
    };
}
```

The #embed directive can also have parameters. The first one we will discuss is the if_empty parameter. If a binary resource is empty (e.g., the file is empty), the if_empty content replaces the directive. If the resource is not empty, the content of the if_empty token is ignored. Let us modify the previous example to check if the file is empty, and if so, put some content into our char array using the if_empty parameter.

Example:

```
#include <stdio.h>
int main(void)
{
const char arr[] = {
#embed "myfile.txt" if_empty('N', 'o ', ' ', 'd', 'a', 't', 'a'), '\0'};
}
```

In this example, we also added the value of '\0', which is a null-terminating character.

In a scenario where we want to initialize a single variable, the if_empty token can simply contain zero:

```
#include <stdio.h>
int main(void)
{
int x = {
#embed "somefile.dat" if_empty(0)
    };
}
```

If we only want to embed a portion of the resource, we can limit the number of read resource elements (not bytes, but resource elements). An example where we want to embed only the first ten elements from an external resource:

```
#include <stdio.h>
int main(void)
{
const char arr[] = {
#embed "myfile.txt" limit(10)
    };
}
```

Now, our array should have only ten elements.

Attributes

There have been many implementation-defined language extensions throughout the years. The adoption of attributes in C23 is an attempt to present a uniform, standard syntax for specifying these extensions/attributes. Attributes are mainly used in declarations and definitions and can relate to types, variables, declarations, and code.

The attributes syntax is:

[[attribute-list]] what_the_attribute_relates_to

One of the attributes can be [[deprecated]]. It marks the declaration as deprecated/obsolete, causing the compiler to issue a warning.

Example:

```
#include <stdio.h>
// deprecated definition
```

```c
[[deprecated]] void myoldfunction()
{
printf("This is a deprecated function.\n"); }
int main(void)
{
myoldfunction();
printf("Using deprecated code.\n");
}
```

Some of the other attributes are

[[fallthrough]] – Where the fallthrough from the previous case is indeed expected

[[maybe_unused]] – When we want to suppress compiler warnings on unused names

[[nodiscard]] – Where we expect the compiler to issue a warning when the return value is discarded

No Parameters Function Declaration

We can now declare a function that accepts no parameters without the need for the inclusion of a void text inside parentheses. We can now ensure the function's behavior will be as intended.

Example:

```c
#include <stdio.h>
void noparamsfn()
{
printf("This function does not accept parameters.\n"); }
int main(void)
{
noparamsfn();
}
```

Output:

This function does not accept parameters.

The strdup Function

The strdup function returns a pointer to a copy of a string. It does so as if the place for a copy was allocated using malloc. The function is declared inside the <string.h> header and has the following syntax:

```c
char *strdup(const char* arg);
```

The pointer obtained through strdup must be freed afterward.

Example:

```c
#include <string.h>
#include <stdlib.h>
#include <stdio.h>
int main(void)
{
const char *s1 = "This will be duplicated.";
char *s2 = strdup(s1);
printf("The result is: %s\n", s2);
free(s2);
}
```

Output:

The result is: This will be duplicated.

There is also a strndup variant that copies N bytes from the source string and has the following syntax:

```c
char *strndup(const char* arg, size_t N);
```

Example:

```c
#include <string.h>
#include <stdlib.h>
#include <stdio.h>
int main(void)
{
const char *s1 = "This will be duplicated.";
char *s2 = strndup(s1, 17);
printf("The result is: %s\n", s2);
free(s2);
}
```

Output:

The result is: This will be dupl

The memccpy Function

The memccpy function copies characters from a data object pointed to by source to a memory/object pointed to by destination. The function stops copying after any of the two conditions are met:

N characters were copied. The character c is found.

The function is declared inside the <string.h> header and has the following syntax:

void *memccpy(void *restrict destination, const void *restrict source, int c, size_t N);

Example:

```
#include <stdio.h>
#include <string.h> int main(void)
{
const char source[] = "Copy this until ~ is found.";
char destination[sizeof source];
const char stopchar = '~';

void *p = memccpy(destination, source, stopchar, sizeof destination);
if (p)
    {
        printf("Terminating character found. The result is:\n");
        printf("%s\n", destination);
    } else
    {
        printf("Terminating character not found. The result is:\n");
        printf("%s\n", destination);
    }
}
```

Output:

Terminating character found. The result is:

Copy this until ~

If the terminating character stopchar is found, the function returns a pointer to the next character in the destination string after the stopchar. The function returns a null pointer if the terminating character is not found.

Conclusion: The Lasting Impact of C11 and Modern C Features on Software Development

The introduction of the C11 standard marked a significant turning point in the evolution of the C language, reaffirming its place in modern programming. Despite C's established reputation as a low-level, high-performance language, it faced the challenge of keeping pace with the ever-growing demands for concurrency, safety, and portability in today's software development landscape. With its comprehensive updates, C11 not only addresses the limitations of previous standards but also reinforces C's utility in multi-core and real-time systems, making it better equipped for the needs of current and future developers.

1. Native Multi-threading Support: Meeting the Demands of Concurrency

Concurrency is integral to modern computing, given the ubiquity of multi-core processors. Previous versions of C lacked native multi-threading, which required developers to rely on non-standard libraries like POSIX Threads (pthreads) or platform-specific APIs. While these libraries were effective, they introduced portability issues and increased complexity for developers working across multiple platforms.

C11's standardized approach to multi-threading directly addresses these issues, enabling portable and consistent thread management across different systems. With the introduction of the threads.h library, C11 simplifies thread creation, synchronization, and lifecycle management through a unified interface. C11's mutexes and condition variables further enhance control over thread interactions, making it easier to handle complex synchronization tasks and avoid common pitfalls like race conditions and deadlocks.

By providing built-in multi-threading, C11 helps C developers embrace concurrent programming more readily. This feature is essential not only for high-performance applications but also for responsive, real-time systems that demand parallel execution. This update thus modernizes C for applications such as embedded systems, network servers, and scientific computing, where efficiency and concurrency are paramount.

2. Atomics and a Defined Memory Model: Ensuring Data Integrity in Multi-threaded Environments

With C11's support for atomics and a defined memory model, developers now have better tools to write safer concurrent code. In multi-threaded applications, shared data must be managed carefully to avoid inconsistencies. Prior to C11, implementing atomic operations and memory order control required low-level manipulation or dependency on external libraries, which was both complex and error-prone.

The memory model provided in C11 clearly defines how operations on shared data should behave in a concurrent context. It establishes different levels of memory ordering—relaxed, acquire-release, and sequential consistency—giving developers flexibility in choosing the appropriate level of synchronization for their needs. This control over memory order is crucial in high-performance applications, where relaxed memory ordering can enhance performance without compromising data integrity.

Atomics in C11 (stdatomic.h) allow operations on shared data to be both lock-free and thread-safe. Functions like atomic_fetch_add and atomic_store make it easier to perform common tasks, such as counting or flagging, across threads without risking data corruption. In scenarios where lock-free data structures are beneficial (e.g., high-frequency trading platforms or network packet processing), C11's atomics provide an efficient and reliable solution.

In short, C11's atomic operations and memory model make it easier to write safe and efficient multi-threaded code. This contributes to C's suitability for critical systems programming, where performance and correctness are vital.

3. Type-Generic Programming with _Generic: Improving Flexibility and Code Reusability

Type-generic programming in C has historically been challenging due to the language's statically-typed nature. C11's _Generic keyword introduces a level of type-generic programming, allowing functions and macros to work with multiple types without requiring code duplication. This feature is particularly valuable for writing reusable, type-safe code, as it enables developers to implement functions that automatically adapt to different data types based on the arguments provided.

For instance, a generic function that calculates the absolute value of any numeric type (e.g., int, float, or double) can be implemented using _Generic, reducing the need for multiple function overloads. This streamlines code maintenance, as there is less duplication, and improves readability by centralizing similar functionality into a single, type-generic construct.

Type-generic programming is particularly beneficial in library development, where flexibility and ease of use are important. By enabling functions to accept various types safely, C11 expands the potential for creating more versatile and user-friendly libraries in C, which can improve productivity for both library developers and end users.

4. Safety Enhancements: Static Assertions and Bounds-checking Interfaces

Safety is a critical aspect of C programming, especially for systems-level applications where bugs can lead to severe consequences. C11's static_assert feature brings compile-time assertions to the language, empowering developers to catch potential issues early in the development process. With static_assert, developers can enforce constraints at compile-time, such as checking the size of data structures or validating configuration constants. This helps to prevent runtime errors, making code safer and more robust.

Bounds-checking interfaces, while optional in C11, provide safer alternatives to common string and memory operations. Functions like memcpy_s and strcpy_s introduce bounds checks to prevent buffer overflows, a frequent source of vulnerabilities in C programs. Although not universally adopted, these optional interfaces promote safer coding practices, particularly for security-sensitive applications like networking software or embedded systems.

These safety enhancements make C11 more reliable, especially for use cases where stability and security are crucial. By catching errors early and reducing risks associated with unsafe operations, C11 allows developers to write code that is both robust and maintainable.

5. Portability and Cross-Platform Consistency

One of C's enduring strengths is its portability, and C11 further solidifies this by standardizing features that were previously dependent on external libraries or platform-specific implementations. The standardization of multi-threading and atomic operations means that C11 programs can now run consistently across different operating systems and hardware architectures without modification. This reduces development time and testing costs, as developers can rely on the standard rather than adapting code for each target platform.

Portability is crucial in industries like embedded systems, where code may need to run on a wide range of devices with varying resources. C11's features ensure that C remains an optimal choice for developers working in these fields, allowing them to write code that is both efficient and adaptable to different environments.

6. Balancing Low-level Control with Modern Features

C has always been prized for giving programmers direct access to system resources, memory, and processor instructions. C11 preserves this low-level control while also introducing features that address the complexity of modern applications. Unlike languages that abstract away system details, C11 allows developers to leverage advanced hardware capabilities (such as multi-core processors) through its native concurrency features and memory model, without sacrificing performance or predictability.

By balancing traditional control with new safety and concurrency features, C11 positions C as a language that can handle the demands of modern applications, such as high-performance computing, embedded systems, and real-time processing. This makes it possible for developers to write efficient, scalable code without needing to abandon C's low-level capabilities.

7. The Future of C Programming: A Language for Modern Systems

With C11, C has effectively demonstrated its adaptability, ensuring its relevance in the evolving software landscape. C11's updates position C as a language that is not only capable of handling contemporary computing needs but also resilient enough to evolve further. The features introduced in C11—multi-threading, atomics, generic programming, and safety mechanisms—empower developers to build faster, safer, and more flexible applications while preserving the language's defining characteristics.

While newer languages like Rust and Go offer modern concurrency and memory safety features, C11 enables the C language to continue thriving by addressing some of these same needs. For developers invested in C's low-level control, C11 provides a familiar yet enhanced environment, reinforcing C as a pragmatic choice for applications where performance, efficiency, and fine-grained control are critical.

Summary

In summary, C11 enhances C programming by introducing features that address modern programming challenges, such as concurrency, data safety, type-generic programming, and cross-platform consistency. These advancements make it easier for developers to create efficient and reliable code, especially for systems programming, embedded systems, and high-performance applications. C11 strengthens C's position as a powerful language for building complex, resource-intensive software, reaffirming its status as a language that evolves with the demands of contemporary computing while retaining the control and performance that make it uniquely valuable.

15. Numeral Systems In C

Introduction to Numeral Systems

Numeral systems are foundational in computing, as they allow representation of numbers in various bases, which are essential for interpreting data at the machine level. In C programming, understanding numeral systems is crucial for manipulating data, working with low-level hardware, and performing tasks that require binary or hexadecimal values. This chapter will introduce the key numeral systems—binary, decimal, octal, and hexadecimal—explore how to represent and convert them, and demonstrate their applications in C.

1. The Basics of Numeral Systems

Numeral systems are methods of representing numbers. Each system is defined by a **base** or **radix**, which indicates the number of unique symbols used to represent values. Common numeral systems include:

Decimal (Base-10): Uses symbols 0-9. This is the most familiar system and is widely used in daily life.

Binary (Base-2): Uses symbols 0 and 1. This is the fundamental system in computing.

Octal (Base-8): Uses symbols 0-7. Octal is often used in digital systems and permissions in UNIX/Linux systems.

Hexadecimal (Base-16): Uses symbols 0-9 and A-F. This system is prevalent in computing for memory addresses and color codes.

Each numeral system expresses numbers in a positional way, meaning the position of each digit represents its power of the base.

2. Understanding Binary Representation in C

The **binary system** is the language of computers. In binary, each digit (bit) represents a power of 2, starting from 2^0 on the right. For example:

Binary: 1011

Decimal Equivalent: $(1 * 2^3) + (0 * 2^2) + (1 * 2^1) + (1 * 2^0) = 8 + 0 + 2 + 1 = 11$

In C, binary literals are not directly supported, but binary values can be represented in code using integer values, bitwise operations, or hexadecimal equivalents.

Example: Bitwise Operations

Bitwise operators in C, such as &, |, ^, ~, <<, and >>, allow manipulation of binary data at the bit level. For example:

```c
#include <stdio.h>
int main()
{
    unsigned int x = 5;     // Binary: 0101
    unsigned int y = 3;     // Binary: 0011
    printf("x & y = %d\n", x & y); // AND operation: 0001 (1 in decimal)
    printf("x | y = %d\n", x | y); // OR operation: 0111 (7 in decimal)
    return 0;
}
```

These operations are powerful tools when working with binary data and are widely used in low-level programming.

3. Decimal Numbers in C

The **decimal system** (base-10) is the default numeral system in C. Decimal values are typically written as-is in code:

```c
int num = 25;
printf("Decimal: %d\n", num);
```

Decimal is convenient for general-purpose calculations, and it's straightforward to use with C's %d format specifier in printf.

4. Octal Representation in C

Octal (Base-8) is a numeral system that uses digits from 0 to 7. In C, octal numbers are represented by prefixing the value with 0.

```c
#include <stdio.h>
int main()
{
    int octalNum = 075;  // Octal representation of 61 in decimal
    printf("Octal: %o\n", octalNum);
    printf("Decimal: %d\n", octalNum);
    return 0;
}
```

Here, 075 is interpreted as an octal number. This can be useful for encoding permissions in UNIX systems, where 0755 represents read, write, and execute permissions.

Practical Use Case: File Permissions

In UNIX-based systems, file permissions are often set using octal values. For instance, 0755 represents permissions for the owner, group, and others.

```
#include <stdio.h>
#include <sys/stat.h>
int main()
{
    chmod("example.txt", 0755); // Sets the file permissions for example.txt
    return 0;
}
```

5. Hexadecimal Representation in C

Hexadecimal (Base-16) is widely used in programming because it aligns well with binary representation, offering a compact format for binary numbers. In C, hexadecimal values are prefixed with 0x.

```
#include <stdio.h>
int main()
{
    int hexNum = 0x1A;  // Hexadecimal for 26 in decimal
    printf("Hexadecimal: %x\n", hexNum);
    printf("Decimal: %d\n", hexNum);
    return 0;
}
```

Hexadecimal is common for memory addresses, color codes in graphics, and low-level data representation.

Memory Addresses

In many systems, hexadecimal notation simplifies the representation of memory addresses. C pointers, for instance, are often printed in hexadecimal to make them more readable.

```
#include <stdio.h>
```

```
int main()
{
    int x = 10;
    printf("Memory address of x: %p\n", (void*)&x);
    return 0;
}
```

6. Converting Between Numeral Systems in C

Conversions between numeral systems are necessary in programming. Common conversions include:

Binary to Decimal: Summing powers of 2 based on binary digits.

Decimal to Binary: Dividing by 2 and noting remainders.

Hexadecimal to Decimal: Multiplying by powers of 16.

C provides several methods for conversions, including functions like atoi, strtol, and custom logic.

Example: Decimal to Binary Conversion

```
#include <stdio.h>

void decimalToBinary(int n)
{
    int binary[32];
    int i = 0;
    while (n > 0)
    {
        binary[i] = n % 2;
        n = n / 2;
        i++;
    }
    for (int j = i - 1; j >= 0; j--)
        printf("%d", binary[j]);
}

int main() {
    int num = 13;
```

```
    printf("Binary of %d: ", num);
    decimalToBinary(num);
    return 0;
}
```

This function divides the number by 2 and collects the remainders, outputting them in reverse to represent the binary value.

Example: Using strtol for Conversions

The strtol function in C provides a built-in method to convert strings representing numbers in various bases.

```
#include <stdio.h>
#include <stdlib.h>
int main()
{
    char hexStr[] = "1A";
    int num = strtol(hexStr, NULL, 16);
    printf("Hexadecimal %s to Decimal: %d\n", hexStr, num);
    return 0;
}
```

This example converts a hexadecimal string to a decimal integer using strtol.

7. Working with Different Bases in C

C provides format specifiers that allow easy representation of different numeral systems:

Binary: There is no direct format specifier for binary in standard C, but it can be printed using custom functions.

Octal: %o in printf.

Decimal: %d in printf.

Hexadecimal: %x (lowercase) or %X (uppercase) in printf.

Example: Displaying a Number in Different Bases

```
#include <stdio.h>
```

```c
int main()
{
    int num = 29;
    printf("Decimal: %d\n", num);
    printf("Octal: %o\n", num);
    printf("Hexadecimal: %x\n", num);
    return 0;
}
```

This will output the number in all three formats, helping visualize the same value in different numeral systems.

8. Practical Applications of Numeral Systems in C

Numeral systems are more than theoretical constructs; they have practical applications in fields such as:

Embedded Systems: Binary and hexadecimal representations are essential when programming microcontrollers.

Computer Graphics: Hexadecimal is used in color encoding.

Data Compression: Binary data manipulation can lead to efficient data compression techniques.

Networking: IP addresses and MAC addresses often require binary or hexadecimal interpretation.

Let's start

Numeral systems, also known as number systems, are methods of representing numbers that allow us to express quantities and perform computations. These systems have been instrumental to human civilizations for thousands of years, enabling scientific, economic, and technological advancements.

In the simplest terms, a numeral system is a way to express numbers using a consistent set of symbols. The exact symbols and how they are arranged vary from one system to another, but the underlying concept remains the same.

There are several types of numeral systems, each defined by its "base" or "radix" - the number of unique digits, including zero, used to represent numbers. Some commonly used numeral systems include:

1. Decimal (Base-10): This is the system most commonly used in everydaylife. It employs ten symbols, from 0-9.

2. Binary (Base-2): This is the fundamental language of digital electronicsand computer systems, using only two symbols: 0 and 1.

3. Octal (Base-8): This system uses eight symbols, from 0-7. While lesscommon today, it was widely used in early computing systems.

4. Hexadecimal (Base-16): This system uses sixteen symbols: 0-9 and A-F. It is frequently used in computing and digital systems because it represents large binary numbers in a more human-readable format.

These numeral systems, while different in their representation, serve the same purpose: to express and manipulate quantities. Understanding the relationships and conversions between these systems is crucial for various scientific and computing domains.

In the subsequent chapters, we will delve into each of these systems and their interconversion in detail, enabling you to interact with and understand the digital world more effectively.

Converting Binary Formats

Binary, as the term suggests, is a base-2 numeral system, commonly used in digital systems including computers, where only two types of symbols or digits are used: 0 and 1. In contrast, the decimal system that we typically use in everyday life is base-10, composed of ten digits (0-9).

In the realm of digital electronics and computing, the binary system is paramount. Each binary digit, also known as a "bit," represents the fundamental unit of data. A combination of these bits creates larger units, such as a byte (8 bits), kilobyte (1024 bytes), and so forth.

Converting Decimal to Binary

To convert from decimal to binary, one can use the method of repeated division by 2. The process includes the following steps:

1.   Divide the decimal number by 2.
2.   Record the remainder.
3.   Replace the original decimal number with the quotient from step 1.
4.   Repeat the process until the quotient is 0.

The binary equivalent of the decimal number is the string of remainders read from bottom to top (i.e., in reverse order of generation).

Example

Let's convert the decimal number 13 to binary:

1.   13 divided by 2 equals 6 remainder 1.

2.   6 divided by 2 equals 3 remainder 0.
3.   3 divided by 2 equals 1 remainder 1.

4.   1 divided by 2 equals 0 remainder 1.

Reading the remainders from the bottom up gives the binary representation of 13 as 1101.

Converting Binary to Decimal

The process of converting from binary to decimal involves multiplying each binary digit by 2 raised to an appropriate power, then summing these products.

Here's the step-by-step process:

1. Identify the rightmost bit in the binary number. This is the least significant bit. The next bit to the left is two times more significant, and so on. Assign each bit a power of 2 starting from 0 for the rightmost bit and incrementing by 1 as you move left.

2. Multiply each binary digit by the corresponding power of 2.

3. Sum up all the values obtained from step 2. The result is the decimal equivalent of the binary number.

Example

Let's convert the binary number 1011 to decimal:

1. Assign powers of 2 to each digit:

$1 (2^3), 0 (2^2), 1 (2^1), 1 (2^0)$.

2. Multiply each binary digit by the corresponding power of 2:

$1*2^3, 0*2^2, 1*2^1, 1*2^0 = 8, 0, 2, 1$.

3. Sum up all the values obtained:

$8 + 0 + 2 + 1 = 11$.

Therefore, the binary 1011 is equivalent to the decimal number 11. In summary, understanding binary format and conversion between decimal and binary is fundamental to grasping how data is represented and manipulated within digital systems. These skills provide the foundation for more advanced concepts such as binary arithmetic, logical operations, and computer programming.

Converting Hexadecimal Formats

The hexadecimal numeral system, often shortened to hex, is a base-16 system, meaning it uses sixteen distinct symbols. It includes the digits 0-9 to represent values zero to nine, and the letters A-F (or alternatively a-f) to represent values ten to fifteen. Hexadecimal is particularly useful in computing and digital systems because it's a human-friendly representation of binary-coded values.

Converting Decimal to Hexadecimal

The process of converting decimal numbers to hexadecimal is similar to the method used for binary conversion. Instead of dividing by 2, we divide by 16. Here are the steps:

1. Divide the decimal number by 16.

2. Record the remainder in hexadecimal (i.e., if the remainder is 10-15, write down A-F).

3. Replace the original decimal number with the quotient.

4. Repeat the process until the quotient is 0.

The hexadecimal equivalent of the decimal number is the sequence of remainders read from bottom to top.

Example

Let's convert the decimal number 255 to hexadecimal:

1. 255 divided by 16 equals 15 remainder 15.

2. 15 divided by 16 equals 0 remainder 15.

Writing down the remainders in hexadecimal (15 is F), from bottom to top, gives us FF. So, 255 in decimal is FF in hexadecimal.

Converting Hexadecimal to Decimal

Converting a hexadecimal number to decimal involves a similar method to that used in binary-to-decimal conversion. The process is as follows:

1. Identify the rightmost digit in the hexadecimal number. This is the least significant digit. The next digit to the left is sixteen times more significant, and so forth. Assign each digit a power of 16, starting from 0 for the rightmost digit and incrementing by 1 as you move left.

2. Multiply each hexadecimal digit (converted to decimal) by the corresponding power of 16.

3. Sum up all the values obtained from step 2. The result is the decimal equivalent of the hexadecimal number.

Example

Let's convert the hexadecimal number AF to decimal:

1. Assign powers of 16 to each digit:

A (16^1), F (16^0).

2. Convert A and F to decimal and multiply by the corresponding powers of 16:

A = 10, F = 15.
$10*16^1$, $15*16^0$ = 160, 15.

3. Sum up all the values obtained:

160 + 15 = 175.

Therefore, the hexadecimal AF is equivalent to the decimal number 175.

Understanding hexadecimal format and the conversion process between decimal and hexadecimal is key to mastering data representation in digital systems. It is used extensively in various fields of computer science and digital electronics, such as in coding, addressing, identifying, and color representation.

Bit Manipulation Techniques

Bit manipulation involves the construction and modification of data at the level of individual bits. It's a powerful technique that can lead to more efficient code, especially in systems programming and embedded systems.

Bitwise Operators

Bitwise operators perform operations on the binary representations of integers. Here are the bitwise operators in C:

- Bitwise AND (`&`):

Bitwise AND (`&`) in C (or any other language) operates on the binary representations of integers. It compares each bit of the first operand to the corresponding bit of the second operand. If both bits are 1, the corresponding result bit is set to 1. Otherwise, the result bit is set to 0. Here is the truth table for the bitwise AND operation:

Operand 1 (Bit A)	Operand 2 (Bit B)	A `&` B (Result)
0	0	0
0	1	0
1	0	0

1   1   1

For instance, if you were to perform a bitwise AND operation on two integers 12 and 13:

int a = 12;   // In binary: 1100 int b = 13;   // In binary: 1101 int result = a & b; // Result: 1100 (in binary), which is 12 in decimal.

In this case, the bitwise AND operation would compare the binary bits from `a` and `b` and give the result. The operation is performed on each corresponding pair of bits, and the result is a binary number that represents the decimal number 12, as demonstrated above.

- Bitwise OR (`|`):

Bitwise OR (`|`) in C (or any other language) operates on the binary representations of integers. It compares each bit of the first operand to the corresponding bit of the second operand. If either bit is 1, the corresponding result bit is set to 1. Only if both bits are 0, the result bit is set to 0.

Here is the truth table for the bitwise OR operation:

Operand 1 (Bit A)	Operand 2 (Bit B)	A `|` B (Result)
0	0	0
0	1	1
1	0	1
1	1	1

For instance, if you were to perform a bitwise OR operation on two integers 12 and 13:

int a = 12; // In binary: 1100 int b = 13;   // In binary: 1101 int result = a | b; // Result: 1101 (in binary), which is 13 in decimal.

In this case, the bitwise OR operation would compare the binary bits from `a` and `b` and give the result. The operation is performed on each corresponding pair of bits, and the result is a binary number that represents the decimal number 13, as demonstrated above.

- Bitwise XOR (`^`):

Bitwise XOR (`^`) in C (or any other language) operates on the binary representations of integers. It compares each bit of the first operand to the corresponding bit of the second operand. If the bits are different, the corresponding result bit is set to 1. If the bits are the same, the result bit is set to 0.

Here is the truth table for the bitwise XOR operation:

Operand 1 (Bit A)	Operand 2 (Bit B)	A `^` B (Result)

0	0	0
0	1	1
1	0	1
1	1	0

For instance, if you were to perform a bitwise XOR operation on two integers 12 and 13:

int a = 12; // In binary: 1100 int b = 13; // In binary: 1101 int result = a ^ b; // Result: 0001 (in binary), which is 1 in decimal.

In this case, the bitwise XOR operation would compare the binary bits from `a` and `b` and give the result. The operation is performed on each corresponding pair of bits, and the result is a binary number that represents the decimal number 1, as demonstrated above.

- Bitwise NOT (`~`):

Bitwise NOT (`~`) in C (or any other language) operates on the binary representation of an integer. It flips each bit of the operand. If a bit is 1, it becomes 0. If a bit is 0, it becomes 1.

Here is the truth table for the bitwise NOT operation:

Operand (Bit A)	`~`A (Result)
0	1
1	0

For instance, if you were to perform a bitwise NOT operation on an integer 12:

int a = 12; // In binary: 1100 int result = ~a; // Result: 0011 (in binary for a 4-bit system), which is 3 in decimal.

However, keep in mind that integers in C are typically represented using more than 4 bits. In a 32bit system, the integer 12 is actually represented as `00000000000000000000000000001100`, and the result of `~a` would be `11111111111111111111111111110011`, which is -13 in decimal, because the most significant bit is used for sign (1 means negative in a two's complement representation, which is usually used in modern computers).

So, for actual C code, the `~a` operation for `a = 12` would give `-13`.

- Left shift (`<<`):

The left shift (`<<`) operator in C (or any other language) operates on the binary representation of an integer. It shifts each bit of the operand to the left by the specified number of positions. Zeroes are filled in from the right, and the leftmost bits that 'fall off' are discarded.

Here is an example of the bitwise left shift operation:

int a = 3;   // In binary: 00000011 int result = a << 2; // Result: 00001100 (in binary), which is 12 in decimal.

In this case, the `<<` operator moves each bit in the binary representation of `a` two positions to the left. Two zeros are added from the right, and the two leftmost bits are dropped.

Here's another example:

int b = 5;   // In binary: 00000101 int result2 = b << 3; // Result: 01010000 (in binary), which is 40 in decimal.

In this case, the `<<` operator moves each bit in the binary representation of `b` three positions to the left. Three zeros are added from the right, and the three leftmost bits are dropped.

- Right shift (`>>`):

The right shift (`>>`) operator in C operates on the binary representation of an integer. It shifts each bit of the operand to the right by the specified number of positions. The bits that 'fall off' to the right are discarded.

If the number is an unsigned integer, zeros are filled in from the left. If the number is a signed integer, the sign bit (i.e., the leftmost bit) is used to fill in from the left. This is called sign extension and it preserves the sign of the number when bits are shifted.

Here's an example of right shift with a positive number:

int a = 12;   // In binary: 00001100 int result = a >> 2; // Result: 00000011 (in binary), which is 3 in decimal.

In this case, the `>>` operator moves each bit in the binary representation of `a` two positions to the right. Two zeros are added from the left because `a` is a positive number, and the two rightmost bits are dropped.

And an example with a negative number:

int b = -12;   // In binary: 11110100 (assuming 8-bit two's complement representation) int result2 = b >> 2; // Result: 11111101 (in binary), which is -3 in decimal (again, under 8-bit two's complement representation).

In this case, the `>>` operator moves each bit in the binary representation of `b` two positions to the right. Since `b` is negative and represented in two's complement form, ones are added from the left (sign extension), and the two rightmost bits are dropped. This preserves the negative sign of the number.

Setting a Bit

To set a bit (change it to 1), you can use the bitwise OR operator with a mask that has a 1 in the position of the bit you want to set.

Here's an example:

unsigned int x = 0; // Binary: 0000 0000 x = x | (1 << 3); // Binary: 0000 1000

// To set the 3rd bit, we perform the following steps:

// 1. (1 << 3) shifts 1 three positions to the left, resulting in 0000 1000.

// 2. x | (1 << 3) performs a bitwise OR operation between x and the shifted value.

//   This sets the 3rd bit of x to 1 while leaving other bits unchanged.

//   Binary: 0000 0000 OR
//   0000 1000
//   --
//   0000 1000

In the given code, we have a variable `x` initially assigned the value `0`, which in binary is `0000 0000`. The line `x = x | (1 << 3);` performs the bitwise OR operation to set the third bit of `x`. Here's the step-by-step process:

1. `(1 << 3)` shifts `1` three positions to the left, resulting in `0000 1000`, which is a mask with a `1` only in the third bit.

2. `x | (1 << 3)` performs the bitwise OR operation between `x` and the shifted value. This operation sets the third bit of `x` to `1` while leaving other bits unchanged.

After executing `x = x | (1 << 3);`, the value of `x` becomes `8`, as shown in the binary representation `0000 1000`.

Therefore, the third bit of `x` has been successfully set to `1`.

Clearing a Bit

To clear a bit (change it to 0), you can use the bitwise AND operator with a mask that has a 0 in the position of the bit you want to clear.

Here's an example:

unsigned int x = 9; // Binary: 0000 1001 x = x & ~(1 << 3); // Binary: 0000 0001

// To clear the 3rd bit, we perform the following steps:

// 1. (1 << 3) shifts 1 three positions to the left, resulting in 0000 1000.

// 2. ~(1 << 3) performs a bitwise NOT operation, flipping all bits of the shifted value. Result: 1111 0111.

// 3. x & ~(1 << 3) performs a bitwise AND operation between x and the complement of the shifted value.

//   This clears the 3rd bit of x while leaving other bits unchanged.

//   Binary: 0000 1001 AND
//   1111 0111
//   ---------------------------------------
//   0000 0001

In the given code, we have a variable `x` initially assigned the value `9`, which in binary is `0000 1001`.

The line `x = x & ~(1 << 3);` performs the bitwise AND operation to clear the third bit of `x`. Here's the step-by-step process:

1. `(1 << 3)` shifts `1` three positions to the left, resulting in `0000 1000`, which is a mask with a `1` only in the third bit.

2. `~(1 << 3)` performs a bitwise NOT operation on the mask, inverting all the bits except the third bit. The result is `1111 0111`.

3. `x & ~(1 << 3)` performs the bitwise AND operation between `x` and the complemented mask. This operation clears the third bit of `x` while leaving other bits unchanged. After executing `x = x & ~(1 << 3);`, the value of `x` becomes `1`, as shown in the binary representation `0000 0001`.

Therefore, the third bit of `x` has been successfully cleared.

Toggling a Bit

To toggle a bit (change it from 0 to 1 or from 1 to 0), you can use the bitwise XOR operator with a mask that has a 1 in the position of the bit you want to toggle.

Here's an example:

```
unsigned int x = 9; // Binary: 0000 1001 x = x ^ (1 << 3); // Binary: 0000 0001

// To toggle the 3rd bit, we perform the following steps:

// 1. (1 << 3) shifts 1 three positions to the left, resulting in 0000 1000.

// 2. x ^ (1 << 3) performs a bitwise XOR operation between x and the shifted value.

//    This toggles the 3rd bit of x, leaving other bits unchanged.

//    Binary: 0000 1001 XOR
//            0000 1000
//    --------------------------------------
//            0000 0001
```

In the given code, we have a variable `x` initially assigned the value `9`, which in binary is `0000 1001`.

The line `x = x ^ (1 << 3);` performs the bitwise XOR operation to toggle the third bit of `x`. Here's the step-by-step process:

1. `(1 << 3)` shifts `1` three positions to the left, resulting in `0000 1000`, which is a mask with a `1` only in the third bit.

2. `x ^ (1 << 3)` performs the bitwise XOR operation between `x` and the shifted value.

This operation toggles the third bit of `x`, leaving other bits unchanged.

After executing `x = x ^ (1 << 3);`, the value of `x` becomes `1`, as shown in the binary representation `0000 0001`.

Therefore, the third bit of `x` has been successfully toggled.

Bit manipulation is a powerful technique that can lead to more efficient and compact code. However, it can also be tricky to get right, so it's important to understand it well and use it carefully.

Checking the Value of a Bit

To check whether a bit is set (1) or not set (0), you can use the bitwise AND operator with a mask that has a 1 in the position of the bit you want to check.

Here's an example:

```
unsigned int x = 8; // Binary: 0000 1000 unsigned int mask = 1 << 3; // Binary: 0000 1000
if (x & mask) {    printf("The 3rd bit is set.\n");
} else {    printf("The 3rd bit is not set.\n");
}
```

In the above code, we have two variables: `x` and `mask`. Here are their binary values:

-        `x`:   0000 1000

-        `mask`:   0000 1000

The variable `mask` is created by shifting `1` three positions to the left (`1 << 3`), which sets the third bit to `1` and leaves all other bits as `0`.

The `if` condition checks if the bitwise AND operation between `x` and `mask` evaluates to a nonzero value. If the third bit of `x` is set (i.e., `1`), the condition is true. Otherwise, if the third bit is not set (i.e., `0`), the condition is false.

Based on the condition, the appropriate message is printed: "The 3rd bit is set." or "The 3rd bit is not set."

In this example, since `x` is `8` (which has its third bit set), the output will be "The 3rd bit is set."

Bitwise Operators In Certain Mathematical Operations

There are specific scenarios where bitwise operators can be used to achieve certain mathematical operations or optimizations.

Here are a few examples:

1. **Multiplication by powers of two:** Multiplication by powers of two can be accomplished using left bit shifting (<<). Shifting a number to the left by n positions is equivalent to multiplying it by 2 to the power of n. For example, x << 3 is equivalent to x * 8.

2. **Division by powers of two:** Division by powers of two can be achieved using right bit shifting (>>). Shifting a number to the right by n positions is equivalent to dividing it by 2 to the power of n. For example, x >> 2 is equivalent to x / 4.

3. **Addition and subtraction of powers of two:** Addition and subtraction of powers of two can be accomplished using bitwise OR (|) and bitwise XOR (^) operations. For example, adding x and y, where y is a power of two, can be achieved using x | y. Similarly, subtracting y from x can be achieved using x ^ y.

Multiplication By Powers Of Two

Multiplication by powers of two refers to multiplying a number by 2 raised to some exponent. Left bit shifting provides a convenient way to achieve this multiplication by shifting the bits of the number to the left.

Here's an example to illustrate the concept:

Suppose we have a variable `x` with an initial value of 5, represented in binary as `00000101`. If we want to multiply `x` by 8 (which is 2 raised to the power of 3), we can use left bit shifting as follows:

int x = 5; // Binary: 00000101 int result = x << 3;

The expression `x << 3` means shifting the bits of `x` to the left by 3 positions. After the left shift, the value of `result` will be: result:

Binary: 00000101 << 3 Result: 00101000

The binary representation `00101000` is equivalent to the decimal value 40. Therefore, the operation `x << 3` effectively multiplies `x` by 8, yielding the result of 40.

In general, left shifting a number by `n` positions is equivalent to multiplying the number by 2 raised to the power of `n`. Each shift to the left effectively doubles the value of the number. For example, shifting by 1 is equivalent to multiplying by 2, shifting by 2 is equivalent to multiplying by 4, and so on.

It's important to note that left shifting is applicable for unsigned integer types and signed integer types (as long as the left-shifted value does not result in overflow). When dealing with signed integers, care must be taken to handle potential sign extension or overflow scenarios.

Using left bit shifting for multiplication by powers of two provides a more efficient and direct approach compared to using the arithmetic multiplication operator (`*`). It can be particularly useful in scenarios where performance optimizations or bit-level manipulations are required.

Division By Powers Of Two

Division by powers of two refers to dividing a number by 2 raised to some exponent. Right bit shifting provides a convenient way to achieve this division by shifting the bits of the number to the right.

Here's an example to illustrate the concept:

Suppose we have a variable `x` with an initial value of 16, represented in binary as `00010000`. If we want to divide `x` by 4 (which is 2 raised to the power of 2), we can use right bit shifting as follows:

int x = 16; // Binary: 00010000 int result = x >> 2;

The expression `x >> 2` means shifting the bits of `x` to the right by 2 positions. After the right shift, the value of `result` will be: result:

Binary: 00010000 >> 2 Result: 00000100

The binary representation `00000100` is equivalent to the decimal value 4. Therefore, the operation `x >> 2` effectively divides `x` by 4, yielding the result of 4.

In general, right shifting a number by `n` positions is equivalent to dividing the number by 2 raised to the power of `n`. Each shift to the right effectively halves the value of the number. For example, shifting by 1 is equivalent to dividing by 2, shifting by 2 is equivalent to dividing by 4, and so on.

It's important to note that right shifting is applicable for unsigned integer types and signed integer types. When dealing with signed integers, the behavior of right shifting depends on the implementation-defined sign extension. If the sign bit (the leftmost bit) is set, right shifting can perform an arithmetic right shift (preserving the sign) or a logical right shift (filling with zeros). The specific behavior may vary depending on the compiler and the signed Ness of the integer type.

Using right bit shifting for division by powers of two provides a more efficient and direct approach compared to using the arithmetic division operator (`/`). It can be particularly useful in scenarios where performance optimizations or bit-level manipulations are required.

Bit manipulation is a powerful technique that can lead to more efficient and compact code. However, it can also be tricky to get right, so it's important to understand it well and use it carefully. As you continue to learn C, you will encounter more complex uses of bit manipulation and learn how to use it to write more advanced programs.

Addition And Subtraction Of Powers Of Two

1. Addition of Powers of Two:

When adding a number `x` to a power of two `y`, where `y` represents a single bit set to `1`, we can use the bitwise OR operation (`|`).

Here's an example:

int x = 10; // Binary: 00001010 int y = 4; // Binary: 00000100 (2^2) int result = x | y;

The expression `x | y` performs the bitwise OR operation between `x` and `y`. This operation combines the bits of `x` and `y`, setting any bit where at least one of the operands has a corresponding bit set. After the operation, the value of `result` will be: result:

Binary: 00001010 | 00000100

Result: 00001110

The binary representation `00001110` is equivalent to the decimal value 14. Therefore, the operation `x | y` effectively adds the power of two `y` to `x`, yielding the result of 14.

2. Subtraction of Powers of Two:

When subtracting a power of two `y` from a number `x`, where `y` represents a single bit set to `1`, we can use the bitwise XOR operation (`^`).

Here's an example:

```
int x = 15; // Binary: 00001111 int y = 8; // Binary: 00001000 (2^3) int result = x ^ y;
```

The expression `x ^ y` performs the bitwise XOR operation between `x` and `y`. This operation compares the corresponding bits of `x` and `y`, setting a bit to `1` if the bits differ. After the operation, the value of `result` will be: result:

Binary: 00001111 ^ 00001000
Result: 00000111

The binary representation `00000111` is equivalent to the decimal value 7. Therefore, the operation `x ^ y` effectively subtracts the power of two `y` from `x`, yielding the result of 7.

It's important to note that the examples given assume `y` represents a power of two with only a single bit set. If `y` has multiple bits set, the bitwise operations will produce different results.

Using bitwise OR (`|`) and bitwise XOR (`^`) operations for addition and subtraction of powers of two can provide a more efficient and direct approach compared to using the arithmetic operators (`+` and `-`). These operations take advantage of the binary representation of numbers and can be useful in scenarios involving bit-level manipulations and optimizations.

LIST, SET, AND MAP

Unlike languages such as Python or Java, C does not provide built-in support for data structures like lists, sets, or maps. However, these data structures can be implemented in C using its fundamental building blocks, such as arrays for lists, and structures and pointers for sets and maps. In this chapter, we will explore how to implement and use these data structures in C.

List

A list is a collection of elements with a specific order. In C, we can use an array to implement a list. Here's an example:

```
#include <stdio.h>

int main()
{
```

```c
int list[5] = {1, 2, 3, 4, 5};
for (int i = 0; i < 5; i++)
{
printf("%d ", list[i]);

    }
return 0;

}
```

In this example, we declare an array of integers and initialize it with five elements. We then print out each element of the list.

Set

A set is a collection of unique elements. In C, we can implement a set using an array along with some additional logic to ensure uniqueness.

Here's a simple example:

```c
#include <stdio.h>

int main()
{
int set[5] = {1, 2, 3, 4, 5};
int value = 3;
int exists = 0;

for (int i = 0; i < 5; i++)
{
if (set[i] == value) {
exists = 1;

break;

}

    }
if (exists) {
        printf("%d exists in the set\n", value);
    } else
{
printf("%d does not exist in the set\n", value);

    }
return 0;

}
```

In this example, we declare an array of integers and initialize it with five elements. We then check if a certain value exists in the set.

Map

A map, also known as a dictionary or associative array, is a collection of key-value pairs. In C, we can implement a map using an array of structures, where each structure represents a key-value pair.

Here's an example:

```c
#include <stdio.h>
#include <string.h>
typedef struct
{
char key[20];
int value;

}
KeyValuePair;
int main() {
KeyValuePair map[2] = {{"apple", 1}, {"banana", 2}};
char key[20] = "banana";
int value = 0;
for (int i = 0; i < 2; i++) {
    if (strcmp(map[i].key, key) == 0)
{
value = map[i].value;
break;
    }
  }
if (value != 0) {
    printf("The value of %s is %d\n", key, value);
  } else {
printf("%s does not exist in the map\n", key);
  }
return 0;
}
```

In this example, we declare an array of `KeyValuePair` structures and initialize it with two key-value pairs. We then search for a certain key in the map and print out its value.

Please note that these are simple implementations and may not be efficient for large collections of data. For more efficient implementations, you might want to use a linked list for the list, a hash table for the set, and a binary search tree or hash table for the map. There are also libraries available, such as the GLib library, which provide implementations of these data structures.

Usage Of List, Set, And Map With Glib

GLib is a utility library that provides support for many data structures that are not natively supported in C, such as lists, sets, and maps. In this chapter, we will explore how to use these data structures in C with GLib, focusing on adding, iterating, finding, updating, and deleting elements.

Before we start, you need to install GLib on your system and include the necessary header files in your program:

```
#include <glib.h> #include <glib/gprintf.h>
```

List

In GLib, lists are implemented as doubly-linked lists. Here's an example of how to use a `GList`:

```
// Create a list
GList* list = NULL;

list = g_list_append(list, "Hello");
list = g_list_append(list, "World");
// Iterate over the list for (GList* iter = list; iter != NULL; iter = iter->next)
{
g_printf("%s ", (char*)iter->data);
}
// Find an element in the list
GList* element = g_list_find_custom(list, "World", (GCompareFunc)g_strcmp0);
if (element != NULL)
{
g_printf("\nFound: %s\n", (char*)element->data);
}
// Update an element in the list element->data = "GLib";
// Delete an element from the list list = g_list_remove(list, "Hello");
// Print the updated list for (GList* iter = list; iter != NULL; iter = iter->next)
{
g_printf("%s ", (char*)iter->data);
}
// Free the list g_list_free(list);
```

Set
GLib does not have a specific set data structure, but it can be easily implemented using a `GHashTable`.

Here's an example:

```
// Create a set
```

```c
GHashTable* set = g_hash_table_new(g_str_hash, g_str_equal);
```

```c
// Add elements to the set g_hash_table_add(set, "Hello");
g_hash_table_add(set, "World");
```

```c
// Check if an element exists in the set gboolean exists = g_hash_table_contains(set, "Hello");
g_printf("\nHello %s in the set\n", exists ? "exists" : "does not exist");
```

```c
// Remove an element from the set g_hash_table_remove(set, "Hello");
```

```c
// Check again if the element exists in the set exists = g_hash_table_contains(set, "Hello");
g_printf("Hello %s in the set\n", exists ? "exists": "does not exist");
```

```c
// Destroy the set
```

```c
g_hash_table_destroy(set);
```

Map

In GLib, maps are implemented as hash tables. Here's an example of how to use a `GHashTable`:

```c
// Create a map
```

```c
GHashTable* map = g_hash_table_new(g_str_hash, g_str_equal);
```

```c
// Insert key-value pairs into the map g_hash_table_insert(map, "apple", GINT_TO_POINTER(1));
g_hash_table_insert(map, "banana", GINT_TO_POINTER(2));
```

```c
// Look up the value of a key in the map int value = GPOINTER_TO_INT(g_hash_table_lookup(map, "banana")); g_printf("\nThe value of banana is %d\n", value);
```

```c
// Update a value in the map g_hash_table_insert(map, "banana", GINT_TO_POINTER(3));
```

```c
// Look up the updated value value = GPOINTER_TO_INT(g_hash_table_lookup(map, "banana"));
g_printf("The updated value of banana is %d\n", value);
```

```c
// Remove a key-value pair from the map g_hash_table_remove(map, "apple");
```

```c
// Check if the key exists in the map gboolean exists = g_hash_table_contains(map, "apple");
g_printf("apple %s in the map\n", exists ? "exists" : "does not exist");
```

```c
// Destroy the map g_hash_table_destroy(map);
```

In this example, we create a `GHashTable`, insert two key-value pairs into it, look up the value of a certain key in the map, update a value in the map, remove a key-value pair from the map, check if a key exists in the map, and finally destroy the map.

Please note that GLib uses pointers to store data in these data structures, so you need to be careful with memory management. In these examples, we use strings and integers that are not dynamically allocated, but if you store dynamically allocated data in these data structures, you need to ensure that the data is properly freed when it is no longer needed.

Conclusion

The study of numeral systems is fundamental to both theoretical and applied computer science. As we have seen throughout this chapter, C programming leverages numeral systems to interact closely with computer hardware, making it a powerful language for low-level operations and resource-efficient programs. The four primary numeral systems covered—binary, decimal, octal, and hexadecimal—each serve unique roles and offer distinct advantages in various computing contexts. This conclusion will examine the importance of understanding numeral systems in C, explore additional applications in advanced fields, and consider how numeral systems influence computational efficiency, security, and problem-solving.

1. Numeral Systems and Their Role in Low-Level Programming

Binary, octal, and hexadecimal systems are not just abstract mathematical constructs; they are embedded into the very architecture of digital computing. Binary, the language of bits (0s and 1s), is the foundation upon which all other numeral systems in computing are built. Understanding binary operations enables programmers to directly manipulate data at the bit level, which is crucial for working with flags, performing logical operations, and interacting with system memory.

Binary Manipulation: Bitwise operations (AND, OR, XOR, NOT, and bit shifts) allow C programmers to perform fast, low-level operations on data. This level of control is beneficial for tasks like optimizing memory usage, implementing algorithms that require specific bit-pattern manipulations, and writing code for embedded systems where resources are constrained.

Hexadecimal and Octal in System Design: While binary is the base of computing, hexadecimal and octal systems provide a shorthand for representing binary values. Hexadecimal notation is particularly valuable for its conciseness, especially when dealing with memory addresses or color codes in graphics programming. Octal, though less commonly used, finds application in specific domains like UNIX permissions.

2. Enhancing Computational Efficiency

One of the main advantages of numeral systems in C programming is the potential for efficiency gains, both in terms of performance and memory usage. C is renowned for giving developers control over memory management and data representation, which is further enhanced by a solid grasp of numeral systems.

Memory Efficiency: By choosing the appropriate numeral system, programmers can reduce memory overhead. For example, binary-coded decimal (BCD) representation or octal notation might save memory in specific applications, such as embedded systems, where memory is limited.

Optimizing Computation: Manipulating data directly in binary enables faster calculations for certain operations, especially when they can be expressed as bitwise shifts rather than arithmetic operations. This approach is often seen in encryption algorithms, data compression, and error-checking codes.

Efficient Storage and Transmission: Numeral systems enable the compact storage and transmission of data. Hexadecimal and octal are especially useful in encoding large binary data efficiently, reducing the space required for storage or transmission in networked applications.

3. Real-World Applications of Numeral Systems

Beyond theoretical and performance benefits, numeral systems are indispensable in real-world applications. From hardware programming and networking to security protocols and software engineering, understanding numeral systems can significantly enhance a programmer's ability to develop robust and optimized solutions.

Embedded Systems: Embedded programming relies heavily on efficient numeral representation. Binary and hexadecimal representations are crucial for configuring hardware registers, setting control flags, and encoding data efficiently.

Networking and Data Transmission: In networking, IP addresses, MAC addresses, and subnet masks are typically represented in hexadecimal or binary formats. Understanding these numeral systems enables developers to perform subnetting, address parsing, and other network-related operations.

Cryptography and Security: Many cryptographic algorithms operate at the bit level, requiring binary manipulation to encode, decode, and securely store data. Hash functions and encryption protocols often use hexadecimal representations for digest outputs, making it easier to handle long binary sequences compactly.

Color Encoding and Graphics Programming: In graphics programming, hexadecimal values are frequently used to represent colors (e.g., #FFFFFF for white). This allows easy manipulation and understanding of colors in applications, which is particularly useful in web development and game programming.

4. Numeral Systems as Problem-Solving Tools

Understanding numeral systems provides programmers with problem-solving strategies that go beyond simple arithmetic. Numeral conversions, for example, enable developers to translate data into forms that are easier to manipulate, analyze, or display.

Data Parsing and Validation: Conversion between numeral systems allows developers to parse data from multiple sources, validate its correctness, and present it in the most appropriate format. For instance, converting binary data into hexadecimal for display purposes or back to binary for internal processing is common in diagnostics and debugging tools.

Algorithm Development: Numeral systems play an essential role in algorithm design, especially in fields like artificial intelligence, data science, and machine learning, where data must often be pre-processed, converted, or encoded in various forms.

Problem Solving with Modulo Operations: Many algorithms leverage binary-based modulo operations to simplify calculations, enabling faster solutions for problems involving powers, parity checking, and bitwise shifts. These techniques are often critical in fields like cryptography, where modular arithmetic is used extensively.

5. Influence on Computational Thinking

The numeral systems provide a framework for computational thinking, encouraging programmers to approach problems from a foundational, logical perspective. C programming's support for direct memory manipulation, pointers, and low-level operations makes understanding numeral systems especially valuable. It reinforces the importance of viewing data as abstract representations that can be manipulated in various ways to achieve desired outcomes.

Binary Thinking: The binary system's on/off states encourage programmers to think in terms of Boolean logic, which is essential in control structures, conditional statements, and logic gates.

Efficient Problem Representation: Different numeral systems facilitate specific types of thinking and problem representation. For example, hexadecimal notation is particularly useful in debugging, as it allows programmers to interpret large binary numbers quickly and accurately.

Memory Addressing and Pointer Arithmetic: The hexadecimal system's alignment with 4-bit binary clusters makes it ideal for memory addressing, pointer arithmetic, and understanding computer architecture. This skill is invaluable for C programmers working in environments where memory management is paramount.

6. Advancing Software Engineering Practices

Beyond individual programming skills, understanding numeral systems enhances software engineering as a discipline by promoting efficient, maintainable, and secure code.

Code Optimization: Code that effectively leverages numeral systems can minimize computational complexity and increase performance, especially in high-performance computing environments.

Security Considerations: Numeral systems impact security practices, especially in cryptographic applications. By encoding data in binary or hexadecimal, sensitive information can be better protected, as these formats allow for more secure hashing and encryption.

Debugging and Diagnostics: Hexadecimal notation is a staple in debugging tools and error diagnostics. Being able to read and interpret memory addresses, machine code, and error codes in hexadecimal is essential for diagnosing issues and understanding system behavior.

7. Bridging Numeral Systems and Future Technologies

As technology advances, numeral systems remain foundational. Emerging technologies like quantum computing, artificial intelligence, and blockchain rely on data representation and manipulation principles that are rooted in these systems. For instance:

Quantum Computing: While it departs from traditional binary computation, quantum computing still relies on representing and manipulating data at a fundamental level. A strong understanding of numeral systems provides a foundation for grasping quantum bits (qubits) and their potential states.

Artificial Intelligence and Machine Learning: In machine learning, data preprocessing often involves encoding and transforming data into various formats. Converting numeric and categorical data efficiently is essential for training machine learning models effectively.

Blockchain and Cryptographic Hashing: Hexadecimal notation is prevalent in blockchain, where transaction hashes and block identifiers are represented in hex format for compactness and readability.

Conclusion Summary

In conclusion, mastering numeral systems is a vital skill for any C programmer aiming to build a strong foundation in low-level computing, data manipulation, and problem-solving. These systems are not merely theoretical concepts but practical tools that shape the way data is represented, processed, and stored. The ability to move seamlessly between binary, decimal, octal, and hexadecimal representations empowers programmers to optimize performance, write secure code, and tackle complex challenges with confidence.

Understanding numeral systems deepens one's knowledge of computer architecture and data encoding, paving the way for advanced programming in fields such as systems programming, embedded development, and cybersecurity. By leveraging these systems, C programmers can make informed decisions that result in efficient, maintainable, and high-performance software—a goal at the heart of software engineering. As computing evolves, the skills gained through mastery of numeral systems will continue to be invaluable in driving innovation and achieving excellence in programming.

16. Common C Programming Errors

Introduction

C programming is a powerful and efficient language, yet it is also prone to errors due to its complexity, lower-level access, and lack of built-in safeguards. Even experienced programmers encounter bugs and pitfalls in C, often leading to crashes, memory leaks, or unexpected behaviors. Understanding these common errors can enhance code reliability, optimize debugging processes, and improve the overall quality of applications. In this comprehensive guide, we will explore some of the most frequent C programming errors, detailing why they occur and how to avoid them.

1. Syntax Errors

Syntax errors arise when the code does not follow the language's grammatical rules, such as missing semicolons or mismatched parentheses. These are often caught by the compiler, making them easier to fix.

Example:

```c
int main() {
    printf("Hello, World!" // Missing closing parenthesis and semicolon
    return 0;
}
```

Solution: Carefully check your code for missing characters and ensure all statements are properly terminated.

2. Uninitialized Variables

Uninitialized variables contain garbage values, which may lead to unpredictable behavior. In C, unlike some higher-level languages, variables are not automatically initialized.

Example:

```c
int main() {
    int x; // Uninitialized
    printf("%d\n", x); // May print any random value
    return 0;
}
```

Solution: Always initialize variables before using them. You can initialize integers to 0 or pointers to NULL if unsure of the starting value.

3. Memory Leaks

Memory leaks occur when allocated memory is not freed, causing the program to consume excessive memory over time. This is particularly common in applications that frequently allocate and deallocate memory.

Example:

```
int main() {
    int *ptr = (int*) malloc(sizeof(int) * 5); // Allocated memory
    // Forget to free ptr
    return 0;
}
```

Solution: Always free dynamically allocated memory after it is no longer needed. Tools like Valgrind can be helpful for detecting memory leaks.

4. Dangling Pointers

A dangling pointer occurs when a pointer still references memory that has been freed. Accessing this memory can lead to crashes or undefined behavior.

Example:

```
int *ptr = (int*) malloc(sizeof(int));
free(ptr);  // Memory is freed
printf("%d\n", *ptr); // Undefined behavior
```

Solution: After freeing a pointer, set it to NULL to avoid accidental dereferencing.

5. Null Pointer Dereferencing

Dereferencing a null pointer is a common cause of crashes. This occurs when you attempt to access memory through a pointer set to NULL.

Example:

```
int *ptr = NULL;
```

```
printf("%d\n", *ptr); // Null pointer dereference
```

Solution: Always check if a pointer is NULL before dereferencing it. For example:

```
if (ptr != NULL) {
    printf("%d\n", *ptr);
}
```

6. Buffer Overflows

Buffer overflows happen when data exceeds the bounds of allocated memory, potentially overwriting adjacent memory and leading to security vulnerabilities.

Example:

```
char buffer[5];
strcpy(buffer, "This is too long"); // Overwrites buffer bounds
```

Solution: Use safer functions like strncpy instead of strcpy, and ensure that data fits within the allocated space.

7. Integer Overflow and Underflow

In C, integers have a fixed size, so exceeding their limits causes overflow (for unsigned types) or underflow (for signed types). This may lead to unexpected values or incorrect calculations.

Example:

```
unsigned int x = UINT_MAX; // Maximum value
x = x + 1; // Overflows back to 0
```

Solution: Use appropriate data types based on the expected range and check for overflow conditions before performing arithmetic operations.

8. Off-By-One Errors

These errors are common in loops or array indexing, where the loop runs one iteration too many or too few. This can result in accessing invalid memory or skipping elements.

Example:

```
int arr[5] = {1, 2, 3, 4, 5};
```

```
for (int i = 0; i <= 5; i++) { // Off-by-one: should be i < 5
    printf("%d\n", arr[i]);
}
```

Solution: Be careful with loop conditions and array bounds. Using < instead of <= (or vice versa) can make a big difference.

9. Misusing Assignment Operators

Using = instead of == in conditional statements is a frequent mistake, leading to unexpected assignments instead of comparisons.

Example:

```
int x = 5;
if (x = 10) { // Assignment, not comparison
    printf("x is 10\n");
}
```

Solution: Use == for comparisons. Some programmers reverse the operands (if (10 == x)) to catch this error at compile time.

10. Incorrect Pointer Arithmetic

Pointer arithmetic is a powerful feature in C, but it's easy to misuse. Incrementing or decrementing pointers incorrectly can result in accessing invalid memory regions.

Example:

```
int arr[3] = {1, 2, 3};
int *ptr = arr + 3; // Points outside the array bounds
printf("%d\n", *ptr); // Undefined behavior
```

Solution: Ensure that pointer operations stay within the bounds of the allocated memory, especially when traversing arrays.

11. Using the Wrong Format Specifiers

In printf and scanf statements, using the wrong format specifier for a data type can lead to incorrect output or runtime errors.

Example:

int x = 10;

printf("%f\n", x); // Wrong specifier for int

Solution: Match the format specifier with the variable type (%d for int, %f for float, etc.).

12. Improper Use of the sizeof Operator

The sizeof operator returns the size of a type or variable, but its misuse in memory allocation or typecasting can lead to unintended behavior.

Example:

int *ptr = (int*) malloc(sizeof(ptr)); // Incorrect: allocates size of pointer, not int

Solution: Use sizeof(*ptr) or sizeof(int) for correct allocation:

int *ptr = (int*) malloc(5 * sizeof(int));

13. Recursion Errors

Recursion errors, like infinite recursion, can lead to stack overflow. This often happens when the base case is missing or incorrect.

Example:

```
void recurse() {
    recurse(); // No base case
}
```

Solution: Always define a clear base case to stop the recursion.

14. Not Using const Correctly

The const keyword prevents modification of variables, and it should be used in pointer declarations when applicable. Not using const can lead to unintended modifications.

Example:

void printMessage(char *msg) {

```
    // Potential modification of msg
}
```

Solution: Use const to enforce read-only behavior:

```
void printMessage(const char *msg) {
    // Now msg cannot be modified
}
```

15. Resource Leaks

Besides memory leaks, file and socket handles can also leak if not properly closed, leading to resource exhaustion in long-running applications.

Example:

```
FILE *fp = fopen("file.txt", "r");
// Forgot to close fp
```

Solution: Always fclose files, close sockets, and release other resources after use.

16. Floating-Point Precision Issues

Floating-point numbers in C are inherently imprecise. Comparisons and calculations can yield unexpected results due to rounding errors.

Example:

```
float a = 0.1;
if (a == 0.1) { // May fail due to precision errors
    printf("Equal\n");
}
```

Solution: Avoid direct equality checks with floating-point numbers. Instead, use a tolerance value:

```
if (fabs(a - 0.1) < 0.0001) {
    printf("Approximately equal\n");
}
```

17. Undefined Behavior in Expressions

Certain expressions, such as modifying and accessing a variable in the same statement, lead to undefined behavior.

Example:

```
int x = 10;
x = x++ + ++x; // Undefined behavior
```

Solution: Avoid complex expressions that modify and access the same variable in different ways.

Introduction To Bug

A software bug is an error, flaw, failure, or fault in a computer program or system that causes it to produce an incorrect or unexpected result, or to behave in unintended ways. Most bugs arise from mistakes and errors made by people in either a program's source code or its design, or in frameworks and operating systems used by such programs, and a few are caused by compilers producing incorrect code.

A program that contains a large number of bugs, and/or bugs that seriously interfere with its functionality, is said to be **buggy**. Reports detailing bugs in a program are commonly known as bug reports, defect reports, fault reports, problem reports, trouble reports, change requests, and so forth.

How bugs get into software

In software development projects, a "mistake" or "fault" can be introduced at any stage during development. Bugs are a consequence of the nature of human factors in the programming task. They arise from oversights or mutual misunderstandings made by a software team during specification, design, coding, data entry and documentation.

For example,

In creating a relatively simple program to sort a list of words into alphabetical order, one's design might fail to consider what should happen when a word contains a hyphen. Perhaps, when converting the abstract design into the chosen programming language,

Prevention

The software industry has put much effort into finding methods for preventing programmers from inadvertently introducing bugs while writing software. **These include:**

Programming style

While typos in the program code are often caught by the compiler, a bug usually appears when the programmer makes a logic error. Various innovations in programming style and defensive programming are designed to make these bugs less likely, or easier to spot.

In some programming languages, so-called typos, especially of symbols or logical/mathematical operators, actually represent logic errors, since the mistyped constructs are accepted by the compiler with a meaning other than that which the programmer intended.

Programming techniques

Bugs often create inconsistencies in the internal data of a running program. Programs can be written to check the consistency of their own internal data while running. If an inconsistency is encountered, the program can immediately halt, so that the bug can be located and fixed. Alternatively, the program can simply inform the user, attempt to correct the inconsistency, and continue running.

Development methodologies

There are several schemes for managing programmer activity, so that fewer bugs are produced. Many of these falls under the discipline of software engineering (which addresses software design issues as well). For example, formal program specifications are used to state the exact behavior of programs, so that design bugs can be eliminated.

Unfortunately, formal specifications are impractical or impossible [citation needed] for anything but the shortest programs, because of problems of combinatorial explosion and indeterminacy.

In modern times, popular approaches include automated unit testing and automated acceptance testing (sometimes going to the extreme of test-driven development), and agile software development (which is often combined with, or even in some cases mandates, automated testing).

All of these approaches are supposed to catch bugs and poorly-specified requirements soon after they are introduced, which should make them easier and cheaper to fix, and to catch at least some of them before they enter into production use.

Programming language support-

Programming languages often include features which help programmers prevent bugs, such as static type systems, restricted namespaces and modular programming, among others. For example, when a programmer writes (pseudocode) LET REAL_VALUE PI = "THREE AND A BIT", although this may be syntactically correct, the code fails a type check. Depending on the language and implementation, this may be caught by the compiler or at run-time.

In addition, many recently invented languages have deliberately excluded features which can easily lead to bugs, at the expense of making code slower than it need be: the general principle being that, because of Moore's law, computers get faster and software engineers get slower; it is almost always better to write simpler, slower code than "clever", inscrutable code, especially considering that maintenance cost is considerable.

For example, the Java programming language does not support pointer arithmetic; implementations of some languages such as Pascal and scripting languages often have runtime bounds checking of arrays, at least in a debugging build.

Code analysis

Tools for code analysis help developers by inspecting the program text beyond the compiler's capabilities to spot potential problems. Although in general the problem of finding all programming errors given a specification is not solvable (see halting problem), these tools exploit the fact that human programmers tend to make the same kinds of mistakes when writing software.

Instrumentation-

Tools to monitor the performance of the software as it is running, either specifically to find problems such as bottlenecks or to give assurance as to correct working, may be embedded in the code explicitly (perhaps as simple as a statement saying PRINT "I AM HERE"), or provided as tools. It is often a surprise to find where most of the time is taken by a piece of code, and this removal of assumptions might cause the code to be rewritten.

Debugging

Debugging is a methodical process of finding and reducing the number of bugs, or defects, (Errors) in a computer program, thus making it behave as expected. Finding and fixing bugs, or "debugging", has always been a major part of computer programming.

Maurice Wilkes, an early computing pioneer, described his realization in the late 1940s that much of the rest of his life would be spent finding mistakes in his own programs. As computer programs grow more complex, bugs become more common and difficult to fix.

Often programmers spend more time and effort finding and fixing bugs than writing new code. Software testers are professionals whose primary task is to find bugs, or write code to support testing. On some projects, more resources can be spent on testing than in developing the program.

Usually, the most difficult part of debugging is finding the bug in the source code. Once it is found, correcting it is usually relatively easy. Programs known as debuggers exist to help programmers locate bugs by executing code line by line, watching variable values, and other features to observe program behavior.

Without a debugger, code can be added so that messages or values can be written to a console (for example

with printf in the C programming language) or to a window or log file to trace program execution or show values.

However, even with the aid of a debugger, locating bugs is something of an art. It is not uncommon for a bug in one section of a program to cause failures in a completely different section, [citation needed] thus making it especially difficult to track (for example, an error in a graphics rendering routine causing a file I/O routine to fail), in an apparently unrelated part of the system.

Introduction

This Chapter lists the common C programming errors that the author sees time and time again. Solutions to the errors are also presented.

Beginner Errors

These are errors that beginning C students often make. However, the professionals still sometimes make them too!

Forgetting to put a break in a switch statement.

Remember that C does not break out of a switch statement if a case is encountered.

For example:

```
int x = 2; switch(x)
{
case 2:
printf("Two\n");
case 3:
printf("Three\n");
}
```

Output:

Two

Three

Put a break to break out of the switch:

```
int x = 2; switch(x)
{
case 2:
printf("Two\n");
break;
case 3:
printf("Three\n");
break;   /* not necessary, but good if additional cases are added later */
}
```

Using = instead of ==

C's = operator is used exclusively for assignment and returns the value assigned. The == operator is used exclusively for comparison and returns an integer value (0 for false, not 0 for true). Because of these return values, the C compiler often does not flag an error when = is used when one really wanted an ==.

For example:

```
int x = 5;
if ( x = 6 )
printf("x equals 6\n");
```

This code prints out x equals 6! Why? The assignment inside the if sets x to 6 and returns the value 6 to the if. Since 6 is not 0, this is interpreted as true.

One way to have the compiler find this type of error is to put any constants (or any r-value expressions) on the left side. Then if an = is used, it will be an error:

```
if ( 6 = x )
```

scanf() errors

There are two types of common scanf() errors:

Forgetting to put an ampersand (&) on arguments scanf() must have the address of the variable to store input into. This means that often the ampersand address operator is required to compute the addresses.

Here's an example:

```
int x;
char * st = malloc(31);

scanf("%d", &x);            /* & required to pass address to scanf()   */
scanf("%30s", st);          /* NO & here, st itself points to variable! */
```

As the last line above shows, sometimes no ampersand is correct!

Using the wrong format for operand

C compilers do not check that the correct format is used for arguments of a scanf() call. The most common errors are using the %f format for doubles (which must use the %lf format) and mixing up %c and %s for characters and strings.

Size of arrays

Arrays in C always start at index 0. This means that an array of 10 integers defined as: int a[10];

Has valid indices from 0 to 9 not 10! It is very common for students go one too far in an array. This can lead to unpredictable behavior of the program.

Integer division

Unlike Pascal, C uses the / operator for both real and integer division. It is important to understand how C determines which it will do. If both operands are of an integral type, integer division is used, else real division is used.

For example:

double half = 1/2;

This code sets half to 0 not 0.5! Why? Because 1 and 2 are integer constants. To fix this, change at least one of them to a real constant.

double half = 1.0/2;

If both operands are integer variables and real division is desired, cast one of the variables to double (or float).

int x = 5, y = 2;
double d = ((double) x)/y;

Loop errors

In C, a loop repeats the very next statement after the loop statement. The code:

```
int x = 5;
while( x > 0 );
x--;
```

Is an infinite loop. Why? The semicolon after the while defines the statement to repeat as the null statement (which does nothing). Remove the semicolon and the loop works as expected.

Another common loop error is to iterate one too many times or one too few. Check loop conditions carefully!

Not using prototypes

Prototypes tell the compiler important features of a function: the return type and the parameters of the function. If no prototype is given, the compiler assumes that the function returns an int and can take any number of parameters of any type.

One important reason to use prototypes is to let the compiler check for errors in the argument lists of function calls. However, a prototype must be used if the function does not return an int. For example, the sqrt() function returns a double, not an int.

The following code:

```
double x = sqrt(2);
```

will not work correctly if a prototype:

```
double sqrt(double);
```

Does not appear above it. Why? Without a prototype, the C compiler assumes that sqrt() returns an int. Since the returned value is stored in a double variable, the compiler inserts code to convert the value to a double. This conversion is not needed and will result in the wrong value.

The solution to this problem is to include the correct C header file that contains the sqrt() prototype, math.h. For functions you write, you must either place the prototype at the top of the source file or create a header file and include it.

Not initializing pointers

Anytime you use a pointer, you should be able to answer the question: What variable does this point to? If you cannot answer this question, it is likely it doesn't point to any variable.

This type of error will often result in a Segmentation fault/core dump error on UNIX/Linux or a general protection fault under Windows. (Under good old DOS (ugh!), anything could happen!)

Here's an example of this type of error.

```
#include <string.h>
int main()

{
char * st;
/* defines a pointer to a char or char array */
strcpy(st, "abc");
/* what char array does st point to?? */
return 0;
}
```

How to do this correctly? Either use an array or dynamically allocate an array.

```
#include <string.h>
int main()

{
char st[20];   /* defines an char array */
strcpy(st, "abc");    /* st points to char array */
return 0;

}
```

Or

```
#include <string.h>
#include <stdlib.h>
int main()

{
char *st = malloc(20); /* st points to allocated array*/
strcpy(st, "abc");     /* st points to char array */

free(st); /* don't forget to deallocate when done! */
return 0;

}
```

Actually, the first solution is much preferred for what this code does. Why? Dynamical allocation should only be used when it is required. It is slower and more error prone than just defining a normal array.

String Errors

Confusing character and string constants

C considers character and string constants as very different things. Character constants are enclosed in single quotes and string constants are enclosed in double quotes. String constants act as a pointer to the actually string.

Consider the following code:

```
char ch = 'A';    /* correct */
char ch = "A";    /* error   */
```

The second line assigns the character variable ch to the address of a string constant. This should generate a compiler error. The same should happen if a string pointer is assigned to a character constant:

```
const char * st = "A"; /* correct */
const char * st = 'A';    /* error   */
```

Comparing strings with ==

Never use the == operator to compare the value of strings! Strings are char arrays.

The name of a char array acts like a pointer to the string (just like other types of arrays in C). So what? Consider the --

following code:

```
char st1[] = "abc";
char st2[] = "abc";
if ( st1 == st2 )
printf("Yes");
else
printf("No");
```

This code prints out No. Why? Because the == operator is comparing the pointer values of st1 and st2, not the data pointed to by them. The correct way to compare string values is to use the strcmp() library function.

(Be sure to include string.h) If the if statement above is replaced with the following:

```
if ( strcmp(st1,st2) == 0 )

printf("Yes"); else   printf("No");
```

The code will print out Yes. For similar reasons, don't use the other relational operators (<,>, etc.) with strings either. Use strcmp() here too.

Not null terminating strings

C assumes that a string is a character array with a terminating null character. This null character has ASCII value 0 and can be represented as just 0 or '\0'.

This value is used to mark the end of meaningful data in the string. If this value is missing, many C string functions will keep processing data past the end of the meaningful data and often past the -end of the character array itself until it happens to find a zero byte in memory!

Most C library string functions that create strings will always properly null terminate them. Some do not (e.g.,strncpy()). Be sure to read their descriptions carefully.

Not leaving room for the null terminator

A C string must have a null terminator at the end of the meaningful data in the string. A common mistake is to not allocate room for this extra character. For example, the string defined below char str[30]; Only has room for only 29 (not 30) actually data characters, since a null must appear after the last data character.

This can also be a problem with dynamic allocation. Below is the correct way to allocate a string to the exact size needed to hold a copy of another.

char * copy_str = malloc(strlen(orig_str) + 1); strcpy(copy_str, orig_str);

The common mistake is to forget to add one to the return value of strlen(). The strlen() function returns a count of the data characters which does not include the null terminator.

This type of error can be very hard to detect. It might not cause any problems or only problems in extreme cases. In the case of dynamic allocation, it might corrupt the heap (the area of the program's memory used for dynamic allocation) and cause the next heap operation (malloc(), free(), etc.) to fail.

Input/Output Errors

Using fgetc(), etc. incorrectly

The fgetc(), getc() and getchar() functions all return back an integer value.
For example, the prototype of fgetc()is: int fgetc(FILE *);

Sometimes this integer value is really a simple character, but there is one very important case where the return value is **not** a character!

What is this value?   **EOF**   A common misconception of students is that files have a special EOF character at the end. There is no special character stored at the end of a file. EOF is an integer error code returned by a function.

Here is the**wrong** way to use fgetc():

```
int count_line_size( FILE * fp )
{
char ch;  int cnt = 0;
 while( (ch = fgetc(fp)) != EOF && ch != '\n')   cnt++;  return cnt;
}
```

What is wrong with this? The problem occurs in the condition of the while loop. To illustrate, here is the loop rewritten to show what C will do behind the scenes.

```
while( (int) ( ch = (char) fgetc(fp) ) != EOF && ch != '\n')   cnt++;
```

The return value of fgetc(fp) is cast to char to store the result into ch. Then the value of ch must be cast back to an int to compare it with EOF. So what?

Casting an int value to a char and then back to an int may not give back the original int value. This means in the example above that if fgetc() returns back the EOF value, the casting may change the value so that the comparison later with EOF would be false.

What is the solution? Make the ch variable an int as below:

```
int count_line_size( FILE * fp )
{
int ch;
int  cnt = 0;
while( (ch = fgetc(fp)) != EOF && ch != '\n')
cnt++;
return cnt;
}
```

Now the only hidden cast is in the second comparison.

```
while( (ch = fgetc(fp)) != EOF &&  ch != ((int) '\n') )   cnt++;
```

This cast has no harmful effects at all! So, the moral of all this is: **always** use an int variable to store the result of the fgetc(), getc() and getchar().

Using feof() incorrectly

There is a wide spread misunderstanding of how C's feof() function works. Many programmers use it like Pascal'seof() function. However, C's function works differently!

What's the difference? Pascal's function returns true if the next read will fail because of end of file. C's function returns true if the last function failed.

Here's an example of a misuse of feof():

```c
#include <stdio.h>
int main()

{
FILE * fp = fopen("test.txt", "r");
char line[100];
while( ! feof(fp) )
{
fgets(line, sizeof(line), fp);
fputs(line, stdout);
}

fclose(fp);
return 0;

}
```

This program will print out the last line of the input file twice. Why? After the last line is read in and printed out,feof() will still return 0 (false) and the loop will continue. The next fgets() fails and so the line variable holding the contents of the last line is not changed and is printed out again. After this, feof() will return true (since fgets()failed) and the loop ends.

How should this fixed? One way is the following:

```c
#include <stdio.h>
int main()
{
FILE * fp = fopen("test.txt", "r");
char line[100];
while( 1 )
{
fgets(line, sizeof(line), fp);
if ( feof(fp) )   /* check for EOF right after fgets() */
break;
fputs(line, stdout);

}

fclose(fp);
return 0;

}
```

However, this is not the best way. There is really no reason to use feof() at all. C input functions return values that can be used to check for EOF. For example, fgets returns the NULL pointer on EOF.

Here's a better version of the program:

```
#include <stdio.h>
int main()
{
FILE * fp = fopen("test.txt", "r");
char line[100];
while( fgets(line, sizeof(line), fp) != NULL )
fputs(line, stdout);
fclose(fp);
return 0;

}
```

The author has yet to see any student use the feof() function correctly! Incidentally, this discussion also applies to C++ and Java. The eof() method of an istream works just like C's feof().

Leaving characters in the input buffer

C input (and output) functions buffer data. Buffering stores data in memory and only reads (or writes) the data from (or to) I/O devices when needed. Reading and writing data in big chunks is much more efficient than a byte (or character) at a time. Often the buffering has no effect on programming.

One place where buffering is visible is input using scanf(). The keyboard is usually line buffered. This means that each line input is stored in a buffer. Problems can arise when a program does not process all the data in a line, before it wants to process the next line of input.

For example, consider the following code:

```
int x;
char st[31];
printf("Enter an integer: ");
scanf("%d", &x);

printf("Enter a line of text: ");

fgets(st, 31, stdin);
```

The fgets() will not read the line of text that is typed in. Instead, it will probably just read an empty line. In fact, the program will not even wait for an input for the fgets() call. Why? The scanf() call reads the characters needed that represent the integer number read in, but it leaves the '\n' in the input buffer. The fgets() then starts reading data from the input buffer. It finds a '\n' and stops without needing any additional keyboard input.

What's the solution? One simple method is to read and dump all the characters from the input buffer until a '\n' after the scanf() call. Since this is something that might be used in lots of places, it makes sense to make this a function.

Here is a function that does just this:

```
/* function dump_line
This function reads and dumps any remaining characters on the current input*line of a file.
```

Parameter:

fp - pointer to a FILE to read characters from* Precondition: * fp points to a open file Postcondition: the file referenced by fp is positioned at the end of the next line* or the end of the file. */

```
void dump_line( FILE * fp )
{
 int ch;
 while( (ch = fgetc(fp)) != EOF && ch != '\n' )
    /* null body */;
}
```

Here is the code above fixed by using the above function:

```
int x; char st[31];
printf("Enter an integer: ");
scanf("%d",    &x);
dump_line(stdin);
printf("Enter a line of text: ");
fgets(st, 31, stdin);
```

One incorrect solution is to use the following:

```
fflush(stdin);
```

This will compile but its behavior is undefined by the ANSI C standard.

The fflush() function is only meant to be used on streams open for output, not input. This method does seem to work with some C compilers, but is completely unportable! Thus, it should not be used.

Using the gets() function

Do not use this function! It does not know how many characters can be safely stored in the string passed to it. Thus, if too many are read, memory will be corrupted.

Many security bugs that have been exploited on the Internet use this fact! Use the fgets() function instead (and read from stdin). But remember that unlike gets(), fgets() does not discard a terminating \n from the input.

The scanf() functions can also be used dangerously. The %s format can overwrite the destination string. However, it can be used safely by specifying a width. For example, the format %20s will not read more than 20 characters.

Conclusion: Mastering C Programming by Avoiding Common Pitfalls

In the journey of mastering C programming, the importance of understanding and avoiding common pitfalls cannot be overstated. C's low-level capabilities make it powerful but also prone to subtle, tricky errors that can undermine the stability and security of applications. As C continues to be a foundational language for systems programming, embedded applications, and performance-critical software, awareness of common errors will help developers write more efficient, reliable, and maintainable code.

1. The Importance of Careful Syntax and Initialization

A foundational takeaway is the role of careful syntax in C programming. Syntax errors, although typically caught by compilers, can be frustrating and time-consuming. Small mistakes, like missing semicolons, misused operators, or mismatched brackets, can cause a cascade of issues in code logic and functionality.

Uninitialized variables are particularly hazardous in C, where undefined values can wreak havoc on program behavior. Developers are encouraged to initialize variables explicitly. Following a strict code style, using static code analysis tools, and reviewing code thoroughly help prevent these issues.

2. Effective Memory Management: Avoiding Leaks and Dangling Pointers

Memory management is among the most challenging aspects of C programming. Dynamic memory allocation with functions like malloc and free gives C its flexibility, but it also demands careful handling to avoid memory leaks, dangling pointers, and memory fragmentation. Memory leaks occur when allocated memory is not properly freed, gradually consuming system resources and slowing down applications. Dangling pointers, on the other hand, refer to pointers that continue to point to memory that has already been freed. Accessing these can lead to crashes, undefined behavior, and security vulnerabilities.

One effective strategy to avoid memory leaks is to adopt a consistent approach to freeing memory. Ensuring that every malloc or calloc call is paired with a corresponding free statement, even in functions that exit early due to errors, is essential. Automated tools like Valgrind can also detect memory leaks, making debugging memory-intensive applications easier. For dangling pointers, a best practice is to set pointers to NULL immediately after freeing them, ensuring that accidental dereferencing attempts are caught early.

3. Preventing Buffer Overflows and Out-of-Bounds Errors

Buffer overflows and out-of-bounds errors are frequent sources of vulnerabilities in C. When data exceeds the allocated buffer's size, it can overwrite adjacent memory, leading to unpredictable results or exploitable security issues. Techniques to avoid buffer overflows include carefully checking the size of data before copying it into buffers, using safer library functions (like strncpy instead of strcpy), and always allocating enough memory for buffers. With modern compilers offering certain protections against buffer overflows, developers are encouraged to enable these settings to catch potential overflows early in development.

Looping structures also require attention to avoid off-by-one errors. These errors are common in array manipulation, where accessing elements beyond array bounds results in undefined behavior. Checking loop conditions carefully and using tools like bounds-checking compilers or static analysis can reduce the frequency of these errors.

4. Managing Null Pointers and Correct Pointer Arithmetic

Pointers are central to C's power but also to its potential pitfalls. Null pointer dereferencing is a primary cause of segmentation faults in C. Before dereferencing any pointer, it's crucial to check if the pointer is NULL, especially when dealing with dynamic memory allocation or user input. When performing pointer arithmetic, it's essential to ensure that pointer movements stay within the bounds of allocated memory, especially when working with arrays or dynamic data structures. Proper pointer management is critical for avoiding memory corruption and ensuring program stability.

5. Using Appropriate Data Types and Handling Integer Overflows

Data type mismatches can lead to unintended results, especially when using format specifiers in input/output functions. C's primitive data types have fixed sizes and limits, so exceeding these boundaries can lead to overflow or underflow errors. For example, unsigned integers wrapping back to zero after reaching their maximum value can result in logical errors that are challenging to debug.

Choosing data types that match the expected range of values, using constants for boundary checks, and leveraging modern compilers with built-in overflow detection can help. For instance, using size_t for array indices and loop counters helps prevent overflows in counting operations. Regularly checking boundary conditions before performing arithmetic operations is also essential, particularly in performance-sensitive applications.

6. Maintaining Resource Management Practices Beyond Memory

Memory management is a primary focus, but resource management extends beyond memory. Files, sockets, and other system resources require timely handling to prevent resource exhaustion. Failing to close a file or release a socket connection can lead to system instability, especially in long-running applications. The key to preventing these leaks is diligent resource tracking. Implementing clear resource allocation and deallocation protocols, often through the use of helper functions or libraries, helps simplify the process. Adopting structured error handling ensures that resources are released, even when functions exit prematurely due to an error.

7. Precision with Floating-Point Numbers

Floating-point arithmetic in C can lead to errors if not handled carefully due to inherent imprecision. Direct equality checks with floating-point numbers can yield unexpected results because of small rounding errors. Developers are advised to use tolerance-based comparisons for floating-point variables, defining a threshold (epsilon) within which two numbers are considered equal. Understanding the limitations of floating-point representation and applying precision management practices helps maintain accurate results in scientific calculations, graphics, and financial applications.

8. Structuring Code with the const Keyword

The const keyword in C enhances code safety by preventing accidental modification of variables and pointers. When working with complex data structures or API interfaces, const can enforce immutability, making code easier to understand and preventing unintended side effects. In multi-developer projects, this practice becomes especially valuable, as const prevents the unintentional modification of shared resources. Using const strategically in function parameters, return types, and pointers promotes defensive programming and encourages clear, intentional code.

9. Avoiding Undefined Behavior in Expressions and Complex Logic

C is notorious for undefined behavior, where certain expressions and operations yield unpredictable results. Examples include modifying a variable multiple times in a single statement or dividing by zero. These issues arise because the C standard leaves some behavior unstandardized, giving compilers flexibility that may vary by platform. Developers should avoid overly complex expressions that attempt to modify and access variables in ambiguous ways, such as x = x++ + ++x. Simplifying expressions, using intermediate variables, and ensuring straightforward logic can reduce the risk of undefined behavior.

10. Leveraging Tools and Practices for Error Prevention

In addition to following best practices in coding, tools play a critical role in preventing and identifying common C programming errors. Static analyzers, like Clang and GCC's built-in diagnostics, help catch syntax and semantic errors early. Dynamic analysis tools, such as Valgrind for memory leaks and Address Sanitizer for buffer overflows, provide runtime checks that highlight memory and resource management errors. Unit testing frameworks, although less common in C compared to modern languages, are invaluable for verifying code logic and catching bugs during development.

Code reviews and pair programming are equally effective for identifying errors, especially when developers can learn from each other's approaches and discuss potential pitfalls. By adopting practices like code reviews, consistent style guides, and static and dynamic analysis tools, teams can avoid many of the common pitfalls that arise in C programming.

In Summary: Developing a Robust Mindset for C Programming

The journey to mastering C involves more than memorizing syntax or knowing library functions; it requires a disciplined approach to error prevention, debugging, and learning from mistakes. C's flexibility is both its strength and its vulnerability, as it allows developers low-level control over system resources at the cost of safety. Understanding common pitfalls and adopting robust coding practices are essential to leverage C effectively while avoiding its potential dangers.

When you develop a mindset oriented around prevention and learning, errors become opportunities for growth rather than roadblocks. Ultimately, it's this balance of power and caution that defines successful C programming. Embracing rigorous testing, defensive coding, and systematic resource management are key elements in producing efficient, reliable, and maintainable C code. With these principles in mind, developers can navigate C's complexities and harness its full potential, creating programs that stand the test of time and perform seamlessly in critical environments.

17. Generic Lists, Trees, Reference Counting Garbage Collection, and Allocation Pools in C

1. Introduction

C is a statically typed language, which traditionally lacks support for generic data structures. Generic data structures, like lists and trees, allow developers to create flexible, reusable structures that can store elements of any data type. Unlike languages with built-in generics (e.g., C++ templates), implementing generic data structures in C requires careful use of pointers and typecasting.

2. Implementing Generic Lists in C

2.1 Basics of Linked Lists

A linked list is a linear data structure where each element (node) contains a pointer to the next node. Unlike arrays, linked lists offer dynamic sizing and efficient insertion/deletion operations.

2.2 Struct Definition for Generic Lists

To create a generic linked list, you need to design a Node structure that can store any data type. This can be achieved by using a void* pointer, which allows a pointer to any data type.

```
typedef struct Node {
    void *data;
    struct Node *next;
} Node;
```

Here, void *data enables storing any data type, while Node *next points to the next node in the list.

2.3 Adding Nodes to a Generic List

Adding nodes typically involves:

Creating a new node.

Setting its data pointer to the element's address.

Adjusting pointers to maintain list integrity.

```
Node* createNode(void *data, size_t dataSize) {
    Node *newNode = (Node*)malloc(sizeof(Node));
```

```
        newNode->data = malloc(dataSize);

        memcpy(newNode->data, data, dataSize);

        newNode->next = NULL;

        return newNode;

}
```

Here, dataSize allows flexible memory allocation for data of varying sizes.

2.4 Traversing and Operating on Generic Lists

Traversal and manipulation of generic lists in C involves iterating through nodes and using void * data handling to apply operations. Since the data type is unknown, typecasting is necessary when accessing data.

```
void printIntList(Node *head) {

    Node *current = head;

    while (current != NULL) {

        printf("%d ", *(int*)current->data);

        current = current->next;

    }

}
```

2.5 Freeing Memory in Generic Lists

To prevent memory leaks, free each node's data before freeing the node itself.

```
void freeList(Node *head) {

    Node *temp;

    while (head != NULL) {

        temp = head;

        head = head->next;

        free(temp->data);

        free(temp);

    }

}
```

3. Introduction to Generic Trees in C

3.1 Basics of Trees and Binary Trees

Trees are hierarchical data structures with nodes that branch out to multiple children. The binary tree, a common variant, restricts each node to two children (left and right). Trees provide efficient data storage and retrieval methods for structured data.

3.2 Struct Definition for Generic Trees

Like lists, trees in C can be made generic by using void* pointers for the node's data.

```
typedef struct TreeNode {
    void *data;
    struct TreeNode *left;
    struct TreeNode *right;
} TreeNode;
```

The TreeNode structure uses void *data to allow storing any data type and pointers to the left and right children.

3.3 Creating Nodes in a Generic Tree

Creating nodes in a generic tree involves allocating memory for the node, setting its data pointer, and initializing child pointers.

```
TreeNode* createTreeNode(void *data, size_t dataSize) {
    TreeNode *newNode = (TreeNode*)malloc(sizeof(TreeNode));
    newNode->data = malloc(dataSize);
    memcpy(newNode->data, data, dataSize);
    newNode->left = newNode->right = NULL;
    return newNode;
}
```

3.4 Inserting Nodes in a Binary Search Tree (BST)

A binary search tree (BST) stores data in a sorted manner, where each left child has a value less than the parent, and each right child has a value greater. Generic BST insertion involves comparing the stored data, which may require a custom comparison function due to unknown data types.

```
TreeNode* insertTreeNode(TreeNode *root, void *data, size_t dataSize, int (*compare)(void*, void*))
{
    if (root == NULL)
        return createTreeNode(data, dataSize);
```

```
    if (compare(data, root->data) < 0)
        root->left = insertTreeNode(root->left, data, dataSize, compare);
    else
        root->right = insertTreeNode(root->right, data, dataSize, compare);
    return root;
}
```

Here, the compare function allows data-type-independent comparisons.

3.5 Traversing a Generic Tree

Tree traversal (inorder, preorder, postorder) in generic trees requires typecasting to access the node's data.

Here's an example for inorder traversal:

```
void inorderTraversal(TreeNode *root, void (*printData)(void*))
{
    if (root != NULL) {
        inorderTraversal(root->left, printData);
        printData(root->data);
        inorderTraversal(root->right, printData);
    }
}
```

The printData function pointer facilitates custom printing based on data type.

4. Key Considerations and Challenges in Generic Data Structures in C

4.1 Memory Management

Since C doesn't have automatic garbage collection, dynamic memory allocation in lists and trees must be handled carefully. Every malloc requires a corresponding free to prevent memory leaks.

4.2 Type Safety

With void * pointers, C lacks type safety. Developers must manage type consistency and typecasting carefully to avoid runtime errors.

4.3 Function Pointers for Custom Operations

Using function pointers enables flexibility for operations like comparisons and printing. However, they add complexity, as each operation must be customized per data type.

5. Example Applications of Generic Lists and Trees in C

5.1 Implementing a Generic Queue with Linked Lists

Queues are FIFO structures often implemented with linked lists. Using generic nodes, you can implement an adaptable queue that stores any data type.

5.2 Implementing a Search System with Binary Search Trees

BSTs are efficient for searching, making them ideal for directory and database applications. A generic BST can store various data types, allowing adaptability.

6. Advantages and Disadvantages of Generic Data Structures in C

6.1 Advantages

Reusability: The same structure can handle multiple data types, saving development time.

Memory Efficiency: Linked lists and trees dynamically allocate memory, adjusting to storage needs.

6.2 Disadvantages

Complexity: Managing pointers and typecasting increases code complexity.

Lack of Compile-Time Type Checking: Errors may only appear at runtime, as the compiler cannot verify data types within generic structures.

Generic Lists and Trees

We now return to lists and trees and consider what it will take to make them generic the way we make generic dynamic arrays in Chapter 10. The techniques we used there, working with void pointers or generating code using macros, will also work with lists and trees, but we will take a different approach.

With lists and trees, we are not working with contiguously allocated chunks of memory, so in principle, links and nodes can have any size. A generic data structure needs to know about the bits that define a link or a node, but if we allocate memory to store additional data alongside links and nodes, it will not affect the generic code at all. If we put a link or node structure in a user data structure, the generic code can use those.

We have to leave it to the user to allocate all data. If the generic code does not know about user data, it cannot allocate space for it nor can it initialize it—but once the memory exists, it doesn't matter that it was allocated as part of a larger block.

We cannot implement the data structures utterly independent of the user data, however. We need a way to delete links and nodes, for example. Maybe we could unlink links and nodes from the structure and return it to the user for him to free them to get around that. Or we could make the user give us a function pointer to handle deallocation. For search trees, we need to compare nodes, to keep the search tree order, and here we need the user to provide a comparison operator.

A function pointer is a natural choice. Generally, there will be functions that the user must supply for various operations. It is a design choice whether they should provide a function when they invoke a data structure operation, or whether we should store the functions with the data structure, and often it will be a mix of the two approaches. It will be a mix in the following sections, where we will add function pointers to lists and trees for the operations, we expect to be constant throughout the lifetime of a data structure instance, and where we will add function pointer arguments to operations where we could expect the user to want to use different callbacks.

Generic Lists

If we remove all user data from a (doubly linked) list, which admittedly was only an integer in our previous implementation, we are left with two pointers to a link.

```
typedef struct link

{
struct link *prev;
struct link *next;
}
link;
```

Most of the operations we had on links didn't look at the data in the link; they only manipulated the pointers, and those functions will work just as well on our reduced structure.

```
static inline void connect (link *x, link *y)
{
x->next = y; y->prev = x;
}
static inline void connect_neighbours(link *x)
{ x->next->prev = x; x->prev->next = x; }
static inline void link_after(link *x, link *y)

{
y->prev = x; y->next = x->next;
connect_neighbours(y);

} static inline void link_before(link *x, link *y)

{

  link_after((x)->prev, y);
}
```

// This time, unlink will set x's pointers to NULL.

// We don't want to risk the callback function modifying

// the list after the link is removed.

```
static inline void unlink(link *x)

{
if (!x->prev || !x->next) return;
x->next->prev = x->prev;
x->prev->next = x->next;
x->prev = x->next = 0;
}
```

For links, however, we might want to store function pointers so the user can parameterize them. I will add a function for freeing the memory of a link and for printing a link. The operations you might need will, of course, depend on your applications. You might have no need for printing lists, so you can leave that function out. Your application might hold references to all links you want to delete, so you don't need the list to know about the deallocation function. On the other hand, you might have other operations that you want a list to provide, which will depend on user-provided functions. The code you need to write will be similar regardless of which functions you add to a list.

I will write a structure that contains function pointers and call it a list_type. When you create a new list, you must provide its "type" through such a struct. A list will contain the functions and the "head" link we use for a circular list.

```
typedef struct list_type
{
void (*free)(link *);
void  (*print)(link *);

}
list_type;
typedef struct list
{
link head;
list_type type;
}
list;
```

Many of the list operations we had in Chapter 4 need only a slight modification to work with the new list structure. We need to work in the head member of the struct instead of directly on the dummy element in the list. Aside from that, though, there is nothing surprising:

```
static inline

link *head(list *x)
{
return &x->head;
} static inline
```

```
link *front(list *x)
{
return head(x)->next;
}

static inline

link *back(list *x)
{ return head(x)->prev;
} static inline

bool is_empty(list *x)
{
return head(x) == front(x);
} static inline

void append(list *x, link *link)
{
link_before(head(x), link);
} static inline
void prepend(list *x, link *link)
{
link_after(head(x), link);
}
```

To create a list, we need the user to provide a list_type. When can then allocate the list structure, set the pointers in the head member to point to the head, and copy the list pointers into the new struct.

```
list *new_list(list_type type)
{
  list *list = malloc(sizeof *list);
if (list) {
*list = (struct list){
.head = { .next = &list->head,
          .prev = &list->head },
    .type = type
  };
 }
  return list;
}
```

I have chosen to copy the function pointers into the struct rather than have a pointer to a list_type object. This is a somewhat arbitrary choice. It saves the user from having to worry about memory management of a list_type object, but at the cost of having copies of the list_type in every list structure. However, I don't expect there to be many lists of the same type in my imaginary application. There might be many links, so I wouldn't want to put function pointers there if I don't need them—and in any case, the list implementation won't know about what I put in user-defined links—but I am okay with embedding the pointers in the list objects.

To free a list, we must run through the links and free them. We have the embedded free function pointer to help us. We have to make a choice about what happens if the user provided a NULL pointer here, however. We could consider that an error and ignore the issue. It would crash the program if we tried to call the function, but that would be part of the interface if we don't allow NULL pointers. We could also decide to provide a default, for example, free(). That way, if the user doesn't provide a function, we assume that links are heap-allocated objects that we can free(). I will pick a third option and say that if there isn't a free function provided, then we don't free the links.

```
void free_list(list *x)
{
  void (*free_link)(link *) = x->type.free;   // We can only free if we have a free function.
  // Otherwise, assume that we shouldn't free.
  if (free_link)
  {
    link *lnk = front(x);
    while (lnk != head(x))
    {
      link *next = lnk->next;
      free_link(lnk);
      lnk = next;
    }
  }
  free(x);
}
```

A user might put stack-allocated or global variables in a list. Who knows what users get up to when you aren't looking? As long as they don't provide a free function pointer, we won't free links. If they want the links freed, they must provide a function—otherwise, we might leak memory here. It is a design choice, and you can choose to do it differently.

For printing a list, I will make a different choice. I will provide a default print function that we use if the user doesn't provide one:

```
// Default print function static void print_link(link *lnk)
{
  printf("<link %p>", (void *)lnk);
}
void print_list(list *x)
{
  void (*print)(link *) = (x->type.print) ? x->type.print : print_link;     printf("[ ");
  for (link *lnk = front(x);
  lnk != head(x); lnk = lnk->next)
  {
    print(lnk);
    putchar(' ');
```

```
  }
  printf("]\n");
}
```

This is again an arbitrary choice.

For some operations, we might wish to provide a function pointer to the operation itself rather than the list. There are operations where we can imagine we want to parameterize the operation itself, and not expect each invocation of the operation to use a (list) global callback. For example, we could want a function that finds the next link in a chain that satisfies some predicate. The predicate is part of the operation and not a property of the list, and it would give us a way to iterate through a subset of a list.

We could implement such a function like this:

```
link *find_link(list *x, link *from, bool (*p)(link *))
{
  for (link *lnk = from;
lnk != head(x);
lnk = lnk->next)
  {
if (p(lnk)) return lnk;
  }
return 0;
}
```

Here, we search from the link from and forward to the end of the list, but we will return if we find a link that satisfies the predicate p, a function that takes a link as input and returns a Boolean. We return NULL if we do not find a link; it seems like a good way to indicate that we couldn't find what we were searching for.

If you want to iterate through links, you should start from the front element in the list (the link after the head, or front(x) for a list x) and use the function like this:

```
for (link *lnk = find_link(x, front(x), p);
lnk;
lnk = find_link(x, lnk->next, p))
{
  // do something
}
```

How we write a predicate that can look at user data, and how we can get user data out from a link, is covered later. Notice that you have to continue the search from lnk>next in the increment. Otherwise, you get lnk right back because it already satisfies the predicate (unless you change that in "do something").

We had a function that would delete all links with a certain value. With a function pointer, we can generalize this and simultaneously have a generic function. Give the function, let us call it delete_if(), a predicate function pointer as argument, and delete the links that satisfy the predicate.

```
void delete_if(list *x, bool (*p)(link *))
{
void (*free)(link *) = x->type.free;
link *lnk = front(x);
while (lnk != head(x))
{
link *next = lnk->next;
if (p(lnk))
{
unlink(lnk);
if (free) free(lnk);

}
lnk = next;

  }

}
```

To delete a link, we, of course, need the free pointer from the type. If it is NULL, we cannot deallocate a link, but we will always unlink() it, so it will still be removed from the list. Generic Lists and trees

These are enough operations for our list, I think. I am convinced that you can work out how to add more functions from the example given. It is time to explore how we can provide user data to links, given that the list implementation doesn't know about that data. Somehow, user data must provide link structures to the list, and we should be able to cast between the user structures and the link structures as needed.

Casting to Links

We can implement a form of polymorphism by exploiting that the data you put at the top of a struct will, when properly cast, look like that kind of data. If you have a type T and we define

```
typedef struct S {
  T t;
  // more here
} S;
```

then we can cast any pointer to an object of type S to a T pointer and treat the top of the S object as a T object, and we can cast the pointer back from T * to S * and get the original object. Be careful here, though. You cannot safely cast any T * to S *. You obviously can't dereference and access any T object as if it were an S object—such objects won't have the "more here" data. Depending on how pointers are represented, you might not even be able to represent all pointers to T as pointers to S, since the structure S can have stricter alignment requirements, and that can affect the representation of pointers. But if you stick to pointers to objects of type S, you can safely cast them to T *, pass those pointers to functions, and get results back, and the T * pointers you get—because they really point to S objects—can be cast back to S *.

For lists, this means that we can define link structs with any data we wish if we put a link as the first element in the struct. A list's head will have type link, not the larger link type we define, so you cannot necessarily cast the head link to a user type, but you shouldn't be doing that to begin with. It doesn't have any of the user data. The preceding generic list functions do not call user functions with the head of the data, and it is easy enough to avoid if you want to.

As an example, we could want a list of integers, and we could define this struct for links:

```
struct int_link
{
link link;
int value;

};
```

```
typedef struct int_link ilink; ilink *new_int_link(int value)

{
 ilink *lnk = malloc(sizeof *lnk);
if (lnk) lnk->value = value;   return lnk;
}
```

The print and free pointers in a list_type are functions that take link as arguments, but if we only insert pointers to ilink, then we can safely cast from link * to ilink * in functions we intend to use with an integer list, and we can define the type of integer lists as

```
void print_int_link(link *lnk)

{
 printf("%d", ((ilink *)lnk)->value);
}
void free_int_link(link *lnk)

{
 free(lnk); // Nothing special
}
list_type int_list = { .free = free_int_link,

 .print = print_int_link

};
```

A predicate we might use for find_link() or delete_if() could check if the value in a link is an even number, but casting the link to the integer link type and checking the value:

```
bool is_even(link *l)

{
```

```c
    ilink *link = (ilink *)l;
    return link->value % 2 == 0;
}
```

and you could use an integer list as in this small program:

```c
int main(void)
{
    list *x = new_list(int_list);   for (int i = 0; i < 10; i++)
    {
        ilink *lnk = new_int_link(i);
        if (!lnk) abort();
        append(x, (link *)lnk);

    }
    print_list(x);
    ilink *lnk = (ilink *)find_link(x, front(x), is_even);
    printf("%d\n", lnk->value);

    lnk = (ilink *)find_link(x, lnk->link.next, is_even);
    printf("%d\n", lnk->value);
    for (link *lnk = find_link(x, front(x), is_even);
    lnk;
    lnk = find_link(x, lnk->next, is_even))
    {
        printf("%d ", ((ilink *)lnk)->value);

    }
    printf("\n");

    delete_if(x, is_even);
    print_list(x);
    free_list(x);
      // using stack-allocated links
    ilink l1 = { .value = 13 };
    ilink l2 = { .value = 42 };
    struct list_type type = {     .print = print_int_link,

    .free = 0 // Do not free stack allocated links

    };
    x = new_list(type);
    append(x, (struct link *)&l1);
    append(x, (struct link *)&l2);
    print_list(x);
    free_list(x);

    return 0;
}
```

Using Offsets

Putting a link struct at the top of a user-defined link structure works fine until you want to put to use your data with more than one generic data structure. But imagine that you want to put your data into more than one list—or a list and a tree simultaneously. If the generic struct must sit at the top of your struct, then you would need to copy the actual data, so it can go into more than one object. Or put your data somewhere else and only have pointers to it your links and nodes. Having to put the generic struct first in your data structs seems too restrictive, and it is because the generic code will work just fine whether you put the generic data at the top of your structs or not. That code just needs their addresses and doesn't worry about whether those addresses are at offset zero of your struct or not. It is to get your data structs back from the generic code that is the issue. And there is a solution that will let you embed the generic structure—or structures—wherever you want.

Let's imagine that I want to put the same data into two lists, one that lets me run through it in the forward direction and one that lets me run through it in the backward direction. I know that we can already do this with a single doubly linked list, but go along with it; it is only an example. We then need to link the same object into two separate lists, so it needs to contain two link structures.

It could look like this:

```
typedef struct double_link
{
link forward_link;
link backward_link;
int value;
}
dlink;

dlink *new_dlink(int value)

{
dlink *link = malloc(sizeof *link);
if (link) link->value = value;
return link;
}
```

If I give you a link * pointer, and you want to look at the dlink * pointer, how do you get it? In the general case, the answer is that you don't. We don't have a general way of determining if we are pointing to the forward_link or backward_link part of a dlink. There might be some (probably unportable) trickery we can do, but I doubt there is much to be done in entirely portable C. However, we don't just get random link * values thrown at us. We know which list we get a link from. And if it comes from the forward list, our link * must point to a forward_link, and if it comes from the backward list, it must point to a backward_link. And if I know which of the two the link * points to, I can get the address of the dlink structure that contains the link.

The offsetof() macro from <stddef.h> (that we have seen before) tells us at which offset any member sits in a struct. If I call offsetof(dlist,forward_link)

I will get the offset of forward_link in a dlink. That value is how many bytes (technically char) I have to go from the beginning of the dlink to get to forward_link. So, with a pointer p to a dlink, forward_link will sit at

(char *)p + offsetof(dlist,forward_link)

The (char *) cast is necessary here because offsetof() gives us the number of bytes to go up, but adding to p will move us in jumps of sizeof(dlink). Anyway, if I can go from a pointer to a dlink to its forward_link by adding this offset, I can also go the other way. If I have a pointer to a forward_link, I can subtract

offsetof(dlist,forward) and get the dlink it sits in. The following macro will get you the containing struct from a pointer to a member inside it, using that computation:

```
#define struct_ptr(p,type,member) \
  (type *)((char *)p - offsetof(type, member))
```

In the following code, we use this struct_ptr() macro to get the user-defined link from the two generic link structs inside it. Notice that we have to provide different functions to the two list types because the struct_ptr() macro needs to know which member we are using. The callback functions will know which of the embedded links we should use, and it is the only way we can keep track of that in this implementation.

```
void print_dlink(dlink *link)
{
  printf("%d", link->value); }
void print_forward(link *link)
{
  print_dlink(struct_ptr(link, dlink, forward_link));
}
void print_backward(link *link)
{
  print_dlink(struct_ptr(link, dlink, backward_link)); }
void free_dlink(dlink *link)
{
  // We have to unlink from both lists
  // before we can safely free the link.
  unlink(&link->forward_link);  unlink(&link->backward_link);   free(link);
}
void free_forward(link *link)
{
  free_dlink(struct_ptr(link, dlink, forward_link));
}
void free_backward(link *link)
{
  free_dlink(struct_ptr(link, dlink, backward_link)); }
  list_type forward_type = {    .free = free_forward,
```

```
    .print = print_forward
  };
  list_type backward_type = {    .free  = free_backward,
    .print = print_backward
  };
  bool is_forward_even(link *l)
  {
    dlink *link = struct_ptr(l, dlink, forward_link);    return link->value % 2 == 0;  }
  int main(void)
  {
list *forward = new_list(forward_type);
list *backward = new_list(backward_type);
if (!forward || !backward) abort(); // error handling

for (int i = 0; i < 10; i++)
{
dlink *link = new_dlink(i);
if (!link) abort();
append(forward, &link->forward_link);
prepend(backward, &link->backward_link);

}
print_list(forward);    print_list(backward);

  // Try changing the first link in forward...
dlink *link = struct_ptr(front(forward), dlink, forward_link);
link->value = 42; // Now both lists have changed (because it is the same link)
print_list(forward);
print_list(backward); // deleting even numbers...

delete_if(forward, is_forward_even); // removes them from both lists
print_list(forward);
print_list(backward);

free_list(forward);
free_list(backward);

return 0;
}
```

Generic Search Trees

For search trees, we can, not surprisingly, take the same approach as for lists. We can make a generic struct that holds the structure of nodes only and let the user allocate larger objects that contain such a node struct.

The node could look like this:

```
typedef struct node
{
struct node *parent;
struct node *left;
struct node *right;
}
node;
```

I have chosen a node with a parent pointer for this chapter. Most of the operations we will implement do not need the extra pointer, but I want to be able to delete a node from a tree through a pointer to the node. When the data we put in the tree has an existence separate from the tree, which they will if the nodes are merely embedded structs, it can be convenient to be able to remove a node from a tree using just the pointer. If we have a node, but we do not know which tree it sits in, we can still remove the node. If we have a parent pointer, we can do this. Otherwise, we would need to find the node's location in its tree through a search, and we can only do that if we also have a reference to the tree—which we might not have. You will see how we exploit the parent pointer to do this when we implement removal later.

For the tree structure, we need function pointers to handle what we cannot do directly from the generic nodes. I will add a print and free function to the type, as for lists, but we also need something that lets us compare nodes, so we can determine the order of nodes. Here, we could choose to have a comparison function on nodes, but I will split comparisons into two steps. One step is to get a key from a node, the relevant data in the node for comparisons, and another that compares keys. This will make it easier to use search trees as tables. If, for example, we want a table from strings to integers, nodes would have to hold both the strings as keys and the integers as values, but when we look up a string in the tree, we do not need to make a node for doing that. We can look up using only the string as a key.

I will implement the function pointer table and the tree struct like this:

```
typedef struct stree_type
{
void const * (*key) (node *n);
int (*cmp) (void const *x, void const *y);
void (*print)(node *n);
void (*free) (node *n);

}
stree_type;
typedef struct stree
{
node root; // dummy node
stree_type type;
}
stree;
```

In the stree structure, we use a dummy node as the tree's root. The purpose of the dummy is the same as for all dummy elements; we can avoid dealing with some special cases. If we have a dummy root of the tree, we can ensure that all "real" nodes have a non-NULL parent pointer. The real tree will start at the root's left child.

This is the interface we will implement:

```
stree *new_tree(stree_type type);
static inline bool is_empty_tree(stree *tree)
{
return tree->root.left == 0;
}

void   insert_node(stree *tree, node *n);
void    print_tree(stree *tree);
void     free_tree(stree *tree);

node    *find_node(stree *tree, void const *key);
void   remove_node(node *n);
void   delete_node(stree *tree, node *n);
static inline bool contains(stree *tree, void const *key)
{
return !!find_node(tree, key);
}
static inline void delete_key(stree *tree, void const *key)

{
node *x = find_node(tree, key);
if (x) delete_node(tree, x);
}
```

Given a type struct, we can create a tree. We can check if it is empty (which it is if the dummy root's left child is NULL). We can insert nodes, print and free trees, which is self-explanatory. We will have a function that finds a node by key (or return NULL if there is no node with the given key). We can remove a node from the tree—it will remove it from the tree structure but not delete it. This function does not need a tree as input. It is one we can use to decouple a node we have a reference to from the tree it sits in, without having a reference to the tree. We can also delete a node, which will remove it from the structure and then use the stored free function. For that, you need the tree, because the tree holds the free pointer. If you want to check if a key is in the tree, you can get the corresponding node and check if it is NULL. If you want to delete a key, you can also find the node and delete it if it isn't NULL.

Nothing surprises in the function for allocating a tree. We have to require that the key and cmp functions are provided, as they are essential for the workings of a search tree, but other than this, it is a simple initialization function.

```
stree *new_tree(stree_type type)

{
  // key and cmp are always needed. The rest

  // are optional.
if (!(type.key && type.cmp)) return 0;
stree *tree = malloc(sizeof *tree);
if (tree)
{
```

```
    *tree = (stree) {
      .root = { .parent = 0, .left = 0, .right = 0 },
      .type = type
    };
  }
  return tree;
}
```

When searching in a tree, we use a modified find_loc() function. It has to use the key and cmp functions from the tree's type for comparisons. Otherwise, it follows the same logic.

```
// Find parent and child
node **find_loc(stree *tree, void const *key, node **n, node **p)

{
void const * (*get_key)(node *n) = tree->type.key;
int (*cmp)(void const *x, void const *y) = tree->type.cmp;

while (*n) {
int cmpres = cmp(key, get_key(*n));
if (cmpres == 0) return n;

*p = *n;

if (cmpres < 0) n = &(*n)->left;
else
n = &(*n)->right;

  } return n;
}
```

The function for finding a node is trivial once we have find_loc():

```
node *find_node(stree *tree, void const *key)

{
node *parent = &tree->root;
node **real_tree = &parent->left;
return *find_loc(tree, key, real_tree, &parent);

}
```

When we insert a node, we expect that the user has already allocated and initialized the memory for it, so we cannot have allocation failures. However, we need to deal with what happens if the key in the new node is already in the tree because as we have implemented the tree, we cannot have two nodes with the same key. An easy solution is to get rid of the old node. The semantics is that if we use the tree as a table, we have replaced the old value for the key with the new.

```
void insert_node(stree *tree, node *n)
```

```
{
    node *parent = &tree->root;
    node **real_tree = &parent->left;
    void const *key = tree->type.key(n);

    node **target = find_loc(tree, key, real_tree, &parent);
    if (*target)
    { // remove the old node delete_node(tree, *target);
    }

    *target = n;
    n->parent = parent;

    n->left = n->right = 0; // leaf
}
```

In this function, we find the location where we should insert the node, deleting the old node if the key was already there. Then we insert the new node at the right location and connect the node's parent pointer to its new parent and set its children to NULL to make it a leaf.

The remove_node() function behaves exactly as the delete function we had previously, except that we do not need the initial search for the node. We already have the node and its parent, so we can go right ahead and remove it. We can remove it directly if it has an empty child, and otherwise we have to replace it with its rightmost child.

```
node **rightmost(node **n, node **p)
{
    while ((*n)->right) {
        *p = *n;    n = &(*n)->right;
    }
    return n;
}
void remove_node(node *n)
{
    if (!n->parent)
    {
        // parentless nodes are not in the tree
        // (they have probably been removed before)
        return;
    }
    // Get the location to replace.   node **loc = (n == n->parent->left) ? &n->parent->left : &n->parent->right;   if (!(n->left && n->right))
    {    // has an empty child...

        *loc = n->left ? n->left : n->right;
        if (*loc) (*loc)->parent = n->parent;
```

```
} else
{
node *rm_parent = n;

node **rm_ref = rightmost(&n->left, &rm_parent);
node *rm = *rm_ref;
*rm_ref = rm->left;

if (*rm_ref) (*rm_ref)->parent = rm_parent;

// we cannot simply move the value now, but must // reconnect the pointers...

*loc = rm; // makes *loc point to rm

*rm = *n;  // copies the struct (i.e. the pointers)

    // When copying the structs like this, we only copy

    // the bits that are in the type they have, so only the

    // three pointers and not whatever else might sit in the      // actual nodes.

  }
  // now, to make our code safer, we NULL the pointers

  // before we call the free function.
n->left = n->right = n->parent = 0;

}
```

We set the pointers in the node to NULL before we return from the call. This can be helpful when we call remove_node() in callback function calls, where having NULL pointers here can prevent us from any unnecessary recursion or from accessing data that might have been freed.

The delete_node() function removes the node and uses the stored free function to deallocate it:

```
void delete_node(stree *tree, node *n)

{
  remove_node(n);
  if (tree->type.free)

  tree->type.free(n);
}
```

The functions to print and free a tree need to use the function pointers, but otherwise they do not change. I have listed recursive versions in the following; you are welcome to implement the recursion and stack free variants if you feel for it.

```
// Just recursion this time; the techniques for avoid it

// hasn't changed. static void default_print(node *n)

  {
  printf("<node %p>", (void*)n);

  }
```

```
void print_node(void (*print)(node *n), node *n)
{
  if (!n) return;  putchar('(');
  print_node(print, n->left);
  putchar(','); print(n); putchar(',');
  print_node(print, n->right);
  putchar(')');
}
void print_tree(stree *tree)
{
  void (*print)(node *) = tree->type.print ? tree->type.print : default_print;
  print_node(print, tree->root.left);
}
void free_nodes_rec(void (*free)(node *n), node *n)
{
  if (!n) return;  free_nodes_rec(free, n->left);
  free_nodes_rec(free, n->right);
  if (free) {
    // remove pointers before callback
  n->left = n->right = n->parent = 0;
  free(n);
  }
}
void free_tree(stree *tree)
{
  free_nodes_rec(tree->type.free, tree->root.left);
  free(tree);
}
```

Imagine that we want to put the same data in both a list and a tree—now that we have the option with generic data structures for both. We can use the struct_ptr() macro to get the struct that contains both the link and the node of user data, so that should be straightforward. We could, for example, use that in an application where we want to have strings in some given order, for example, insertion order in a table, and at the same time have efficient lookup to remove strings from the table.

A data type that contains nodes, links, and strings could look like this:

```
typedef struct ordered_string
{
node node;
```

```c
    link link;
    char const *str;
}
ostring;
ostring *new_ostring(char const *str)
{
    ostring *n = malloc(sizeof *n);
    if (!n) abort();
    n->str = str;
    return n;
}
```

Print and delete functions could look like this:

```c
void print_ordered_string(ostring *str)
{
    printf("\"%s\"", str->str);
}
void free_ordered_string(ostring *str)
{
// Remove from data structures...    unlink(&str->link);
remove_node(&str->node);
    // and then free...
    free(str);
}
```

We can't use those directly with the data structures because they have the wrong type (and with the callbacks, we need to go from nodes/links to ostring using contains()), but they are the functions we can use once we have converted links and nodes. When we free an ostring, we should remove it from both the list and the node, so we use the unlink() and remove_node() functions. Here, where we only have the structure and not the list or tree, it is useful that these functions do not need the list or tree as arguments, but only the link or node.

To get the functions for the search tree, we must adapt the functions to its interface and put them in a stree_type structure:

```c
void const *strnode_key(node *n)
{
    return struct_ptr(n, ostring, node)->str;
}
```

```c
int strnode_cmp(void const *x, void const *y)
{
return strcmp(x, y);
}
void strnode_print(node *n)
{
print_ordered_string(struct_ptr(n, ostring, node));
}
void strnode_free(node *n)
{
free_ordered_string(struct_ptr(n, ostring, node));
}
stree_type strnode_type = {
  .key   = strnode_key,
  .cmp   = strnode_cmp,
  .print = strnode_print,
  .free  = strnode_free
};
```

Likewise for the list interface:

```c
void strlink_print(link *lnk)
{
print_ordered_string(struct_ptr(lnk, ostring, link));
}
void strlink_free(link *lnk)
{
free_ordered_string(struct_ptr(lnk, ostring, link));
}
list_type strlink_type = {   .print = strlink_print,
  .free  = strlink_free
};
```

If we now want a data structure with strings in insertion order, and with a search tree as a map, we can define it like this:

```c
typedef struct ordered_strings
{
```

```
stree *map; list *order;
}
ordered_strings;
ordered_strings *new_ordered_strings(void)
{
ordered_strings *os = malloc(sizeof *os);
if (!os) abort(); // handle alloc errors   os->map = new_tree(strnode_type);
os->order = new_list(strlink_type);
if (!os->map || !os->order) abort(); // handle errors
return os;
}
void add_string(ordered_strings *os, char const *str)
{
ostring *ostr = new_ostring(str);
if (!ostr) abort(); // handle alloc errors
insert_node(os->map, &ostr->node);
append(os->order, &ostr->link);
}
void remove_string(ordered_strings *os, char const *str)
{
node *n = find_node(os->map, str);
if (n) {
ostring *x = struct_ptr(n, ostring, node);
free_ordered_string(x);
  }
}
```

When we add a string, we append it to the list, so we have the insertion order there, and we insert it in the tree, so we can get fast lookup. When we remove a string, we find the data from the tree and remove it, where free_ordered_string() removes it from both the list and the tree.

If you want to remove data by index, in the ordered list, we can implement it like this, where using a negative index will look from the back of the list:

```
link *take_front(list *x, int idx)
{
  for (link *lnk = front(x);
  lnk != head(x); lnk = lnk->next)
```

```
{
if (idx-- == 0)
return lnk;
}
return 0;
}

link *take_back(list *x, int idx)

{
for (link *lnk = back(x);

lnk != head(x); lnk = lnk->prev)
{
if (idx-- == 0)
return lnk;

}
return 0;
}

void remove_index(ordered_strings *os, int idx)

{
link *lnk;   if (idx < 0)
{
lnk = take_back(os->order, -idx - 1);

} else {

lnk = take_front(os->order, idx);
}
if (!lnk) {

   // report an error...     return;

  }
ostring *x = struct_ptr(lnk, ostring, link);
free_ordered_string(x);
}
```

It is linear time operations, so it might not be optimal for your use, but the functions are there as an example, so I can live with that.

If we free both tree and list, the order will affect the running time. If you delete the list first, you will delete each link, which will call the free function. When the function is called, the link is already unlinked, but there is no harm in unlinking it again—the unlink() function recognizes that there is nothing to unlink and that will be all. You also call remove_node() from the callback deallocator, and this can involve a search for rightmost(). Each deletion might thus trigger a search in the tree. If you delete the tree first, however, the tree deletion code will set the node's pointers to NULL before it calls the callback, so the remove_node() call there will not trigger a search. The unlink() call never triggers a search. So, deleting the nodes/links via the tree will be faster than deleting them through the list, so that is what we will do.

```c
void free_ordered_strings(ordered_strings *os)
{
  free_tree(os->map);   free_list(os->order);   free(os);
}
```

I didn't really have any exciting application in mind with this data structure, but you can see it in use here:

```c
int main(void)
{
ordered_strings *os = new_ordered_strings();
add_string(os, "foo");
add_string(os, "bar");
add_string(os, "baz");
add_string(os, "qux");
add_string(os, "qax");
print_list(os->order);
print_tree(os->map);
printf("\n\n");
printf("removing 'bar'\n");
remove_string(os, "bar");
print_list(os->order);
print_tree(os->map);
printf("\n\n");
printf("Removing index 1 (baz)\n");
remove_index(os, 1); // baz   print_list(os->order);
print_tree(os->map);
printf("\n\n");
printf("Removing index -3 (foo)\n");
remove_index(os, -3);
print_list(os->order);
print_tree(os->map);
printf("\n\n");
printf("all done\n");
free_ordered_strings(os);
return 0;
```

}

As long as we can delegate the allocation of memory to the user of a data structure, it is not hard to implement a generic data structure. We have a minimal struct with the information the data structure needs, and this must be embedded in the user's data. Everything else is handled with generic code, supplemented with callback functions provided as function pointers. Lists and trees are not special in this regard; you can do this with any data structure where you can let the user handle memory allocation.

Reference Counting Garbage Collection

1. Introduction

Reference counting is a form of garbage collection where each allocated object keeps a count of the references pointing to it. When a new reference to an object is created, the reference count increments; when a reference is removed or goes out of scope, it decrements. When an object's reference count reaches zero, the object is no longer in use, so the memory it occupies can be safely freed.

This method is commonly used in languages with some level of memory management automation, like Python and Objective-C. However, it's possible to implement it in C by explicitly managing reference counts for each allocated object.

2. Structuring Reference Counting in C

2.1 Defining a Reference Counted Object

To implement reference counting, we'll define a struct that includes:

A void* pointer for the actual data.

A reference count integer to track how many references point to the data.

Here's an example:

```
typedef struct RefCountedObject
{
    void *data;
    int ref_count;
}
RefCountedObject;
```

In this setup:

data is a pointer to the allocated data.

ref_count holds the current reference count.

2.2 Allocating a Reference Counted Object

A helper function, createRefCountedObject, initializes a new object, allocates memory for data, and sets ref_count to 1.

```
RefCountedObject* createRefCountedObject(size_t dataSize)
{
    RefCountedObject *obj = (RefCountedObject*) malloc(sizeof(RefCountedObject));
    obj->data = malloc(dataSize); // Allocate memory for the actual data
    obj->ref_count = 1; // Initialize reference count
    return obj;
}
```

This function allocates memory for both the struct and the object's data, making it ready for use with an initial reference count.

2.3 Increasing the Reference Count

When a new reference to the object is created, we increment the reference count using a retain function:

```
void retain(RefCountedObject *obj)
{
    if (obj) {
    obj->ref_count++;
    }
}
```

This function simply increments ref_count, signaling that another reference to the object now exists.

2.4 Decreasing the Reference Count

Similarly, when a reference to the object is removed, release is called to decrement ref_count. If the count drops to zero, the object is freed:

```
void release(RefCountedObject *obj)
{
    if (obj)
    {
        obj->ref_count--;
        if (obj->ref_count == 0)
        {
            free(obj->data); // Free the actual data
```

```
        free(obj); // Free the struct itself
    }
  }
}
```

This function frees both the object's data and the struct itself, ensuring that no memory leaks occur once the object is no longer referenced.

3. Practical Example: Managing a Reference Counted String

Consider a scenario where we want to manage dynamically allocated strings with reference counting.

```c
#include <stdio.h>
#include <stdlib.h>
#include <string.h>
RefCountedObject* createString(const char *str)
{
    RefCountedObject *stringObj = createRefCountedObject(strlen(str) + 1);
    strcpy((char*)stringObj->data, str);
    return stringObj;
}
void printString(RefCountedObject *stringObj)
{
    if (stringObj && stringObj->data)
    {
        printf("%s\n", (char*)stringObj->data);
    }
}
int main()
{
    RefCountedObject *hello = createString("Hello, world!");
    // Use the object
    printString(hello);
    // Add another reference
    retain(hello);
    // Release references
    release(hello);
    release(hello);  // Frees the memory as ref_count reaches zero
    return 0;
```

}

This example demonstrates the essential steps of creating, retaining, and releasing a reference-counted object.

4. Advantages of Reference Counting in C

4.1 Manual Memory Management Relief

Reference counting offloads the responsibility of freeing memory from the programmer, reducing the risk of memory leaks and errors.

4.2 Deterministic Destruction

With reference counting, objects are freed immediately when they're no longer referenced, leading to predictable and efficient memory management. This is especially useful in environments where low latency and real-time performance are crucial.

4.3 Reusability

This approach enables reusable code across projects, especially for frequently used data structures or libraries, enhancing development efficiency and reliability.

5. Limitations and Challenges of Reference Counting

5.1 Cyclic References

A significant limitation of reference counting is its inability to handle cyclic references, where two or more objects reference each other. Cyclic dependencies prevent reference counts from reaching zero, resulting in memory that can't be freed.

For example:

```
struct Node {
    RefCountedObject *next;
    RefCountedObject *data;
};
```

If two nodes reference each other, the cyclic dependency will cause a memory leak. Solving cyclic references requires more advanced garbage collection techniques, like mark-and-sweep algorithms.

5.2 Performance Overhead

Every retain and release call involves incrementing or decrementing ref_count, which can introduce overhead in high-frequency operations. However, this impact is typically minimal in most applications.

5.3 Lack of Type Safety

Since void* pointers are used for the data in each reference-counted object, type safety is not enforced by the compiler. Developers must be cautious about type consistency, using appropriate casting when accessing data.

6. Extending Reference Counting with Custom Free Functions

Some objects may require additional cleanup beyond simply freeing memory, such as closing file handles or releasing network connections. By adding a custom free function to the RefCountedObject struct, you can provide specific cleanup instructions:

```
typedef struct RefCountedObject {
    void *data;
    int ref_count;
    void (*customFree)(void*);  // Custom free function pointer
} RefCountedObject;
```

With this setup, the release function can check if customFree is set, and call it before freeing the memory:

```
void release(RefCountedObject *obj) {
    if (obj) {
        obj->ref_count--;
        if (obj->ref_count == 0) {
            if (obj->customFree) {
                obj->customFree(obj->data);  // Call custom free if provided
            } else {
                free(obj->data);        // Default free if no custom function
            }
            free(obj);
        }
    }
}
```

This addition allows for a more versatile reference counting system, adaptable to resources that need specific cleanup actions.

7. When to Use Reference Counting in C

Reference counting is beneficial in scenarios where:

Deterministic destruction is essential, such as in real-time systems.

Memory leaks pose a major risk, like in long-running applications or embedded systems.

Cross-module resource sharing occurs, and no single module should be responsible for the sole cleanup.

Keeping track of when memory should be freed, so we always remember to do it and never call free() on the same memory twice, is at times complicated. The scenario where you have a function that allocates some memory, uses it, and then frees it before the function returns is hardly ever problematic. If you have many exit points, that is, you return multiple places, you must ensure that you free everything regardless of how you exit the function, but unless it is an incredibly complicated function, it is manageable. However, once you start working with heap-allocated data structures, even as simple as lists and trees, things can get more complicated. The same memory can be referenced from multiple places, and you cannot free it before you remove the last reference (at which point you must).

Consider the first version of singly linked lists, where we had the new_link() function for creating a new link with a next pointer to the next link in the list.

With that, we could create lists:

list x = new_link(11, new_link(12, NULL)); list y = new_link(1, new_link(2, x));

where now x is a list with elements 11 and 12, and y is a list with the elements 1, 2, 11, and 12. The two last links in y are shared with x. We cannot free y as long as we need x because we would destroy x's links. We cannot free x while we use y because we would destroy its last two links.

This is a simple example, and of course we could code our way around deleting the first two, but not the last two links of y if we want to free y, but it should not surprise you to learn that things can get a lot more complicated than this. When we start wiring up data structures with pointers to substructures, keeping track of what memory, we have a reference to, and what we can and should free, gets complicated. It is why most modern programming languages have automatic garbage collection to a varying degree. But C does not, so we have to deal with it on our own and implement our own strategies.

One of the simplest approaches to memory management, when we find ourselves in a situation such as this, is reference counting. The idea is as trivial as this: you give each object a counter that tracks how many references you have to it. When you add another reference, you increment the counter, and when you remove one, you decrement the counter. If the counter hits zero, you no longer need the object, and you free it.

As a trivial example, imagine that we have heap-allocated integers. We can add a counter to each, as in the following code, and initialize each new object with a count of one—whoever creates the object probably wants a reference to it and will have a pointer to it, so that is the reference we are counting. We can free these objects with free(), since they do not contain anything we must recursively free, but in the example, I have added a function that prints when an object is freed, so it is easier to track. We don't call that function directly; however, we use two other functions for memory management: incref() for adding a reference and decref() for removing one.

When you want another pointer to the object, you incref(), and when you want to remove a reference, you use decref():

```
#include <stdio.h>
#include <stdlib.h>
struct rc_int
{
int refcount;
int value;
};
struct rc_int *new_rc_int(int i)

{
struct rc_int *p = malloc(sizeof *p);
if (p) {    *p = (struct rc_int)
{
    .refcount = 1, .value = i
  };
 }
return p;
}
void free_rc_int(struct rc_int *i)

{
  printf("Freeing %d\n", i->value);   free(i); } struct rc_int *incref(struct rc_int *p)

{
  if (p) p->refcount++;   return p; } struct rc_int *decref(struct rc_int *p)

{
  if (p && --p->refcount == 0) {    free_rc_int(p);    return 0;
 }
return p;
}
int main(void)

{
struct rc_int *i = new_rc_int(42);
struct rc_int *j = incref(i);
decref(i); // decrements...
decref(j); // decrements and deletes...
return 0;
```

}

In both incref() and decref(), we allow NULL pointers. When we can get away with it, it is easier to write code where we do not need to treat NULL as a special case, and if we let these two functions return NULL on NULL input, we can write simpler code. In the main() function, for example, we don't check for an allocation error because the code will work correctly on NULL pointers as well. In practice, of course, we need non-N ULL pointers somewhere, but we can defer worrying about that to the point where we have to.

That is the whole idea behind reference counting, but of course there are some practices you need to make it work as well, or the chapter would be finished by now. We are not entirely out of the woods with respect to memory management simply because we add a counter. We still have to know when to increment and decrement the counter. This, however, we can mostly handle on a per-function basis and doesn't require an overview of the entire program and how pointers are connected globally. To demonstrate how we can use reference counting traditionally, I will return to our trusted lists and trees.

Immutable Links with Reference Counting

Imagine that we have an application where we want to work with lists, and we want the lists to be immutable, in the sense that if you have a reference to a list, then that list never changes. It will always be the same elements in the same order. Such immutability makes it easy to share data. If we have two lists, and one is a suffix of the other, they can share all the links in the shorter list. Since we cannot change any links, the longer list doesn't have to worry about its suffix changing because we do something to the shorter list.

Immutable data structures can reduce our memory usage when different structures can share substructures, they are useful for so-called persistent data structures that have their uses in various algorithms, and they alleviate some problems in concurrent programs. So immutable lists are not an artificial constraint I made up for this chapter; there really are applications where you want them. And if you want them, and you want to share suffixes between them, then reference counting is the ideal strategy for memory management.

We can define an immutable list link like this:

```
struct link {
int refcount;
struct link * const next;

int const value;

};
typedef struct link *list;
```

The next pointer and the value are const, so we cannot modify the link's data or the list that follows the link. The refcount is not const, obviously, since even if the list is immutable, we need to keep track of how many references we have to any given link.

The lists are much like the first version of singly linked lists in Chapter 11, and there we had a problem with differentiating between operations that would give us an empty list and operations that would report errors, as both errors and empty lists were represented by a NULL pointer. To avoid this, we can explicitly represent empty lists as a special link. If we have a NULL pointer for a list, it is an error, and if we have an empty list, it is the designated link.

So, a NULL pointer to a list is an error:

```
static inline bool is_error(struct link *x) { return x == 0; }
```
and we define a special address that we can get through a function get_NIL() to be the empty list:

```
struct link *get_NIL(void); static inline bool is_nil(struct link *x) { return x == get_NIL(); }
```

We can define the special link as a static variable in the get_NIL() function:

```
struct link *get_NIL(void)
{
  static struct link NIL_LINK = { .refcount = 1 };
  return &NIL_LINK;
}
```

That way, we get the same link every time we get the empty list. The initial reference count for the empty list is one, but it should be incremented and decremented like other objects—but never decremented more than incremented, because we obviously do not want to risk deleting it.

To avoid accidentally decrementing the empty list more than we increment it, we can use a macro to access it. The macro will increment the reference each time we use it in an expression.

```
#define NIL incref(get_NIL())
```

We shouldn't use this macro to check if we have an empty list because a test such as NIL == NIL will increment the reference count twice. It isn't really a problem, since as long as we never decrement the counter in an empty list to zero, we are fine. Still, for consistency, we should only increment a reference counter when we are also going to decrement it later. When we use NIL, we increment, so we should only use it in expressions where we will eventually decrement as well. Writing NIL gives us a "new" empty list, and we should think about it as such.

The incref()/decref() and deallocation code look much like the example with reference counted integers. The decref() function will call another function, free_link(), when we need to actually free a link. It is listed later.

```
struct link *incref(struct link *link)
{
if (link) link->refcount++;
return link;
}
```

```
void free_link(struct link *link);
struct link *decref(struct link *link)
{
  if (link && --link->refcount == 0)
  {
   free_link(link);
   return 0;

  }

  return link;
}
```

Now we are almost ready to write list functions, but before we start, we need to lay down the ground rules for how we work with incrementing and decrementing lists. These are the rules that ensure that we increment and decrement correctly, so we always have a valid reference when we need it, and we always decrement references when we no longer need them. Essentially, it boils down to deciding when a function is responsible for incrementing a reference it gets as input and when it is responsible for decrementing a reference that it holds.

Consider as an example a function for computing the length of a list. We will see two versions later, but for now let us just assume that we have a function, length(), that gives us the length, and that new_link(). Now consider this code:

```
list x = new_link(1, new_link(2, NIL));
int len1 = length(x);

int len2 = length(new_link(1, new_link(2, NIL)));
```

We use NIL for the empty list, so we have separate references to the empty list we create in the two lists we construct, the first when we create x and the second when we create an anonymous list that we immediately call length() on. When we call length(), does it increment/decrement its input? Let us assume that it does neither, and x holds the only reference to the front link it points to. Then, if length() doesn't change anything, we get the length and x remains the same, with the single reference to the list. That would work fine, but then the second call to length() could be problematic. Here, we create a list with the two calls to new_link(), then we call length() which doesn't increment or decrement anything— and once length() returns, we have lost access to the new list. We have leaked the memory for two links.

On the other hand, if length() decrements its input, so we would free the new list in the third line of the code, then it would also decrement the reference to x in the first line. If x is the only reference to that list, decrementing in length() would free the list, and x would point at freed memory. If length() decrements, and we want to keep x around after the call to length(), we should incref(x) before we call length():

```
int len1 = length(incref(x));
```

Either version of length(), the one that takes ownership of the input and frees it and the one that doesn't, is a fine choice. We just need to be careful, so we always know what kind of function we are using.

I will write functions of both kinds in this section to illustrate how we write both types, but in practice I would recommend choosing one convention and using it for all your functions, or at least all the functions you provide to a user, to minimize confusion. To avoid confusion ourselves in this chapter, I will annotate our functions with two "keywords," borrows and takes, for when a function will leave an input as it is (borrows) or when it takes ownership of the reference (takes) and will decrement the reference.

We can add the keywords to our code using preprocessor definitions:

```
#define borrows
#define takes
```

The preprocessor will expand them to empty strings, so they have no semantic meaning in the code, but we can write the keywords together with function arguments. This is not something I will generally recommend that you do in your code.

A function that borrows an argument should not decrement the argument, nor should it give the argument to another function that takes it because that amounts to passing on a reference that the borrowing function doesn't own. A function that takes an argument should always decref() the argument or give it to another function that takes ownership of the argument.

To make the "passing of ownership" more explicit in our code, we can use another macro, transfer():

```
#define transfer(x) x
```

The macro doesn't do anything either; the only purpose it serves is to make explicit that we are passing on ownership to someone else. Don't transfer() a reference you do not own. If you have borrowed a reference, and you want to give it away, incref() it first. That gives you your very own reference, and you are allowed to give your own reference away.

Rules for references in arguments are half the strategy. The other is what we expect from pointers that functions return. Do functions return new references that we are responsible for decrementing, or do they give us "borrows" references that we should incref() if we want to keep them? Both approaches are valid, but in this case, for me, the rule that says that functions always give you a reference feels more reasonable.

When you get the result of a function call, the function doesn't have a reference any longer— the function call is done, after all—so either it created a reference, which you definitely have to own, or it borrowed a reference and then gave it to you, while it wasn't its to give. I will follow the rule that if a function returns a reference, it is giving the reference to the caller. If it borrowed the reference, it must incref(), so it is allowed to give it away.

With these rules in place, let's write the functions for creating and freeing links:

```
list new_link(int head, takes list tail)
{
```

```
if (is_error(tail)) return tail;
list link = malloc(sizeof *link);
if (!link)
{
decref(tail);
return 0;
}
struct link link_data = {
  .refcount = 1,
  .next = transfer(tail), // gives away the reference
  .value = head
};

// explanation below for memcpy()   memcpy(link, &link_data, sizeof *link);   return transfer(link);
}
```

When we create a new link, we provide new_link() with a value and a link, and we give the function that link, as we have made clear with the takes keyword before the tail argument. If tail is a NULL pointer, that is, if it is the result of something we consider an error, we won't put it into the new link. We will generally return an error if we get any error lists as input. So, we check for errors first and propagate it if tail is one.

Otherwise, we allocate the new link. That can fail, in which case we should return NULL to indicate that we had an error. Before we can return, however, we must decrement tail. The function owns it at this point, and it is responsible for decrementing tail.

If we successfully allocated, we initialize the link. We transfer() the tail to the link, so it now owns the reference. The construction where we first initialize a stack-allocated link and then move the data with memcpy() is to get around the const'ness of value and next and doesn't serve any other purpose. Once the new link is initialized, we give it to the caller. The link is initialized with a reference count of one, and the caller now owns that single reference.

When we need to free a link, when its reference count reaches zero in decref(), we call free_link():

```
void free_link(struct link *link)
{
  decref(link->next);   free(link);
}
```

We must decref(link->next) because the link we are deleting has a reference to its next that now disappears.

To warm up for writing list functions, consider first a function for printing a list.

A version that borrows a reference could look like this:

```
void print_list(borrows list x)
{
assert(!is_error(x));
printf("[ ");
while (!is_nil(x))
{
    printf("%d[%d] ", x->value, x->refcount);
x = x->next;
  }
  printf("]\n");
}
```

Since we borrow the list, we don't need to decref() it when we are done. If we take the list instead, we would have to void print_list(takes list x)

```
{
assert(!is_error(x));
printf("[ ");
struct link *l = x; // use separate pointer
while (!is_nil(l)) {
printf("%d[%d] ", l->value, l->refcount);
l = l->next;
}
printf("]\n");
decref(x); // remember to decref a taken list
}
```

We loop through the list, so we need a separate variable for that. Otherwise, we couldn't decref() the correct list when we are done. We don't take ownership of the links that follow x in either function. As long as we have a reference to x, the following links will not be freed—they cannot go away as long as there is a reference to them, and as long as x exists, there will be.

What about the now infamous length() function from earlier? A borrowing version could look like this:

```
int length_rec(borrows list x, int acc)
{
  assert(!is_error(x));
if (is_nil(x))
return acc;
else
```

```
return length_rec(x->next, acc + 1);
}
static inline
int length(borrows list x)

{
return length_rec(x, 0);
}
```

I have chosen to implement it as a tail-recursive function for no other reason than to make it a little more interesting when we get to the version that takes its argument. The compiler will turn it into a loop, and we could easily do so as well if we wanted to. The recursive function uses an accumulator, acc, to count the number of links we have run through, and I use another function to give the accumulator a default of zero.

With a version that borrows, there is nothing interesting in using reference counting; we run through the list in the recursions as we would with any pointer data structure. With this function, the code from earlier

```
list x = new_link(1, new_link(2, NIL));
int len1 = length(x);
int len2 = length(new_link(1, new_link(2, NIL)));
```

will leak memory in the second call to length(), where we get a reference that we never decrement. For the second call to work, we need a function that takes its argument, and that could look like this:

```
int length_rec(takes list x, int acc)
{
assert(!is_error(x));
if (is_nil(x))
{
decref(x);
return acc;
} else
{
struct link *next = incref(x->next);
decref(x);
return length_rec(transfer(next), acc + 1);
    }
} static inline
int length(takes list x)
{
```

```
  return length_rec(transfer(x), 0);
}
```

There is a little more meat on this one. Because we take the x argument, we are responsible for decrementing it as well, which we have to do in both the base case and the recursive case. It is strictly speaking not essential that we decrement in the base case, where we have an empty list, since we will never free the empty list anyway, but the general rule is to decref() if we take a reference, so that is what we do. In the recursive case, we need x->next, but if decref(x) frees x—it will if we have the only reference to x—then that might free x->next as well.

To prevent this, we need to get our own reference to x->next, so we incref(x->next). Even if we weren't worrying about how x->next could disappear when we decref(x), it is only proper that we incref(x->next) in any case. We are going to transfer() it to the recursive call, and it is not ours to give away. It is x that has a reference to x->next, not us, and if we want to give it away, we need our own reference. So based merely on considerations of criminal conduct, we should incref(x->next) before we can call recursively. That we must do it before we decref(x) is because decrementing x's reference counter could free it.

Generally, we have to consider decref(x) as analogous to free(x), and with free(x) we know better than to access x->next after we have freed x. It is the same with decref(x). We need to incref(x->next) so we can transfer() it to the recursive call, we need to decref(x) because we have taken it, and we need to do it in the order we do, because we cannot get x->next after calling decref(x).

With this version, when we write

```
list x = new_link(1, new_link(2, NIL));
int len1 = length(x);
int len2 = length(new_link(1, new_link(2, NIL)));
```

the second call to length() works as intended and frees the link we create, so we do not leak memory. The first call, however, is giving x to length(x), so we should either write

```
int len1 = length(transfer(x));
```

to make clear that x is not around after the call, or we should write

```
int len1 = length(incref(x));
```

to keep our own reference after the call.

A borrowing function for reversing a list will look like this:

```
list reverse_rec(borrows list x, borrows list acc)
{
  if (is_error(x) || is_error(acc))
{
return 0;
}
if (is_nil(x))
{
return transfer(incref(acc));
} else {    return reverse_rec(x->next, new_link(x->value, transfer(incref(acc))));
```

```
}
} static inline list reverse(borrows list x)
{return reverse_rec(x, get_NIL());
}
```

We are not actually reversing a list. Lists are immutable, so we can't. We are creating a new list that has the elements in the original list but in reverse order. It is a recursive function with an accumulator once again and with a helper function to give the accumulator a default value. We should start with an empty list, but we can't use NIL here. That creates a new reference to the empty list, and since this function doesn't take ownership of its input, we shouldn't create new references for it. So get_NIL() is what we need.

The function recurses along with the list x, at each level taking the value in x and putting it into a new link, which prepends the new value to the current acc. Once we reach the end of the recursion, where x is empty, acc contains the reversed list. Since acc is a reference that we have borrowed, and since our rule is that functions should return new references to objects, we must incref(acc) when we return the accumulator. In the recursive calls, where we create new links, we should also remember to incref(acc). The new_link() function takes its reference argument, and since we have only borrowed acc, we must get a reference so we can give it away.

A function that takes both arguments would look like this:

```
list reverse_rec(takes list x, takes list acc)
{
  if (is_error(x) || is_error(acc))
{
decref(x);
decref(acc);
return 0;

}
if (is_nil(x))
{
decref(x);
return transfer(acc);

} else {
int value = x->value;
struct link *next = incref(x->next);
decref(x);
return reverse_rec(transfer(next), new_link(value, transfer(acc)));

  }
} static inline list reverse(takes list x)

{
return reverse_rec(x, NIL);
}
```

The default argument to the accumulator is now NIL because we want to give the function a new reference to the empty list. If either of the input lists has an error value, we report an error, but because we have ownership of the lists, we must decref() them before we return, also when we have errors, so we do that first. In the base case, we should return acc. We own it, so we can give it away without incref(), but since we also own x, and we do not give it away, we must decref() it. In the recursive case, we need to extract x's value and next before we can decref(x). We need to give x->next to the recursive call, so as with length(), we get a new reference to it before we can call recursively. In the recursive call, we transfer() the accumulator to the recursive call, so we shouldn't decref() that reference.

If you want to concatenate two borrowed lists, you can use this function:

```
list concat(borrows list x, borrows list y)
{
  if (is_error(x) || is_error(y)) {
return 0;
  }
  if (is_nil(x)) {
    return transfer(incref(y));
} else {    return new_link(x->value, concat(x->next, transfer(incref(y))));
  }
}
```

The only reference counting related part of it is remembering that we have only borrowed y, so we cannot give it away. We are giving a reference away when we return it or when we give it to a function that takes the argument, so in both cases, we need to get a reference to y first.

A concatenation function that takes ownership of the lists would look like this:

```
list concat(takes list x, takes list y)
{
  if (is_error(x) || is_error(y))
{
decref(x); decref(y);
return 0;
  }
  if (is_nil(x))
{
decref(x);
return transfer(y);
  } else {
    int value = x->value;
    struct link *next = incref(x->next);
decref(x);
```

```
      return new_link(value, concat(transfer(next), transfer(y)));
  }
}
```

Adding a Compiler Extension (Not Portable!)

The code for decref()'ing all arguments that a function "takes," scattered throughout functions, can make the code harder to read. There isn't any way around it if we take ownership of a reference, we are responsible for decrementing it unless we give it away. Still, some compilers, at least clang, gcc, and icc that I know of, have an extension that makes it a little easier. This is not standard C, but if you are writing code for a specific compiler, and you know that it doesn't have to compile elsewhere, you can exploit it.

Very briefly, I will give an example here.

The extension I have in mind is __attribute__((cleanup(f))) that, if you place it where you declare a variable, will tell the compiler to call the function f() with the address of the variable, when the variable goes out of scope. We will use it for lists, so we can define

```
void list_cleanup(struct link **x)
{
decref(*x);
}
#define autoclean_list \ list __attribute__((cleanup(list_cleanup)))
```

The callback function will be called with the address of the variable, and since we are working with lists, which are struct link * pointers, the address will be a pointer to those, so struct link **. When the callback is called, we want to decrement the variable's value, what it points at, since that is the pointer to the link. That is what list_ cleanup() does. The autoclean_list macro defines a new type, autoclean_list, that is a list with the callback attribute. Declare a variable as autoclean_list, and the callback will be called when the variable goes out of scope.

The list x here

```
autoclean_list x = new_link(1, new_link(2, NIL));
```

will automatically be decremented (and freed) when x goes out of scope.

The compiler extension doesn't work for function arguments—which would otherwise be nice for our purposes—but it does work for local variables. To use it with function arguments, we can reassign parameters to local variables. A version of new_ link() that automatically deletes tail in case of allocation errors could look like this:

```
list new_link(int head, takes list tail_)
{
autoclean_list tail  = tail_;
if (is_error(tail)) return 0;
list new_link = malloc(sizeof *new_link);
```

```
  if (new_link)
  {
    struct link link_data = {
      .refcount = 1,
      .next = incref(tail),
      .value = head
    };
    memcpy(new_link, &link_data, sizeof *new_link);
  }
  return transfer(new_link);
}
```

We need to incref(tail) when we add it to the link, rather than transfer(tail), since it will be decref()'ed when the function returns.

We don't get much out of it with new_link(), but consider length():

```
int length_rec(takes list x_, int acc)
{
  autoclean_list x = x;
if (is_nil(x)) {
return acc;
} else {
return length_rec(incref(x->next), acc + 1);
  }
}
```

Now we get rid of the code for getting x->next before we call recursively, since decref(x) isn't called until x goes out of scope, which doesn't happen until after we have made the function call. So, the recursive case gets more natural code.

The same is the case for reverse() and concat():

```
list reverse_rec(takes list x_, takes list acc_)
{
autoclean_list x = x_, acc = acc_;
if (is_error(x) || is_error(acc)) return 0;
if (is_nil(x)) {
return incref(acc);
} else
{
return reverse_rec(incref(x->next), new_link(x->value, incref(acc)));
  }
```

```
}
```

list concat(takes list x_, takes list y_)

```
{
autoclean_list x = x_, y = y_;
if (is_error(x) || is_error(y)) return 0;
if (is_nil(x)) {
return incref(y);
} else
{
return new_link(x->value, concat(incref(x->next), incref(y)));

  }

}
```

Simply by assigning the input to local variables of type autoclean_list, we automatically insert decref() at every exit point of the functions. We do not need to worry about accessing links after we have decref()'ed them—that doesn't happen because we do not decref() them as long as they are in scope.

The tail recursion optimization will not be applied, at least not on the compilers I have checked it on, so you will suffer some in speed efficiency if you take this approach, though. Because of that, and because it will no longer be standard-compliant C, this is not an approach I will recommend, but now you know that the possibility exists.

A Generic Reference Counter

With a reference counter for integers and lists under our belts, we might ask ourselves if we could implement generic code for reference counting garbage collection, and the answer, not surprisingly, is yes. All our tricks for generic data structures will work for adding a reference counter to user data. We can embed a counter in our data, and if it is at the top of a struct, we can cast, and if it isn't, we can use the struct_ ptr(p,type,member) macro from Chapter 14. To learn something new, however, we will take a different approach, where we can also make the reference counter data structure opaque to the user.

We will provide the following interface:

```
void *rc_alloc(size_t size, void cleanup(void *, void *));
void *incref(void *p);

// Use this one when decref'ing from a callback
void *decref_ctx(void *p, void *ctx); // Use this one otherwise

static inline void decref(void *p)
{
decref_ctx(p, 0);
}
```

where we only expose reference counted memory through void pointers. If you want reference counted memory, you allocate it with rc_alloc() that takes a callback for freeing memory as the second argument. That function will be called with the memory you need to free plus a "secret" data structure we use to avoid recursion when freeing cascades to free other objects. The incref() and decref() functions work as before, but there is a second decref_ctx() function for when you decrement from a callback. If you call this version, with the second argument to the callback, you avoid recursion.

To make our code easier to follow, we will still use these macros, but do keep in mind that for a general user interface, we probably want better names.

```
// Annotation macros
#define borrows
#define takes
#define transfer(x) x
```

Those are all the functions and macros we expose in a header file. The rest of the functionality, we hide away in a .c file, so we can change it as we see fit.

The data we need to represent a reference counter must reside somewhere in memory, but the addresses we provide the user are theirs to do with as they please, so we cannot put the addresses there. Instead, we will put our bookkeeping information before those addresses. In effect, we are placing reference counters at the top of a structure, except that we do not need a structure. The user doesn't have to use structs but can reference count any data—for example, strings—and we do not need the user to know anything at all about how we handle bookkeeping. We will allocate memory, with malloc(), put our bookkeeping information at the first addresses of the memory we get, and then return a pointer to the memory after that data.

Here, we have to be careful, and I feel that I must stress this because I have seen people forget it countless times. If you do this trick, and you give a user an address higher than the one you got from malloc() yourself, you have to consider alignment. The address we get from malloc() is guaranteed to be such that any data structure can be placed there. That isn't also true for any offset from that address. If we write a function that puts some information at the first addresses and then returns an offset, we must make sure that the user's data can reside at that offset. Otherwise, on some architectures, and for some data, our reference counters will break. Debugging why is going to be hell on Earth.

If your compiler supports C11, and that standard is nine years old at the time of writing so I think it should, it is easy to get right. Then, there is a type, defined in <stddef.h> called max_align_t, that is guaranteed to have the maximum alignment constraints of any type. If a max_align_t can sit at an address, then anything can. We can combine max_align_t with a flexible array. If we put an empty array with type max_align_t[] after our data, the offset it gets will be valid to return, regardless of what data the user wants reference counted.

If you do not have max_align_t because you are using a compiler for an earlier version of the C standard, then I don't think that there is a portable way to work out what the maximum alignment is from within your program. There is a reason they added the type to the standard, after all. If you cannot get the information out of your system's documentation, a probabilistic approach would be to malloc() a lot of small memory blocks and check how many lower bits are zero. With malloc(), you are guaranteed to get addresses that are maximally aligned, and if it has a non-zero bit somewhere, that is higher than the maximum alignment. This, of course, is not an optimal approach, as you could get unlucky and infer a higher alignment than you need. But I am not aware of anything better that you can do if you don't get the information from the documentation.

I will assume that we have a C11 compiler and that we can use max_align_t. Our reference counter will look like this:

```
struct refcount {
union { size_t rc; void *stack; };
void (*cleanup)(void *, void *);
max_align_t user_data[];
};
```

The rc member is the counter, the cleanup() pointer is for the cleanup callback, and the user_data[] array is there for alignment. The stack pointer is the one we will use to avoid recursing when we delete objects, and I will explain it later. The rc and stack variables are in an anonymous union, since we will never use them both at the same time. We use rc while we have references to the object and stack when we are deleting them. Putting them in a union saves space. On my computer, pointers and size_t are 8 bytes.

With rc and stack in a union, the entire struct takes up 16 bytes, which also happens to be the alignment constraint of max_align_t. If you want to know that the maximum alignment is on your machine, you can include <stdalign.h> and use alignof(max_align_t). It might differ from mine, but on my computer, the 16 bytes I use for reference counting is the minimal possible memory I can use if I want to add bookkeeping to general data.

If we put our reference counting data before the user data, we need operations to move back and forth between the addresses. We can use the user_data member to get the user's data, and we can use struct_ptr() to get the reference counting data:

```
#define struct_ptr(p,type,member)                \
   (type *)((char *)p - offsetof(type, member))
#define refcount_mem(p)                   \    struct_ptr(p, struct refcount, user_data)
#define user_mem(rc)                 \
   (void *)(rc->user_data)
```

When we allocate memory, we allocate the number of bytes the user wants plus the size of the reference counter data, initialize the reference counter, and return the user data:

```
void *rc_alloc(size_t size, void (*cleanup)(void *, void *))
{
  struct refcount *mem = malloc(sizeof *mem + size);   if (!mem) return 0;
  mem->rc = 1;   mem->cleanup = cleanup;
  return user_mem(mem);
}
```

With flexible array members, sizeof of a struct won't necessarily give us the location of the array, whereas offsetof() will, so you could also use

```
#define RCSIZE offsetof(struct refcount, user_data) void *rc_alloc(size_t size, void (*cleanup)(void *,
void *))
{
  struct refcount *mem = malloc(RCSIZE + size);
if (!mem) return 0;

  mem->rc = 1;
mem->cleanup = cleanup;

return user_mem(mem);
}
```

I wouldn't worry about that, however. When there is a difference between sizeof and the offset of a flexible array member, it is because of alignment. It happens when the array has lower alignment constraints than the struct itself. That cannot happen with max_align_t, so sizeof(struct refcount) should be the same as offsetof(struct refcount, user_data). The padding at the end of a structure is there to make alignment work, and it isn't necessary when we explicitly go for alignment to max_align_t.

There is nothing new in incref(). It works exactly as before, except that we need to adjust the address we get as input to get to the reference counting metadata. We get a pointer to the user's data, and we should return the same, but we need the address of the reference counter to update it.

```
void *incref(void *p)
{
  if (!p) return p;

  struct refcount *mem = refcount_mem(p);
  mem->rc++;  return p;
}
```

Because I want to avoid recursion when deleting objects—we don't want to run out of stack space, after all—there is more work in decrementing. Here, the idea is to use the embedded stack variable that we are free to use once we no longer need the counter. If we call decref_ctx(p,x), we use x as a pointer to a stack of objects to be deleted. If x is NULL, we have a top-level deletion, and we will delete the object. If x isn't NULL, we simply put the object on the stack to be deleted later.

We use the function cleanup() for deleting objects:

```
void cleanup(struct refcount *stack)
{
  while (stack)
{
if (stack->cleanup)
stack->cleanup(user_mem(stack), stack);
struct refcount *next = stack->stack;
```

```
free(stack);
stack = next;

   }

}
```

It will iteratively delete objects as long as there are some on the stack, but before it deletes, it calls the user's callback. If the user remembers to use the decref_ctx() function for decrementing, the recursive deletion will go on the stack. Otherwise, the user's objects are still deleted, but with recursive calls to cleanup() via decref().

The decref_ctx() decrements the counter, and if it has to delete, it will do one of two things. If it has a second argument, I call it ctx for "deletion context," it will put the object on the cleanup stack. When that happens, we are already in the process of deleting, and putting the object on the stack schedules it for later deletion. If ctx is NULL, we immediately start a cleanup of the object.

```
void *decref_ctx(void *p, void *ctx)
{
if (!p) return p; // accept NULL as free() would...

struct refcount *mem = refcount_mem(p);
if (--mem->rc == 0)
{
   // change the memory for rc/stack to a NULL stack
mem->stack = 0;
if (ctx)
{
   // Schedule for deletion
struct refcount *stack = ctx;
mem->stack = stack->stack;
stack->stack = mem;
} else {
   // Start cleanup      cleanup(mem);
}    return 0; // reference is now gone...

   }
return p;
}
```

Search Trees with Reference Counting

Let us take our fancy new generic reference counter for a spin by implementing immutable search trees. An immutable tree consists of immutable nodes, and an immutable node is one where all of the value and the left and the right subtrees are const:

```
struct node
{
int const val;
```

```
struct node * const left;
struct node * const right;

};
```

We are going to use reference counting on the nodes, but we do not need to embed any counter information in them when we use the generic reference counting functions.

As with the lists earlier in the chapter, we want to distinguish between "empty" and "error," and we will use NULL pointers to indicate that some allocation error has occurred. This means that we have to use a real object for empty trees, and since all empty trees are alike, we can use a global object for this. However, if we use reference counting on nodes, and we intend to use empty trees as a kind of nodes with no special cases, then the empty tree node must be allocated with the rc_alloc() function.

We cannot do this for a global variable, but we can take the approach we did with empty lists and have a function that gives us a special address that represents the empty tree. It will hold a static variable that we cannot initialize where we define it, but we can check if it is NULL, and then initialize it, before we return it.

```
struct node *get_EMPTY(void)

{
static struct node *empty_node = 0;
if (!empty_node)
 empty_node = rc_alloc(sizeof *empty_node, 0);
if (!empty_node) abort(); // nothing works without it   return empty_node;
}
```

We can use a macro to get new references to the empty tree and predicates to test if a node is empty or an error, just as we did for lists.

```
#define EMPTY incref(get_EMPTY())

static inline bool is_empty(borrows struct node *t)

{
return t == get_EMPTY();
}
static inline bool is_error(borrows struct node *t)
{
return t == 0;
}
```

We do not initialize the node part of the empty tree, because we do not intend to use it as a proper node. The purpose of the object is to indicate an empty tree and nothing more. For real nodes, of course, we need initialization, and a function for that can look like this:

```
struct node *new_node(int val, takes struct node *left, takes struct node *right)

{
```

```
struct node *n = 0;
if (is_error(left) || is_error(right)) goto done;

n = rc_alloc(sizeof *n, free_node);

if (!n) goto done;

memcpy(n,  &(struct node) {

 .val = val, .left = incref(left), .right = incref(right)

}, sizeof *n);

done:

decref(left); decref(right);

return n;
}
```

The control flow is a little different from what we have seen before, but it is this way, so I only have one exit point from the function, which makes it easier for me to remember to decref() the two tree arguments the function takes. The result will be the node n that we keep NULL until we have passed the points where errors can occur. If either input tree is an error, we jump to the end of the function, at label done, and decref() both trees. At least one of them will be NULL, but decref() can handle that.

If we cannot allocate memory for n, we also jump to done, where we decref() the two trees and return NULL (which n will still be). If we make it through the error test and allocation, then we create a node and move the data into the newly allocated memory. Here, we incref() the two trees. If we didn't, we would lose them before we return, when we decref() them. If we didn't incref() them here, we would need a separate exit point for failure and success.

It could look something like this:

```
void free_node(void *p, void *ctx); // callback (see below) struct node *new_node(int val, takes struct
node *left, takes struct node *right)
{
if (is_error(left) || is_error(right)) goto error;
struct node *n = rc_alloc(sizeof *n, free_node);
if (!n) goto error;

memcpy(n, &(struct node) {

    .val   = val,

    .left  = transfer(left),

    .right = transfer(right)

  }, sizeof *n);

 // success   return n; error:

  decref(left); decref(right);
return 0;
}
```

As long as we remember to decrement the references, or give them away, through any path through the function, we are fine. But you cannot both give them to the new node and decref() them. I find the first version easier to read, but your mileage may vary.

The callback for the rc_alloc() function looks like this:

```
void free_node(void *p, void *ctx)
{
struct node *n = p;
decref_ctx(n->left, ctx);
decref_ctx(n->right, ctx);
}
```

When a node reaches reference count zero, we get it here, as a void pointer. It points at a struct node, since we allocated it as such, so we can cast it. To free it, we must decrement the subtrees to release the reference that this node has to them. We use the ctx argument we get when the function is used as a callback, so the reference counting code can avoid recursive calls.

A contains() function on these trees is simple to implement. We can try a borrows version, under the assumption that a user doesn't want us to delete a tree simultaneously with querying it:

```
bool contains(borrows struct node *tree, int val)
{
assert(!is_error(tree));
if (is_empty(tree))

return false;

if (tree->val == val) return true;

if (val < tree->val)

return contains(tree->left, val);

else

return contains(tree->right, val);
}
```

Because we borrow the reference, there is nothing unusual in the function. There is no incref() or decref() necessary, since we should not decrement borrowed nodes, and we are not returning a node that would have needed a new reference.

The usage pattern of contains() is likely to be something like if (contains(tree, val)) { /* do stuff */ }

so borrowing is fine, but with insert() we are more likely to write code such as t = insert(t, val);

which tells us that insert() should probably take ownership of its input. We are implementing immutable trees, so we are not getting t back in a modified form. Whatever we get back from the function call is a new tree that holds the elements from the old tree plus val. If we do not get the old tree back, we have lost a reference to it, and we haven't decremented it.

We cannot write t = insert(decref(t), val); since that might free t before insert() gets to work with it, so instead we must make insert() handle the decrementing. So, we will implement insert(), so it takes its tree argument:

```
struct node *insert(takes struct node *tree, int val)
{
  if (is_error(tree))
return 0;
if (is_empty(tree))
{
decref(tree);
return new_node(val, EMPTY, EMPTY);
}
if (val == tree->val) return transfer(tree);
int tval = tree->val;
struct node *left = incref(tree->left);
struct node *right = incref(tree->right);
decref(tree);
if (val < tree->val)
{
return new_node(tree->val, insert(transfer(left), val), transfer(right));
} else
{
return new_node(tree->val, transfer(left), insert(transfer(right), val));
  }
}
```

The two base cases are error handling, where tree is NULL, and we return NULL, and an empty tree, where we decrement tree and return a new node. Since we decremented the input, we are okay with the ownership, and since new_node() gives us a new reference, we are returning a fresh reference to the user, so we are also fine there. If we find that the value is already in the tree, we can return tree. We own a reference to it, so we can give it to the caller. In the remaining two cases, we will create a new node, with the value we have in tree, one of the existing subtrees, and the result of a recursive call for the remaining tree. Since we intend to give the subtrees to either the new node or the recursive call, we need new references to them. We own a reference to tree, but not its subtrees, so we must incref() them to get our own references. After that, we can safely decref(tree), since the trees we own references to cannot be deallocated. After that, it is a straightforward recursive call in the correct branch.

When removing values, we need to get the rightmost value in the left tree in the general case. We cannot modify the node we find there in any case, so we might as well just get the value in that tree, and for that, we can borrow references:

```
int rightmost_value(borrows struct node *tree)
{
assert(!is_error(tree) && !is_empty(tree));
while (!is_empty(tree->right)) tree = tree->right;
return tree->val;
}
```

For the same reasons as for insert(), we want delete() to take ownership of its input tree. We want to be able to write t = delete(t, val); to "update" an otherwise immutable tree t.

The function can look like this:

```
struct node *delete(takes struct node *tree, int val)
{
if (is_empty(tree)) return transfer(tree);
int tval = tree->val;
struct node *left = incref(tree->left);
struct node *right = incref(tree->right);
decref(tree);
if (val < tval)
{
return new_node(tval, delete(transfer(left), val), transfer(right)
} else if (val > tval)
{
return new_node(tval, transfer(left), delete(transfer(right), val)
} else {
if (is_empty(left))
{
decref(left);
return transfer(right);
}
if (is_empty(right)) {
decref(right);
return transfer(left);
}
int rmval = rightmost_value(left);
return new_node(rmval, delete(transfer(left), rmval), transfer(right));

}

}
```

We reply to an error with a NULL pointer, and if we get an empty tree, we give it back. Otherwise, we are going to return a new node where we have modified either the left or right tree, so we need new references to the subtrees and then decref() the reference we have to tree. Searching left or right to find the node we should delete is straightforward. We create a node that we will hold one of the existing subtrees, which we give to it, and the result of a recursive call, which we give the reference to the other tree. When we have the node we should delete, if either subtree is empty, we decrement that tree and give the other to the caller.

Otherwise, we get the value in the rightmost node in the left tree. We are only lending left to rightmost_value(left), so we still have the tree after the call. With the rmval in hand, we create a new node with that value, we give left to a recursive delete(), and we give right to the new node. The new node is the result.

Circular Structures?

What happens if you have data with a circular structure, for example, circular lists? Can you still use reference counting? The short answer is no. If you want to replace all of your pointers with reference counting pointers, you cannot free memory with cyclic dependencies. Objects that refer to each other in a cyclic structure will never reach count zero—at least not unless you explicitly break the cycle, which is something you probably want to avoid, as that requires the global knowledge of the data structure that we use referencing counting to avoid having.

In many data structures, however, we can have circular dependencies without this issue. There, the trick is to mix reference counting pointers and "raw" or "weak" pointers. For example, if you want to add parent pointers to the nodes in your search trees, you introduce a circular dependency from a node to its children and from the children to the node. But you can use a raw pointer for the parent, for example. Then the reference counter will keep children alive as long as there is a parent that holds a reference to them, but the children will not keep the parent around. If you choose such a strategy, you will have to deal with parents disappearing from children, if that is a problem. If a child can survive longer than a parent, you might, for example, want the deletion callback of a node to set the children's nodes' parent pointers to NULL. It isn't elegant, but it gets the job done.

There are more advanced garbage collection strategies than reference counting and strategies that deal with cyclic dependencies, but they are more complex and beyond the scope of this book. Reference counting gets most of the job done, with little effort and little overhead. It is the method of choice for many applications, including the runtime system of many programming languages. If you find that you need a little extra in terms of memory management, it should be the first strategy you explore.

Allocation Pools

1. What are Allocation Pools?

Allocation pools involve reserving a contiguous block of memory in advance and using it to fulfill allocation requests within the application. This memory management technique is commonly used in systems programming, embedded environments, game development, and high-performance applications where memory fragmentation and allocation speed are critical considerations.

In an allocation pool:

Memory is pre-allocated in bulk.

Memory chunks are provided for use from within the pool.

Freed memory within the pool is managed internally, rather than being returned to the system immediately.

2. Why Use Allocation Pools?

The traditional approach of using malloc and free has overhead, particularly when handling many small allocations. Using allocation pools offers several advantages:

Reduced Overhead: Allocation pools allow for faster memory allocations since no system calls are required once the pool is created.

Minimized Fragmentation: By keeping allocations within a fixed block of memory, memory fragmentation is reduced, which is beneficial in long-running programs or systems with limited memory.

Predictable Performance: Memory pools provide more predictable allocation and deallocation times, essential for real-time or performance-sensitive applications.

Simplified Deallocation: Instead of freeing each object individually, some pools allow for bulk deallocation, where the entire pool is cleared at once.

3. Implementing an Allocation Pool in C

3.1 Basic Pool Structure

To create an allocation pool, we typically define a structure that includes:

A pointer to the block of allocated memory.

The total size of the pool.

The current position or offset within the pool where the next allocation will happen.

Optionally, additional metadata, such as free lists for efficient deallocation.

```c
#include <stdlib.h>
#include <string.h>
typedef struct AllocationPool
{
    char *pool;        // Pointer to the start of the memory pool
    size_t pool_size;   // Total size of the memory pool
    size_t offset;      // Current offset for the next allocation
}
AllocationPool;
```

3.2 Creating and Initializing the Pool

The first step in using an allocation pool is to initialize it by allocating a large block of memory.

```
AllocationPool* createPool(size_t size) {
    AllocationPool *pool = (AllocationPool*) malloc(sizeof(AllocationPool));
    if (pool) {
        pool->pool = (char*) malloc(size);  // Allocate the memory block
        pool->pool_size = size;
        pool->offset = 0;  // Start at the beginning of the pool
    }
    return pool;
}
```

This function initializes the pool, reserving a block of memory of the specified size and setting the offset to zero, indicating that no memory has been allocated yet.

3.3 Allocating Memory from the Pool

When allocating memory from the pool, we use the current offset to find the next free block. After each allocation, the offset is incremented by the size of the requested block.

```
void* poolAlloc(AllocationPool *pool, size_t size) {
    if (pool->offset + size > pool->pool_size) {
        return NULL;  // Out of memory in the pool
    }
    void *ptr = pool->pool + pool->offset;
    pool->offset += size;
    return ptr;
}
```

This function checks if there's enough space left in the pool for the requested allocation size. If not, it returns NULL, indicating that the allocation has failed. Otherwise, it increments the offset by the size of the allocated block.

3.4 Resetting or Freeing the Pool

Since freeing individual allocations within a pool can be complex, many allocation pools are reset in bulk. Resetting the pool involves simply resetting the offset, making all memory within the pool available for reuse without releasing the allocated memory back to the operating system.

```
void resetPool(AllocationPool *pool) {
    pool->offset = 0;  // Reset the offset to reuse the entire pool
```

```
}

void freePool(AllocationPool *pool) {
    if (pool) {
        free(pool->pool);  // Free the allocated memory block
        free(pool);        // Free the pool structure
    }
}
```

Resetting the pool is very efficient, as it only requires setting the offset to zero. When the entire pool is no longer needed, freePool releases the allocated memory back to the system.

4. Example Usage of Allocation Pool

The following example demonstrates how to use an allocation pool to manage memory for a set of integer arrays:

```c
#include <stdio.h>
int main() {
    AllocationPool *pool = createPool(1024);  // Create a pool of 1024 bytes

    int *arr1 = (int*)poolAlloc(pool, 10 * sizeof(int));
    int *arr2 = (int*)poolAlloc(pool, 20 * sizeof(int));

    if (arr1 && arr2) {
        for (int i = 0; i < 10; i++) arr1[i] = i;
        for (int i = 0; i < 20; i++) arr2[i] = i * 2;

        printf("Array 1: ");
        for (int i = 0; i < 10; i++) printf("%d ", arr1[i]);
        printf("\nArray 2: ");
        for (int i = 0; i < 20; i++) printf("%d ", arr2[i]);
        printf("\n");
    }

    resetPool(pool);  // Reuse the pool for new allocations
    freePool(pool);   // Release memory
    return 0;
```

}

In this example:

A memory pool of 1024 bytes is created.

Two arrays of integers are allocated within the pool.

The pool is reset, making all memory available again.

The pool is finally freed, releasing all memory.

5. Advanced Allocation Pool Strategies

5.1 Free Lists

A **free list** tracks memory blocks that have been deallocated within the pool. When a block is freed, it's added to the free list, allowing it to be reused by future allocations without expanding the pool.

5.2 Chunk-Based Allocation

Some allocation pools divide memory into fixed-size chunks. This approach is efficient for applications requiring frequent, uniform-sized allocations, such as managing objects of a specific type. When a chunk is freed, it's added back to a list of available chunks for rapid reallocation.

5.3 Pool Expansion

While basic pools have a fixed size, some pools support expansion by allocating additional blocks when they run out of space. The pool structure maintains a linked list of memory blocks, allowing the pool to grow as needed while keeping the allocation mechanism consistent.

6. Advantages of Allocation Pools

Efficiency: Pool allocations are faster than repeated calls to malloc, as they avoid the overhead associated with general-purpose allocators.

Fragmentation Reduction: By allocating memory in large contiguous blocks, pools reduce fragmentation, which is beneficial in long-running applications.

Predictability: Memory pools provide predictable allocation times, crucial for real-time systems where timing consistency is necessary.

Bulk Deallocation: Instead of freeing each individual allocation, pools allow for efficient memory clearing by resetting or freeing the pool at once.

7. Limitations of Allocation Pools

Fixed Size: Simple allocation pools are fixed in size, which means that they may run out of memory if the pool is too small, leading to allocation failures.

Manual Management: Developers must handle pool allocation and deallocation carefully to avoid memory leaks or segmentation faults.

No Built-in Object Tracking: Pools do not inherently track individual allocations, so memory leaks may occur if the pool is not managed carefully.

Limited Reusability: Custom memory pools are often tailored for specific applications, making them less flexible than system-wide memory allocators.

8. When to Use Allocation Pools

Allocation pools are beneficial in scenarios where:

High-performance memory allocation is needed, such as in gaming or networking.

Embedded systems have limited resources and require efficient memory usage.

Real-time applications demand predictable memory allocation times.

We will implement our own memory allocation routine. We won't implement the full generality of malloc() and friends. There is rarely a need to try to replicate something we already have code for, presumably optimized and thoroughly tested. Instead, we will implement allocation routines optimized for cases where we need to allocate many equally sized objects, and here we can improve upon the performance of the general code that needs to handle the allocation of objects of any size.

There is some overhead to allocating memory, even though malloc() is usually very fast. It might involve a system call, and those can be expensive, although with most runtime systems, the allocation and free() functions usually have a pool of memory that they can hand out memory from, which alleviates that problem. Still, to keep track of which memory is in use and to correctly handle that you get the right size of memory blocks, and free the right size again, it involves some bookkeeping. A common case, however, is that you have a data structure where you need multiple objects of the same size, like links in a linked list or nodes in a tree.

For such an occurrence, we can implement a pool of memory, where we hand out blocks of that size each time we need one. We do not need to search for a block of memory of the right size because all our blocks have the same size, so any free block will do. We need to get memory for the pool of blocks, of course, and for that, we need malloc(), but as long as we allocate large chunks of memory, we can minimize the expensive allocations and use the cheap ones most of the time.

If you use such an allocation pool with a data structure, you get another benefit on top of it. When you are done with the data structure and need to free it, you do not need to free all the objects from the pool individually. You don't have to, for example, traverse a tree to free all its nodes, as you would with free(). Instead, you can free the allocation pool as a whole and that way free the memory that the tree's nodes use.

So, let's dig into implementing an allocation pool.

A Simple Pool for Tree Nodes

We start with the simplest situation. Assume that we have a struct node that we need a pool for, and assume that we have a cap on how many nodes we will need. If we use nodes in a tree such that we only allocate and never free them—not until we free the entire tree and can free the allocation pool, at least— we can implement an allocation pool similarly to how we implemented the simplest dynamic array. We allocate a chunk of memory that can hold a fixed number of nodes, and every time we need a new, we get the next free block.

The struct for the allocation pool looks like the struct for dynamic arrays:

```
struct node_pool {  size_t size, used;  struct node *pool; };
```

When we allocate a new pool, we allocate memory for this struct and a block of memory for struct node objects:

```
struct node_pool *new_pool(size_t capacity)
{
struct node_pool *pool = malloc(sizeof *pool);
if (!pool) return 0;
pool->pool = malloc(capacity * sizeof *pool->pool);
if (!pool->pool) {
free(pool);
return 0;
}
pool->size = capacity;
pool->used = 0;
return pool;
}
```

When we free a pool, we need to free the block of memory that holds the nodes and then the struct node_pool itself:

```
void free_pool(struct node_pool *pool)
{
  free(pool->pool);
  free(pool);
}
```

Finally, when we need a node, we get the next free block in the pool:

```
struct node *node_alloc(struct node_pool *pool)
{
  if (pool->used == pool->size) return 0; // Pool is used up   return &pool->pool[pool->used++];
}
```

If we need more nodes than we allocated memory for, we are out of luck. It is not too bad; there are many applications where we know how many nodes of a tree, or links in a list, that we need a priori. But it is not most of them, so it would be better if we can grow a pool if we need to.

Adding Resizing

The natural instinct when we have to grow an array is to use realloc(). Repress that instinct for memory pools. When we hand out nodes from our allocation pools, we are handing out addresses into the array in the pool. If we realloc() that array, we have to copy the data to new memory locations. The pointers we have already handed out won't be updated, however. They will still point into the original memory buffer. If you move an object in memory, all the pointers to it have to be updated to its new address. Finding and updating all pointers to an object's address is not for the faint-hearted, and not something I will suggest that you ever attempt. It is, practically, impossible.

We need to grow our memory pool without moving any of the existing objects. That is not really a problem, though, as long as we don't need to store the objects in contiguous memory. We need to do that for arrays, but we don't need memory pools to behave like arrays, after all, so we are not limited in this way. If we need to enlarge the pool, we can allocate a new chunk of memory for more nodes and start to take them from there. That chunk can sit anywhere in memory, as far as we are concerned.

So, we can split a pool into several sub-pools, where each sub-pool is a chunk of contiguous memory, but where the sub-pools are free to be located anywhere. We can chain them together in a linked list to keep track of them that way.

The most straightforward implementation of this idea is to have sub-pools contain a pointer to the next sub-pool and an array of nodes of some constant time:

```
#define SUBPOOL_SIZE 1P24 // an arbitrary number...
struct subpool
{
struct subpool *next;
struct node nodes[SUBPOOL_SIZE];
};
struct subpool *new_subpool(struct subpool *next)
{
struct subpool *pool = malloc(sizeof *pool);
if (pool) pool->next = next;
```

```
  return pool;
}
```

We could also use a flexible array member for the nodes in a sub-pool for the data and precede it with a pointer to the next sub-pool and allocate them like this:

```
struct subpool {
struct subpool *next;
struct node nodes[];
};
struct subpool *new_subpool(size_t capacity, struct subpool *next)
{
struct subpool *pool = 0;
size_t size = offsetof(struct subpool, nodes) + (sizeof *pool->nodes) * capacity;
pool = malloc(size);
if (pool) pool->next = next;
return pool;
}
```

With this approach, we can allocate sub-pools of different sizes and perhaps adapt the size of the sub-pools to the algorithm we use them for at runtime. I will assume that we use a constant size for each sub-pool, though.

We still need to keep track of how many empty slots we have in a pool, but there is no need to do this in the sub-pools. We will do the bookkeeping in the pool proper, where we keep track of how many empty slots we have in the top sub-pool:

```
struct node_pool
{
size_t free_slots;
struct subpool *subpools;
};
```

When we create a pool, we also create the top sub-pool, and then we set the free_ slots counter to SUBPOOL_SIZE to indicate that all the slots in the top sub-pool are free for use:

```
struct node_pool *new_pool(void)
{
  struct node_pool *pool = malloc(sizeof *pool);
if (!pool) return 0;
```

```
    struct subpool *subpool = new_subpool(0);
if (!subpool) {
free(pool);
return 0; }
  pool->free_slots = SUBPOOL_SIZE;
return pool;
  }
```

When we free a pool, we need to free all the sub-pools. Since we are familiar with how we run through a linked list, there is nothing complicated in that:

```
void free_pool(struct node_pool *pool)
{
struct subpool *sp = pool->subpools;
while (sp) {
struct subpool *next = sp->next;
free(sp);
sp = next;
  }
  free(pool);
}
```

It is when we allocate nodes that we need to manage the sub-pools. We will have the invariant that the free slots are all in the top node and that the free slots sit at index free_ slots - 1 and down to zero. If we still have free slots left, the next we can give away will thus sit at index free_slots - 1 in the top sub-pool, so we can return the address of that node and decrement the free slots counter. If there are no free slots available, we must allocate a new sub-pool first:

```
struct node *node_alloc(struct node_pool *pool)
{
if (!pool->free_slots) {
struct subpool *new_top = new_subpool(pool->subpools);
if (!new_top) return 0;
pool->subpools = new_top;
pool->free_slots = SUBPOOL_SIZE;
}
return &pool->subpools->nodes[--(pool->free_slots)];
}
```

Adding Deallocation

Can we also free nodes we have allocated from a pool? We can, of course, free all the memory when we deallocate the entire pool, so the real question is whether we can mark the memory a node occupies as free to be reused by a later allocation. We can do this by chaining free node slots in a linked list, where allocations take the slot at the front of the list, and deallocation prepends a newly freed node to the list.

We do not need to implement such a list of available slots as links containing nodes. Any memory that is used as a node shouldn't be in the free list, and any node in the list shouldn't be used as a node. So, we can embed the list in the same memory as the nodes using a union that is either a linked list pointer or a node:

```
union node_free_list {
union node_free_list *next_free;
struct node node;

};
struct subpool {
struct subpool *next;

union node_free_list nodes[SUBPOOL_SIZE];

};
```

When we allocate a new sub-pool, it will consist of SUBPOOL_SIZE free nodes, and we should chain these into a free list. If we run through all the slots in the nodes[] array, interpret them as free list pointers in the union, and point them to the address of the next index in the array, we will have chained them. For the last index, we will set next_free to NULL to indicate that it is the last free slot.

```
struct subpool *new_subpool(struct subpool *next)

{

  struct subpool *pool = malloc(sizeof *pool);
if (!pool) return 0;

  // chain sub-pools   pool->next = next;

  // chain free node-slots

for (size_t i = 0; i < SUBPOOL_SIZE - 1; i++) pool->nodes[i].next_free = &pool->nodes[i + 1];
pool->nodes[SUBPOOL_SIZE - 1].next_free = 0;

  return pool;
}
```

The pool proper will have a pointer to the front of the free list, and when we create a new pool, we set the free pointer to the first index in the top sub-pool. That index is the first free slot in the chain we created for the sub-pool.

```
struct node_pool {

  union node_free_list *next_free;
struct subpool *subpools;
};
struct node_pool *new_pool(void)
```

```c
{
  struct node_pool *pool = malloc(sizeof *pool);
  if (!pool) return 0;

  struct subpool *subpool = new_subpool(0);
  if (!subpool) { free(pool); return 0; }
  pool->subpools = subpool;
  pool->next_free = &subpool->nodes[0];
  return pool;
}
```

We do not need to change anything in the function that frees pools. We do not need to iterate through the free list or handle the individual nodes in any way, so freeing a pool is still just a matter of freeing all the sub-pools it contains.

```c
void free_pool(struct node_pool *pool)
{
  struct subpool *sp = pool->subpools;
  while (sp) {
    struct subpool *next = sp->next;
    free(sp);
    sp = next;
  }
  free(pool);
}
```

To allocate a node from a pool, we can return the node at the front of the free list and update the free list to point at the next in the chain. If the next_free pointer is NULL, there are no available slots, and we must allocate a new sub-pool. Once we have done that, we have a new list of free nodes that start at the first index in the sub-pool's array.

```c
struct node *node_alloc(struct node_pool *pool)
{
  if (pool->next_free == 0) {
    struct subpool *new_top = new_subpool(pool->subpools);
    if (!new_top) return 0;
    // Success, so add new pool to list
    new_top->next = pool->subpools;
    pool->next_free = &new_top->nodes[0];
  }
  struct node *node = &pool->next_free->node;
  pool->next_free = pool->next_free->next_free;
  return node;
}
```

When we want to free a node, we can reinterpret the memory it holds as the union type, we use in the pool. It is memory of that type that we have handed to the user, and while they have used it as a struct node, we are allowed to cast it back to its true form.[10] If we interpret the memory as the union type, we can write to the next_free pointer in it and that way put it at the front of the free list.

```
void free_node(struct node_pool *pool, struct node *node)
{
  union node_free_list *free_list = (union node_free_list *) node;
  free_list->next_free = pool->next_free;

  pool->next_free = free_list;
}
```

A Generic Pool

If we can write an allocation pool for struct node objects, we can write it for any other type, of course. But as with the other data structures we have considered in the book, it is worthwhile considering one implementation that can handle all types. Can we implement such a generic allocation pool that is oblivious to the concrete types we will allocate memory from?

With the node allocation pools, we never explicitly exploited that the objects in the pools were of any particular type, so it seems as if it should be straightforward to generalize the code. And it is not that difficult. But we did exploit that we knew the underlying type implicitly in a couple of ways, and now we need to handle that without the assistance of the compiler. When we worked with arrays of struct node in the sub-pools, the compiler worked out the size of the array for us and made sure that the alignment constraint for nodes was satisfied. That is what we have to handle manually now.

We will handle raw memory, in the form of a buffer we access through a char * pointer, in chunks of size block_size. We will compute this size, so it satisfies both size and alignment requirements. What that means is the same as sizeof(T) means for type T: if we can place an object at an address a, then we can also place one at a + i * block_size for all integers i. In sub-pools, we will have a pointer to the next sub-pool and a pointer to raw data:

```
struct subpool {  char *data;

  struct subpool *next;
};
```

We won't embed the data in the sub-pool this time. We could, but it would have to be at an offset that is a multiple of block_size, so it would require some extra bookkeeping. We wouldn't be able to use a struct member for the data, as we could with the array of nodes. Instead, we would have to allocate memory for both the pointer, SUBPOOL_SIZE * block_size memory for the data, and some extra header, so we could access the data at a multiple of block_size from the beginning of the sub-pool memory.

This is not impossible to do, but it is cumbersome. If we use a separate malloc() memory allocation for the data, we know that the first address has maximum alignment and thus that we can place any object there.

Thus, allocating a sub-pool now involves two calls to malloc(): one for allocating the pool and one for allocating the data. The function looks like this:

```
struct subpool *new_subpool(size_t block_size, struct subpool *next)
{
  struct subpool *spool = malloc(sizeof *spool);
if (!spool) return 0;
  spool->data = malloc(SUBPOOL_SIZE * block_size);
if (!spool->data) { free(spool); return 0; }
spool->next = next;
chain_subpool(spool->data, block_size);
return spool;
}
```

where the chain_subpool() is responsible for creating a linked list of free blocks.

We do not have a data structure for the blocks and the free pointers, as we are working with raw memory now, but if block_size is large enough—and we will ensure that it is we can place void pointers in each block and chain them together like that:

```
void chain_subpool(char *data, size_t block_size) {
  // We need a void ** so we can write a void * into each block.
void **p = (void **)data + (SUBPOOL_SIZE - 1) * block_size;
  *p = 0;
  for (size_t i = 0; i < SUBPOOL_SIZE; i++)
{
p = (void **)(data + i * block_size);
*p = data + (i + 1) * block_size;
  }
}
```

We go through each block and cast its address to void **. If it is a pointer to a void pointer, we can write a void pointer into it. So, we take the address of the next block, computed as data + (i + 1) * block_size. Since data is a char pointer, we are getting addresses block_size apart. It is a char * pointer we get out of this pointer arithmetic, but we can write those into void pointers. If p is the address of a block, interpreted as void **, then *p is a void pointer that we can write to, and that is where we write the address of the next block. The code might be a little hard to decipher, but the result is that for each of the blocks, the first sizeof(void *) of the block_size bytes holds an address.

In the last of the blocks, the value is a NULL pointer; we set it in the line *p = 0, and for the remaining blocks, the address is the start of the next block.

The tricky part of making all this work is to have a block_size that will allow you to both embed pointers in the blocks and allow you to place the objects you want the pool to handle. There are two constraints that we must meet. The size of a block must be large enough to both hold void * and the objects, so it must be at least MAX(sizeof(void *), sizeof(T)) if you plan to put objects of type T in the pool. Blocks must also be aligned so you can place both void * and T objects at the beginning of each, so the alignment must be the maximum of the two type's alignment: MAX(alignof(void *), alignof(T)). (Remember that you need to include <stdalign.h> to get alignof().)

To satisfy both constraints, block_size must be a multiple of MAX(alignof(void *), alignof(T)) of size at least MAX(sizeof(void *), sizeof(T)), and naturally we want the smallest such multiple. The following function computes such a block size, where the type's size and alignment are in type_size and type_align:

```
#define MAX(a,b) (((a) > (b)) ? (a) : (b))
static inline
size_t aligned_block_size(size_t type_size, size_t type_align)
{
  // The block size must be a multiple of align of size
  // at least min_size.
size_t min_size  = MAX(sizeof(void *), type_size);
size_t align = MAX(alignof(void *), type_align);
size_t block_size = ((min_size - 1) / align + 1) * align;
return block_size;
}
```

To get the block size for objects of type T, you would use aligned_block_size (sizeof(T),alignof(T).

Our plan is to have allocation pools for one type of object only, so we can compute the block size when we create a pool and store it with the pool (together with the sub- pool list and the free list): struct pool {

struct subpool *top_pool;   size_t block_size;   void *next_free; };

We cannot write a function that takes a type as an argument, so we write one that creates a pool based on the size and alignment values instead:

```
struct pool *new_pool_type(size_t type_size, size_t type_align)
{
size_t block_size = aligned_block_size(type_size, type_align);
  // check size overflow...   if (SIZE_MAX / SUBPOOL_SIZE < block_size) return 0;
struct pool *pool = malloc(sizeof *pool);
if (!pool) return 0;
pool->top_pool = new_subpool(block_size, 0);
```

```
if (!pool->top_pool) {
free(pool);
return 0;
}
pool->block_size = block_size;
pool->next_free = pool->top_pool->data;
return pool;
}
```

This function looks much like the one from the previous section, except that we need to ensure that we do not have a size overflow when we combine the SUBPOOL_SIZE with the block_size, and we get the first free block in the free list as the address of the sub- pool's data.

It is, of course, more convenient if we can allocate a pool based on a type, and while we cannot write a function that takes a type as an argument, we can write a macro that does it. Therefore, we can write a new_pool() macro that takes a type as an argument, get the type's size and alignment specification, and call the new_pool_type() function with those:

```
#define new_pool(type) new_pool_type(sizeof(type), alignof(type))
```

When we free an allocation pool, we must remember to free sub-pools' data as well as the sub-pool, but otherwise that function is straightforward.

```
void free_pool(struct pool *pool)
{
  struct subpool *sp = pool->top_pool;
while (sp) {
struct subpool *next = sp->next;
free(sp->data);
free(sp);
sp = next;
  }
  free(pool);
}
```

When we hand out new memory blocks, and when we return them to the free list, the free list is a linked list of void pointers. There is no information about what is at the other end of a void *, so we must cast what we see there to manipulate it. To deliver the next free memory block to the user, we can return the address that pool->next_free points to, but to update the free list, we must also update pool->next_free so it now points at the next block in the list. However, if next_free points at a memory block, that block is free, which means that it should hold data that we can interpret as a pointer in the free list. So, we can cast pool->next_free to void ** and read the void * it points at. That will be the address of the next free block, and we should update pool->next_free to point there:

```
void *pool_alloc(struct pool *pool)
{
  if (pool->next_free == 0) {
struct subpool *new_top = new_subpool(pool->block_size, pool->top_pool);
if (!new_top) return 0;
    pool->top_pool = new_top;
pool->next_free = new_top->data;
  }
void *p = pool->next_free;
pool->next_free = *(void **)pool->next_free;
return p;
}
```

When we return a block to the pool, we do the same in reverse. We take the memory we are getting back and interpret it as void **. That means that we now consider it as pointing to an address where we can write a pointer to the current free list, after which we can update next_free to point to the now freed block.

```
void pool_free(struct pool *pool, void *p)
{
  void **next_free = (void **)p;
  *next_free = pool->next_free;
  pool->next_free = next_free;
}
```

Manipulating raw memory, the way we do with the free lists here means that we have to be super careful. But we made sure that the size and alignment constraints on blocks allow us to put void * data at the beginning of each block, and since we are also careful with casting when we read and write into blocks, we make it work.

We now have a generic allocation pool, from which we can obtain equal-sized blocks of memory and return the blocks to when done using them. If we use the pool in an algorithm, after which we can release all the memory blocks, we can do so as a single operation, and we do not need to free them individually.

We could try to extend our pool so it can handle variable-size memory blocks, but that will add substantially to the bookkeeping, and we would end up implementing our own version of the malloc()/free() runtime system we already have available. And our solution would likely be inferior to a system that is highly optimized and tested by thousands of users every day.

We could also consider improving the pool, so it deletes sub-pools when they are no longer used. Again, however, I would discourage it. The implementation we currently have doesn't keep track of which sub-pool a block of memory is in, and doing that would incur substantial bookkeeping overhead. Without knowing that, tracking when the last memory block in a sub-pool is released is difficult.

No, I think this is as far as I would take an allocation pool. At least, I have never taken it further, and yet I have managed to implement many data structures with custom allocators for links, nodes, and whatnot. Now you can do so as well.

Conclusion on Generic Lists, Trees, Reference Counting Garbage Collection, and Allocation Pools in C

In C programming, effective memory and data structure management is essential for writing efficient, reliable, and scalable code. The concepts of generic lists and trees, reference counting garbage collection, and allocation pools provide fundamental mechanisms to manage dynamic memory and data structures, reduce fragmentation, and handle complex relationships among objects.

1. Generic Lists and Trees

Generic lists and trees are foundational data structures that allow developers to organize data hierarchically or sequentially without a fixed size, making them crucial for applications that handle dynamic data. Lists, such as singly or doubly linked lists, enable linear data storage with efficient insertions and deletions. Trees, including binary trees and AVL trees, support hierarchical data organization, providing faster access times for structured searches and allowing efficient representation of nested relationships.

Advantages: Generic data structures eliminate the need for type-specific structures, making code reusable and simplifying the development process. Lists and trees, in particular, facilitate flexible data handling, as they allow dynamic resizing without the memory overhead associated with arrays.

Challenges: In C, creating truly generic structures is challenging due to the lack of built-in generic data types. Developers often rely on void* pointers for generic implementations, but this approach can increase complexity and risk type safety issues. Additionally, manual memory management is required, which can introduce memory leaks or errors if not handled carefully.

Best Practices: To ensure safety and efficiency, generic lists and trees should be implemented with clear interfaces and encapsulated in a way that abstracts the complexity from the user. Proper use of macros, function pointers, or a limited subset of type-safe templates can improve usability and reduce type safety risks. Using well-tested libraries or implementing consistent naming conventions for custom functions can also enhance code readability and maintainability.

2. Reference Counting Garbage Collection

Reference counting is a simple yet effective garbage collection strategy that helps manage dynamically allocated memory in C by tracking the number of references to each object. When the reference count of an object reaches zero, the object is deallocated, freeing memory that is no longer in use.

Advantages: Reference counting is predictable and easy to implement, particularly in scenarios where memory needs to be freed deterministically. This method is ideal for programs with complex object graphs where explicit tracking of object usage is feasible.

Challenges: A key limitation of reference counting is its inability to detect and collect cyclic references, where objects refer to each other, preventing their reference counts from reaching zero. Additionally, reference counting introduces some runtime overhead, as the counter must be updated every time a reference is added or removed, potentially impacting performance in high-frequency reference scenarios.

Best Practices: To avoid memory leaks due to cyclic references, developers should combine reference counting with additional techniques, such as weak references or manual cycle-breaking. Careful consideration of where and when references are updated can also reduce unnecessary counter adjustments, thus enhancing performance. For complex applications, using existing libraries or frameworks that handle reference counting automatically can significantly reduce the risk of errors.

3. Allocation Pools

Allocation pools, or memory pools, are a technique for managing dynamic memory by preallocating a block of memory and dividing it into smaller, reusable chunks. Instead of repeatedly allocating and deallocating memory from the heap, which can lead to fragmentation and overhead, memory pools provide a mechanism for efficient allocation and deallocation within a fixed memory space.

Advantages: Allocation pools can improve performance significantly by reducing memory fragmentation and providing faster allocations. This technique is particularly useful in real-time systems or embedded applications where memory usage must be predictable and efficient.

Challenges: While allocation pools reduce fragmentation, they require careful design to avoid inefficient use of memory within the pool. If a pool's size is underestimated, memory may still need to be allocated from the heap, which undermines the purpose of the pool. Conversely, overestimating can lead to wasted memory. Furthermore, managing complex pool hierarchies in larger applications can become cumbersome without rigorous planning and management.

Best Practices: Proper analysis of memory usage patterns is essential when designing allocation pools. Developers should create pools tailored to specific data types or usage scenarios, ensuring that each pool's size and chunk arrangement meet the application's demands. To enhance flexibility, pools can be segmented or dynamically resized, when necessary, though caution should be exercised to balance flexibility with efficiency. Implementing boundary checks and monitoring tools can help track pool usage and prevent leaks.

Integrating the Concepts

These three concepts – generic lists and trees, reference counting, and allocation pools – form an essential toolkit for effective memory and data structure management in C. By integrating these techniques thoughtfully, developers can craft robust, efficient applications that handle complex data structures with minimal overhead.

Combining Generic Lists and Reference Counting: Using generic lists with reference counting ensures that memory is freed when no longer in use, which is beneficial for managing linked structures like trees where each node may have multiple references. The combination also mitigates risks of memory leaks in dynamically allocated structures that are often reused or modified during runtime.

Reference Counting within Allocation Pools: By using reference counting alongside allocation pools, developers can achieve fine-grained memory control and avoid fragmentation. Memory pools can be designated for objects with varying lifetimes and usage patterns, while reference counting ensures that objects are freed only when they are no longer referenced, making memory management more predictable and efficient.

Allocation Pools for Lists and Trees: Allocation pools can also enhance the efficiency of generic lists and trees, particularly in applications with predictable data structures. For example, a pool allocated for tree nodes minimizes allocation time and ensures consistent memory usage. With this approach, the data structure's integrity is maintained without the overhead of frequent allocations.

Final Takeaways

C programming requires a meticulous approach to memory management, especially in applications where performance and reliability are paramount. Generic lists and trees, reference counting, and allocation pools are invaluable tools for managing memory and data structures effectively, though each comes with unique considerations:

Safety and Type Management: In generic structures, type safety must be carefully managed to prevent errors during data access and manipulation. Type-specific operations may be necessary, even within generic structures, to maintain code integrity.

Efficient Memory Usage: Allocation pools and reference counting reduce overhead by streamlining memory management, though they require precise planning and monitoring to avoid fragmentation or leaks. In applications where speed and memory usage are critical, these techniques offer a balanced approach to dynamic allocation.

Performance Optimization: The use of these techniques together can greatly enhance the performance of C applications by reducing allocation time and minimizing memory waste. Careful design and implementation of these structures are essential for optimizing application runtime and resource utilization.

In summary, by mastering these techniques, C developers can build applications that handle complex data efficiently, reduce memory-related errors, and ensure predictable behavior even in high-stakes, resource-constrained environments. Each of these methods – generic lists and trees, reference counting, and allocation pools – plays a unique role in elevating the reliability, efficiency, and maintainability of C applications, making them indispensable for advanced C programming.

18. Dos and Don'ts in C

Introduction

The C programming language, one of the oldest yet most powerful languages, provides low-level access to memory and is widely used in systems programming, embedded systems, and performance-critical applications. However, C is also prone to errors and vulnerabilities due to its lack of built-in safety mechanisms. This guide will cover essential "Do's" and "Don'ts" in C, aiming to make your code safer, cleaner, and more efficient.

1. Memory Management

Do:

Use malloc and free Carefully: Always pair malloc (or calloc) with free to avoid memory leaks. For every dynamic memory allocation, ensure there's a corresponding free.

Initialize Pointers: Initialize pointers to NULL and check before dereferencing. It reduces the chance of accessing invalid memory locations.

Use calloc for Zero-Initialized Memory: calloc initializes allocated memory to zero, which is useful if zero initialization is needed.

Don't:

Don't Use Uninitialized Pointers: Accessing uninitialized pointers can lead to unpredictable behavior and crashes.

Avoid Memory Leaks: Failing to free allocated memory can result in memory leaks, especially in long-running applications.

Don't Double-Free Memory: Freeing the same memory twice can cause undefined behavior.

2. Pointers and Arrays

Do:

Use Array Bounds Checking: Carefully manage array sizes and ensure index variables don't exceed the allocated array length.

Use sizeof Operator Properly: When allocating memory for an array, use sizeof(type) instead of hardcoding sizes. For example, malloc(sizeof(int) * length);

Don't:

Don't Mix Up Array and Pointer Syntax: Avoid treating arrays and pointers interchangeably, as they have subtle differences in memory handling and indexing.

Avoid Pointer Arithmetic Without Caution: Ensure that pointer arithmetic stays within valid memory bounds to prevent accessing unintended memory areas.

3. Control Structures

Do:

Use Braces with Conditionals: Even for single-line statements following if or else, use braces { } to prevent errors in case of later modifications.

Handle All Cases in Switch Statements: Use a default case in switch statements to handle unexpected values gracefully.

Don't:

Don't Use goto Unnecessarily: The goto statement can create hard-to-follow code paths and should generally be avoided. Use structured control flow instead.

Avoid Deeply Nested Loops and Conditionals: Complex nesting makes code hard to read and maintain. Refactor to reduce nesting.

4. Error Handling

Do:

Check Return Values of Functions: Always check the return values of library functions like malloc, scanf, fopen, etc., as they may return error codes or NULL in failure cases.

Use errno for Error Checking: The errno variable is helpful for diagnosing errors from system and standard library functions.

Don't:

Don't Ignore Errors: Failing to handle errors or log them can lead to unpredictable issues that are difficult to debug.

Don't Return Uninformative Error Codes: Returning 0 for success and non-zero for errors is a good practice; make sure the error codes are descriptive.

5. Code Readability and Maintenance

Do:

Follow Naming Conventions: Use meaningful names for variables, functions, and constants. For example, buffer_size instead of bsize.

Use Comments Wisely: Add comments to explain complex logic, but avoid over-commenting. Well-named functions and variables reduce the need for excessive commenting.

Don't:

Don't Write Cryptic Code: Obfuscated or overly compact code may save lines but will reduce readability. Write code that is intuitive and maintainable.

Avoid Magic Numbers: Use constants or macros instead of hardcoding numbers, making the code self-explanatory.

6. File Handling

Do:

Check File Open Success: Always verify that file pointers returned by fopen are not NULL.

Close Files Properly: Use fclose to close files after they're no longer needed to prevent file descriptor leaks.

Don't:

Don't Forget to Close Files: Leaving files open will cause resource leaks, especially in programs that handle many files.

Avoid Hardcoding File Paths: Use relative paths where possible and configurable file paths for flexibility and portability.

7. Using Standard Library Functions

Do:

Use Standard String Functions Carefully: Functions like strcpy and strcat assume enough buffer space, so ensure you're aware of the destination's capacity.

Use snprintf Instead of sprintf: snprintf allows specifying the buffer length, reducing the risk of buffer overflow.

Don't:

Avoid Dangerous Functions: Functions like gets are unsafe because they lack bounds checking. Prefer fgets or safer alternatives.

Don't Ignore Function Documentation: Standard library functions have specific behaviors that need to be understood, such as assumptions about null-terminated strings.

8. Concurrency and Thread Safety

Do:

Use Mutexes for Shared Resources: When using threads, use mutexes or locks to prevent race conditions when accessing shared data.

Prefer Atomic Operations When Possible: For basic operations, atomic functions can prevent data races without the overhead of locking.

Don't:

Don't Assume Functions Are Thread-Safe: Many standard library functions are not thread-safe. If unsure, use synchronization mechanisms.

Avoid Global Variables in Multithreaded Contexts: Shared global variables in a multithreaded program are prone to race conditions unless carefully managed.

9. Macros and Preprocessor Directives

Do:

Use Constants Over Macros When Possible: Use const variables instead of #define for constant values, as they provide type safety.

Wrap Complex Macros in Parentheses: When defining complex macros, enclose expressions in parentheses to avoid precedence issues.

Don't:

Don't Overuse Macros: Macros can make code harder to debug and read. Prefer inline functions for short code snippets.

Avoid Undefined Macro Behavior: Always ensure macros are defined as expected, and use #ifdef to handle conditional compilation safely.

10. Best Practices in C Style

Do:

Follow Indentation and Style Guidelines: Use consistent indentation, brace styles, and spacing to improve readability.

Break Long Functions into Smaller Ones: Long functions can be hard to understand; break them down for better modularity and reusability.

Don't:

Avoid Non-Standard C Extensions: Stick to the C standard for portability. Non-standard extensions may not work across different compilers or platforms.

Don't Ignore Compiler Warnings: Compiler warnings often indicate potential issues. Address them to make code safer and more reliable.

Do Not Use the gets Function

The gets function is declared inside the <stdio.h> header, reads the input into a character array pointed to by str, and has the following syntax:

char *gets (char* str);

This function is hazardous as it can cause a buffer overflow and allows for potential buffer overflow attacks. The function is deprecated in the C99 standard and removed in the C11 standard. Do not use this function!

The workaround is to use the fgets alternative. Unlike gets, the fgets function performs bounds checking and is safe from buffer overflow scenarios.

To use the fgets, we simply pass in the pointer to a buffer buff, the maximum number of characters that can be read, and stdio representing our standard input/keyboard.

A simple example:

```
#include <stdio.h>
int main(void)
{
    char buff[100];
```

```
    printf("Please enter a string:\n");
    fgets(buff, 100, stdin);
    printf("The result is: %s\n", buff);
}
```

Output:

Please enter a string:
Do not use the gets function!
The result is: Do not use the gets function!

Alternatively, opt for a gets_s function, which might be available on our C implementation as part of the optional bounds-checking interfaces extension.

Initialize Variables Before Using Them

When we declare local variables, they are not initialized. Their values are undetermined. Trying to access uninitialized variables causes undefined behavior. One use case would be trying to print local, uninitialized variables.

The following example demonstrates what should be avoided:

```
#include <stdio.h>
int main(void)
{
char c;    int x;    double d;
printf("Accessing uninitialized variables...\n");
printf("%c, %d, %f\n", c, x, d); // undefined behavior
}
```

Possible Output:

Accessing uninitialized variables...
[, 32767, 0.000000

We are trying to access/print out uninitialized local variables in this example. This leads to undefined behavior and is best avoided.

We should always initialize (or assign values to) our variables before using them.

Example:

```
#include <stdio.h>
```

```c
int main(void)
{
    char c = 'a';       int x = 0;       double d = 0.0;
    printf("Accessing initialized variables...\n");
    printf("%c, %d, %f\n", c, x, d); // OK
}
```

Output:

Accessing initialized variables...

a, 0, 0.000000

Do Not Read Out of Bounds

Trying to access an array element that is not there invokes undefined behavior. We say we are reading out of bounds. The following example demonstrates a common scenario of trying to access a nonexistent, out-ofbounds array element:

```c
#include <stdio.h>
int main(void)
{
    int arr[5] = {10, 20, 30, 40, 50};
    printf("Trying to read out of bounds...\n");
    printf("The non-existent array element is: %d\n", arr[5]);
}
```

Possible Output:

Trying to read out of bounds...

The non-existent array element is: 32767

In this example, we declared an array of five integers. We then try to access a sixth array element using a[5]. But since there is no element a[5], we are invoking undefined behavior. This might cause our program to do anything, including the strange output result earlier. The same effect would be if we tried to access a[10], a[256], etc. We can only access elements a[0] through a[4]. If we want to access only the last array element, we can rewrite the preceding example to be:

```c
#include <stdio.h>
int main(void)
{
    int arr[5] = {10, 20, 30, 40, 50};
    printf("Accessing the existing array element...\n");
```

```
        printf("The existent array element is: %d\n", arr[4]);
}
```

Output:

Accessing the existent array element...

The existent array element is: 50

Do Not Free the Allocated Memory Twice

Trying to free the allocated memory two times causes undefined behavior. The following example shows the wrong usage of two free statements:

```
#include <stdio.h>
#include <stdlib.h>
int main(void)
{
    printf("Allocating memory...\n");
    int *p = malloc(sizeof(int));
    *p = 123;
    printf("The value is: %d\n", *p);
    printf("Freeing twice - undefined behavior.\n");
    free(p);
    free(p); // undefined behavior
}
```

Possible Output:

Allocating memory...

The value is: 123

Freeing twice - undefined behavior.

free(): double free detected in tcache 2 Aborted (core dumped)

In this example, we wrongly tried to free the already freed memory by invoking a second free(p); statement.

The correct way is to free the allocated memory only once:

```
#include <stdio.h>
#include <stdlib.h>
int main(void)
```

```
{
printf("Allocating memory...\n");
int *p = malloc(sizeof(int));

    *p = 123;

    printf("The value is: %d\n", *p);
    printf("Freeing the memory only once.\n");
    free(p); // OK
}
```

Output:

Allocating memory...

The value is: 123 Freeing the memory only once.

Do Not Cast the Result of malloc

In C, we do not need to cast the result of malloc. The following example wrongly performs the cast:

```
#include <stdio.h>
#include <stdlib.h>
int main(void)
{
    printf("Casting the result of malloc. Not needed!\n");
    int *p = (int *) malloc(sizeof(int));
    *p = 123;
    printf("The result is: %d\n", *p);
    free(p);
}
```

Output:

Casting the result of malloc. Not needed!

The result is: 123

This example casts the result of malloc to type int*. This is unnecessary as the malloc's return value type is void*. And void* is safely and implicitly convertible to the correct pointer type. The cast also adds unneeded code clutter.

The proper example would be:

```
#include <stdio.h>
#include <stdlib.h>
```

```c
int main(void)
{
    printf("Allocating memory without casting.\n");
    int *p = malloc(sizeof(int));
    *p = 123;
    printf("The result is: %d\n", *p);
    free(p);
}
```

Output:

Allocating memory without casting.

The result is: 123

Furthermore, we could also replace the sizeof(int) expression with the sizeof *p expression to not depend on the type name.

Example:

```c
#include <stdio.h>
#include <stdlib.h>
int main(void)
{
    printf("Allocating memory without casting.\n");
    int *p = malloc(sizeof *p);
    *p = 123;
    printf("The result is: %d\n", *p);
    free(p);
}
```

Output:

Allocating memory without casting.

The result is: 123

This casting habit probably stems from the world of C++, where the cast is needed. The rule of thumb is as follows: in C, we do not need to cast the result of malloc, while in C++, we should. We should remember that C and C++ are two different programming languages with different sets of rules.

Do Not Overflow a Signed Integer

There are lower and upper limits to values a signed integer can hold. An INT_MAX macro represents the maximum signed integer value, and the minimum signed integer value is represented by the INT_MIN macro. These macros are declared inside the <limits.h> header.

Trying to store the value that is higher than the allowable maximum or lower than the allowable minimum causes undefined behavior.

Example:

```
#include <stdio.h>
#include <limits.h>
int main(void)
{
    int x = INT_MAX;
    printf("The maximum integer value is: %d\n", x);
    printf("Trying to store a value higher than the maximum...\n");
x = INT_MAX + 1; // undefined behavior
printf("The variable value is now: %d\n", x);
}
```

Output:

The maximum integer value is: 2147483647 Trying to store a value higher than the maximum...

The variable value is now: -2147483648

This example tries to store the number that is higher than the allowable maximum for type int. This causes undefined behavior and the so-called integer overflow, resulting in strange negative value output. We should make sure we do not try to store signed integer values outside the allowable range.

Cast a Pointer to void* When Printing Through printf

When printing out a pointer's value (the memory address it points to) using a printf function and a %p format specifier, we need to cast that pointer to type void* first. Simply trying to print out the pointer value through printf causes undefined behavior.

Example:

```
#include <stdio.h>
int main(void)
{
    int x = 123; int *p = &x;
```

```
        printf("The pointer value is: %p\n", p); // undefined behavior
}
```

Possible Output:

The pointer value is: 0x7ffc57d762ec

This example causes undefined behavior because the %p format specifier expects a type void*, and we are passing in int*. The same applies when trying to print out any other pointer type.

We need to cast the pointer to type void* when printing out the pointer's value using a printf function and the %p conversion specifier.

Example:

```
#include <stdio.h>
int main(void)
{
        int x = 123; int *p = &x;
        printf("The pointer value is: %p\n", (void *)p); // OK
}
```

Possible Output:

The pointer value is: 0x7ffe9d9262dc

Do Not Divide by Zero

Trying to divide by zero (0) causes undefined behavior, as shown in the following example:

```
#include <stdio.h>
int main(void)
{
        printf("Trying to divide with zero...\n");       int x = 123;
        int y = x / 0; // undefined behavior
        printf("The result is: %d\n", y);
}
```

Possible Output:

Trying to divide with zero...

Floating point exception (core dumped)

Similar to math rules, we should not divide by zero in C either. The preceding example causes undefined behavior.

Conclusion

The "Do's and Don'ts" of C programming provide a roadmap for developing clean, efficient, and secure code in a language known for its power and complexity. Each of these best practices is a building block for creating software that stands the test of time. By following these guidelines, developers can mitigate the inherent risks of C's low-level capabilities while harnessing its strengths in performance, flexibility, and control.

1. Mastery of Memory Management

Memory management in C is a responsibility rather than a luxury. In languages like Python or Java, garbage collection abstracts memory handling away from the developer, but in C, understanding memory management is central to the discipline. Proper use of malloc, calloc, and free can prevent memory leaks, segmentation faults, and inefficient memory usage. These guidelines not only improve stability but also prepare developers to work in environments where resources are constrained, such as embedded systems or high-performance computing.

In the broader software ecosystem, the importance of memory management cannot be overstated. Many critical vulnerabilities, such as buffer overflows, arise from improper handling of memory, often due to overlooking simple best practices. By mastering memory management, developers can produce robust software less prone to catastrophic failures and security risks.

2. Effective Use of Pointers and Arrays

Pointers are among C's most powerful tools, enabling efficient data manipulation, but they are also the source of frequent errors. Correct use of pointers and arrays is a skill that separates experienced C programmers from novices. Mistakes with pointers can lead to undefined behavior, difficult-to-trace bugs, and potential security vulnerabilities.

Pointers are also a distinguishing feature that makes C suitable for systems programming and other resource-critical applications. Efficient use of pointers can reduce the overhead of copying large data structures and enable more direct control over hardware resources. By adhering to best practices in pointers and arrays, developers can write optimized and reliable code that meets the demands of high-performance applications.

3. Control Structures and Code Readability

Clear, well-structured control flows improve code readability and reduce the risk of logic errors. Using braces consistently, avoiding excessive nesting, and minimizing the use of goto contribute to more maintainable code. Well-organized control structures make it easier to extend or modify code and simplify debugging.

Control structures are a primary tool for implementing program logic. In professional environments, maintainable code is paramount, as other developers often need to understand, extend, or debug the code. Clear, consistent structure improves collaboration and ensures that the original intent of the code is preserved. This cultural aspect of software development is critical, as developers rarely work in isolation; by following these best practices, they show respect for their fellow developers and contribute to a healthier coding environment.

4. Error Handling as a Discipline

Error handling is not merely a technical skill but a discipline that reflects a programmer's attention to detail. In C, where errors are often silent, conscientious error checking becomes essential. By checking return values, understanding error codes, and using tools like errno, developers create code that is resilient to unexpected issues.

This level of diligence builds trust in software. Proper error handling is especially crucial in systems programming, embedded devices, and critical applications where failures can lead to severe consequences. By making error handling a priority, C programmers can build systems that maintain integrity under a wide range of conditions, enhancing reliability and user trust.

5. Readability and Maintainability

Readable code is maintainable code. Good naming conventions, meaningful comments, and clear structuring improve code quality by making it accessible to future developers, including the original author. Readability ensures that bugs are easier to locate, intentions are clear, and the codebase can evolve with minimal friction.

In C, this practice takes on even greater importance due to the language's verbosity and lower-level syntax. Well-structured and documented C code allows developers to use this language's power without sacrificing clarity. This approach is particularly valuable for teams, as it ensures that knowledge transfer is seamless and that developers with varying levels of experience can contribute effectively to the project.

6. File Handling and I/O Safety

File handling is another area where discipline is crucial. C provides powerful tools for file manipulation, but these tools come with risks. Properly checking file open operations, closing files, and handling errors ensures that applications avoid file descriptor leaks and that data integrity is maintained.

In modern software development, data is often the most valuable asset. File handling best practices help safeguard data, ensuring that applications handle files correctly without risking data corruption or loss. As data privacy and security become more prominent concerns, following these practices demonstrates a commitment to responsible software design.

7. Use of Standard Library Functions

The C standard library provides a wealth of tools, but not all are equally safe or efficient. Understanding which functions to use and which to avoid is essential for creating secure applications. Functions like strcpy and gets may introduce vulnerabilities if not used carefully, so opting for safer alternatives, such as snprintf and fgets, minimizes risks.

Choosing the right standard library functions demonstrates a mature approach to C programming. Using the library effectively requires knowledge of the language's evolution and awareness of security practices. By mastering these functions, C developers produce code that is both efficient and secure, reflecting a nuanced understanding of the language's strengths and limitations.

8. Concurrency and Thread Safety

As modern applications increasingly rely on concurrency to improve performance, managing shared resources and ensuring thread safety are paramount. In C, these aspects require special attention due to the lack of built-in synchronization. Best practices in this area—such as using mutexes for shared resources and avoiding global variables in multithreaded contexts—prevent race conditions and improve stability.

Concurrency is challenging even in high-level languages, but in C, the responsibility lies entirely with the developer. By adhering to best practices in concurrency, developers write code that can safely run on multiple cores or in environments where simultaneous execution is critical. This skill is particularly valuable as software moves towards parallelism, making developers who can manage C concurrency effectively in high demand.

9. Effective Use of Macros and Preprocessor Directives

Macros and preprocessor directives are powerful but potentially dangerous. Misusing them can lead to unexpected bugs, reduced code clarity, and difficulties in debugging. Best practices in using #define, conditional compilation, and macros enhance code readability, portability, and reliability.

By using macros wisely, C developers can leverage these features to write more flexible and reusable code without compromising safety or maintainability. The preprocessor offers unique advantages, but it requires a disciplined approach to use effectively. Developers who master macros demonstrate their ability to balance power with clarity, an essential skill in professional programming.

10. Adherence to C Style and Standards

Coding style is not just about aesthetics; it reflects the professionalism and consistency of the codebase. Following a consistent style for indentation, brace placement, and naming conventions makes C code more readable and easier to debug. Adhering to the C standard and avoiding compiler-specific extensions improve portability, allowing code to run across various platforms.

A consistent style fosters a collaborative development environment, as team members can easily understand each other's code. Professional C programming isn't just about getting the code to work; it's about crafting code that others can build upon, a vital aspect of successful software projects.

Closing Thoughts

The "Do's and Don'ts" of C programming are more than a checklist; they form a philosophy of responsible, disciplined development. By following these guidelines, C developers can overcome the language's challenges while leveraging its strengths. These best practices create a foundation for writing code that is efficient, secure, and maintainable.

As the programming landscape evolves, C remains relevant in systems programming, embedded systems, and performance-critical applications. Each best practice covered in this guide equips developers to write code that is not only functionally correct but also durable and trustworthy. Adhering to these principles is a testament to a programmer's dedication to the craft, ensuring that C continues to be a cornerstone of high-performance computing for decades to come.

By integrating these "Do's and Don'ts" into daily practice, C programmers embody the discipline, rigor, and attention to detail that define the best of software engineering.

Thank You

www.ingramcontent.com/pod-product-compliance
Lightning Source LLC
LaVergne TN
LVHW081750050326
832903LV00027B/1879